Effective Company Disclosure in the Digital Age

International Banking and Finance Law Series

VOLUME 28

Series Editors

Professor Joseph Norton, Professor Ross Buckley and Professor Douglas Arner.

Subjects

Topical issues in international banking and financial services law, such as regulatory responses to the global financial crisis or regulation of alternative investment funds.

Objective & Readership

To provide authoritative analysis of trends and complex subjects for academics, regulators and practitioners involved in international banking and financial services law.

The titles published in this series are listed at the end of this volume.

Effective Company Disclosure in the Digital Age

Gill North

Wolters Kluwer

Published by:
Kluwer Law International
PO Box 316
2400 AH Alphen aan den Rijn
The Netherlands
Website: www.wklawbusiness.com

Sold and distributed in North, Central and South America by:
Aspen Publishers, Inc.
7201 McKinney Circle
Frederick, MD 21704
United States of America
Email: customer.service@aspenpublishers.com

Sold and distributed in all other countries by:
Turpin Distribution Services Ltd
Stratton Business Park
Pegasus Drive, Biggleswade
Bedfordshire SG18 8TQ
United Kingdom
Email: kluwerlaw@turpin-distribution.com

Printed on acid-free paper.

ISBN 978-90-411-3815-6

Printed and Bound by CPI Group (UK) Ltd, Croydon, CR0 4YY.

Table of Contents

Foreword

This book is particularly timely as it is important at this stage in the evolution of our global financial markets. It is a masterful comparative analysis of disclosure laws and practices in a broad range of jurisdictions including the United States, Canada, Germany, UK, Japan, Hong Kong, Australia and Singapore. The legal analysis of each jurisdiction's rules is supported by the case studies of the disclosure practices of two leading corporations in each jurisdiction.

The groundwork for this extensive comparative analysis is laid in the first four chapters which examine the theory of mandatory corporate disclosure regimes, their impact on insider trading, and the prevalence of selective disclosure to certain analysts and other privileged parties at the expense of the general public.

The eight comparative chapters form the core of the book. After them, the work concludes with three substantial chapters which examine and pull together conclusions about periodic and continuous disclosure regulation and practice, and then develops a best practice disclosure framework. The author concludes with a strong endorsement for the rules and practices of the Securities and Exchange Commission in the US and American approaches to disclosure generally.

To write a work of this depth and rigor requires a certain fire in the belly. In this author's case, the fire appears to have been stoked by long years as an asset manager and financial analyst in some of the principal global financial centres. The practice of selective disclosure is widespread with corporations conducting briefings for privileged analysts and others. It is a practice that has galled this author and provided the impetus for this major contribution to the literature. We have, regrettably, moved a long way from the guiding ethos of the 1930s US reforms which was that, in Louis Brandeis' words, 'sunlight is the best disinfectant'.

I, for one, hope this author turns her considerable forensic and analytical capacities to the next most pressing issues in global disclosure which, to my mind at least, include the rapid rise in the past decade of algorithmic high frequency trading and 'dark pools'. A high proportion of the orders placed in high frequency trading are, apparently, placed to mislead other investors or, at the least, obfuscate which trades are actually being implemented; and dark pools involve removing trades from the lit exchange during the trading day thereby placing participants on the lit exchange at an informational disadvantage. Both of these developments, therefore, represent further significant departures from transparency in our markets in my view. Appropriately neither have been addressed in this book as this is a global analysis of disclosure regimes and high frequency trading and dark pools are therefore rightly beyond its purview. However, both topics would benefit if the forensic and analytical excellence on display here were brought to bear on them.

Disclosure has come under sustained criticism as an organising regulatory principle in recent years in light of its apparent failure to prevent the crisis of 2008. Many have questioned whether disclosure is an adequate approach to the increasing complexity and opacity of many modern financial products. I have argued elsewhere that the problem lies not in the disclosure regimes, but in the complexity and opacity of the products. While continued criticism and analysis is always to be encouraged in our system, to criticise disclosure as an organising principle in the absence of something better does not seem particularly productive. It is possible that the calls by some regulators for the power to ban certain products outright may be the right way to go, but certainly I, for one, doubt the capacity of any regulator to consistently get those sorts of judgment calls right over the longer term.

Associate Professor Gill North clearly has not given up on disclosure as the organising principle for our markets. Instead she has written a clarion call for us collectively to turn our backs on selective disclosure and support to the fullest extent possible clear, transparent and uniform disclosure across the markets. This is a call, contained in a book, that I heartily endorse.

Ross P. Buckley
CIFR King & Wood Mallesons Professor of International Finance Law
UNSW Australia, Sydney, September 2015

List of Abbreviations

AASB	Australian Accounting Standards Board
ADR	American Depositary Receipt
AIM	Alternative Investment Market
AIMR	Association for Investment Management and Research
AIRA	Australian Investor Relations Association
ASIC	Australian Securities and Investment Commission
ASX	Australian Securities Exchange
ASXSR	ASX Supervisory Review Pty Limited
BHP	BHP Billiton Limited
BP	BP Plc
CBA	Commonwealth Bank of Australia Limited
CEO	Chief Executive Officer
CFO	Chief Financial Officer
China Mobile	China Mobile Limited
CICA	Canadian Institute of Chartered Accountants
Citigroup	Citigroup Inc
Compliance Department	Listed Company Compliance Department
CRR	Corporate Responsibility Reporting
CSA	Canadian Securities Administrators
CSR	Corporate Social Responsibility
Deutsche Bank	Deutsche Bank AG
DTR	Disclosure Rules and Transparency Rules
EBIT	Earnings before Interest and Tax

EBITA	Earnings before Interest, Tax and Amortisation
EBITDA	Earnings before Interest, Tax, Depreciation and Amortisation
EC	European Commission
ECMH	Efficient Capital Markets Hypothesis
EDGAR	Electronic Data Gathering, Analysis, and Retrieval System
EPS	Earnings per Share
ESAs	Exchange Supervisory Authorities
EU	European Union
Exchange Act	*Securities Exchange Act of 1934* (US)
FCA	Financial Conduct Authority
FIEA	*Financial Instruments and Exchange Act* (Japan)
FINRA	Financial Industry Regulatory Authority
FLI	Forward Looking Information
FSA	Financial Services Authority
FWB	Frankfurter Wertpapierbörse
GAAP	generally accepted accounting principles
GEM	Growth Enterprise Market
GFC	Global Financial Crisis
GRI	Global Reporting Initiative
Guidance Note 8	ASX Guidance Note 8 to Listing Rule 3.1 *Continuous Disclosure Listing Rule 3.1-3.1B*
HKEC	Hong Kong Exchanges and Clearing Limited
HKEx	Hong Kong Exchange
HKEC	Hong Kong Exchange and Clearing Ltd
HKSE	Stock Exchange of Hong Kong Limited
ICMM	International Council on Mining and Metals
IFRS	International Financial Reporting Standards
IIRC	International Integrated Reporting Council
IMF	International Monetary Fund
Impact Report	European Commission 2012 Impact Assessment Report
IMSs	interim management statements
IOSCO	International Organization of Securities Commissions
IOSCO Principles	Objectives and Principles of Securities Regulation

JORC Code	Australasian Code for Reporting of Exploration Results, Minerals Resources and Ore Reserve
JPX	Japan Exchange Group, Inc
Kay Final Report	Kay Review Final Report
Kay Interim Report	Kay Review Interim Report
Kay Review	Kay Review of UK Equity Markets
Keppel	Keppel Corporation
KPIs	Key Performance Indicators
LSE	London Stock Exchange
MAS	Monetary Authority of Singapore
MD&A	Management Discussion and Analysis
Microsoft	Microsoft Corporation
MSCD	Market Surveillance and Compliance Department
MSE	Market Surveillance and Enforcement
NASD	National Association of Securities Dealers
NGO	Non-governmental Organisation
NYSE	New York Stock Exchange Euronext
NYSER	NYSE Regulation, Inc
OFRs	Operating & Financial Reviews
OSC	Ontario Securities Commission
PBT	Profit before Tax
PEID	Participants Examination and Inspection Department
PetroChina	PetroChina Company Limited
Promina	Promina Group Limited
RBC	Royal Bank of Canada
RCC	Regulatory Conflicts Committee
Reg AC	Regulation Analyst Certification
Reg FD	Regulation Fair Disclosure
RIS	Regulatory Information Service
Rmb	Renminbi
Sainsbury	J Sainsbury Plc
SEC	Securities and Exchange Commission
SEDAR	System for Electronic Document Analysis and Retrieval
SESC	Securities and Exchange Surveillance Commission
SFC	Securities and Futures Commission

SFCO	Securities and Futures Commission Ordinance
SGX	Singapore Exchange
SGX Code	Singapore Code of Corporate Governance
Siemens	Siemens AG
Singtel	Singapore Telecommunications Limited
SLR	Securities Listing Regulations
Sony	Sony Corporation
Sumitomo	Sumitomo Mitsui Financial
TD	Transparency Directive
Teck	Teck Resources Ltd
TMX	Toronto Stock Exchange
TSE	Tokyo Stock Exchange
TSER	Tokyo Stock Exchange Regulation
TSO	Trading Surveillance Office
UK	United Kingdom
UKLA	United Kingdom Listing Authority
US	United States
VaR	Value-At Risk Model
WpHG	Wertpapierhandelsgesetz

Acknowledgements

There are two people who contributed enormously to this book and their significant efforts and support enabled me to deliver the manuscript to the publishers by the middle of 2015. Martin, my husband, provided support in innumerable ways that allowed me time and space to deliberate and write. Stephanie Babic edited drafts of the book at various stages and provided invaluable and timely feedback and encouragement. Many thanks and best wishes Steph.

The publication processes ran smoothly thanks to the efficiency and friendliness of all those I worked with at Kluwer Law. In particular, I acknowledge the efforts and efficiency of Simon Bellamy, Eleanor Taylor and Mrs Sudha. My thanks extends to Professors Norton, Buckley and Arner. It is an honour to be an author within the International Banking and Finance Law series.

Many thanks also to the editors and publishers of the articles that are incorporated within the book. The publication of a series of articles allowed me to develop my knowledge and critique of specific aspects of company disclosure frameworks, to obtain authoritative feedback, and to develop the overall structure and content of the book. The following publishers kindly provided written permission to include content from published material with appropriate acknowledgment:

Thomson Reuters – Sweet and Maxwell (United Kingdom)

- Gill North, 'Listed Company Disclosure and Financial Market Transparency: Is this a Battle Worth Fighting or Merely Policy and Regulatory Mantra?' (2014) 6 *Journal of Business Law* 486-513.

Thomson Reuters (Professional) Australia Ltd

- Gill North, 'Timely Public Disclosure of Company Information: A Likely Precondition for Optimal Long-Term Corporate and National Outcomes' (2014) 32 *Company and Securities Law Journal* 560-582.

Lexis Nexis Australia Ltd

- Gill North, 'A Re-examination of the Manne Efficiency Theory and the Insider Trading and Company Disclosure Efficiency Rationales' (2011) 25 *Australian Journal of Corporate Law* 209-225.

University of New South Wales Law Journal

- Gill North, 'A Theoretical Basis for Selective Disclosure Regulation' (2009) 32 *University of New South Wales Law Journal* 143-168.

Written permission to replicate content from the Listed Company Manual of the Intercontinental Exchange (NYSE) was also generously provided.

Finally, I would like to dedicate this book to my father Dennis who passed away in late 2014. You were loved and cherished by all those who knew you well. We miss you greatly.

Gill North
Associate Professor, Faculty of Law,
Monash University

Part I Introduction

CHAPTER 1
Overview

> Great corporations exist only because they are created and safeguarded by our institutions; and it is our right and our duty to see that they work in harmony with these institutions. ... The first requisite is knowledge, full and complete – knowledge which may be made public to the world.[1]

Most nations in the world have established company disclosure regulation. Indeed, some countries, such as the United States, have had comprehensive disclosure frameworks in operation for many decades. The book discusses the efficacy of this regulation and corporate disclosure in practice from varying perspectives. It considers the scholarly theoretical debates on company disclosure regimes, reviews the continuing disclosure regulation applicable to listed companies in countries spanning the Americas, Europe and Asia/Pacific, and examines company reports and disclosures. It is not possible to discuss all aspects of company disclosure law and practice across the jurisdictions reviewed, nor all of the related case law and enforcement proceedings. The primary purpose of the book is to identify policies and practices to improve the overall quality of listed company reporting and communication within public domains. Accordingly, the regulation, case law, and issues highlighted are primarily focused on the relatively unexplored areas concerning: the tensions between direct and indirect investment in financial markets; the continued assumptions by the judiciary and others of the need to maintain a privileged role for financial intermediaries; and the intersection between private and public company disclosure frameworks. The book concludes with consideration of the principles, processes and practices that should be implemented within best practice company disclosure frameworks.

Company disclosure legislation is structured hierarchically in most jurisdictions, with increasing disclosure requirements and obligations as a company moves from private to public registration and from unlisted to listed status. The disclosure obligations imposed on private companies are relatively minimal because a small pool of private individuals and institutions provide the equity capital and it is assumed that

1. Theodore Roosevelt, State of the Union Message to Congress (3 December 1901).

these capital providers have the capacity and wherewithal to communicate with the company directors and managers and to monitor their investments. The disclosure obligations become progressively onerous for public companies and companies that list on exchanges in order to allow public trading of the company's securities and or to raise capital from the public. This tiered disclosure regulation reflects the more dispersed and vulnerable nature of the investor base of listed companies. Investors with smaller holdings lack negotiating power with company boards and managers, so their interests could potentially be disregarded following a listing or the raising of capital.

Listed company disclosure regulation generally includes periodic disclosure reporting requirements and continuous disclosure rules requiring timely disclosure of material information on a continuous, ad hoc or episodic basis between reporting periods.[2] This regulation requires listed companies to publicly disclose material information, to enable well-informed decision-making and to ensure market transparency. Market transparency has been defined as 'the widespread availability of relevant, reliable information about the ... governance, value, and risk of publicly traded firms.'[3] Accepting this definition, market transparency is achieved through best practice periodic reporting and continuous disclosure because these combined reporting regimes and disclosure processes provide the most relevant and reliable information on publicly traded companies.[4] When considering whether the existing disclosure frameworks achieve their objectives, this book recognises that investors and stakeholders are not generally concerned with the discrete disclosure regime under which information is provided, or with the provisions that may have been breached when required disclosures have not been made. Instead, these participants must consider and process company information on a holistic basis.

Some of the most significant barriers to achieving high quality public reporting and disclosures arise from fixed perceptions held by companies, regulators, scholars and others regarding the appropriate role and capacity of retail and institutional investors, and their levels of sophistication, requirement for company information, analytical skills, and long-term portfolio performance.[5] However, broad generalisations about institutional and retail investors mask the true spectrum of professionalism, competency and diligence across both groups. In practice, there are, and always will be, people who require professional assistance because of a lack of skills, resources or time. Thus, there is a continued role for analysts or professional intermediaries who are genuinely skilled at spotting arbitrage opportunities or who can provide a valued service to clients. Nevertheless, not all individuals want or require the assistance of

2. Some countries and jurisdictions refer to continuous disclosure as ad hoc or episodic disclosure. These terms are generally equivalent, and are used as such in the book.
3. Robert M Bushman and Abbie Smith, 'Transparency, Financial Accounting Information, and Corporate Governance' (2003) 9 *Economic Policy Review* 65, 66.
4. In most of the jurisdictions reviewed, the periodic and continuous disclosure regimes are supported by regulation that prohibits insider trading and selective disclosure, and by provisions dealing with misstatements. The scope of the book does not allow for comprehensive discussion of these rules.
5. Caroline Bradley, 'Disorderly Conduct: Day Traders and the Ideology of "Fair and Orderly Markets"' (2000) 26 *Journal of Corporation Law* 63, 96.

analysts and other intermediaries, with some preferring to invest on an independent or direct basis. The investor categories used in the book are simply 'institutional' or 'retail', and this categorisation depends only on whether an investment involves an intermediary. 'Retail investors' are persons who invest directly on their own behalves. 'Institutional investors' include asset managers who manage investment portfolios, buy-side analysts who research on behalf of invested clients, sell-side brokers who implement security transactions on behalf of clients, and sell-side analysts who publish research for clients including security transaction recommendations.

Corporate disclosure is no longer about merely sending an occasional report to shareholders. The audiences that public companies communicate and interact with are extensive, including shareholders, analysts, regulators, creditors, employees, trade unions, industry associations, rating agencies, environmental groups, human rights advocates, researchers, public bodies, and so forth. Effective corporate disclosure should provide high quality information through non-discriminatory channels as a means to promote vigorous competition and optimal performance. This disclosure should be timely, comprehensive, clear, and balanced. Companies should explain their strategies, developments, and performance on a layered basis to enable all interested persons to access the type and level of information they require. Layered disclosure requires the availability of information in varying forms and detail to suit a broad audience with differing interests, time constraints, knowledge and abilities.

Effective corporate communication involves more than mere disclosure. Communication is a 'two-way process of reaching mutual understanding, in which participants not only exchange ... information, news, ideas and feelings but also create and share meaning.'[6] Companies need to embrace appropriate modes of communication to remain connected and engaged with their investor base and stakeholders. Facilities and forums that allow continuous deliberation, engagement and response are essential limbs of best practice communication frameworks in contemporary markets.

This book contends that public disclosure and communication of listed company information is an essential precondition to the long-term efficient operation of financial markets. There are many definitions and measures of efficiency in financial markets. For the purposes of this book, 'price efficiency' is defined as an individual security price that accurately reflects its underlying economic value; 'market efficiency' is defined as a financial market in which security prices closely reflect their underlying economic values; and 'economic efficiency' is defined as an economy that optimally allocates its capital and real resources. In order to focus on core issues, the book makes some important assumptions. First, it assumes that company results, or more specifically, company earnings, drive security prices over the longer-term. In other words, security prices in financial markets generally follow long-term trend lines that equate with the underlying earnings or potential earning capacity of the relevant companies.[7] Second,

6. Business Dicionary.com, 'Communication definition' http://www.businessdictionary.com/definition/communication.html viewed 17 August 2014.
7. D Craig Nichols and James Wahlen, 'How Do Earnings Numbers Relate To Stock Returns? A Review of Classic Accounting Research with Updated Evidence' (December 2004) *Accounting Horizons* 263, 264 citing William Beaver, *Financial Reporting: An Accounting Revolution* (Prentice Hall, 3rd ed., 1998). Beaver suggests that there are links between earnings and share prices;

it assumes that investors search for information about listed companies in order to obtain informational advantages, in the belief that mispriced company securities and profitable trading opportunities can be discovered.[8] Third, empirical studies from legal, accounting, finance, and economic scholars are outlined and discussed throughout the book to provide critical links between theoretical, policy, and empirical outcomes. Some scholars suggest there is minimal evidence or commentary on disclosure practices and compliance issues because researchers cannot accurately measure occurrences of non-disclosure and company insiders are unlikely to admit to non-disclosure because this would be tantamount to confessing a crime.[9] Such conclusions are too sweeping and defeatist. There are extensive bodies of scholarly work that examine the effects and regulation of company disclosure, insider trading and selective disclosure, and this research provides valuable insights on the efficacy of existing disclosure regulation and practice. The author acknowledges the many challenges in presenting empirical work to a broad spectrum of readers. Empirical research is open to varying interpretations, individual studies can become dated or less relevant over time, and it is not always possible to extrapolate the results of country-specific research to other countries or the global arena.

§1.01 OUTLINE

Part II of this book discusses the theoretical and conceptual bases for company disclosure regulation. Initially, the arguments for and against mandatory disclosure regimes are outlined and considered. This debate closely connects with the theoretical debates concerning regulation that prohibits trading on private or 'inside' company information by persons employed by, or related to, the company (insiders) and by participants external to the company (outsiders). Hence Part II comprises three chapters that discuss the theoretical frameworks supporting mandatory company disclosure regulation, regulation that prohibits trading by insiders and outsiders on material company information that has not been publicly disclosed (insider trading), and regulation that prohibits the disclosure of materially price-sensitive information to selected outsiders, such as financial intermediaries, without disclosure to the wider market (selective disclosure). It concludes that an essential question across these debates is whether information privately disclosed by companies to some market participants should be publicly disclosed through mandatory reporting processes.

Part III of the book provides an overview of global disclosure regulation and practice. It includes country profiles that summarise the significant disclosure obligations that apply to listed companies, including an introductory overview and a summary of the important periodic reporting and continuous disclosure rules. The

current period earnings provide information to predict future periods' earnings; which provides information to develop expectations about dividends in future periods; which provides information to determine share value.

8. The motivations of investors in financial markets vary.
9. Usah Rodrigues and Mike Stegemoller, 'Placebo Ethics: A Study in Securities Disclosure Arbitrage' (2010) 96 *Virginia Law Review* 1, 4.

countries that are profiled are the United States (US), Canada, Germany, the United Kingdom (UK), Japan, Hong Kong, Australia, and Singapore. This selection of nations includes countries with the largest securities exchanges by market capitalisation, such as the US, and countries that are expected to become more prominent in future decades, such as Hong Kong. The content of the national profiles is intentionally sourced from information available on public websites in accordance with the proposition that modern financial markets should operate on a broadly transparent basis. The country profiles are supported by empirical evidence, including comprehensive reviews of corporate disclosures by national regulators and a survey conducted by the author that looks at the company reports, disclosures and websites of two large listed companies in each of the selected countries. The primary purpose of these disclosure reviews is to highlight sound initiatives for possible broader application.

Part IV builds on the earlier chapters. It outlines and discusses the key principles of periodic and continuous disclosure regulation. In doing so, it draws on the company disclosure rationales and principles published by the International Organization of Securities Commissions (IOSCO).[10] IOSCO indicates in its document entitled 'Objectives and Principles of Securities Regulation' that the primary rationales for corporate disclosure regimes are protecting investors, ensuring fair, efficient and transparent markets, and reducing systemic risk.[11] Part IV concludes that to achieve these IOSCO goals, company disclosure structures need to provide publicly available information that is sufficiently regular, complete, and timely to enable meaningful decision making and engagement by all persons with a warrantable interest.

Part V seeks to promote high quality disclosure standards and effective supervisory structures at both national and global levels. It draws on the regulatory reviews discussed in Part III to identify common disclosure issues that arise across jurisdictions, and to provide useful feedback and insight on processes and measures to improve company disclosure standards. Further, it uses the author's examination of a sample of listed company reports, disclosures and websites in the selected countries to identify noteworthy corporate reporting and communication practices for consideration within a best practice company disclosure framework.

This book concludes that best practice company disclosure principles and practices are relatively straightforward.[12] When a listed company or entity wishes to communicate in a manner that is clear, concise and effective, this can generally be done without undue angst or cost. Directors are required to oversee and steer companies through corporate, economic and financial life cycles that include significant challenges, uncertainties and volatility. The real character and resilience of a listed company is revealed during these stormy periods. Effective corporate disclosure and

10. The International Organization of Securities Commissions is the primary international cooperative forum for securities market regulatory agencies. Its members regulate more than 95% of the world's securities markets.
11. International Organization of Securities Commissions, *Objectives and Principles of Securities Regulation* (June 2010) 3.
12. This conclusion is supported by the author's thirty years' experience around the globe working in small and large companies, advising corporations, valuing companies and corporate securities, and researching corporate disclosure matters.

communication involves far more than mere technical compliance with regulation. Good corporate communication, like most human interaction, is ultimately built on trust, so listed companies need to develop and sustain a culture of continuous disclosure, engagement, and accountability with all investor and stakeholder groups. This book suggests that to promote and deeply embed such cultures across major financial markets, company boards and executives, policy makers, scholars and lawyers should consider company disclosure regulation and practice anew.

PART II

Company Disclosure Regulation: Theoretical and Conceptual Bases

> The Principles on which the [Corporate Governance] Code is based are those of openness, integrity and accountability. They go together. Openness on the part of companies, within the limits set by their competitive position, is the basis for the confidence which needs to exist between business and all those who have a stake in its success. An open approach to the disclosure of information contributes to the efficient working of the market economy, prompts boards to take effective action and allow shareholders and others to scrutinise companies more thoroughly.[1]

INTRODUCTION

Part II includes three consecutive chapters that discuss the theoretical frameworks supporting mandatory disclosure, insider trading and selective disclosure regulation. There are common theories, concepts and themes across these debates. These scholarly theoretical debates centre on either the justification or lack of support for mandatory disclosure regimes. This primary debate is outlined and analysed in Chapter 2, but the mandatory disclosure debate inherently overlaps with the theories concerning trading on 'inside' company information by insiders and outsiders. Most commentators adopt or assume a particular stance on the role of financial markets and its participants, and the appropriate level and type of regulation. These assumed positions strongly influence authors' theoretical frameworks and adopted efficiency, fairness and rationality concepts. For example, some disclosure theories assume that financial markets operate most efficiently with minimal regulatory interference. Others argue that financial markets work best when there is broad confidence in the integrity of a market and participants believe they are trading with equal access to company information. Behavioural scholars generally argue that economic rationalist models, which assume that individuals will act rationally in their own interests, are not

1. Report of the Committee on the Financial Aspects of Corporate Governance (1 December 2012) [3.2] available at www.jbs.ac.uj/cadbury/report/index.html.

entirely credible because participant behaviour is often, sometimes even predictably, irrational.[2]

It is important for readers to understand the role, nature and limitations of individual scholarly models and theories. Theoretical assumptions are not intended to fully reflect real world complexities. A theory is by necessity based on abstraction. Nonetheless, an 'important test of a theory is its ability to explain reality.'[3] Bridging the gap between theory and reality sometimes requires the use of extrapolation and human judgment for the theory to have practical application.[4] Theoretical frameworks that are narrowly constructed can present difficulties for policy makers, who determine company disclosure and insider trading rules, and for judiciaries, who are required to interpret this regulation. To be effective, company disclosure and insider trading regulation must take into account the fact that financial markets are controlled largely by human participants and that we do not always act entirely rationally or within the law, particularly within financial spheres when there are large potential monetary gains involved.

2. See, e.g., John Keynes, *The General Theory of Employment, Interest and Money* ((Macmillan, London, 1936) 156.
3. Richard Posner, *Economic Analysis of Law* (Aspen, 6th ed., 2003) 17. See also Karl L Popper, *The Logic of Scientific Discovery* (Hutchinson, 1959) 59. Popper argues that a 'theory' is a net 'cast to catch ... "the world"; to rationalize, to explain, and to master it.'
4. John McMillan, 'Market Design: The Policy Uses of Theory' (2003) 93 *American Economic Review* 139, 143.

CHAPTER 2
Mandatory Corporate Disclosure*

> Our era aptly has been styled, and well may be remembered as, the 'age of information.' Francis Bacon recognized nearly 400 years ago that 'knowledge is power,' but only in the last generation has it risen to the equivalent of the coin of the realm. Nowhere is this commodity more valuable or volatile than in the world of high finance, where facts are worth fortunes while secrets may be rendered worthless once revealed.[1]

§2.01 OVERVIEW

Most developed nations have established listed company disclosure frameworks that encompass periodic reporting and some form of disclosure between reporting periods.[2] Nevertheless, scholarly debates concerning the need for, and justification of, disclosure regulation continue. One legal commentator concludes that '[p]roponents of the third-party externality rationale have not specified what information requirements the rationale justifies, let alone whether that information is the focus of ... disclosure requirements.'[3] Some accounting and economics academics suggest that 'it is surprising how little we still know about fundamental issues such as the reasons for disclosure regulation in developed markets and the determinants of the format of this regulation ...[and] the objectives of managers in making voluntary disclosures.'[4] Company

* Some of the material discussed in this chapter is contained in a published article: Gill North, 'Timely Public Disclosure of Company Information: A Likely Precondition for Optimal Long-Term Corporate and National Outcomes' (2014) 32 *Company and Securities Law Journal* 560.

1. *SEC v. Materia*, 745 F.2d 197, 198 (2d Cir. 1984).
2. Companies are typically required to provide specified information to the market under periodic reporting and continuous disclosure regulation. In addition, failures to provide mandated information, selective disclosure, or misleading disclosure may be governed by insider trading, selective disclosure, market abuse, or misleading and deceptive conduct regulation.
3. Roberta Romano, 'Empowering Investors: A Market Approach to Securities Regulation' (1998) 107 *Yale Law Journal* 2359, 2380. An 'externality' is an uncompensated cost or benefit that may be intentional, accidental, or incidental.
4. Anne Beyer, Daniel Cohen, Thomas Lys and Beverly Walther, 'The Financial Reporting Environment: Review of the Recent Literature' (2010) 50 *Journal of Accounting and Economics* 296, 336.

managers and advisers often claim such regulation is burdensome, too prescriptive and costly.[5] Others argue that disclosure is a limited tool and it is time for the main debate to shift to fresh policy options.[6] The Kay Review of UK Equity Markets (Kay Review) even suggested that '[d]isclosure and transparency have become mantras in policy and in regulation.'[7] These views reflect the highly political nature of company disclosure law and the varying perspectives and incentives of the groups involved. The disclosure debates will undoubtedly remain robust and contentious given the power imbalances and high monetary stakes involved.

A major weakness in the existing literature is the lack of an overarching theory, making it difficult to capture and assess existing and potential disclosure models and arguments. It is notoriously difficult to develop a theoretical structure that comprehensively encompasses financial market and corporate environments, given the interdependencies or endogenous nature of the variables and drivers involved. There are distinct differences across the disclosure literature between contributors' assumed financial market and company disclosure environments, and many of the efficiency and fairness notions are imprecise or ambiguous. Commentators tend to emphasise models or definitions from a particular discipline, such as economics, accounting, finance or law, and the adopted research methodologies and assumptions can vary markedly. This chapter acknowledges the many difficulties and complexities that arise when discussing theoretical and empirical issues regarding corporate disclosure. Nonetheless, it concludes that company periodic and continuous disclosure regimes are likely to deliver better investor protection, more efficient, fair and transparent financial markets, lower systemic risk, and superior long-term corporate, economic and community outcomes, compared to those achieved in voluntary disclosure environments. It suggests that public disclosure frameworks in the twenty-first century should be wholeheartedly accepted as being in the long-term interests of listed corporations, and the communities and countries in which they operate. The arguments advanced for mandatory disclosure regimes are outlined in this chapter in three ways. First, the chapter responds to arguments that are generally accepted as the rationales for opposing company disclosure regulation. Second, it highlights the critical interconnections between financial market incentives, efficiency, fairness, and governance factors. Third, it outlines interdisciplinary empirical research that suggests that there are significant associations between high quality company disclosure in financial markets and superior long-term corporate, economic and community outcomes.[8]

5. See, e.g., European Commission, Report from the Commission Staff Working Paper *Impact Assessment* (SEC(2011) 1280 final) 13.
6. See, e.g., *The Kay Review of UK Equity Markets and Long-Term Decision Making: Final Report* (July 2012) 72.
7. *The Kay Review of UK Equity Markets and Long-Term Decision Making: Final Report* (July 2012) 70. See Gill North, 'Listed Company Disclosure and Financial Market Transparency: Is this a Battle Worth Fighting or Merely Policy and Regulatory Mantra?' (2014) 6 *Journal of Business Law* 484.
8. The definitions of variables and outcomes within individual scholarly empirical studies vary. These definitions are generally defined in the studies.

Global events and developments over the last decade clearly highlight the interconnections and alignments between corporations, real economies, and communities. Country-specific and global empirical studies of financial markets consistently link improved corporate and national outcomes to high disclosure standards, vigorous enforcement of securities laws, broad investor participation, protection of minority shareholder rights, and public trust. Growing bodies of empirical research also suggest there are associations between mandatory disclosure frameworks and sound corporate governance and corporate sustainability practices. This combined research suggests that the mandatory disclosure theoretical debates should not be characterised as simply a 'turf war' between different classes of shareholders. Instead, it points to compelling commercial and societal imperatives for comprehensive regulatory frameworks governing listed company communication in financial markets.

The debates concerning mandatory disclosure regimes have been running strongly for many decades. The literature on mandatory disclosure generally focuses on two essential questions; first, whether the information provided in a voluntary company disclosure environment is sufficient, and second, the appropriate nature and scope of the disclosure regulation.[9] The main issues discussed in the interdisciplinary theoretical debates concern the incentives companies have to disclose information to the market, and the relative efficiency and fairness of voluntary and mandatory disclosure regimes.[10]

§2.02 INFORMATION INCENTIVES

The discussion concerning company disclosure begins with the lifeblood of all modern developed financial markets – information. Scholars agree that the efficient operation of financial markets requires the disclosure of timely and accurate information. Views differ, however, on the expected quantity and quality of information provided in discretionary disclosure environments in the absence of disclosure regulation.

[A] The Information Conundrum

General information can operate as a public or private good, or it may have a dual character and be produced and used in both spheres.[11] Within the public sphere, information is viewed as a resource to be shared and spread as widely as possible, and

9. See, e.g., John Coffee Jr, 'Market Failure and the Economic Case for a Mandatory Disclosure System' (1984) 70 *Virginia Law Review* 717, 722, 725–737; Merritt Fox, 'Required Disclosure and Corporate Governance' (1996) 62 *Law and Contemporary Problems* 113; Merritt Fox, 'The Issuer Choice Debate' (2001) 2 *Theoretical Inquiries in Law* 563; James Cox, 'Premises for Reforming the Regulation of Securities Offerings: An Essay' (2000) 63 *Law and Contemporary Problems* 11; Stephen Bainbridge, 'Contemporary Issues in the Law of Business Organizations: Mandatory Disclosure: A Behavioural Analysis' (2000) 68 *University of Cincinnati Law Review* 1023.
10. Anne Beyer, Daniel Cohen, Thomas Lys and Beverly Walther, 'The Financial Reporting Environment: Review of the Recent Literature' (2010) 50 *Journal of Accounting and Economics* 296, 315–316.
11. James Boyle, 'A Theory of Law and Information: Copyright, Spleens, Blackmail, and Insider Trading' (1992) 80 *California Law Review* 1413, 1433–1437.

the emphasis is on fairness and equality.[12] Once produced, information can be disseminated at virtually zero marginal cost.[13] However, information providers are unable to receive full value for their efforts, so they tend to under-produce unless a government or other third parties intervene.[14] Within private markets, information is a resource that cannot be infinitely distributed without diminishing its value.[15] Private resources are subject to the same economic laws as other goods within the private sphere.[16] An information provider requires a profit or an incentive to continue to produce, and rights to the information may therefore be required to avoid under-production and inefficient allocation.[17] Free markets are assumed to promote the most efficient or profitable outcomes – and equality is not a relevant concern.[18]

The complexities arising from the dual public/private nature of information are reflected in the company disclosure debates. When company information is considered a property right, it may be treated as a private or public resource. That is, the property right may remain with the company that generated the information, a non-exclusive right may be granted to third parties such as analysts, or the information may be considered a necessary public good.[19] These property right arguments represent an important limb of the mandatory disclosure theoretical debates. Scholars who criticise mandatory disclosure frameworks typically argue or imply that any rights to information generated by a public company are held by the company as a separate legal entity, and that company managers should retain discretion around whether to disclose information, who to disclose it to, and the form in which it is disclosed. As discussed more fully in Chapters 3 and 4, some of these commentators also believe that it is appropriate for company managers to provide information privately to third parties such as analysts on a selective basis. In contrast, other scholars argue for disclosure regulation that requires public disclosure of material company information, and for

12. Kimberly Krawiec, 'Fairness, Efficiency and Insider Trading: Deconstructing the Coin of the Realm in the Information Age' (2001) 95 *North Western University Law Review* 443, 453; James Boyle, 'A Theory of Law and Information: Copyright, Spleens, Blackmail, and Insider Trading' (1992) 80 *California Law Review* 1413, 1438.
13. James Boyle, 'A Theory of Law and Information: Copyright, Spleens, Blackmail, and Insider Trading' (1992) 80 *California Law Review* 1413, 1438.
14. James Boyle, 'A Theory of Law and Information: Copyright, Spleens, Blackmail, and Insider Trading' (1992) 80 *California Law Review* 1413, 1439, 1445.
15. James Boyle, 'A Theory of Law and Information: Copyright, Spleens, Blackmail, and Insider Trading' (1992) 80 *California Law Review* 1413, 1439.
16. James Boyle, 'A Theory of Law and Information: Copyright, Spleens, Blackmail, and Insider Trading' (1992) 80 *California Law Review* 1413, 1439.
17. Kimberly Krawiec, 'Fairness, Efficiency and Insider Trading: Deconstructing the Coin of the Realm in the Information Age' (2001) 95 *North Western University Law Review* 443, 502.
18. Kimberly Krawiec, 'Fairness, Efficiency and Insider Trading: Deconstructing the Coin of the Realm in the Information Age' (2001) 95 *North Western University Law Review* 443, 460.
19. James Cox, 'Insider Trading and Contracting: A Critical Response to the "Chicago School"' (1986) 4 *Duke Law Journal* 628; Michael Whincorp, 'Towards A Property Rights and Market Microstructural Theory of Insider Trading Regulation - The Case of Primary Securities Markets Transactions' (1996) 7 *Journal of Business and Finance Law* 212; Jonathan Macey, 'Securities Trading: A Contractual Perspective' (1999) 50 *Case Western Reserve Law Review* 269; Stephen Choi, 'Regulating Investors Not Issuers: A Market-Based Proposal' (2000) 88 *California Law Review* 279; Edmund Kitch, 'Proposals for Reform of Securities Regulation: An Overview' (2001) 41 *Virginia Journal of International Law* 629.

insider trading and selective disclosure regulation that prohibits private or selective disclosure of material information that has not been disclosed publicly. This latter group of scholars typically draws on the public good theory of company information. The property right theories and arguments in relation to company information are closely connected to information incentive arguments, as decisions within listed companies concerning disclosure of company information are normally made by managers and are motivated by various incentives.

[B] Company Manager Information Incentives

When considering the incentives to provide and disseminate company information in financial markets, it is important to clearly differentiate between information generated and disclosed by a listed company and additional information and analysis provided by third parties outside of the company. This section discusses incentives within listed companies to provide information to market participants, while the next section considers third party information incentives.

Commentators agree that listed company managers have some incentives to voluntarily disclose information to the market. While listed companies are not generally required to disclose proprietary confidential information (even in countries with mandatory disclosure regimes),[20] some information must be disclosed to satisfy the demands for ongoing news from existing investors and encourage interest from potential investors.[21] Empirical research confirms that listed companies voluntarily disclose information when they need to raise new capital,[22] reduce information asymmetry,[23] or lower the cost of capital.[24] Managers may also voluntarily provide or verify information to mitigate litigation risks.[25] Critics argue that listed companies have sufficient incentives to ensure information provided to investors is credible and accurate without the need for mandatory disclosure regimes.[26] However, market variables that encourage high quality disclosure and optimal long-term performance do not always exist. Many listed companies operate for long periods without raising new

20. Ronald Dye, 'Disclosure of Nonproprietary Information' (1985) 23 *Journal of Accounting Research* 123. Certain categories of information possessed by a listed entity, which may otherwise go to value, are properly excluded from mandatory disclosure regimes.
21. Kimberly Krawiec, 'Fairness, Efficiency and Insider Trading: Deconstructing the Coin of the Realm in the Information Age' (2001) 95 *North Western University Law Review* 443, 489.
22. Roberta Romano, 'Empowering Investors: A Market Approach to Securities Regulation' (1998) 107 *Yale Law Journal* 2359, 2374; Richard Frankel, Maureen McNichols and G Peter Wilson, 'Discretionary Disclosure and External Financing' (1995) 70 *Accounting Review* 135, 141.
23. Maribeth Coller and Teri Yohn, 'Management Forecasts and Information Asymmetry: An Examination of Bid-Ask Spreads' (1997) 35 *Journal of Accounting Research* 181.
24. Christine Botosan, 'Evidence that Greater Disclosure Lowers the Cost of Equity Capital' (2000) 12 *Bank of America Journal of Applied Corporate Finance* 60.
25. See, e.g., Jennifer Francis, Douglas Philbrick and Katherine Schipper, 'Shareholder Litigation and Corporate Disclosures' (1994) 32 *Journal of Accounting Research* 137; Douglas Skinner, 'Earnings Disclosures and Stockholder Lawsuits' (1997) 23 *Journal of Accounting and Economics* 249.
26. Frank Easterbrook and Daniel Fischel, 'Mandatory Disclosure and the Protection of Investors' (1984) 70 *Virginia Law Review* 669, 673–676, 684, 694, 709; Roberta Romano, 'Empowering Investors: A Market Approach to Securities Regulation' (1998) 107 *Yale Law Journal* 2359, 2373.

capital, and a takeover bid may be avoided by participating in a buy-out or private equity bid, or by establishing takeover protections.[27] In these circumstances, the security prices may not accurately reflect their underlying economic value, thereby reducing the efficiency of the relevant market.

Senior executives are undoubtedly well positioned to provide valuable information about a company to the market because they manage the day-to-day operations of the business, and this provides them with a comprehensive and nuanced understanding of company developments and issues.[28] Nevertheless, there are significant information asymmetries between senior managers and outside investors and other stakeholders. And when short-term managerial incentives intrude on or dominate the corporate decision making processes, these differences in knowledge can be manipulated and abused. The primary areas of concern arise when managers have incentives to hide or disguise information needed by outsiders, such as impending losses that would significantly decrease security prices if discovered by outsiders. These incentives can be so powerful that some companies misrepresent or fail to disclose material information,[29] particularly when performance trends are negative or the company's financial position is ailing.[30]

Some commentators suggest that companies are forced to disclose unfavourable news, otherwise sophisticated institutional investors will interpret the lack of disclosure as bad news.[31] However, a company's silence does not provide unambiguous signals to the market of impending bad news. When negative corporate news is publicly announced, and it is clear that the relevant executives were aware of the information earlier than its public release, the prices of the company's listed securities may fall as a result of poor transparency and a loss of trust. Nonetheless, there are forceful countervailing motivations for managers to avoid disclosure of unfavourable news or to delay its public release, particularly when accountability or blame may attach. Public disclosure of negative events or issues may harm managers' reputations, employment prospects, and remuneration packages.

Private disclosure of company information allows managers to have control over information dissemination processes and limits their accountability for poor business

27. Zohar Goshen and Gideon Parchomovsky, 'The Essential Role Of Securities Regulation' (2006) 55 *Duke Law Journal* 711, 760–761.
28. See, e.g., Orie Barron, Charles Kile and Terrence O'Keefe, 'MD&A Quality and Analysts' Earnings Forecasts' (1999) 16 *Contemporary Accounting Research* 75; Michael Guttentag, 'An Argument for Imposing Disclosure Requirements on Public Companies' (2004) 32 *Florida State University Law Review* 123, 173.
29. See, e.g., Victor Brudney, 'Insiders, Outsiders, and Informational Advantages Under the Federal Securities Laws' (1979) 93 *Harvard Law Review* 322, 327.
30. Jennifer Arlen and William Carney, 'Vicarious Liability for Fraud on Securities Markets: Theory and Evidence' (1992) *University of Illinois Law Review* 691, 701; Marc Steinberg, 'Insider Trading, Selective Disclosure, and Prompt Disclosure: A Comparative Analysis' (2001) 22 *University of Pennsylvania Journal of International Economic Law* 635, 658; Zohar Goshen and Gideon Parchomovsky, 'The Essential Role Of Securities Regulation' (2006) 55 *Duke Law Journal* 711, 760.
31. Roberta Romano, 'The Need for Competition in International Securities Regulations' (2001) 2 *Theoretical Inquiries in Law* 387.

judgments and suboptimal company performance. Consequently, in voluntary disclosure environments, company information is likely to be disclosed privately to a narrow spectrum of investors, and the quantity and quality of publicly available information may be limited. Regulation that mandates public disclosure of all material price-sensitive information can assist to promote disclosure of negative corporate news. As Fama and Laffer noted in 1971:

> [i]n some cases where the firm would be the producer of information about itself, a social optimum can be achieved by means of legal disclosure provisions... That is, the firm is restricted by law both from selling information about itself and from giving preferential treatment to either its shareholders or outsiders in increasing information. Such a law destroys the firm's incentive to generate information for trading purposes.[32]

While empirical research indicates that many executives remain reluctant to disclose negative news even within mandatory disclosure jurisdictions,[33] potential action by public or private litigants can alter the disclosure incentive equation.

[C] Third Party Information Incentives

An assessment of potential gains in efficiency and fairness from the imposition of mandatory disclosure regulation requires assumptions to be made about the relationship between the information produced by listed companies and additional information provided by third parties. As will be discussed in Chapter 4, only minimal consideration has been given to this important area until now. While many scholars and practitioners assume that sell-side analyst research plays a critical role in enhancing share price efficiency,[34] the extent to which sell-side reports provide useful content and enhance financial market efficiency in addition to, and independent from, the information provided by companies remains open to question.

Many commentators claim that retail investors require professional analysts to interpret company information and to present it to them in a way that they can

32. Eugene Fama and Arthur Laffer, 'Information and Capital Markets' (1971) 44 *Journal of Business Law* 289, 298.
33. See, e.g., Wilbur Lewellen, Taewoo Park and Byung Ro, 'Self-Serving Behaviour in Managers' Discretionary Information Disclosure' (1996) 21 *Journal of Accounting and Economics* 227; Donald Langevoort, 'Organized Illusions: A Behavioral Theory of Why Corporations Mislead Stock Market Investors (and Cause Other Social Harms)' (1997) 146 *University of Pennsylvania Law Review* 101; Gregory Miller, 'Earnings Performance and Discretionary Disclosure Decisions' (2002) 40 *Journal of Accounting Research* 173; John Graham, Campbell Harvey and Shiva Rajgopal, 'The Economic Implications of Corporate Financial Reporting' (2005) 40 *Journal of Accounting and Economics* 3; SP Kothari, Susan Shu and Peter Wysocki, 'Do Managers Withhold Bad News?' (2009) 47 *Journal of Accounting Research* 241; Dushyantkumar Vyas, 'The Timeliness of Accounting Write-Downs by U.S. Financial Institutions During the Financial Crisis of 2007-2008' (2011) 49 *Journal of Accounting Research* 823; Catherine Schrand and Sarah Zechman, 'Executive Overconfidence and the Slippery Slope to Financial Misreporting' (2012) 53 *Journal of Accounting and Economics* 311.
34. See Jill Fisch and Hillary Sale, 'The Securities Analysts as Agent: Rethinking the Regulation of Analysts' (2003) *88 Iowa Law Review* 1035.

understand.[35] Some argue that retail investors can obtain the benefits of private information by purchasing analyst reports, investing with fund managers, or trading at the market price and free riding on the presumption of market efficiency.[36] However, arguments that suggest that all investors, especially those saving for retirement, should protect themselves or should be required to pay for company information from financial intermediaries is objectionable. As Mitchell notes, 'this results in these investors giving their money to the very institutions whose informational superiority drove them out of the market in the first place.'[37]

The argument that retail investors concerned about informational access should invest through intermediaries,[38] heightens managerial incentives to disclose privately rather than publicly. However, when company information is exchanged privately on a regular basis, this results in a cycle of institutional reliance on managers to provide most or all of the required company information and commentary through private exchanges. As discussed more fully in Chapter 4, it also leads to analyst relationships based on favour and a high stakes race by analysts and investors to gain better and or faster access to private earnings related information.

§2.03 EFFICIENCY

A key issue of any company disclosure debate concerns the extent to which mandatory reporting regimes alter information incentives and enhance market efficiency and fairness outcomes. Most commentators argue for or against mandatory disclosure regimes on either 'efficiency' or 'fairness' grounds, rather than on a holistic basis. Commentators in favour of voluntary or discretionary disclosure environments argue that financial markets operate *most* efficiently by allowing listed company directors and managers to determine the most appropriate disclosure processes. These parties suggest that efficiency is optimised when companies are able to choose:

- whether to disclose specific information to the market;
- whether to disclose information privately or publicly;
- when to disclose information; and
- the specific investors to whom information is disclosed.

Those who support mandatory disclosure regimes argue instead that efficiency is best optimised by enactment of disclosure regulation because it ensures timely disclosure of material company information to all investors.

35. See, e.g., Scott Russell, 'Regulation Fair Disclosure: The Death of the Efficient Capital Market Hypothesis and the Birth of Herd Behaviour' (2002) 82 *Boston University Law Review* 527, 550; Linda Yi, 'Road Shows On The Internet: Taking Individual Investors For A Ride On The Information Highway' (2002) 52 *Duke Law Journal* 243, 259–261.
36. See, e.g., Scott Russell, 'Regulation Fair Disclosure: The Death of the Efficient Capital Market Hypothesis and the Birth of Herd Behaviour' (2002) 82 *Boston University Law Review* 527, 550.
37. Lawrence Mitchell, 'Book Review –The Cult of Efficiency' (1992) 71 *Texas Law Review* 217, 226.
38. See, e.g., Kimberly Krawiec, 'Fairness, Efficiency and Insider Trading: Deconstructing the Coin of the Realm in the Information Age' (2001) 95 *North Western University Law Review* 443, 479.

Efficiency concepts that are commonly discussed within the mandatory disclosure literature include: agency costs, information production costs, information utility, price efficiency, and externalities. These efficiency concepts and models are evaluated in turn.

[A] Agency Costs

Many scholars assess corporate disclosure issues through the prism of an agency model.[39] The agency theories typically assume that when the principals (the shareholders and other corporate stakeholders) and agents (the managers and directors) are utility or profit maximisers, company directors and managers will be motivated to act in their own interests and to maximise personal returns.[40] Shareholders (and sometimes other stakeholders) can try to prevent or limit potential and actual conflicts between managers and the company as a whole by structuring the remuneration of managers and directors to incentivise desired outcomes.[41] They may also establish a range of processes to enable effective monitoring of manager and director conduct.

Contributors to the mandatory disclosure debate tend to draw on elements of the agency theory that reflect a particular model of market efficiency. Those who support voluntary disclosure environments argue that agency costs are reduced and market efficiency is enhanced when institutional investors and analysts receive information privately and act as market 'gatekeepers'.[42] Many commentators argue these investors have comparative advantages vis-à-vis individual investors in the monitoring process. Some further assume or assert that only large institutional investors have the resources and ability to monitor companies.[43] Such sweeping investor characterisations should not be accepted without detailed explanation and substantiation. Market observation and empirical studies suggest that institutional investors are not always effective corporate monitors.[44] Moreover, even if these participants are consistently proactive and engaged as corporate overseers, this does not necessarily minimise agency costs.

The purpose of corporate monitoring under an agency model is to minimise the multilayered conflicts that arise within listed companies. As Davies et al. indicate:

39. See, e.g., Anne Beyer, Daniel Cohen, Thomas Lys and Beverly Walther, 'The Financial Reporting Environment: Review of the Recent Literature' (2010) 50 *Journal of Accounting and Economics* 296.
40. See, e.g., Michael Jensen and William Meckling, 'Theory of the Firm: Managerial Behaviour, Agency Costs and Ownership Structure' (1976) 3 *Journal of Financial Economics* 305.
41. Michael Jensen and William Meckling, 'Theory of the Firm: Managerial Behaviour, Agency Costs and Ownership Structure' (1976) 3 *Journal of Financial Economics* 305, 308.
42. See, e.g., Stephen Thurber, 'The Insider Trading Compensation Contract as an Inducement to Monitoring by the Institutional Investor' (1994) 1 *George Mason University Law Review* 119, 134.
43. See Michael Jensen and William Meckling, 'Theory of the Firm: Managerial Behaviour, Agency Costs and Ownership Structure' (1976) 3 *Journal of Financial Economics* 305, 354.
44. Bipin Ajinkya, Sanjeev Bhojraj and Partha Sengupta, 'The Association Between Outside Directors, Institutional Investors and the Properties of Management Earnings Forecasts' (2005) 43 *Journal of Accounting Research* 343; Jana Fidrmuc, Marc Goergen and Luc Renneboog, 'Insider Trading, News Releases, and Ownership Concentration' (2006) 61 *Journal of Finance* 2931.

> Within corporate law, agency problems fall into three categories: those between the management (agent) and the shareholders as a class (principal) where shareholdings in a company are dispersed; those between controlling (agent) and non-controlling (principal) shareholders where shareholdings are concentrated; and those between the controllers of the company (agent) and non-shareholder stakeholders ...[45]

As previously noted, the personal interests of managers are not always fully aligned with the long-term interests of the company and senior executives are unlikely to willingly discuss negative developments or instances of poor managerial judgment, suboptimal performance, or misconduct in voluntary disclosure environments. Furthermore, the interests of controlling shareholders such as institutional investors can diverge from the interests of non-controlling shareholders and other stakeholders. Controlling shareholders naturally prefer to obtain information privately from listed companies in order to gain informational advantages, leaving other investors and stakeholders in a disadvantaged position. Hence, critical issues that arise when listed company information is communicated voluntarily include potential misalignments of corporate, managerial, institutional and other outsider incentives, and the consequential suboptimal long-term outcomes. The essential question that needs to be addressed is whether the long-term interests of corporations and the communities they operate in, and interact with, are better served by mandatory disclosure frameworks.

[B] Information Production Costs

Commentators that favour minimal regulatory interference argue that market forces reduce unnecessary information production costs or research. They suggest that listed companies have incentives to provide information at lower costs because the valuations of companies with high information acquisition costs are discounted.[46] It is not clear though how uninformed investors can practically adjust their valuations of companies to take into account information acquisition costs (or lack of access to information), particularly in financial markets that permit private or selective disclosure.

Evidence from the early part of the twentieth century suggests that in the absence of disclosure regulation, large institutional investors would negotiate for information exchanges with companies.[47] The costs to produce this information may have been similar to the costs incurred under a mandatory disclosure regime. However, the quality of the reported financial results and management discussion and analysis may have been lower if these were not prepared in accordance with generally accepted

45. See Paul Davies, Guido Ferrarini, Klaus Hopt, Alain Pietrancosta, Rolf Skog, Satanislaw Soltysinski, Jaap Winter and Eddy Wymeersch, 'European Company Law Experts' *Response to the European Commission's Green Paper* "The EU Corporate Governance Framework"' (22 July 2011) 1 http://papers.ssrn.com/sol3/papers.cfm?abstract_id=1912548 viewed 10 April 2013.
46. Gordon Walker, Brent Fisse and Ian Ramsay, *Securities Regulation in Australia and New Zealand* ((Lawbook Co, 1st ed., 1994) 69.
47. See, e.g., Richard Morris, 'Corporate Disclosure in a Substantially Unregulated Environment' (1984) 20 *Abacus* 52.

accounting standards and not subject to independent scrutiny and verification by external auditors.

Parties agree that information is essential to the efficiency of financial markets, but views differ on the issue of whether in the absence of mandatory disclosure, company information would be under or over-produced.[48] Valuable resources may be wasted in voluntary disclosure environments if investors spend undue time trying to obtain company information or generating similar information relating to listed company securities.[49] Listed company information is produced for multiple purposes, with ongoing requirements for information from various government and private entities and participants, regardless of the content of any disclosure regulation.[50] Listed company directors and senior managers are generally required by their employers, and by law, to keep abreast of trading conditions and the company's financial and operational positions. Companies have established structures, technologies, and processes to provide regular (usually monthly) reports to assist managers and directors to monitor developments and performance and to run the business efficiently.[51] The costs to produce mandated information are therefore marginal as much of the information that would be required within a mandatory disclosure regime is already being regularly produced by companies.[52] Subsequent electronic dissemination of this information to outsiders is also now relatively easy and low cost. In fact, it is now considerably more expensive and cumbersome for companies to provide information to investors at a series of private meetings, because this requires senior managers to present the same material and respond to similar questions at each meeting.

[C] Information Utility

Some commentators suggest that information provided under mandatory disclosure regulation is not useful[53] because it is predominantly historical

48. Jack Hirshleifer, 'The Private and Social Value of Information and Reward To Inventive Activity' (1971) 61 *American Economic Review* 561, 565–566; Frank Easterbrook and Daniel Fischel, 'Mandatory Disclosure and the Protection of Investors' (1984) 70 *Virginia Law Review* 669, 682.
49. Jack Hirshleifer, 'The Private and Social Value of Information and Reward To Inventive Activity' (1971) 61 *American Economic Review* 561, 565–566; Frank Easterbrook and Daniel Fischel, 'Mandatory Disclosure and the Protection of Investors' (1984) 70 *Virginia Law Review* 669, 682.
50. Kimberly Krawiec, 'Fairness, Efficiency and Insider Trading: Deconstructing the Coin of the Realm in the Information Age' (2001) 95 *North Western University Law Review* 443, 488. See also Harold Demsetz, 'The Private Production of Public Goods' (1970) 13 *Journal of Law and Economics* 293, 295; J onathan Oever, 'Insider Trading and the Dual Role of Information' (1997) 106 *Yale Law Journal* 1325; Kimberly Krawiec, 'Fairness, Efficiency and Insider Trading: Deconstructing the Coin of the Realm in the Information Age' (2001) 95 *North Western University Law Review* 443, 488.
51. Zohar Goshen and Gideon Parchomovsky, 'The Essential Role Of Securities Regulation' (2006) 55 *Duke Law Journal* 711, 757–758.
52. James Cox, 'Premises for Reforming the Regulation of Securities Offerings: An Essay' (2000) 63 *Law and Contemporary Problems* 11, 17.
53. Homer Kripke, 'The SEC, The Accountants, Some Myths and Some Realities' (1970) 45 *New York University Law Review* 1151; Jonathan Macey, 'Administrative Agency Obsolescence and Interest Group Formation: A Case Study of the SEC at Sixty' (1994) 15 *Cardozo Law Review* 909; Edmund Kitch, 'The Theory and Practice of Securities Disclosure' (1995) 61 *Brooklyn Law*

information.[54] These theoretical assumptions are poorly informed. Financial reports that present a company's position and performance on a regular basis are necessary to ensure that all internal and external groups are kept apprised of a company's financial and operational positions. Managers and directors use these historical numbers and trends as the baseline for determining future strategies, plans and budgets. Similarly, investors and others engaged in corporate analysis and security valuation use the reported figures as the starting position for estimating future earnings or cash flow. In any event, jurisdictions with mandatory disclosure regimes generally require companies to explain and analyse the reported results, including discussion of isolated and recurring items. Executives are also required to outline and discuss company prospects and longer-term strategies and plans.[55]

Some critics concede that mandated disclosures might be useful to institutional investors, but claim the idea that retail investor decisions are informed by mandated reports is a myth.[56] These commentators suggest that retail investors as a group lack the time, desire and skill to analyse securities information. These arguments assume a complete divide between institutional and retail investors, and are regularly expressed within scholarly publications and policy reviews, but are rarely substantiated or supported by empirical research. In reality, some institutional investors have a poor fundamental understanding of the securities that they trade or invest in,[57] while some retail investors are skilled, sophisticated and understand well the companies and securities within their portfolios.[58] Institutional and retail investors exist on a highly diversified spectrum, and simple assumptions or generalisations do not encompass the levels of professionalism, competency and diligence across both groups.

Review 763; Roberta Romano, 'Empowering Investors: A Market Approach to Securities Regulation' (1998) 107 *Yale Law Journal* 2359, 2359-2361, 2428.

54. Homer Kripke, 'The SEC, The Accountants, Some Myths and Some Realities' (1970) 45 *New York University Law Review* 1151, 1197-1201; Frank Easterbrook and Daniel Fischel, 'Mandatory Disclosure and the Protection of Investors' (1984) 70 *Virginia Law Review* 669, 703-704; Christopher Donald, 'A Critique of Arguments for Mandatory Continuous Disclosure' (1999) 62 *Saskatchewan Law Review* 85, 116-117.
55. See, e.g., Regulation S-K Item 303, *Management's Discussion and Analysis of Financial Condition and Results of Operations* (2005); United States Securities and Exchange Commission, Securities Release 33-8350 (29 December 2003) Financial Reporting Release 72, *Interpretation: Commission Guidance Regarding Management's Discussion and Analysis of Financial Conditions and Results of Operations.*
56. See, e.g., Jeff Schwartz, 'Fairness, Utility, and Market Risk' (2010) 89 *Oregon Law Review* 175, 183. See also Scott Russell, 'Regulation Fair Disclosure: The Death of the Efficient Capital Market Hypothesis and the Birth of Herd Behaviour' (2002) 82 *Boston University Law Review* 527, 550; Linda Yi, 'Road Shows On The Internet: Taking Individual Investors For A Ride On The Information Highway' (2002) 52 *Duke Law Journal* 243, 259-261.
57. The fact that most of the trading and portfolio losses accumulated during the global financial crisis resulted from institutional decision making seems to have been quickly forgotten.
58. See, e.g., Ron Kaniel, Shuming Liu, Gideon Saar and Sheridan Titman, 'Individual Investor Trading and Return Patterns Around Earnings Announcements' (2012) 57 *Journal of Finance* 639; Joshua Coval, David Hirshleifer and Tyler Shumway, 'Can Individual Investors Beat the Market?' (Working Paper 04-025, Harvard University, September 2005).

[D] Price Efficiency

Critics of mandatory disclosure regimes argue that listed company information is sufficiently disclosed and factored into share prices by means of voluntary disclosures, insider trading, independent research, and the media.[59] These commentators rely on notions of price efficiency. Security price efficiency theories derive from the efficient markets theory and efficient capital markets hypothesis (ECMH) developed by Eugene Fama in the 1960s. The Fama efficient markets theory is discussed more fully in Chapter 3. To summarise, this theory centres on the speed and accuracy with which share prices achieve equilibrium when new information becomes available.[60] Markets are commonly described as fundamentally efficient when security prices respond to available information quickly and accurately, and prices across the market reflect the best possible estimates of the underlying economic value of the securities in terms of their expected risks and returns, given all available information.[61] The mechanisms to achieve share price accuracy involve a number of steps, including information searching and analysis, accuracy verification and trading.[62]

[E] Externalities

Most scholarly empirical models are not able to measure or encompass all of the direct and indirect financial and social costs that arise when companies either fail to publicly disclose significant developments at all, or when they only partially or selectively disclose material information.[63] Some commentators include the benefits of disclosure to a company's competitors as an externality in their efficiency analysis.[64] However, broader and more significant externalities are generally excluded from efficiency models and theories. Such externalities involve harm or damage suffered by corporate stakeholders (including employees, creditors, tort claimants, and fraud victims) resulting from disclosure omissions or delays, or from misleading and deceptive reporting. Indirect costs to the community, including the cost to bail out companies using

59. Jonathan Macey, 'Administrative Agency Obsolescence and Interest Group Formation: A Case Study of the SEC at Sixty' (1994) 15 *Cardozo Law Review* 909, 928; Roberta Romano, 'Empowering Investors: A Market Approach to Securities Regulation' (1998) 107 *Yale Law Journal* 2359, 2373, 2380, 2428.
60. D Craig Nichols and James Wahlen, 'How Do Earnings Numbers Relate To Stock Returns? A Review Of Classic Accounting Research With Updated Evidence' (December 2004) *Accounting Horizons* 263, 281.
61. Lynn Stout, 'The Mechanisms of Market Inefficiency: An Introduction to the New Finance' (2003) 28 *Journal of Corporation Law* 635, 640. See also William Sharpe, 'Efficient Capital Markets: A Review of Theory and Empirical Work' (1970) 25 *Journal of Finance* 418, 418.
62. Zohar Goshen and Gideon Parchomovsky, 'The Essential Role Of Securities Regulation' (2006) 55 *Duke Law Journal* 711, 714, 721.
63. Gill North and Ross Buckley, 'A Financial Transaction Tax: Inefficient or Needed Systemic Reform?' (2012) 43 *Georgetown Journal of International Law* 745.
64. Anne Beyer, Daniel Cohen, Thomas Lys and Beverly Walther, 'The Financial Reporting Environment: Review of the Recent Literature' (2010) 50 *Journal of Accounting and Economics* 296, 315.

taxpayer monies or consequential harm resulting from inappropriate corporate behaviour, such as losses borne by shareholders, creditors and employees when the assets of a company are seriously depleted by conduct that is not motivated by sound commercial rationales are also excluded from most theoretical and empirical efficiency frameworks.

Efficiency rationales and effects in financial markets are interrelated with fairness factors. While fairness factors are difficult to define and measure, public trust and fair conduct are important factors underpinning broad financial market participation.[65]

§2.04 FAIRNESS

Most policy and scholarly commentary on fairness issues within financial markets focuses on notions of equal access, investor protection, fraud minimisation, and investor confidence. These fairness concepts and measures are tightly interwoven. Equal access is the foundational step, in the sense that investor protection, fraud minimisation, and investor confidence depend on broadly equivalent information access rights. It is difficult to provide credible investor protection and to sustain investor confidence in markets where listed company information is regularly provided on a private or selective basis. Similarly, when the levels and quality of publicly disclosed company information are poor, public scrutiny and other control processes that deter or mitigate fraud cannot fully operate.

[A] Equal Access

The morality of investors trading without equal access to information has been the subject of heated debate among philosophers and legal scholars for many centuries.[66] Most equal access theories involving company information are based on concepts of consent, or notions that rules are only fair if disinterested individuals who will be bound by them would agree to them in advance.[67] A narrower model developed by Brudney does not seek to offset individual disparities of power, wealth, diligence or intelligence,[68] but it prohibits parties from possessing informational advantages that others cannot lawfully overcome (known as unerodable information advantages).[69] Global disclosure regimes that require listed companies to publicly disclose material price-sensitive information are generally based on the Brudney model.

65. See, e.g., Luigi Guiso, Paola Sapienza and Luigi Zingales, 'Trusting the Stock Market' (2008) 63 *Journal of Finance* 2557.
66. Garry Lawson, 'The Ethics of Insider Trading' (1988) 11 *Harvard Journal of Law and Public Policy* 727, 737, 753.
67. Kim Scheppele, '"It's Just Not Right": The Ethics of Insider Trading' (1993) 56 *Law & Contemporary Problems* 123, 151–154; David Gauthier, *Morals By Agreement* (Oxford University Press, Oxford, 1986).
68. Victor Brudney, 'Insiders, Outsiders, and Informational Advantages Under the Federal Securities Laws' (1979) 93 *Harvard Law Review* 322, 356–361.
69. Victor Brudney, 'Insiders, Outsiders, and Informational Advantages Under the Federal Securities Laws' (1979) 93 *Harvard Law Review* 322, 357, 360.

Some commentators argue that a policy mandating the disclosure of financial information does not favour or defend a specific group of investors; rather it aims to benefit all.[70] Others suggest regulation requiring equal access may adversely affect some investors while improving the lot of others.[71] These arguments reflect, at least in part, the differences between utilitarian or Pareto efficiency measures (the total return across a market or an economy; sometimes referred to as the size of the pie),[72] and those concerned with the distribution of the absolute return (the allocation of the pie).[73] The absence or imposition of mandatory disclosure regulation alters the

70. Baruch Lev, 'Toward a Theory of Equitable and Efficient Accounting Policy' (1988) 63 *Accounting Review* 1, 19.
71. Nils Hakansson, 'Interim Disclosure and Public Forecasts: An Economic Analysis and a Framework for Choice' (1977) 52 *Accounting Review* 396, 413.
72. The Pareto optimum was introduced by Vilfredo Pareto in 1896. The Pareto efficiency approach asks whether a transaction or change will make somebody better off while making no one worse off. Pareto efficiency is a form of utilitarianism, and the inherent theoretical and practical difficulties that arise from utilitarian models apply. There are no criteria for weighing up preferences and excluding those that may not deserve recognition and issues of unequal distribution may be skewed. In addition, the assumptions of voluntariness, complete information and a lack of 'externalities' may not be valid. In practice, 'few policies have no losers'. A pareto optimal allocation may be theoretically possible despite taxes and transaction costs. However, the allocation of resources may be privately optimal but publicly suboptimal when externalities cause a divergence between private and social costs and benefits. Difficulties in measuring and applying the Pareto efficiency criteria led to the development of the Kaldor-Hicks approach, which asks whether a transaction or change will result in a net benefit to all affected individuals. Under the Kaldor test, redistributions are possible in order to achieve an allocation that is superior to the other state according to the Pareto criterion. The Hicks test is met when it is not possible to further redistribute to make everyone better off within a Pareto superior state. The Pareto and Kaldor-Hicks measurements of economic efficiency exclude distributive considerations in an attempt to be value-free. Kaldor argued that an economist cannot be concerned with distributional questions because it is impossible to decide on economic grounds what pattern of income-distribution maximizes social welfare. Similarly, Hicks notes that if measures making for efficiency are to have a fair chance, they should be freed from distributive complications.
73. Some scholars adopt economic models that incorporate income distribution considerations and notions of fairness and equality. See, e.g., Louis Kaplow and Shavell Shavell, *Fairness versus Welfare* (Harvard University Press, Oxford, 2002) 18; Louis Kaplow and Shavall Shavall, 'Fairness versus Welfare' (2001) 114 *Harvard Law Review* 961. Kaplow and Shavall interpret individual preferences broadly in their social welfare model. Individual tastes for a notion of equality and for legal rules that 'comport with some personally held notions of fairness' are included in their assessment of individuals' well-being and thus in determining social welfare. No weight is given to notions of fairness that are independent from individual well-being. However, they suggest that 'redistributing income from the rich to the poor will tend to raise social welfare, assuming that the marginal utility of income is greater for the poor than for the rich.'

    There is a broad range of views among law scholars on the applicability of efficiency and economic models. See, e.g., Laurence Tribe, 'Constitutional Calculus: Equal Justice or Economic Efficiency?' (1985) 98 *Harvard Law Review* 592, 596; Lynne Dallas, 'Two Models of Corporate Governance: Beyond Berle and Means' (1988) 22 *University of Michigan Journal of Law Reform* 19, 45; Alex Johnson Jr, 'An Appeal for the Liberal Use of Law and Economics: The Liberals Fight Back' (1989) 67 *Texas Law Review* 659, 667; Herbert Hovenkamp, 'The First Great Law & Economics Movement' (1990) 42 *Stanford Law Review* 993, 1045; Lawrence Mitchell, 'Book review –The Cult of Efficiency' (1992) 71 *Texas Law Review* 217, 218, 226–228, 241–242. Tribe argues that the appeal of utilitarian policy analysis, as well as its power, lies in its ability to reduce the various dimensions of a problem to a common denominator. He suggests that the law and economics school of thought typically argues that rights should be awarded on grounds of

distribution of returns or trading profits across a market as a result of changes to the positioning and degree of informational advantages between investors. Commentators who adopt a utilitarian or Pareto efficiency model may argue that redistributions of wealth in financial markets do not matter because security trading is zero sum and social welfare outcomes are not impacted.[74] However, such arguments fail to address the substantive empirical evidence that associates superior financial market, corporate and national outcomes with high quality public disclosure, protection of minority shareholder rights, and broad participation.

[B] Investor Protection

Notions of investor protection in modern financial markets often seek or involve a rebalancing of power between the interests of majority and minority shareholders, between large financial institutions and individual investors, and between the interests of corporations and their stakeholders. Adolf Berle and Gardiner Means argued in the 1930s that shareholder power is determined primarily through control, rather than through contractual rights. They suggested that:

---

efficiency to reflect the discontinuous preferences of those who would refuse any inducement to cede those 'rights'. Further, one of the most persistent myths of policy analysis based on a utilitarian approach is that the analytical techniques *in themselves* lack significant substantive bias or controversial content. The disregard of those for distributive concerns cannot be corrected merely by punching in one or more dummy variable labelled 'values'. The cost-benefit comparisons and marginal analyses are already engineered, whether intentionally or not, to serve a specific agenda. Mitchell suggests that the economic models used have enormous public policy consequences, including exacerbating the potentially dangerous trend towards the concentration of corporate wealth in the hands of a relatively small group of institutional investors. Moreover, they draw conclusions based on their model, expressed with characteristic certitude that are debatable even on their own terms. Mitchell describes the approach as ultra-utilitarian, openly discriminatory and lacking any conception of justice or distributional fairness. He notes that Adam Smith accommodated the goals of altruism and concern for others in his economic theories.

There is also a broad range of views among scholars on the use of economic models and analysis within public policy decision making. See, e.g., John Chipman and James Moore, 'The New Welfare Economics 1939-1974' (1978) 19 *International Economic Review* 547, 548; Robert Frank, 'If Homo Economicus Could Choose His Own Utility Function, Would He Want One with a Conscience?' (1987) 77 *American Economic Review* 593, 603; Amitai Etzioni, *The Moral Dimension: Toward a New Economics* (Free Press, 15 June 1990); Amartya Sen, *On Ethics and Economics* (Wiley-Blackwell, 1987) 22–28. Chipman and Moore argue that economics must be considered a failure judged in relation to its basic objective of enabling economists to make welfare prescriptions without having to make value judgments and, in particular, interpersonal comparisons of utility. They suggest that policy recommendations must be made on the basis of value judgments, and these value judgments should be made explicit. Sen suggests that public choice theory is made unduly narrow by the insistence that individuals invariably behave as *Homo Economicus* because such restrictions can significantly misrepresent the nature of social concerns and values. Hammond agrees that value-free measures are undesirable and impossible. Frank indicates that it is neither necessary nor productive for modern economists to exclude behavioural factors such as conscience and other moral sentiments from utility maximisation models.

74. See, e.g., Jeff Schwartz, 'Fairness, Utility, and Market Risk' (2010) 89 *Oregon Law Review* 175, 189.

> Control lies in the hands of the individual or group who have the actual power to select the board of directors (or its majority) ... In most cases ... if one can determine who does actually have power to select the directors, one has located the group of individuals who for practical purposes may be regarded as the 'control'.[75]

This procedural notion of control is a key element within mandatory disclosure debates. In developed nations, institutional investors hold majority stakes in many listed companies and for practical purposes often have 'control' of these companies. The largest market participants can and do use their significant political and financial power to demand superior private access to information from listed companies, leaving other investors and stakeholders in a disadvantaged position. The informational interests of shareholders and stakeholders outside of this core group of investors can potentially be ignored in a voluntary disclosure environment.

An investor protection rationale impliedly accepts that in a voluntary company disclosure environment, uninformed investors are likely to suffer harm when trading against counterparties with private (inside or selectively disclosed) company information. While some critics argue that unsophisticated investors do not require mandatory disclosure as a protective mechanism because of the efficiency of the market,[76] these arguments infer or assume that no investors can gain from receipt of 'inside' or private information. However as discussed in more detail in Chapter 3, empirical evidence of financial market efficiency suggests that uninformed investors are not protected when trading against counterparties with private company information.[77]

75. Adolph Berle and Gardiner Means, *The Modern Corporation and Private Property* (Transaction Publishers, 1932) 66–67.
76. See, e.g., Merritt Fox, 'Civil Liability and Mandatory Disclosure' (2009) 109 *Columbia Law Review* 237.
77. See Eugene Fama, 'Efficient Capital Markets: A Review of Theory and Empirical Work' (1970) 25 *Journal of Finance* 383. Fama argued in the 1960s that an efficient market is one in which prices 'fully reflect' available information. His efficient capital market hypothesis is designed to empirically test the extent to which security prices reflect particular information subsets. Commentators generally agree that markets are only either semi-strong or weak form efficient, which means that security price do not fully reflect private information. See William Bratton and Michael Wachter, 'The Case Against Shareholder Empowerment' (2010) 158 *University of Pennsylvania Law Review* 653, 691. Empirical studies generally find that company insiders can in many instances outperform the general market. See H Nejat Seyhun, 'Insider's Profits, Costs of Trading and Market Efficiency' (1986) 16 *Journal of Financial Economics* 189; H Nejat Seyhun, 'The Effectiveness of the Insider Trading Sanctions' (1992) 35 *Journal of Law and Economics* 149; Michael Rozeff and Mir Zaman, 'Market Efficiency and Insider Trading: New Evidence' (1988) 61 *Journal of Business* 25; Stephen Penman, 'Insider Trading and the Dissemination of Firm's Forecast Information' (1982) 55 *Journal of Business* 479; John Elliott, Dale Morse and Gordon Richardson, 'The Association Between Insider Trading and Information Announcements' (1984) 15 *RAND Journal of Economics* 521. See also Thomas Eyssell, 'Corporate Insiders and the Death of the Firm: Evidence on the Incidence of Insider Trading in Corporate Dissolutions' (1991) 26 *Financial Review* 517; H Nejat Seyhun and Michael Bradley, 'Corporate Bankruptcy and Insider Trading' (1997) 70 *Journal of Business* 189; Philip Brown, Mark Foo and Iain Watson, 'Trading by Insiders in Australia: Evidence on the Profitability of Directors' Trades' (2003) 21 *Company and Securities Law Journal* 248; Jana Fidrmuc, Marc Goergen and Luc Renneboog, 'Insider Trading, News Releases, and Ownership Concentration' (2006) 61 *Journal of Finance* 2931; Hollis Skaife, David Veenman and Daniel Wangerin, 'Internal Control Over Financial Reporting and Managerial Rent Extraction: Evidence From The Profitability of Insider Trading' (2013) 55 *Journal of Accounting and Economics* 91.

Some scholars suggest that individual shareholders do not require protection because they can sell their shares when they are dissatisfied with the disclosure practices or other aspects of a company's activities or performance. This argument is, at best, incomplete. In extreme cases, investors may lose their total investment without the capacity to sell if the company moves into some form of external administration. In less extreme circumstances, selling one's shares at a large loss when a company's security price is falling with no accompanying disclosures to explain the decline cannot be characterised as an optimal situation. Such instances leave the affected investors with a deep-seated sense of disillusionment and, over time, these occurrences severely weaken confidence and public trust in the integrity of the market.

Other critics argue that long-term investors do not suffer loss from inadequate disclosure provided they hold diversified portfolios, because any loss suffered from one transaction is countered by gains from other transactions. In other words, a diversified investor will suffer a mix of gains and losses, thereby negating any investor protection concerns.[78] This argument may be valid to some extent when an investor is entirely passive and the portfolio is intended to reflect general market movements over a specified period, but even then the gains and losses incurred across the portfolio or relevant index may not be equally borne. The diversified investor argument becomes even more problematic when the private exchange of material 'inside information' is involved. Inadequate disclosure involves both failures to disclose material information to all investors, and disclosing material information to only select investors. These categories are often blurred in practice, because investors with private access to company executives can ask for additional information or seek clarification of ambiguous or incomplete disclosures.

[C] Mitigation of Fraud Related Losses

Several scholars suggest the central aim of securities law is to deter fraud.[79] One critic dismisses the fraud protection argument on the basis that there is limited evidence of rampant fraud prior to the introduction of disclosure regulation in the US.[80] Others

78. Paul Davies, 'Liability for Misstatements to the Market: Some Reflections' (2009) 9 *Journal of Corporate Law Studies* 295, 300. See also, Merritt Fox, 'Civil Liability and Mandatory Disclosure' (2009) 109 *Columbia Law Review* 237, 253. Davies points out [at 300] that it is crucial to note that this argument does not negate the rationales or need for mandatory continuing disclosure obligations to be placed on companies. He indicates these obligations can be well supported on allocative efficiency and governance grounds.
79. Jennifer Arlen and William Carney, 'Vicarious Liability for Fraud on Securities Markets: Theory and Evidence' (1992) *University of Illinois Law Review* 691, 704; Joel Seligman, 'The Historical Need for a Mandatory Corporate Disclosure System' (1983) 9 *Journal of Corporation Law* 1, 7–8; Lynn Stout, 'The Unimportance of Being Efficient: An Economic Analysis of Stock Market Pricing and Securities Regulation' (1988) 87 *Michigan Law Review* 613, 700-01.
80. Roberta Romano, 'Empowering Investors: A Market Approach to Securities Regulation' (1998) 107 *Yale Law Journal* 2359, 2381.

suggest there is no evidence that mandatory disclosure regimes have reduced incidences of fraud.[81] The proposition that company disclosure regulation is designed to prevent all instances of corporate fraud is misconceived. Mandatory disclosure regimes are not intended to prevent all corporate fraud; however, regulation that promotes transparent corporate disclosure to the public can mitigate the consequences of corporate fraud or failures. Regulatory frameworks that mandate public reporting and enable public scrutiny of company developments significantly broaden the spectrum of possible monitors and critics. This increased scrutiny deters, or draws attention to, possible instances of fraud, poor business practices and performance issues, and it invites stakeholder response.[82] As Lowenstein suggests, the power of public scrutiny stems from the principle that 'corporate executives, like the rest of us, behave more honestly, diligently and competently, when they know that their stewardship of other people's money is open to scrutiny.'[83]

Some commentators suggest the usefulness of company disclosure in deterring fraud is limited because the bulk of mandated information is provided for security valuation purposes, rather than for public consumption.[84] Yet, there are many instances of fraud and corporate misconduct that are directly or indirectly reflected in company reporting. Moreover, when valuing a company's securities using fundamental analysis, the skill and integrity of the company managers are key assessment factors. Thus it is not clear how one can draw boundaries around information required to value company securities and information used to identify possible misconduct or fraud. These classes of information overlap to such an extent that they are arguably indistinguishable.[85]

[D] Investor Confidence

The investor confidence rationale generally centres on the need to ensure that a broad spectrum of investors are sufficiently confident in the integrity of the market that they are willing to participate. Concepts of market integrity and investor confidence are linked to arguments supporting equality of access and notions that market participants should operate on a 'level playing field'. Proponents argue that investor confidence is undermined 'by a sense of systematic discriminatory treatment between those "in the

81. See, e.g., Frank Easterbrook and Daniel Fischel, 'Mandatory Disclosure and the Protection of Investors' (1984) 70 *Virginia Law Review* 669, 673–674.
82. See, e.g., Commonwealth of Australia, HIH Royal Commission, *The Failure of HIH Insurance* (2003) vol. 1 68; Andrew McRobert and Ronnie Hoffman, *Corporate Collapse: An Early Warning System for Lenders, Investors and Suppliers* (McGraw Hill, Sydney, 1997) 1279, 1332, 1352, 1358.
83. Louis Lowenstein, 'Financial Transparency and Corporate Governance: You Manage What You Measure' (1996) 96 *Columbia Law Review* 1335, 1339. See also Robert Bushman, Joseph Piotroski and Abbie Smith, 'What Determines Corporate Transparency?' (2004) 42 *Journal of Accounting Research* 207; Victor Brudney, 'Insiders, Outsiders, and Informational Advantages Under the Federal Securities Laws' (1979) 93 *Harvard Law Review* 322, 335–336.
84. Jeff Schwartz, 'Fairness, Utility, and Market Risk' (2010) 89 *Oregon Law Review* 175, 185.
85. Based on the authors many years of experience as a professional analyst and user of global company disclosures.

know" and the average investor.'[86] One scholar suggests that it is now recognised that regulation governing the use of price-sensitive information is required to sustain investor confidence in the integrity of a market.[87]

However, some scholars reject all fairness-based justifications for mandatory disclosure, including equal access, investor protection, fraud deterrence, and investor confidence.[88] It is even suggested that investors expect inside information 'as part of the gamble of investing in the stock market,'[89] and an effort to install confidence may 'actually mislead ... the unsophisticated by suggesting that the stock market is a more secure investment than it really is.'[90] These arguments are narrowly framed and ultimately counterproductive. People do not act in a social vacuum. Research confirms that many people make investment choices relying on fairness principles,[91] and their perceptions of the integrity and fairness of a market significantly influence their willingness to invest.[92] The Financial Commission in the US expressed the investor confidence argument more broadly, noting that the 'integrity of our financial markets and the public's trust in those markets are essential to the economic well-being of ... [a] nation.'[93] Greg Tanzer, the Secretary General of IOSCO, confirms that investor confidence is at the core of its aims. He suggests that investor confidence depends on the integrity, comprehensiveness and transparency of financial reporting,[94] because a well-informed market is an essential factor in stable financial systems, management of systemic risk, continuing market investment and economic growth.[95]

86. Donald Langevoort, 'Investment Analysts and the Law of Insider Trading' (1990) 76 *Virginia Law Review* 1023, 1048.
87. Kern Alexander, 'UK Insider Dealing and Market Abuse Law: Strengthening Regulatory Law to Combat Market Misconduct' in Stephen Bainbridge (ed.), *Research Handbook on Insider Trading* (Edward Elgar, Cheltenham UK, 2013) 428.
88. Frank Easterbrook and Daniel Fischel, 'Mandatory Disclosure and the Protection of Investors' (1984) 70 *Virginia Law Review* 669; Roberta Romano, 'Empowering Investors: A Market Approach to Securities Regulation' (1998) 107 *Yale Law Journal* 2359, 2381; John Barry, 'The Economics of Outside Information and Rule 10b-5' (1981) 129 *University of Pennsylvania Law Review* 1307, 1352–1353.
89. John Barry, 'The Economics of Outside Information and Rule 10b-5' (1981) 129 *University of Pennsylvania Law Review* 1307, 1352.
90. John Barry, 'The Economics of Outside Information and Rule 10b-5' (1981) 129 *University of Pennsylvania Law Review* 1307, 1352–1353.
91. See, e.g., Cass Sunstein, *Free Markets and Social Justice* (Oxford University Press, 1997) 53–54. See also Elizabeth Hoffman and Matthew Spitzer, 'Entitlement, Rights and Fairness: An Experimental Examination of Subjects' Concepts of Distributive Justice' (1985) 14 *Journal of Legal Studies* 259; Daniel Kahneman, Jack Knetsch and Richard Thaler, 'Fairness as a Constraint on Profit Seeking: Entitlements in the Market' (1986) 76 *American Economic Review* 728; Robert Bloomfield, Robert Libby and M Nelson, 'Confidence and the Welfare of Less-Informed Investors' (1999) 24 *Accounting, Organizations and Society* 623.
92. Donald Langevoort, 'Words From on High about Rule 10b-5: Chiarella's History, Central Bank's Future' (1995) 20 *Delaware Journal of Corporate Law* 865, 885.
93. United States Financial Crisis Inquiry Commission Report 47 (January 2011) xxii.
94. Greg Tanzer, Secretary General, International Organization of Securities Commissions, 'Building a Better Financial System: IOSCO's Role' (Speech delivered to Intergovernmental Working Group of Experts on International Standards of Accounting and Reporting, 12 October 2011) 2.
95. Greg Tanzer, Secretary General, International Organization of Securities Commissions, 'Building a Better Financial System: IOSCO's Role' (Speech delivered to Intergovernmental Working Group of Experts on International Standards of Accounting and Reporting, 12 October 2011).

§2.05 GOVERNANCE

This section extends to broader and more holistic discussion that highlights the importance of corporate governance frameworks. Corporate governance has been described as structures and processes that ensure 'fundamental notions of openness, integrity and accountability.'[96] Corporate governance rules around the world operate as codes containing broad recommendations or principles. Most corporate governance codes include principles or rules regarding the equal treatment of shareholders and timely and simultaneous public disclosure of material company information. Thus the corporate governance rules are now an essential component of the public reporting structures. While these codes are voluntary in most jurisdictions, listed companies that do not follow any of the recommendations, either partially or fully, must generally explain their reasons for not doing so in the annual report or on the company website.[97]

Persons or institutions outside of a listed company that are typically encompassed within a company's governance structure include independent directors, auditors, ratings agencies, analysts, and institutional investors. While these groups play important roles within established corporate governance mechanisms, history tells us that all of these individual controls or gatekeepers can fail.[98] Many of the largest global corporate collapses or losses such as Enron, Madoff, Lehman Brothers, Freddie Mac, Worldcom and American Insurance Group have involved professional gatekeeper failures.[99] The consuming drive within markets to make money is a double-edged sword. While profit incentives are a necessary element of financial markets, conflicts of interest and excesses must be checked or controlled to keep markets optimally efficient.[100] The market disciplines which flow from public scrutiny are needed to

96. Commonwealth of Australia, HIH Royal Commission, *The Failure of HIH Insurance* (2003) Vol. 1, Pt 3, s. 6.6. See also Report of the Committee on the Financial Aspects of Corporate Governance (1 December 1992) [3.2].
97. Most corporate governance codes in developed markets provide high-level principles. These codes, which operate through the listing rules of securities exchanges, require listed companies to include a corporate governance statement in their annual reports indicating whether they have complied with the individual principles and explaining any non-compliance. See, e.g., Australian Securities Exchange Corporate Governance Council, Australian Securities Exchange Corporate Governance Council, *Corporate Governance Principles and Recommendations* (3rd ed., 2014); Financial Reporting Council, *The UK Corporate Governance Code* (September 2012). The New York Stock Exchange (NYSE) Corporate Governance Rules are codified in s. 3030A in the NYSE's Listed Company Manual. Unlike most other jurisdictions, companies listed on the NYSE must comply with some of the standards of the corporate governance rules.
98. William Bratton, 'Does Corporate Law Protect the Interests of Shareholders and Other Stakeholders?: Enron and the Dark Side of Shareholder Value' (2002) 76 *Tulane Law Review* 1275, 1340.
99. William Beaver, 'The Information Content of Annual Earnings Announcements' (1968) 6 *Journal of Accounting Research* 67, 159; Donald Langevoort, 'Investment Analysts and the Law of Insider Trading' (1990) 76 *Virginia Law Review* 1023, 1142; John Coffee Jr., *Gatekeepers: The Professions and Corporate Governance* (Oxford University Press, 2006).
100. See, e.g., Eric Posner, 'The Jurisprudence of Greed' (2003) 151 *University of Pennsylvania Law Review* 1097; Saul Levmore, 'Simply Efficient Markets and the Role of Regulation: Lesson from the Iowa Electronic Markets and the Hollywood Stock Exchange' (2003) 28 *Journal of Corporation Law* 589.

promote genuinely open and competitive markets, discourage institutional, professional and individual excesses, and ensure that losses are not unfairly placed on the most vulnerable participants and community stakeholders. The Global Financial Crisis (GFC)[101] drew attention to these critical principles by highlighting the extent to which externalities can arise when large areas of market activity are based on short-term institutional incentives. While the causal factors of the GFC are complex, it is clear that most people were unaware of the building risks and issues. The activities of many financial companies continued with poor levels of disclosure, transparency and accountability, particularly in unregulated areas of the market.

Unfortunately, it is often easier for company and securities regulators to take action (or attempt to allocate blame) after a corporate collapse, than to engage with companies about poor disclosure and other conduct while they are still trading. Participants who become aware of issues in a corporation are often discouraged from raising the alarm to a broader audience. It is particularly difficult for concerned persons to take action against large establishment companies.[102] There were members of senior management, analysts, media and auditors who warned internal and external parties about various issues at Enron, Mazoff, Lehman Brothers and HIH Insurance - but most of these individuals were ignored, dismissed or blacklisted.[103] Many of the largest global corporate collapses and losses have involved, or been linked to, poor disclosure practices. Too often the public disclosures provided little or no indication of compounding difficulties until the companies became insolvent or moved into bankruptcy or liquidation.[104]

§2.06 MANDATORY DISCLOSURE EMPIRICAL RESEARCH

[A] Overview

Company disclosure theories, models, and assumptions should be examined in real world environments. It is not possible to conclusively prove the need for mandatory disclosure given the complexities of modern financial markets,[105] but empirical studies

101. See United States Financial Crisis Inquiry Commission Report 47 (January 2011) xxii .
102. Andrew McRobert and Ronnie Hoffman, *Corporate Collapse: An Early Warning System for Lenders, Investors and Suppliers* (McGraw Hill, Sydney, 1997); William Bratton, 'Does Corporate Law Protect the Interests of Shareholders and Other Stakeholders?: Enron and the Dark Side of Shareholder Value' (2002) 76 *Tulane Law Review* 1275, 1279, 1332, 1352, 1358; Commonwealth of Australia, HIH Royal Commission, *The Failure of HIH Insurance* (2003) vol. 1 68.
103. Roman Tomasic, 'Corporate Collapse, Crime and Governance - Enron, Anderson and Beyond' (2002) 14 *Australian Journal of Corporate Law* 183, 195; Christine Selb and Alexandra Frean, 'Lehman Vice-President Lost Job After Raising Repo 105 Ethical Concerns', *The Australian* (Sydney), 17 March 2010; Robert Rhee, 'The Madoff Scandal, Market Regulatory Failure and the Business Education of Lawyers' (2009) 35 *Journal of Corporation Law* 363, 365; Commonwealth of Australia, HIH Royal Commission, *The Failure of HIH Insurance* (2003) vol. 1.
104. See, e.g., Commonwealth of Australia, HIH Royal Commission, *The Failure of HIH Insurance* (2003) vol. 1 xviii, 72–73.
105. See e.g., John Coffee Jr, 'Market Failure and the Economic Case for a Mandatory Disclosure System' (1984) 70 *Virginia Law Review* 717, 719–720.

provide valuable evidence on disclosure patterns and the benefits of disclosure regulation. This book outlines recent bodies of work from legal, accounting, finance and economic scholars. Despite the multifaceted nature of this research, it presents a remarkably consistent picture of the potential benefits for corporations and countries that can result from high quality company disclosure through non-discriminatory channels.

Many of the studies outlined in this and other chapters are econometric studies. These studies form an important class of empirical work that use regression analysis as a statistical tool for the investigation of relationships between factors or variables. Regression analysis requires initial hypotheses about the relationships between likely predictors and the outcome. The main purpose of regression analysis is to predict the strength of the relationship between the predictors (the independent variables) and the outcome (the dependent variable). The significance of a relationship in statistical terms is the degree of confidence that the actual relationship is as estimated. A result that is statistically significant accepts the hypothesis as true on the basis that the probability of obtaining the result 'by chance' is less than a specified threshold level, which is usually set at a maximum of 5%. A result that is not statistically significant indicates that the probability of obtaining the result 'by chance' is *more* than the specified threshold level of 5%. When multiple variables are used in a regression analysis, the effects of each of the individual independent variables or predictors are estimated separately by controlling the other variables or, in other words, holding them constant. Legal scholars sometimes argue that econometric studies do not 'prove' anything and that inferences based on probabilities are not sufficient or useful. These arguments misunderstand the fundamental nature and carefully designed parameters of this type of empirical research.[106]

Scholarly studies and models establish only partial relationships and their conclusions and predictions are only valid with respect to the assumptions and arguments specified. These models break up phenomena into more manageable portions by extracting variables believed to have a significant influence on choice and subjecting them to deductive reasoning based on a set of accepted axioms. These models are translated into propositions about the real world and their hypotheses are compared to actual behaviour and experience, either by observation or statistical methods.[107] This process continues progressively with new or adjusted hypotheses according to the evidence adduced. Calabresi and Melamed indicate that model building has two shortcomings. The first is that a model can mistakenly be taken to provide a complete picture of a phenomenon. The second is that models generate categories into which one then feels compelled to force situations that do not truly fit.[108] There are, however, compensating advantages. While legal scholars often review cases on an ad hoc basis looking for patterns, such an approach may ignore, understate

106. See Lynn Stout, 'Derivatives and the Legal Origins of the 2008 Credit Crisis' (2001) 1 *Harvard Business Law Review* 1, 37.
107. Richard Posner, *Economic Analysis of Law* (Aspen, 6th ed., 2003) 17.
108. Guido Calabresi and A Douglas Melamed, 'Property Rules, Liability Rules and Inalienability: One View of the Cathedral' (1972) 85 *Harvard Law Review* 1089, 1128.

or fail to identify the importance of certain relationships among common variables in cases that could be highlighted using a statistical model.

Empirical bodies of work from accounting, finance, economic and legal scholars use many different measures, samples and designs. This work includes studies that examine effects at a microstructure level and research that explores broader connections. Microstructure study designs are easier to control and the results are generally deemed to be more robust. However, individual microstructure studies that examine single factors in a financial market are sometimes so narrowly constructed that their value on a standalone basis is limited. The methodologies and assumptions built into a study design are important to assess its relevance and credibility. While macroeconomic studies are sometimes criticised for their breadth and ambiguity due to the difficulties in controlling and explaining endogenous effects, these studies are essential to understand the broader interconnections between corporations and financial markets, and between financial markets and economic and national outcomes. Scholars should assist by developing sophisticated models that take into account as many connections across financial markets, financial systems, and the real economy as possible. As the scale and complexity of global financial markets and systems increase, processes that highlight systemic effects and issues are vital.

[B] Company Disclosure Studies

[1] Global Studies

La Porta et al. have carried out a series of empirical studies on company disclosure over the last decade. In earlier research, they found evidence suggesting that countries with better investor protection, measured by the character of the legal rules and the quality of law enforcement, have more valuable markets, larger numbers of listed securities per capita, and a higher rate of initial public offering activity than do countries with worse investor protection.[109] They suggested that companies in countries with greater minority shareholder protection are valued more highly than companies in countries without such protection.[110] In a later study, they found evidence suggesting that laws mandating disclosure and facilitating private enforcement through liability rules benefit the stock market.[111] They stated that these results 'point to the importance of regulating the agency conflict between controlling shareholders and outside investors to further the development of capital markets.'[112] They concluded that '[f]inancial

109. Rafael La Porta, Florencio Lopez-de-Silanes, Andrei Shleifer and Robert Vishny, 'Legal Determinants of External Finance' (1997) 52 *Journal of Finance* 1131 (Legal), 1131. See also Rafael La Porta, Florencio Lopez-de-Silanes, Andrei Shleifer and Robert Vishny, 'Law and Finance' (1998) 106 *Journal of Political Economy* 1113 (Law), 1152.
110. Rafael La Porta, Florencio Lopez-de-Silanes, Andrei Shleifer and Robert Vishny, 'Investor Protection and Corporate Valuation' (2002) 62 *Journal of Finance* 1147, 1166–1169.
111. Rafael La Porta, Florencio Lopez-de-Silanos and Andrei Shleifer, 'What Works in Securities Laws?' (2006) 61 *Journal of Finance* 1, 1, 27–28.
112. Rafael La Porta, Florencio Lopez-de-Silanos and Andrei Shleifer, 'What Works in Securities Laws?' (2006) 61 *Journal of Finance* 1, 28. See also Stephen Choi, 'Law, Finance, and Path

markets do not prosper when left to market forces alone ... Extensive disclosure requirements and standards of liability facilitating investor recovery of losses are associated with larger stock markets.'[113]

Jackson and Roe conducted a study that showed a significant relationship between the intensity of public enforcement and the size of a country's capital markets. They also found associations between the quality of disclosure and strong capital markets.[114] They concluded that:

> public enforcement is, overall, as important as disclosure in explaining financial market outcomes around the world and more important than private liability rules. Hence, policy makers who reject public enforcement as useful for financial market development are ignoring the best currently available evidence.[115]

Similarly, a global study by Jayaraman found that enhanced enforcement of securities law leads to the provision of more useful company reporting and more timely recognition of bad news.[116]

A study by Francis et al. concluded that a country's corporate transparency environment contributes to efficient resource allocation.[117] The study authors argue that transparency improves firms' access to lower cost external financing, contributes to more informative stock prices, and plays an important governance role by allowing greater monitoring by outside investors. They suggest 'an improved information environment may enhance intersectoral asset allocation, irrespective of other underlying country characteristics and institutions.'[118] Other international studies have found similar links. Young and Guenther suggest that countries with greater disclosure of value-relevant accounting information are more likely to have higher international

---

Dependence: Developing Strong Securities Markets' (2002) 80 *Texas Law Review* 1657, 1726; Brian Cheffins, 'Law As Bedrock: The Foundations of an Economy Dominated By Widely Held Public Companies' (2003) 23 *Oxford Journal of Legal Studies* 1. Choi suggests that merely pointing to elements of a strong securities market does not address the more difficult question of how to get countries to embrace such elements. Cheffin suggests that the manner in which corporate governance evolved n the US and the UK does not foreclose the possibility that the law could play a significant role in countries that currently have an insider control-oriented system of ownership and control. Instead, law reform could perhaps provide a 'jump start' in an Anglo-American direction by offering outside investors sufficient protection to feel confident about owning tiny percentages of equity in publicly traded companies.

113. Rafael La Porta, Florencio Lopez-de-Silanos and Andrei Shleifer, 'What Works in Securities Laws?' (2006) 61 *Journal of Finance* 1, 27.
114. Howell Jackson and Mark Roe, 'Public and Private Enforcement of Securities Laws: Resource-Based Evidence' (2009) 93 *Journal of Financial Economics* 207, 236. The authors indicate that evidence supports the view that public regulation plays an important role in setting the institutional foundation for securities markets.
115. Howell Jackson and Mark Roe, 'Public and Private Enforcement of Securities Laws: Resource-Based Evidence' (2009) 93 *Journal of Financial Economics* 207, 207.
116. Sudarshan Jayaraman, 'The Effect of Enforcement on Timely Loss Recognition: Evidence From Insider Trading Laws' (2012) 53 *Journal of Accounting and Economics* 77.
117. Jennifer Francis, Shawn Huang, Inder Khurana and Raynolde Pereira, 'Does Corporate Transparency Contribute to Efficient Resource Allocation?' (2009) 47 *Journal of Accounting Research* 943.
118. Jennifer Francis, Shawn Huang, Inder Khurana and Raynolde Pereira, 'Does Corporate Transparency Contribute to Efficient Resource Allocation?' (2009) 47 *Journal of Accounting Research* 943, 982.

capital mobility.[119] Frost et al. found evidence that the strength of a country's disclosure system is positively associated with market development, investor participation, and economic growth.[120]

Laws that protect investors and shareholder rights have been linked to various corporate and national benefits. A global study by McLean et al. concluded that investor protection laws encourage accurate share prices, efficient investment, and improved access to external finance.[121] A study by Brown et al. found that strong shareholder protections and better access to stock market financing led to significantly higher long-run levels of research and development investment, particularly in smaller and younger companies. They suggest that :

> the findings connect law and stock markets with innovative activities key to economic growth, and show that legal rules and financial developments affecting the availability of external equity financing are particularly important for risky, intangible investments not easily financed with debt.[122]

Notably, Cremers and Ferrell found a significantly negative association between restrictions on shareholder rights and company values.[123]

[2] Disclosure and Cost of Capital Studies

There is a significant and growing body of research that shows links between greater disclosure, reduced information asymmetry, and lower costs of capital.[124] One stream of empirical research links reductions in information asymmetry and lower equity

119. Danqing Young and David Guenther, 'Financial Reporting Environments and International Capital Mobility' (2003) 41 *Journal of Accounting Research* 553. See also William Reese and Michael Weisback, 'Protection of Minority Shareholder Interests, Cross-Listings in the United States, and Subsequent Equity Offerings' (2002) 66 *Journal of Financial Economics* 65.
120. Carol Frost, Elizabeth Gordon and Andrew Hayes, 'Stock Exchange Disclosure and Market Development: An Analysis of 50 International Exchanges' (2006) 44 *Journal of Accounting Research* 437.
121. R David McLean, Tianyu Zhang and Mengxin Zhao, 'Why Does the Law Matter? Investor Protection and Its Effects on Investment, Finance, and Growth' (2012) 57 *Journal of Finance* 313.
122. James R Brown, Gustav Martinsson and Bruce C Petersen, 'Law, Stock Markets, and Innovation' (2013) *68 Journal of Finance* 1517.
123. Martijn Cremers and Allen Ferrell, 'Thirty Years of Shareholder Rights and Firm Value' (2014) 69 *Journal of Finance* 1167.
124. Douglas Diamond and Robert Verrechia, 'Disclosure, Liquidity, and the Cost of Capital' (1991) 46 *Journal of Finance* 1325; Christian Leuz and Robert Verrecchia, 'The Economic Consequences of Increased Disclosure' (2000) 38 *Journal of Accounting Research* 91, 121; David Easley and Maureen O'Hara, 'Information and the Cost of Capital' (2004) 59 *Journal of Finance* 1553; Christine Botosan, 'Disclosure and the Cost of Capital: What Do We Know?' (2006) *Accounting and Business Research* International Accounting Policy Forum 31; Stephen Cooper, 'Discussion of Disclosure and the Cost of Capital: What Do We Know?' (2006) *Accounting and Business Research* International Accounting Policy Forum 41; Luzi Hail and Christian Leuz, 'International Differences in the Cost of Equity Capital: Do Legal Institutions and Securities Regulation Matter?' (2006) 44 *Journal of Accounting Research* 485; Richard Lambert, Christian Leuz and Robert Verrechia, 'Information Asymmetry, Information Precision, and the Cost of Capital' (2012) 16 *Review of Finance* 1.

capital costs with a reduction in investor estimation risks. Another stream links reductions in information asymmetry and lower equity capital costs with reduced transaction costs or increased liquidity.[125] There are outstanding issues with all of the methodologies used to measure cost of capital which are not easily resolved. However, Botosan concluded that while individual studies on cost of capital are not perfect, 'the bulk of the literature suggests that greater disclosure reduces the cost of equity capital.'[126] This analysis is affirmed by studies that suggest that companies can lower their cost of capital by disclosing publicly rather than privately.[127]

Barth et al. provide evidence that companies with more transparent earnings enjoy a lower cost of capital.[128] Bhattacharya et al. suggest that an increase in the opacity of reported earnings in a country is linked to a significant increase in the cost of equity and a significant decrease in trading in the relevant stock market.[129] Hail and Leuz suggest that companies from countries with more extensive disclosure requirements, stronger securities regulation, and stricter enforcement mechanisms have a significantly lower cost of capital and higher valuations.[130] Balakrishnan et al. suggest that managers can causally influence their cost of capital by voluntarily providing more timely and informative earnings guidance. They suggest that this reduces information asymmetries between retail and institutional investors and improves liquidity, and in turn, this increases the value of the relevant companies.[131] A study by Fu et al. suggests that higher reporting frequency can also reduce information asymmetry and the cost of equity.[132]

The cost of equity benefits of higher quality disclosure may be greater or more distinct in countries and environments with lower or more variable disclosure standards and practices. Lopes and Alencar found that increased levels of corporate disclosure in Brazil were strongly associated with the *ex ante* cost of equity, especially for companies with limited analyst coverage and low ownership concentration.[133] Xu

125. Christine Botosan, 'Disclosure and the Cost of Capital: What Do We Know?' (2006) *Accounting and Business Research* International Accounting Policy Forum 31.
126. Christine Botosan, 'Disclosure and the Cost of Capital: What Do We Know?' (2006) *Accounting and Business Research* International Accounting Policy Forum 31, 31. Various proxies have been used to date to measure cost of capital and improved levels or quality of disclosure. However, all of these proxies have flaws that are difficult to fully resolve.
127. David Easley, Soeren Hvidkjaer and Maureen O'Hara, 'Is Information Risk a Determinant of Asset Returns?' (2002) 62 *Journal of Finance* 2185, 2219. See also David Easley and Maureen O'Hara, 'Information and the Cost of Capital' (2004) 59 *Journal of Finance* 1553.
128. Mary Barth, Yaniv Konchitchki and Wayne Landsman, 'Cost of Capital and Earnings Transparency' (2013) 55 *Journal of Accounting and Economics* 206.
129. Utpal Bhattacharya, Hazem Daouk and Michael Welker, 'The World Price of Earnings Opacity' (2003) 78 *Accounting Review* 641.
130. Luzi Hail and Christian Leuz, 'International Differences in the Cost of Equity Capital: Do Legal Institutions and Securities Regulation Matter?' (2006) 44 *Journal of Accounting Research* 485. See also Ross Levine, 'Law, Finance, and Economic Growth' (1999) 8 *Journal of Financial Intermediation* 8.
131. Karthik Balakrishnan, Mary Brooke Billings, Bryan Kelly and Alexander Ljungqvist, 'Shaping Liquidity: On the Causal Effects of Voluntary Disclosure' (2014) 69 *Journal of Finance* 2237.
132. Renhui Fu, Arthur Kraft and Huai Zhang, 'Financial Reporting Frequency, Information Asymmetry, and the Cost of Equity' (2012) 54 *Journal of Accounting and Economics* 132.
133. Alexandro Lopes and Roberta de Alencar, 'Disclosure and Cost of Equity Capital in Emerging Markets: The Brazilian Case' (2010) 45 *International Journal of Accounting* 45.

and Lin found transparent companies in Taiwan are more highly valued than opaque companies, and that companies with tightly controlled ownership tend to be ranked lower for disclosure transparency.[134]

The efficiency gains from enhanced disclosure appear to be more pronounced during periods of market crisis or illiquidity. Empirical studies suggest that transparency reduces liquidity uncertainties for individual companies.[135] Sadka found evidence consistent with a flight to information quality during the height of the GFC. An interaction between information quality and illiquidity suggested that investors continue to invest in illiquid stocks when the information quality is high.[136] Ng found that increased information quality can also reduce a company's exposure to systemic liquidity risk.[137]

These studies as a whole suggest that high quality company disclosure within public spheres enhances fairness, efficiency, and transparency in financial markets, and that improvements in these variables may assist to minimise systemic risk.

[3] Disclosure, Governance and Broader Societal Factors

The potential benefits of corporate disclosure regimes appear to extend more broadly. Empirical research that examines corporate governance factors is growing. Some studies find significant associations between corporations with high governance rankings and lower equity capital costs.[138] For example, Bozec and Bozec found significant negative associations between the quality of corporate governance practices of listed Canadian companies and their cost of capital.[139]

Other studies examine the effects of reporting of corporate social responsibility (CSR), and corporate sustainability performance.[140] Reporting on CSR and sustainability factors and impacts[141] is becoming increasingly important within corporate disclosure frameworks, with many companies providing these reports voluntarily in response to demands from various investor and stakeholder groups. Theoretical

134. Hao-Feng Xu and Mei-Feng Lin, 'Controlling Owner and Transparency: Information Transparency and Disclosure Rankings System' (2011) 29 *African Journal of Business Management* 11589.
135. Mark Lang and Mark Maffett, 'Transparency and Liquidity Uncertainty in Crisis Periods' (2011) 52 *Journal of Accounting and Economics* 101.
136. Ronnie Sadka, 'Liquidity Risk and Accounting Information' (2011) 52 *Journal of Accounting and Economics* 144.
137. Jeffrey Ng, 'The Effect of Information Quality on Liquidity Risk' (2011) 52 *Journal of Accounting and Economics* 126.
138. See, e.g., Yves Bozec and Richard Bozec, 'Corporate Governance Quality and the Cost of Capital' (2011) 2 *International Journal of Corporate Governance* 217; Peter Pham, Jo-Ann Suchard and Jason Zein, 'Corporate Governance and the Cost of Capital: Evidence from Australian Companies' (2012) *Journal of Applied Corporate Finance* 84.
139. Yves Bozec and Richard Bozec, 'Corporate Governance Quality and the Cost of Capital' (2011) 2 *International Journal of Corporate Governances* 217.
140. The purposes and content of corporate social responsibility reporting and corporate sustainability reporting overlap and companies that provide these reports often include similar content regardless of the report title.
141. Many larger listed companies publish reports that discuss the company's performance against corporate social responsibility and or sustainability goals and specific targets. These reports

frameworks for considering company disclosure policies and practices should therefore reflect these broader boundaries. Dhaliwal et al. found that companies with superior CSR performance achieved a reduction in the cost of equity capital and attracted dedicated institutional investors and analyst coverage. Further, companies that initiated CSR reporting raised significantly larger amounts of capital than other companies conducting equity offerings.[142] Ioannou and Serafeim examined the effects of mandatory corporate sustainability reporting in fifty-eight countries.[143] They found that adoption of mandatory corporate sustainability reporting lead to heightened managerial awareness of sustainability issues and higher levels of company programmes focused on sustainable development and employee training. In addition, corporate governance levels and ethical practices improved, the levels of bribery and corruption decreased, and managerial credibility was enhanced. Notably, all of these positive benefits were more significant in countries with stronger law enforcement and independent assurance of the reports.[144]

§2.07 SUMMARY

The primary arguments made by critics of mandatory disclosure regimes are that:

- companies have sufficient incentives to voluntarily disclose information;
- market forces work to reduce information production costs;
- mandatory disclosure fails to enhance the monitoring of management;
- retail investors do not need protection; and
- mandated disclosures are not very useful.

The implicit assumption underpinning these arguments is that financial markets operate most efficiently by allowing companies discretion on the content, timing and recipients of their disclosures.

Commentators who support mandatory disclosure regimes respond that:

- incentives to promote voluntary public disclosure of material company information on a timely basis do not always apply;

may be in a standalone form that sit alongside the annual reports or the content may be included within the annual report. Corporate social responsibility and corporate sustainability reporting may be mandated in a country or may be reported on a voluntary basis in response to growing calls from some investor segments and others. The author's empirical reviews include the corporate social responsibility and corporate sustainability reports of the selected companies.

142. Dan Dhaliwal, Oliver Li, Albert Tsang and Yong Yang, 'Voluntary Nonfinancial Disclosure and the Cost of Equity Capital: The Initiation of Corporate Social Responsibility Reporting' (2011) 86 *Accounting Review* 59.

143. Ioannis Ioannou and George Serafeim, 'The Consequences of Mandatory Corporate Sustainability Reporting' (Working Paper 11-100, Harvard Business School, 26 October 2012).

144. Ioannis Ioannou and George Serafeim, 'The Consequences of Mandatory Corporate Sustainability Reporting' (Working Paper 11-100, Harvard Business School, 26 October 2012).

- mandatory disclosure frameworks enable more accurate information production at lower cost, reduce agency costs, and enhance the monitoring of company management; and
- mandatory disclosure regimes are needed to protect investors, promote investor confidence in the integrity of the market, and deter fraud and/or mitigate losses resulting from fraud.

The implicit assumption underlying these arguments is that disclosure rules are needed to ensure timely disclosure of company information to all investors and effective corporate governance processes.

Market efficiency debates concern the relative efficiency of a particular market or disclosure environment. Defined benchmarks are required to examine and assess arguments concerning whether company disclosure regimes enhance market efficiency. Commentators on both sides of the voluntary-mandatory disclosure debate therefore need to explain their efficiency framework, including:

- the adopted efficiency variables;
- the nexus between the efficiency variables and asserted economic outcomes;
- the timeframe during which efficiency gains are anticipated; and
- the participant groups that are expected to benefit from the relevant efficiency and economic frameworks.

Efficiency rationales that are commonly discussed within the mandatory disclosure literature include: agency costs, information production costs, information utility, price efficiency, and externalities. These efficiency measures are highly interdependent, so improvement in one proxy may be countered by reductions in other efficiency measures. The time periods over which efficiency is measured and the expected beneficiaries of efficiency gains are also critical because short-term improvements in one or more efficiency proxies may not accurately reflect the long-term efficiency of the relevant market and economy.

It is difficult to conceive of theoretical company disclosure frameworks that produce optimal market fairness, efficiency and transparency outcomes when listed companies are permitted to raise capital from the public, while retaining full discretion over the content, manner and recipients of their disclosures. In contemporary markets, institutional demands for company information are insistent, making it difficult for managers to keep material information confidential or to withhold it from all parts of the market for long periods. Consequently, the real debate today is not whether mandatory disclosure regulation is required to ensure disclosure of 'new' information to the market, but how much of the information disclosed by companies privately to some participants should be publicly disclosed through mandatory reporting processes. The most significant challenges for persons advocating a return to voluntary disclosure environments are the strong incentives listed company managers and institutional investors have to privately exchange information and to act in their personal and institutional short-term interests.[145]

Listed company disclosure to the world at large is the best means available in modern financial markets to reduce information production and dissemination costs, maximise information utility and economic efficiency, incentivise independent research and analysis, encourage healthy competition between listed companies, and minimise agency costs and externalities.[146] Timely and comprehensive company reporting is also the best available approach to protect investors, optimise the fairness, efficiency and transparency of a financial market and to minimise its systemic risks. Such reporting enables the broadest spectrum of investors and stakeholders to make informed decisions and enables all of these groups to meaningfully respond to issues as they emerge.[147] As Louis Brandeis forcefully argued a century ago, the potent force of publicity can be used as a continuous remedial process in financial markets.[148] Of course company disclosure regimes on their own cannot guarantee well-informed decisions in financial markets, nor sound corporate, economic and national outcomes. Perfect regulatory solutions do not exist in financial markets – all we can do is seek diligently for the best possible market and regulatory structures at a particular time based on a rich and broad evidentiary database. Evidence that highlights the net benefits of these company disclosure frameworks is overwhelming. The empirical research as a whole suggests that financial markets that serve the national public interest well over the long-term require high quality company disclosure, broad and diversified participation, and community trust and confidence.[149]

All debates concerning access to company information have been radically changed by digital developments. Modern communication technologies change the relevant questions that should be asked, and they provide a broad range of innovative models and solutions that did not exist previously. Global communities are rapidly becoming accustomed to digital technologies, and in these fast moving and tech savvy environments, demands for direct access to regular and comprehensive company information will continue to increase. Most scholars agree that the internet can assist

---

145. Laura Unger, 'Corporate Communications Without Violations' (1999) 51 *Administrative Law Review* 1119, 1122–1124; Camilia Lopez-Fernandini, 'Regulation FD of the SEC's Selective Disclosure and Insider Trading Rule: Finally, Full And Fair Disclosure' (2001) 53 *Administrative Law Review* 1353, 1373.
146. See Saul Levmore, 'Simply Efficient Markets and the Role of Regulation: Lesson from the Iowa Electronic Markets and the Hollywood Stock Exchange' (2003) 28 *Journal of Corporation Law* 589.
147. See Louis Lowenstein, 'Financial Transparency and Corporate Governance: You Manage What You Measure' (1996) 96 *Columbia Law Review* 1335, 1361–1362; Donald Langevoort, 'Technological Evolution and the Devolution of Corporate Finance Reporting' (2004) 46 *William & Mary Law Review* 1.
148. See Louis Brandeis, *Other People's Money* (National Home Library Foundation, Washington, 1914) Ch. V.
149. The term national public interest is coined from s. 2 of the *Securities Exchange Act of 1934* in the United States, which states that 'transactions in securities as commonly conducted upon securities exchanges ... are effected with a national public interest, which makes it necessary to provide for regulation and control of such transactions and of practices and matters related thereto, including ... to require appropriate reports ...'.

to reduce information asymmetries.[150] Some suggest that increasing the amount of information available online may overwhelm investors or make them worse off due to excess, overconfident and speculative trading.[151] However, narrow or strict generalisations and assumptions about investor groups and their capacities are not credible reasons for withholding company information from investors and the broader public in the modern age.[152]

Issues concerning private versus public disclosure of company information are discussed more fully in the following two chapters. The insider trading and selective disclosure theoretical debates centre on whether trading on private information should be permitted or prohibited by persons related to, or outside of, the company.

150. Donald Langevoort, 'Information Technology and the Structure of Securities Regulation' (1985) 98 *Harvard Law Review* 747, 749; John Coffee Jnr, 'Brave New World? The Impact(s) of the Internet on Modern Securities Regulation' (1997) 52 *Business Lawyer* 1195, 1196; Nancy Libin and James Wrona, 'The Securities Industry and the Internet: A Suitable Match?' (2001) *Columbia Business Law Review* 601, 631; Caroline Bradley, 'Disorderly Conduct: Day Traders and the Ideology of "Fair and Orderly Markets"' (2000) 26 *Journal of Corporation Law* 63, 81, 87, 96; Laura Unger, 'Corporate Communications Without Violations' (1999) 51 *Administrative Law Review* 1119, 1121.
151. Terrance Odean, 'Volume, Volatility, Price and Profit When All Traders are Above Average' (1998) 53 *Journal of Finance* 1887; Brad Barber and Terrance Odean, 'The Internet and the Investor' (2001) 15 *Journal of Economic Perspectives* 41; Linda Yi, 'Road Shows On The Internet: Taking Individual Investors For A Ride On The Information Highway' (2002) 52 *Duke Law Journal* 243.
152. Camilia Lopez-Fernandini, 'Regulation FD of the SEC's Selective Disclosure and Insider Trading Rule: Finally, Full And Fair Disclosure' (2001) 53 *Administrative Law Review* 1353, 1371.

CHAPTER 3

Insider Trading*

> [W]e do not let Paul rob Peter merely because he may be able to put the stolen property to a better economic use.[1]

§3.01 OVERVIEW

The insider trading theoretical debates intersect with, and strongly influence, the mandatory disclosure debates.[2] Most of the substantive scholarly debate concerning the effects and regulation of insider trading has occurred in the US, and many legal contributors to this debate argue on efficiency grounds. Most of the efficiency arguments within the legal literature derive from, or draw on, the theories developed by Henry Manne to support unfettered insider trading in financial markets. Manne's theories and arguments are discussed in detail in this chapter, given the critical importance of his work to policy, judicial and scholarly developments since the 1970s, and its continuing influence today across the insider trading, mandatory disclosure and selective disclosure theoretical debates.

---

* Some of the material in this Chapter was included in a published article: Gill North, 'A Re-examination of the Manne Efficiency Theory and the Insider Trading and Company Disclosure Efficiency Rationales' (2011) 25 *Australian Journal of Corporate Law* 209.

1. Richard Jennings, 'Book Review of *Insider Trading and the Stock Market* by Henry G Manne' (1967) 55 *California Law Review* 1229, 1234.
2. There are other provisions in the United States apart from Rule 10b-5 relating to insider trading. For example:

   - Section 17 of the *Securities Act of 1933* prohibits insider trading in relation to the 'offer or sale' of a security.
   - Rule 14e-3 prohibits insider trading in relation to a tender offer. Liability under this rule is not premised on breach of a fiduciary duty. Rule 14e-3 was promulgated under s. 14 of the *Securities Exchange Act of 1934.*
   - Section 20 of the *Insider Trading and Securities Enforcement Act 1988* provides a private right of action for individuals against those who have breached Rule 10b-5.
   - Section 16(b) of the *Securities Exchange Act of 1934* 15 USC (1934) provides a right of profit recovery by companies from officers, directors or large shareholders who have traded in the company's stock in specified circumstances.

Manne expressly noted that his work on insider trading was grounded on economic principles.[3] Within economic spheres, the seminal efficiency theory applicable to financial markets is the ECMH, which was developed by Eugene Fama as an economics doctoral candidate in the US during a similar period as Manne was publishing on insider trading. Fama's work is central to all scholarly debates concerning efficiency in financial markets, as well as the theoretical debates concerning the efficiency or otherwise of company disclosure regulation and insider trading regulation. Accordingly, the Fama market efficiency and ECMH are referenced in this Chapter to provide appropriate economic context for discussion of Manne's theories. Brief summaries of financial market behavioural theories and studies are also included, because these bodies of work are increasingly influencing disclosure policy developments, although more so in relation to financial services regulation than in corporate disclosure realms.

While some scholars argue for insider trading regulation on fairness grounds, these papers comprise a relatively minor portion of the scholarly literature. Fairness concepts and arguments were introduced in Chapter 2 and are discussed further in this chapter and in Chapter 4. Some scholars adopt theoretical frameworks that encompass fairness and efficiency concepts. These commentators generally argue that regulation prohibiting insider trading is required to ensure long-term investor confidence in the integrity of markets. They suggest that high-levels of investor confidence and public trust are required to promote and sustain long-term efficiency in financial markets.[4]

Finally, this chapter provides a summary of the development of insider trading case law in the US to highlight the impact of Manne's work on the judiciary, and to show the influence of the broader scholarly theoretical debates on insider trading case law and the development of company disclosure law, principles and practice. The insider trading jurisprudence in the US reflects the perceived tensions between the market efficiency and fairness objectives that underpin insider trading regulation and mandatory disclosure frameworks. It also provides important commentary on the assumed roles of intermediaries within financial markets, such as analysts.[5]

§3.02 THE HENRY MANNE INSIDER TRADING THEORIES (1)

Henry Manne developed a series of theories to support insider trading activity within financial markets without regulatory interference. His earliest theory claimed that

3. Henry Manne, 'Insider Trading and the Law Professors' (1975) 23 *Vanderbilt Law Review* 547, 548.
4. See, e.g., Robert Haft, 'The Effect of Insider Trading Rules on the Internal Efficiency of the Large Corporation' (1982) 80 *Michigan Law Review* 1051; Morris Mendelson, 'Review: The Economics of Insider Trading Reconsidered' (1969) 117 *University of Pennsylvania Law Review* 470; Joel Seligman, 'The Reformulation of Federal Securities Law Concerning Non-Public Information' (1995) 73 *Georgetown Law Journal* 1083.
5. This book includes summaries of the insider trading case law in the United States because this jurisprudence has strongly influenced, and continues to significantly impact, the disclosure and insider trading theoretical debates, and company disclosure principles and practice. The scope of the book does not allow for discussion of insider trading regulation, case law and enforcement across other jurisdictions.

insider trading does no harm. His second theory asserted that profits from insider trading constitute the only effective compensation scheme for entrepreneurial services in large corporations. His final and most influential theory suggested that insider trading enhances efficiency. These theories are outlined and discussed in order.

[A] No Investor Harm

Manne argued in his early published work that careful analysis of insider trading requires considering at least three major questions:

(1) Who gains and who loses from insider trading?
(2) What are the long-term consequences of disallowing insider trading?
(3) Can insider trading be prevented, and if so, at what financial and social cost?[6]

He differentiated between long-term shareholders who select stocks based on fundamental analysis, and short-swing traders or speculators. He asserted that only short-term speculators and traders benefit from insider trading regulation. He claimed that long-term shareholders 'almost never buy or sell because of short-swing fluctuations in the price of a security.'[7] Manne further claimed that if the long-term investor in fact sells to the insider, 'he is normally selling for reasons unrelated to the insider's trading, and would be selling in any event'.[8]

These arguments are not empirically credible. When shareholders invest on a fundamental basis, they value companies and securities on the present value of estimated future earnings and distributions,[9] and they buy or sell securities when the prices move beyond their fundamental value based on available information. The information available to those with no access to inside information is limited to information released through public channels.[10] Traders relying on public disclosures have no reliable means to determine when, or the extent to which, insider trading is occurring.[11] There are no sound mechanisms to know whether another participant is

6. Henry Manne, 'In Defense of Insider Trading' (1966) 44 *Harvard Business Review* 113, 113.
7. Henry Manne, 'In Defense of Insider Trading' (1966) 44 *Harvard Business Review* 113, 114.
8. Henry Manne, 'In Defense of Insider Trading' (1966) 44 *Harvard Business Review* 113, 115.
9. See, e.g., Baruch Lev and S Ramu Thiagarajan, 'Fundamental Information Analysis' (1993) 31 *Journal of Accounting Research* 190.
10. Morris Mendelson, 'Review: The Economics of Insider Trading Reconsidered' (1969) 117 *University of Pennsylvania Law Review* 470, 483.
11. Some scholars suggest or imply that the price signals of insiders can be incorporated within a share price without the relevant news being disseminated. Such a view assumes the rest of the market will effectively adopt and verify insider trading on trust without knowing or understanding the relevant information. However, security valuations based on fundamental analysis is not possible on this basis. It is also suggested that investors can respond to insider trading by widening their bid-ask spreads. Presumably this means that one values a security and then adjusts the valuation by a certain margin. However, such a process is likely to be counterproductive, particularly if a significant proportion of the market participants are 'insiders' that don't make the equivalent margin adjustments. In practice, there are no reliable mechanisms for traders to calculate the necessary amount of compensation and to adjust their trading processes.

better informed or how other participants arrive at their decisions. Moreover, uninformed participants cannot accurately predict the effects of their own actions or the decisions of others on security prices.[12]

Manne argued that insider trading does not harm long-term investors because these investors do not trade on short-term noise.[13] He assumed that the transactions of long-term investors are not influenced by security prices.[14] However, as discussed above, price is often a major consideration in share transactions and informed investors may sell to the insider when the security price goes beyond the fundamental value based on publicly available news.[15] Participants who trade on materially price-sensitive inside information that alters the fundamental valuation of the securities generally profit at the expense of these traders. Hence an appropriate measure of harm is the difference in the amount that would have been made by the sellers if the information had been made public prior to the insider trading event.[16] A growing number of commentators now concede that uninformed investors suffer harm when insider trading is permitted.[17] While it is often difficult in practice to identify investors that have been harmed by insider trading, it must be remembered that individual trades are zero sum. Consequently, all other things being equal, when one or more participant(s) benefit from trading on inside information, other participants suffer harm to an equivalent extent.[18]

---

12. Razeen Sappideen, 'Securities Market Efficiency Reconsidered' (1988) 9 *University of Tasmania Law Review* 132, 146.
13. Henry Manne, 'In Defence of Insider Trading' (1966) 44 *Harvard Business Review* 113, 114.
14. Roy Schotland, 'Unsafe At Any Price: A Reply to Manne, Insider Trading and the Stock Market' (1967) 53 *Virginia Law Review* 1425, 1447.
15. Morris Mendelson, 'Review: The Economics of Insider Trading Reconsidered' (1969) 117 *University of Pennsylvania Law Review* 470, 483.
16. Morris Mendelson, 'Review: The Economics of Insider Trading Reconsidered' (1969) 117 *University of Pennsylvania Law Review* 470, 482. See also John Barry, 'The Economics of Outside Information and Rule 10b-5' (1981) 129 *University of Pennsylvania Law Review* 1307, 1329; Joel Seligman, 'The Reformulation of Federal Securities Law Concerning Non-Public Information' (1995) 73 *Georgetown Law Journal* 1083, 1098.
17. See, e.g., H Nejat Seyhun, 'Insider's Profits, Costs of Trading and Market Efficiency' (1986) 16 *Journal of Financial Economics* 189, 190; Robert Masson and Ananth Madhavan, 'Insider Trading and the Value Of the Firm' (1991) 39 *Journal of Industrial Economics* 333; Nicholas Georgakopoulos, 'Insider Trading as a Transaction Cost: A Market Microstructure Justification and Optimization of Insider Trading Regulation', 26 *Connecticut Law Review* 1, 17; Kim Scheppele, '"It's Just Not Right": The Ethics of Insider Trading' (1993) 56 *Law & Contemporary Problems* 123, 160; Richard Painter, 'Insider Trading And The Stock Market Thirty Years Later' (1999) 50 *Case Western Reserve Law Review* 305, 308; Zohar Goshen and Gideon Parchomovsky, 'The Essential Role Of Securities Regulation' (2006) 55 *Duke Law Journal* 711, 714, 733; David Easley, Soeren Hvidkjaer and Maureen O'Hara, 'Is Information Risk a Determinant of Asset Returns?' (2002) 62 *Journal of Finance* 2185, 2218; Ian Ayres and Stephen Choi, 'Internalizing Outsider Trading' (2002) 101 *Michigan Law Review* 313; Victor Brudney, 'Insiders, Outsiders, and Informational Advantages Under the Federal Securities Laws' (1979) 93 *Harvard Law Review* 322, 357, 360; Ernst Maug, 'Insider Trading Legislation and Corporate Governance' (2002) 46 *European Economic Review* 1569, 1588.
18. William Wang, 'Trading on Material Non-Public Information on Impersonal Stock Markets: Who is Harmed, and Who Can Sue Whom under SEC Rule 10b-5?' (1981) 54 *Southern California Law Review* 1217, 1235; William Wang, 'Stock Market Insider Trading: Victims, Violators And Remedies – Including an Analogy to Fraud in the Sale of a Used Car with a Generic Defect' (2001) 33 *Securities Law Journal* 381, 417.

[B] Insider Trading as a Managerial Compensation Scheme

Manne suggested in his early publications that when it is realised 'how rare significant insider trading must be, one wonders even more what all the shouting has been about.'[19] He further stated that if:

> this is all that could be said for or against insider trading, the matter would not be a very interesting one. But there is another and far more crucial facet ... the argument that profits from insider trading constitute the only effective compensation scheme for entrepreneurial services in large corporations.[20]

This claim has largely been rejected by scholars. There are few, if any, commentators today who agree with Manne that insider trading is the most effective scheme to compensate corporate employees for the implementation of innovative ideas. Manne fails to explain how a return gained from insider trading can only be limited to an amount reflective of the inside trader's contribution to the company.[21] As Boyle notes, Manne's theory: 'cannot separate bad originality from good originality; ... it can neither justify nor limit the class of people entitled to cash in on insider information; ... [and there is only the] most tenuous argument to connect insiders and entrepreneurs in the first place.'[22]

Managerial compensation schemes should be carefully designed to incentivise superior long-term performance in the interests of the relevant corporation.[23] Schemes that permit trading by company insiders are poorly targeted[24] because insider trading rewards the practice of keeping company information confidential, rather than promoting efficient business management.[25] The potential moral hazards arising from insider trading by company managers are significant, and these are compounded by management stock options that allow unlimited upside with no capital at risk.[26]

19. Henry Manne, 'In Defence of Insider Trading' (1966) 44 *Harvard Business Review* 113, 115.
20. Henry Manne, 'In Defence of Insider Trading' (1966) 44 *Harvard Business Review* 113, 116.
21. John Barry, 'The Economics of Outside Information and Rule 10b-5' (1981) 129 *University of Pennsylvania Law Review* 1307, 1329.
22. James Boyle, *Shamans, Software, and Spleens: Law and the Construction of the Information Society* (1996) 96. See also John Barry, 'The Economics of Outside Information and Rule 10b-5' (1981) 129 *University of Pennsylvania Law Review* 1307, 1329; Morris Mendelson, 'Review: The Economics of Insider Trading Reconsidered' (1969) 117 *University of Pennsylvania Law Review* 470, 481, 489–490; Burton Malkiel, 'Review of *Insider Trading and the Stock Market* by Henry Manne' (1968) 41 *Journal of Business* 263, 264; Richard Posner, *Economic Analysis of Law* (Aspen Law & Business, 6th ed., 2003) 433.
23. Mark Klock, 'Mainstream Economics and the Case for Prohibiting Inside Trading' (1994) 10 *Georgia State University Law Review* 297, 317.
24. Burton Malkiel, 'Review of *Insider Trading and the Stock Market* by Henry Manne' (1968) 41 *Journal of Business* 263, 264; Saul Levmore, 'In Defense of the Regulation of Insider Trading' (1988) 11 *Harvard Journal of Law & Public Policy* 101, 104–105.
25. Richard Posner, *Economic Analysis of Law* (Aspen Law & Business, 6th ed., 2003) 433. The US Supreme Court noted in *Dirks v. SEC* 463 US (1983) at 653 that 'a significant purpose of the Securities Exchange Act of 1934 was to eliminate the idea that use of inside information for personal advantage is a normal emolument of corporate office.'
26. Mark Klock, 'Mainstream Economics and the Case for Prohibiting Inside Trading' (1994) 10 *Georgia State University Law Review* 297, 314.

Indeed, insider trading incentives have the potential to distort company decision-making at many levels, with serious adverse consequences.[27]

[C] Manne's Efficiency Theory

Manne published a book titled *Insider Trading and the Stock Market* in 1966.[28] The stated focus of the book was on economics but Manne indicated that its content was of great interest to lawyers.[29] Manne argued that the insider trading debate could be resolved through the application of basic economic principles.[30] Yet, ironically, there is little economic content in the book, particularly given Manne's admitted emphasis on the entrepreneurial compensation scheme. His most significant efficiency or economic arguments are contained in a subsequent article titled 'Insider Trading and the Law Professors'. Manne stated in this paper that:

> the efficient functioning of the stock market is actually one of the strongest arguments for unfettered insider trading ... Efficiency in the stock market refers to both the speed and accuracy with which the market integrates new information into the market price of a security ... An efficient market is one in which capital will be allocated to its highest-return uses, thus ensuring that capital goes into those uses with the greatest individual and social utility ... to the extent that the stock market is functioning efficiently, both the capital markets and the market for corporate control function more effectively.[31]

Thus, Manne claimed that markets that permit systemic insider trading simultaneously lead to optimal individual utility and social utility. He suggested the benefits of efficiency in a market ultimately relate to individual goals, but conceded that the 'gains from efficiency are diffuse and often specifically unidentifiable.'[32]

Manne did not define what he meant by optimal individual or social utility, nor did he explain how insider trading assists with achieving these goals. It is conceptually and practically difficult to reconcile Manne's goals of optimal social utility and optimal

27. Saul Levmore, 'In Defense of the Regulation of Insider Trading' (1988) 11 *Harvard Journal of Law & Public Policy* 101, 104; Morris Mendelson, 'Review: The Economics of Insider Trading Reconsidered' (1969) 117 *University of Pennsylvania Law Review* 470, 489; Roy Schotland, 'Unsafe At Any Price: A Reply to Manne, Insider Trading and the Stock Market' (1967) 53 *Virginia Law Review* 1425, 1440–1442; Saul Levmore, 'Securities and Secrets: Insider Trading and the Law of Contracts' (1982) 68 *Virginia Law Review* 117, 149; Kimberly Krawiec, 'Fairness, Efficiency and Insider Trading: Deconstructing the Coin of the Realm in the Information Age' (2001) 95 *North Western University Law Review* 443, 496; Robert Haft, 'The Effect of Insider Trading Rules on the Internal Efficiency of the Large Corporation' (1982) 80 *Michigan Law Review* 1051, 1053–1064; Boyd Dyer, 'Economic Analysis, Insider Trading, and Game Markets' (1992) 1 *Utah Law Review* 1, 21–25.
28. Henry Manne, *Insider Trading and the Stock Market* (Free Press, 1966).
29. Henry Manne, 'Insider Trading and the Law Professors' (1975) 23 *Vanderbilt Law Review* 547, 548.
30. Henry Manne, 'Insider Trading and the Law Professors' (1975) 23 *Vanderbilt Law Review* 547, 548.
31. Henry Manne, 'Insider Trading and the Law Professors' (1975) 23 *Vanderbilt Law Review* 547, 565.
32. Henry Manne, 'Insider Trading and the Law Professors' (1975) 23 *Vanderbilt Law Review* 547, 566.

individual utility because individual incentives and utility are often poorly aligned with social incentives and utility. It is true that company managers and participants have strong incentives to engage in insider trading. Individual managers and participants may legitimately point to efficiency gains in the form of personal profits from trading on inside information. However, the key issue for scholars and policy makers concerns the differences between the short-term interests of corporate managers and financial institutions and the long-term interests of nations and the global community. Manne validly argued that economic analysis of insider trading should take the costs associated with establishing and maintaining insider trading regulation into account; however, complete economic analysis also includes the significant initial and longer-term costs that arise in financial markets which permit insider trading.

It is not clear whether Manne was aware of Fama's efficient markets theory when he wrote his insider trading book and articles. Fama was an economics PhD student at the time of Manne's publications and did not publish his seminal work until 1970.[33] Certain ideas in a 1975 article published by Manne appear to be similar to Fama's efficient market theory, but there are also critical differences. It is necessary to provide a brief summary of Fama's work on efficiency on financial markets in order to understand these differences and to consider Manne's work within a more complete scholarly framework. This summary will include Fama's efficient markets theory and ECMH, academic criticisms of the theory and ECMH, and Fama's response to these criticisms.

§3.03 FAMA'S EFFICIENT MARKETS THEORY

Fama argued that an ideal market is one:

> in which prices provide accurate signals for resource allocation: that is, a market in which firms can make production-investment decisions, and investors can choose among the securities that represent ownership of firm's activities under the assumption that security prices at any time 'fully reflect' all available information.[34]

Accordingly, under Fama's efficient markets theory, price efficiency is a means to an end. Fama confirms that the primary role of financial markets is to allocate ownership of the economy's capital stock.[35] His theoretical model assumes that investor expectations are homogeneous, companies and investors act rationally in their economic self-interests, and information is costless and freely available to all market participants.[36] These assumptions are necessary to ensure that companies seeking

33. Eugene Fama, 'Efficient Capital Markets: A Review of Theory and Empirical Work' (1970) 25 *Journal of Finance* 383.
34. Eugene Fama, 'Efficient Capital Markets: A Review of Theory and Empirical Work' (1970) 25 *Journal of Finance* 383, 383.
35. Eugene Fama, 'Efficient Capital Markets: A Review of Theory and Empirical Work' (1970) 25 *Journal of Finance* 383, 383.
36. Eugene Fama, 'Efficient Capital Markets: A Review of Theory and Empirical Work' (1970) 25 *Journal of Finance* 383, 387–388.

capital and investors providing capital are competing in a highly transparent and robustly competitive marketplace, thereby driving an efficient allocation of an economy's resources.[37]

[A] Efficient Capital Markets Hypothesis

Fama developed the ECMH to test his efficiency theory. The ECMH is intended to empirically examine whether security prices 'fully reflect' specified information subsets.[38] Markets which reflect these information subsets are categorised as strong, semi-strong or weak form efficient.[39] In a strong form or perfectly efficient market, security prices fully reflect all currently known information, including public and private information. The information subset tested in the semi-strong form is limited to publicly available information. The weak form is limited to historical price sequences. Accordingly, in a strong form market, no investor can benefit from new information, including persons that possess inside information or information not publicly available, because the prices will already reflect such information. Fama does not expect this extreme model to be an exact description of the world; instead it provides the benchmark against which deviations can be measured.[40] In a semi-strong form market, a person may earn superior returns from information that is not publicly available, but no investor can earn excess returns by fundamental research or the identification of mispriced securities on the basis of publicly available information.[41] Finally, in a weak form market, investors cannot earn superior returns by technical analysis, or the study of past security pricing or volume trends.[42] In such a market, price changes occur randomly, so that security prices or patterns of change cannot be objectively valued and future movements cannot be predicted.

37. For more discussion on the Fama efficient markets theory, see Gill North and Ross Buckley, 'A Fundamental Re-examination of Efficiency in Capital Markets in Light of the Global Financial Crisis' (2010) 33 *University of New South Wales Law Journal* 714.
38. The Efficient Capital Markets Hypothesis formally evolved in the 1960s from the PhD dissertation of Fama. However, its origins date back to a dissertation by Bachelier, a student of the French mathematician, Henri Poincare. Bachelier analysed the French commodities market in 1900 and found the market prices to be unbiased estimates of future prices, with changes in pricing the result of new information, the emergence of which was random.
39. Eugene Fama, 'Efficient Capital Markets: A Review of Theory and Empirical Work' (1970) 25 *Journal of Finance* 383, 383, 388.
40. Eugene Fama, 'Efficient Capital Markets: A Review of Theory and Empirical Work' (1970) 25 *Journal of Finance* 383, 414.
41. Fundamental analysis seeks to values companies and their securities based on the present value of the estimated future earnings and distributions. See, e.g., Baruch Lev and S Ramu Thiagarajan, 'Fundamental Information Analysis' (1993) 31 *Journal of Accounting Research* 190.
42. Technical analysis looks at patterns based on security prices and trading volumes and presumes that future patterns are predictable based on previous patterns of security prices and trading volumes.

[B] Criticisms of Fama's Efficient Market Theory and ECMH

Critics claim that the ECMH concept of market efficiency has been severely challenged by growing empirical evidence of short-term inefficiencies. Stock price inaccuracies are caused by many short-term occurrences, including lack of information, wrong assessments of information, speculative trading, liquidity crunches, excess market volatility, random short-run inaccuracies, industry-wide inaccuracies or systematic discounts.[43] There are many studies that suggest financial markets are sometimes slow to fully reflect company earnings announcements.[44] Further, the arbitrage activities of informed investors do not always fully counteract the actions of uninformed speculators.[45] Most financial markets experience periods of boom and bust when security valuations move away from fundamental valuation trend lines.[46]

Other significant criticisms of the ECMH come from behavioural scholars. Commentators who believe that markets are significantly influenced by noise and investor psychology point to market bubbles and crashes as examples of inefficiencies based on non-fundamental signals.[47] Behavioural economists argue that investors are often, if not always, predictably irrational.[48] They argue that most people tend to overreact to unexpected and dramatic news events.[49] International empirical research confirms that investors are sometimes overconfident,[50] prone to overreact,[51] subject to

43. Marcel Kahan, 'Securities Law and the Social Costs of "Inaccurate" Stock Prices' (1992) 41 *Duke Law Journal* 977, 994–997. See also Julian Du and Shang-jin Wei, 'Does Insider Trading Raise Market Volatility?' (2004) 114 *Economic Journal* 916, 916, 940.
44. Stewart Brown, 'Earnings Changes, Stock Prices, and Market Efficiency' (1978) *Journal of Finance* 17; Henry Latane and Charles Jones, 'Standardized Unexpected Earnings – A Progress Report' (1977) 32 *Journal of Finance* 1457; Ross Watts, 'Systematic "Abnormal Returns" After Quarterly Earnings Announcements' (1978) *Journal of Financial Economics* 127; Victor Bernard and Jacob Thomas, 'Post-Earnings-Announcement Drift: Delayed Price Response or Risk Premium?' (1989) 27 *Journal of Accounting Research* 1, 5.
45. Merritt Fox, Randall Morck, Bernard Yeung and Artyom Durnev, 'Law, Share Price Accuracy, and Economic Performance: The New Evidence' (2003) 102 *Michigan Law Review* 331, 348–349. Fox et al. argue that the arbitrage activities of smart money speculators do not always fully counteract the actions of naïve speculators.
46. Jeffrey Gordon and Lewis Kornhauser, 'Efficient Markets, Costly Information and Securities Research' (1985) 60 *New York University Law Review* 761, 769; Sheen Kassouf, 'Towards a Legal Framework for Efficiency and Equity in the Securities Markets' (1974) 25 *Hastings Law Journal* 417, 424; Stephan Schulmeister, 'A General Financial Transactions Tax: A Short Cut of the Pros, the Cons and a Proposal' (Working Paper No. 344, Austrian Institute of Economic Research, October 2009).
47. Joseph Stiglitz, 'Symposium on Bubble' (Spring 1990) *Journal of Economic Perspective* 13, 17; Andrei Shleifer and Lawrence Summers, 'The Noise Trader Approach in Finance' (Spring 1990) *Journal of Economic Perspective* 19, 19.
48. Andrew Lo, 'Reconciling Efficient Markets with Behavioral Finance: The Adaptive Markets Hypothesis' (Working Paper, 8 March 2005) 7.
49. Werner De Bondt and Richard Thaler, 'Does the Stock Market Overreact?' (1985) 40 *Journal of Finance* 793; Werner De Bondt and Richard Thaler, 'Further Evidence On Investor Overreaction And Stock Market Seasonality' (1987) 42 *Journal of Finance* 557.
50. Brad Barber and Terrance Odean, 'Online Investors: Do the Slow Die First?' (2002) 15 *Review of Financial Studies* 455.
51. Werner De Bondt and Richard Thaler, 'Does the Stock Market Overreact?' (1985) 40 *Journal of Finance* 793; Daniel Kent, David Hirshleifer and Avanidhar Subrahmanyam, 'Investor Psychology and Security Market under and Overreactions' (1998) 53 *Journal of Finance* 1839.

herding,[52] incapable of assessing probabilities,[53] subject to regret,[54] biased towards past behaviour or the status quo,[55] and or subject to fads.[56] In practice, participant behaviour such as investor overconfidence can lead to reduced returns, excess volatility and stock mispricing.[57]

Hence there is a large body of empirical studies that potentially challenge Fama's ECMH by identifying security price and market inefficiencies.[58] There is also growing evidence of irrational or cognitively biased market conduct and decision-making across all market participant groups, including regulators, company managers, institutional investors, and retail investors. Nonetheless, the debates concerning how to best respond to market behaviour categorised as irrational or cognitively biased are still nascent, as useful definitions or specific models of rational and irrational behaviour in financial markets remain elusive. Indeed, financial market behaviour defined as irrational or cognitively biased by some parties can be viewed as entirely rational by others. For example, the sort of behaviour underlying contagion models or herd behaviour is viewed as important by all investor groups,[59] and there are sound reasons

52. Robert Shiller, 'Conversation, Information, and Herd Behavior' (1995) 85 *American Economic Review* 181; Gur Huberman and Tomer Regev, 'Contagious Speculation and a Cure for Cancer: A Non-Event that Made Stock Prices Soar' (2001) 56 *Journal of Finance* 387; Stephen Bainbridge, 'Contemporary Issues in the Law of Business Organizations: Mandatory Disclosure: A Behavioural Analysis' (2000) 68 *University of Cincinnati Law Review* 1023, 1038–1041; Herding behaviour occurs when a decision-maker imitates the actions of others, while ignoring his or her own information and judgment with regard to the merits of the underlying decision.
53. See e.g., David Laibson, 'Golden Eggs and Hyperbolic Discounting' (1997) 112 *Quarterly Journal of Economics* 443.
54. See e.g., Roger Clarke, Scott Krase and Meir Statman, 'Tracking Errors, Regret and Tactical Asset Allocation' (1994) 20 *Journal of Portfolio Management* 16.
55. Stephen Bainbridge, 'Contemporary Issues in the Law of Business Organizations: Mandatory Disclosure: A Behavioural Analysis' (2000) 68 *University of Cincinnati Law Review* 1023, 1041–1044. Bainbridge indicates that the status quo bias posits a systematic decision making bias such that actors favour maintaining the status quo rather than switching to some alternative state.
56. Robert Shiller, 'Market Volatility and Investor Behavior' (1990) 80 *American Economic Review* 58; Stephen Choi and AC Pritchard, 'Behavioral Economics and the SEC' (2003) 56 *Stanford Law Review* 1; 72; David Hirshleifer, 'Investor Psychology and Asset Pricing' (2001) 56 *Journal of Finance* 1533, 1576; Stephen Bainbridge, 'Contemporary Issues in the Law of Business Organizations: Mandatory Disclosure: A Behavioural Analysis' (2000) 68 *University of Cincinnati Law Review* 1023, 1040.
57. Daniel Kent, David Hirshleifer and Avanidhar Subrahmanyam, 'Investor Psychology and Security Market under and Overreactions' (1998) 53 *Journal of Finance* 1839, 1867; Andrei Shleifer and Lawrence Summers, 'The Noise Trader Approach in Finance' (Spring 1990) *Journal of Economic Perspective* 19.
58. See Gill North and Ross Buckley, 'A Fundamental Re-examination of Efficiency in Capital Markets in Light of the Global Financial Crisis' (2010) 33 *University of New South Wales Law Journal* 714.
59. Stephen Bainbridge, 'Contemporary Issues in the Law of Business Organizations: Mandatory Disclosure: A Behavioural Analysis' (2000) 68 *University of Cincinnati Law Review* 1023, 1038–1039; John Coffee Jnr, 'Gatekeeper Failure and Reform: The Challenge of Fashioning Relevant Reforms' (2004) 84 *Boston University Law Review* 301, 329; Robert Shiller and John Pound, 'Survey Evidence on Diffusion of Interest and Information among Investors' (1989) August *Journal of Economic Behaviour and Organisation* 44; Marcel Kahan and Michael Klausner, 'Path Dependence in Corporate Contracting: Increasing Returns, Herd Behavior and Cognitive Biases' (1996) 74 *Washington University Law Quarterly* 347, 355–356. Bainbridge indicates that there is lots of evidence that smart, seemingly rational decision-makers are prone

for investors to engage in such conduct. Herding behaviour may be rational when investors play the momentum game in the hope that they can profit from noise trading. Such behaviour may result in speculative bubbles, but it may also enhance short-term profits and ensure job security.[60] Investing against market trends for long periods can be risky and counterproductive, even when security prices or entire markets seem to have become disconnected from real world factors.[61]

[C] Fama's Response to Criticisms of His Efficient Market Theory

In 1998, Fama argued that many of the identified market efficiency anomalies are not inconsistent with the market efficiency model because overreactions to information are as common as under-reactions, suggesting the anomalies are chance occurrences.[62] He indicated that most of the short-term anomalies could be accounted for by reasonable changes in the methods used to measure anomalies. He suggested that the ECMH can only be 'replaced by a better specific model of price formation, itself potentially rejectable by empirical tests.'[63] Alternative or adaptive models to the ECMH have been proposed. Some commentators suggest that a new paradigm founded in modern finance and incorporating the many complex realities and nuances in financial markets

---

to herd behaviour. He suggests that herding can arise because of a reputational pay-off even if the chosen course of action fails, it can be a response to bounded rationality and information asymmetries, or it can be a so-called conformity effect.

60. Ronald Gilson and Reinier Kraakman, 'The Mechanisms of Market Efficiency Twenty Years Later: The Hindsight Bias' (2003) 28 *Journal of Corporation Law* 715, 716. See also John Coffee Jnr, 'Gatekeeper Failure and Reform: The Challenge of Fashioning Relevant Reforms' (2004) 84 *Boston University Law Review* 301, 329; John C Coffee Jr, *Gatekeepers: The Professions and Corporate Governance* (Oxford University Press, 2006). Coffee notes that asset managers who are cautious, or who prematurely respond to new information, may underperform compared to their rivals and may lose their jobs. He suggests that the primary motive of many asset managers is to perform no worse than their major institutional rivals and this provides a strong incentive to herd. He notes that during a market bubble, it is dangerous to be sane in an insane world.
61. It is not easy for policy makers, regulators or scholars to appropriately raise the alarm during potential boom periods, and any that do raise the alarm may find that no one wants to listen. Individuals, particularly those with positions and reputations to protect, may not wish to be responsible for reducing or stopping money flows, or to be shown in hindsight to have made the wrong call As Jane Diplock, a prior Chair of IOSCO has noted, '[w]hen everybody is making money, and there's exuberance in the markets. It's extremely difficult to be the Jeremiah saying: "Look, that's a cliff you're about to run over". Nobody wants to hear that message, least of all politicians whose funds are perhaps being swollen by the very people making all this money.': ASIC, ASIC Summer School 2010, 'Securities and Investment Regulation: Beyond the Crisis' (1–3 March 2010, Melbourne, Australia) 76. It is not possible to eliminate all irrational or cognitively biased participant behaviour in financial markets, but there are policy measures and processes that can mitigate adverse effects. For example, the benefits of transparency and publicity as tools to promote appropriate market conduct are well-understood and acknowledged. Educational programmes and financial experience can mitigate behavioural biases. Regulatory structures that ensure consistent and comprehensive oversight of financial markets can also assist.
62. Eugene Fama, 'Market Efficiency, Long-Term Returns, and Behavioural Finance' (1998) 49 *Journal of Financial Economics* 283, 287.
63. Eugene Fama, 'Market Efficiency, Long-Term Returns, and Behavioural Finance' (1998) 49 *Journal of Financial Economics* 283, 283–284.

is emerging.[64] Others argue that, at this stage, behavioural economics provides only valuable after-the-fact explanations for observed behaviour rather than generating testable predictions.[65]

§3.04 THE HENRY MANNE INSIDER TRADING THEORIES (2)

[A] Manne's Efficiency Theory

Having outlined the basic principles of Fama's efficiency and economic theories and models, it is time to return to Manne's theories and models. Under Manne's efficiency theory, price efficiency appears to be defined in similar terms as those used in the ECMH, but the linkages from short-term price efficiency to economic outcomes remain unexplained, and the long-term economic goals are not defined or clarified. Indeed, Manne's oblique references to optimal individual or social utility are difficult to reconcile to a credible economic model or framework. In order for Manne's efficiency theory to produce optimal social utility (assuming this is a Pareto efficiency goal), short-term price efficiency gains must produce better long-term economic outcomes (or grow the total size of the economic pie).

A series of assumed linkages underpin price efficiency theories which posit that insider trading enhances economic efficiency, including that:

(1) insider trading provides effective price signals to the market;
(2) these price signals are the most efficient mechanism to enable the relevant information to be absorbed within security prices; and
(3) the price signals provided by insider trading and associated price efficiency gains lead to an improved allocation of economic resources.

The validity of these assumptions can be challenged. Low volume insider trading in highly liquid securities is unlikely to impact securities trading patterns sufficiently to provide any meaningful price signals to the market. While finely tuned algorithms or astute participants may pick up signals when insider trading occurs in reasonable volumes, particularly in less liquid stocks, the message behind such trading can easily be misinterpreted. When systemic trading on inside information is permitted in financial markets, price signals are noisier and the factoring of news into share prices

64. Lynn Stout, 'The Mechanisms of Market Inefficiency: An Introduction to the New Finance' (2003) 28 *Journal of Corporation Law* 635, 666–669.
65. Stephen LeRoy, 'Efficient Capital Markets and Martingales' (1989) 27 *Journal of Economic Literature* 1585, 1616; Ronald Gilson and Reinier Kraakman, 'The Mechanisms of Market Efficiency Twenty Years Later: The Hindsight Bias' (2003) 28 *Journal of Corporation Law* 715, 739–742; Alon Brav and JB Heaton, 'Market Indeterminacy' (2003) 28 *Journal of Corporation Law* 517, 519. See also Harrison Hong and Jeremy Stein, 'A Unified Theory of Underreaction, Momentum Trading, and Overreaction in Asset Markets' (1999) 54 *Journal of Finance* 2143.

is slower than when the information is widely disseminated.[66] It takes a period of time for share prices to incorporate new information. During this period, uninformed investors are unable to distinguish between trading volume and price movements based on credible private information and movements due to poorly informed trading. As a result, unexplained insider trading tends to encourage further speculative trading, leading to an overall reduction in share price accuracy and increased price volatility. Even if one accepts Manne's arguments that insider trading allows earlier incorporation of relevant information into share prices thereby optimising price efficiency, any positive impacts on real capital allocations (and not merely secondary trades) are minimal.[67] Commentators who promulgate price efficiency models often assume links to long-term economic gains.[68] However, information that is revealed through trading on inside information often becomes public soon after the insider trading occurs, and in these instances, any economic efficiency gains are negligible.[69] When company information is not incorporated into a security price for a few hours, this may alter the distribution of profits between traders but is unlikely to adversely impact a company's ability to raise capital or its long-term cost of capital.

[B] Manne's Efficiency Theory Assumptions

When Manne considered the long-term consequences of disallowing insider trading, he made a series of assertions or assumptions to support his theories:

(1) The information most commonly affecting share prices are significant changes in earnings. However, all market participants know of instances where earnings news does not have the expected effect on share prices, and the most likely explanation is insider trading.
(2) There is a high-level of insider trading within markets.
(3) A large proportion of inside information is not released publicly for long periods.
(4) Company disclosure regimes are not a credible alternative to permitting insider trading because issues regarding asset valuation, accounting, competitive positions, potential earnings and managerial developments cannot be fully disclosed.

66. See, e.g., Roy Schotland, 'Unsafe At Any Price: A Reply to Manne, Insider Trading and the Stock Market' (1967) 53 *Virginia Law Review* 1425, 1440–1442, 1448–1449; Victor Brudney, 'Insiders, Outsiders, and Informational Advantages Under the Federal Securities Laws' (1979) 93 *Harvard Law Review* 322, 334.
67. Mark Klock, 'Mainstream Economics and the Case for Prohibiting Inside Trading' (1994) 10 *Georgia State University Law Review* 297, 304.
68. See Gill North and Ross Buckley, 'A Financial Transaction Tax: Inefficient or Needed Systemic Reform?' (2012) 43 *Georgetown Journal of International Law* 745. Price efficiency studies do not examine economic outcomes or the relative efficiency of private versus public disclosure of company information.
69. David Pompillo, 'On the Reach of Insider Trading Law' (2007) 25 *Company and Securities Law Journal* 467, 472.

(5) The public is unsophisticated and incapable of ensuring disclosed company information is accurately absorbed into share prices.
(6) There is no evidence that investors lose confidence in markets that allow systemic insider trading.

Most of these assumptions can be challenged on theoretical and empirical grounds.

First, Manne acknowledged that the 'financial news most commonly affecting share prices is a significant change in annual earnings,'[70] but claimed that all market participants knew of cases where earnings news did not have the expected effect on security prices. He suggested that the most likely explanation was that the information was already known by the market and had been anticipated in the relevant security prices.[71] Most commentators would accept the link made by Manne between earnings and share prices. Empirical research suggests that available company information, particularly earnings related news, is generally absorbed into security prices quickly, including information that companies have disclosed publicly and privately. Seminal research by Brown and Ball in the 1960s found that the market anticipated company earnings throughout the year.[72] When the preliminary final results were announced, about 85% of the adjustment was already incorporated within the share price, and by the time the annual report was released, the share price fully reflected its content.[73] Subsequent studies have also found a pattern of adjusting share prices over the year, with a strong correlation between annual stock returns and income changes.[74] The volume and speed of securities trading on leading exchanges have increased exponentially over the last decade, so the time required for information to be absorbed into security prices is also likely to have increased.

Second, Manne assumed that regulation that prohibits insider trading is ineffectual because such trading is routine within markets and cannot be stopped.[75] Most, if not all, commentators would accept that instances of insider trading occur in financial markets, but it is not possible to know the extent of insider trading, regardless of whether a particular financial market has insider trading regulation. The fact that

70. Henry Manne, 'Insider Trading and the Law Professors' (1975) 23 *Vanderbilt Law Review* 547, 571.
71. Henry Manne, 'Insider Trading and the Law Professors' (1975) 23 *Vanderbilt Law Review* 547, 571.
72. Ray Ball and Philip Brown, 'An Empirical Evaluation of Accounting Income Numbers' (1968) 6 *Journal of Accounting Research* 159, 176.
73. Ray Ball and Philip Brown, 'An Empirical Evaluation of Accounting Income Numbers' (1968) 6 *Journal of Accounting Research* 159, 176. See also William Beaver, 'The Information Content of Annual Earnings Announcements' (1968) 6 *Journal of Accounting Research* 67; William Beaver, Richard Lambert and Dale Morse, 'The Information Content of Security Prices' (1980) 2 *Journal of Accounting and Economics* 3; Dale Morse, 'Price and Trading Volume Reaction Surrounding Earnings Announcements: A Closer Examination' (1981) 19 *Journal of Accounting Research* 374.
74. D Craig Nichols and James Wahlen, 'How Do Earnings Numbers Relate To Stock Returns? A Review Of Classic Accounting Research With Updated Evidence' (December 2004) *Accounting Horizons* 263.
75. Henry Manne, 'Insider Trading and the Law Professors' (1975) 23 *Vanderbilt Law Review* 547, 564.

regulation prohibiting insider trading does not prevent all instances of insider trading does not mean the regulation is not beneficial. Regulation that prohibits certain behaviour rarely, if ever, results in complete cessation of the prescribed conduct. Appropriately enforced insider trading regulation can deter insider trading and provide support for effective mandatory disclosure regimes.

Third, Manne assumed the information used by insider traders is not made public for long periods, but he did not provide any evidence or commentary to support this claim.[76] Commentators who argue that most materially price-sensitive inside information is not publicly released, or that it is only released after long delays, need to explain what type of information falls within these categories in contemporary markets, and how important this information is across the total pool of information used by market participants to value and trade company securities. Most insider trading case law in developed markets involves trading on confidential information in advance of public announcements concerning capital raisings, takeover deals, and earnings related news. These classes of information are highly price-sensitive, and when related trading occurs close to public announcements, it is easier for regulators to establish the elements of an insider trading action. Additionally, experienced participants have indicated that insider trading on these classes of information are of most concern because it enables those with access to valuable private information from reliable inside sources to make trading gains on a virtually riskless basis.[77] As noted previously, when insider trading occurs during a short window prior to public release of the information, then price, market and economic efficiency effects are minimal or non-existent. The only substantive impact of such trading is a shift of wealth from uninformed to informed traders.

Fourth, Manne suggested that full disclosure was not a credible alternative to permitting insider trading, as there must be a significant number of instances where insider trading is based on information that cannot be legally divulged, or disclosed in any useful or straightforward manner.[78] He outlined examples of scenarios that an unsophisticated public are unlikely to understand, and suggested that it is better to allow insiders who understand these matters to influence the market by trading in the shares.[79] He concluded by stating that it is clear that:

> [a]sset valuation problems, accounting issues, competitive positions, potential earnings and managerial developments are examples of news items that will always prevent the philosophy of full disclosure, no matter what its theoretical merit, from existing in the real world.[80]

---

76. Henry Manne, 'Insider Trading and the Law Professors' (1975) 23 *Vanderbilt Law Review* 547, 564.
77. See, e.g., Australian Securities and Investments Commission (ASIC), 'Our Financial Markets: The Big Issues' (ASIC Summer School 2008 Report, 18-20 February 2008) 82-83.
78. Henry Manne, 'Insider Trading and the Law Professors' (1975) 23 *Vanderbilt Law Review* 547, 571.
79. Henry Manne, 'Insider Trading and the Law Professors' (1975) 23 *Vanderbilt Law Review* 547, 573.
80. Henry Manne, 'Insider Trading and the Law Professors' (1975) 23 *Vanderbilt Law Review* 547, 574.

This argument is best answered by a review of the public disclosures of listed companies. All of these types of corporate issues are now regularly disclosed and discussed publicly.

Fifth, Manne brazenly questioned the intelligence and capacities of most investors and the public. As already highlighted in Chapter 1, the validity of presumptions about investor groups in contemporary financial markets is doubtful. For example, the fact that most of the losses resulting from the GFC stemmed from institutional analysis and trading seems to have been quickly forgotten.[81] The distinction between individual investors and institutional investors is far from sharp and a more nuanced approach is required.

Finally, Manne claimed there was a lack of evidence suggesting a loss of public confidence and subsequent reluctance to invest in stock markets with regular occurrences of insider trading.[82] Market confidence notions and arguments were discussed in Chapter 2. In the period since the Manne publications, empirical research published by finance, economics and accounting scholars on associations between insider trading and efficiency are extensive. This research, which is summarised later in this chapter, consistently suggests that any short-term price efficiency gains from insider trading are significantly outweighed over longer periods by increases in market volatility and reductions in other efficiency measures, such as bid-ask spreads, liquidity and price accuracy.[83] Broader research on global markets also suggests that countries with enforced insider trading laws benefit over the long-term through enhanced liquidity, more informative stock prices, and lower costs of capital.[84] These bodies of work suggest that sustainable economic growth created through efficient markets requires public confidence and trust, and a belief that financial markets operate on a fair basis. People do not willingly participate and invest their hard-earned money in markets unless they are confident about the quality of information with which they are provided and the integrity of the market processes.[85]

§3.05 INSIDER TRADING JURISPRUDENCE

A summary of the insider trading jurisprudence in the US is provided in this section, because a high proportion of insider trading enforcement actions has occurred in the

81. Tony D'Aloisio, Chairman ASIC, 'Developments in the Global Regulatory System' (Speech Delivered at the Financial Services Council Annual Conference, Melbourne, 12 August 2010) 7.
82. Henry Manne, 'Insider Trading and the Law Professors' (1975) 23 *Vanderbilt Law Review* 547, 577–578.
83. See, e.g., Bradford Cornell and Erik Sirri, 'The Reaction of Investors and Stock Prices to Insider Trading' (1992) 47 *Journal of Finance* 1031, 1055; Raymond Fishe and Michael Robe, 'The Impact of Illegal Insider Trading in Dealer and Specialist Markets: Evidence From a Natural Experiment' (2004) 71 *Journal of Financial Economics* 461, 461–462, 481.
84. See, e.g., Utpal Bhattacharya, Hazem Daouk and Michael Welker, 'The World Price of Earnings Opacity' (2003) 78 *Accounting Review* 641; Laura Beny, 'Insider Trading Law and Stock Markets Around the World: An Empirical Contribution to Theoretical Law and Economics Debate' (2007) 32 *Journal of Corporation Law* 237.
85. Bernard Black, 'The Legal and Institutional Precondition for Strong Securities Markets' (2001) 48 *UCLA Law Review* 781, 782.

US.[86] The insider trading case law in the US provides useful insights on the differences in judicial interpretation of the rationales that underpin most insider trading and disclosure frameworks. It also provides valuable commentary on the theory and practice of selective disclosure.

Insider trading rules in the US are contained within Rule 10b-5 of the *Exchange Act*, a broad provision directed at fraudulent practices.[87] Until 1980, the US judiciary indicated that Rule 10b-5 was based on a 'disclose or abstain rule' or an equality of access approach. In *SEC v. Texas Gulf Sulphur* 401 F.2d 833 (2nd Cir 1968), cert denied 394 US 976 (1969), the Court indicated [at 851-852] that:

> The core of Rule 10b-5 is the implementation of the congressional purpose that all investors should have equal access to the rewards of participation in securities transactions. It was the intent of Congress that all members of the investing public should be subject to identical market risks ... The insiders here were not trading on an equal footing with the outside investors ... Such inequities based upon unequal access to knowledge should not be shrugged off as inevitable ....

Further, in *re Cady, Roberts & Co* 40 SEC 907 (1961), a broker who traded while in possession of non-public information received from a company director was held to have violated Rule 10b-5. The SEC held that the duties of corporate insiders may extend to outsiders when the outsides were effectively 'temporary or constructive insiders'.

The intention of Congress regarding Rule 10b-5 was reconsidered in 1980. In *Chiarella v. United States* 445 US 222 (1980), the Supreme Court reversed the criminal conviction of a printer who obtained non-public information of a proposed merger from tender documents that he was contracted to print and who purchased stock in the target company based on this information. The majority[88] suggested [at 232–233] that the decision by the Court of Appeal:

> rested solely upon its belief that the federal securities laws created a system providing equal access to information necessary for reasoned and intelligent investment decisions [when] neither the Congress nor the Commission ... has adopted a parity-of-information rule.

86. See, e.g., Securities Exchange Commission, 'SEC Enforcement Actions Insider Trading Cases' 5 February 2015, http://www.sec.gov/spotlight/insidertrading/cases.shtml. See also David Enrich and Harriet Agnew, 'U.K. Agency Struggles in Fight Agency Insider Trading', 4 January 2014 wsj.com http://www.wsj.com/articles/SB10001424052702303640604579296520563211360 viewed 9 February 2015. Enrich and Agnew indicates that the Financial Conduct Authority and its predecessor, the Financial Services Authority, did not bring a criminal insider trading case until 2009. Their analysis found twenty-three convictions since 2009 involving profits of less than USD 9 million. By comparison, they note that the US Securities and Exchange Commission filed more than fifity insider trading civil cases in each of the past three years.
87. Rule 10b-5, Employment of Manipulative and Deceptive Devices, Exchange Release No. 3230, 7 Fed Reg 3804 (1942) (codified at 17 CFR s. 240.10b-5 (1991)). Rule 10b-5 forbids any person, in connection with the purchase or sale of any security: (a) 'To employ any device, scheme or artifice to defraud, (b) To make any untrue statement of a material fact or omit to state a material fact necessary in order to make the statements made, in light of the circumstances under which they were made, not misleading, or (c) To engage in any act, practice or course of business which operates or would operate as a fraud or deceit on any person.'
88. Justice Powell delivered the opinion of the Court, in which Stewart, White, Rehnquist and Stevens JJ joined. Burger, Blackmun and Marshall JJ filed dissenting opinions.

It rejected a parity of information approach, indicating that such a broad duty was sufficiently divorced from the established doctrine that a duty to disclose only arises from a specific relationship between parties. It held that the printer owed no duty to the target company shareholders and therefore did not defraud them. The *Chiarella* case altered the legal framework of Rule 10b-5, with liability only arising when the person trading on inside information was in a fiduciary relationship with the relevant company. Among the three dissenters, Burger J highlighted [at 241] that:

> the antifraud provisions were designed in large measure to assure that dealing in securities is fair and without undue preferences or advantages among investors ... An investor who purchases securities on the basis of misappropriated non-public information possesses just such an 'undue' trading advantage; his conduct quite clearly serves no useful function except his own enrichment at the expense of others.

Blackmun J further stated [at 251] that:

> I would hold that persons having access to confidential material information that is not legally available to others generally are prohibited by Rule 10b-5 from engaging in schemes to exploit their structural informational advantage through trading in affected securities.

The SEC responded to the *Chiarella* decision by promulgating Rule 14e-3 under section 14(e) of the *Exchange Act*. Rule 14e-3 makes it illegal for anyone to trade on the basis of material non-public information in relation to tender offers when they know the information source is an insider.

The fiduciary-based approach was modified in 1981 when the Second Circuit developed the misappropriation theory in *United States v. Newman* 664 F.2d 12 (2nd Cir 1981), cert denied, 464 US 863 (1983). In this case, Newman was found to have contravened Rule 10b-5 when he traded the securities of a company while in possession of information obtained from two investment bankers, because the bankers had misappropriated the information from their employers. The misappropriation approach was further developed in *Dirks v. SEC.* 463 US 646 (1983). Justice Powell speaking for the majority of the Supreme Court[89] outlined the principle of 'constructive insiders' who receive confidential information in the course of providing services to the corporation and who acquire the fiduciary duties of the true insider when the insider is bound to keep the information confidential. Dirk, the tippee, escaped liability in this instance, because the original tipper disclosed the information to expose a fraud and not for personal gain. Justice Powell stated [at 667] that:

> there must be a breach of the insider's fiduciary duty before the tippee inherits the duty to disclose or abstain ... Moreover, to constitute a violation of Rule 10b-5, there must be fraud ... Dirks ... had no duty to abstain from use of the inside information that he obtained.

---

89. Powell J delivered the opinion of the Court, in which Burger, White, Rehnquist, Stevens and O'Conner joined. Blackmun J filed a dissenting opinion, in which Brennan and Marshall JJ joined.

It confirmed that a tippee is only liable as a constructive insider if he or she knew or had reason to believe that the tipper had breached a fiduciary duty in disclosing the confidential information and the tipper received a benefit from the disclosure. Blackmun J in dissent suggested [at 936] that the majority's improper purpose requirement:

> seems little different from the theory that insider trading should be permitted because it brings relevant information to the market... [and the] extreme theory, which postulates that insider trading causes no harm at all to those who purchase from the insider ... Th[is] theory rejects the existence of any enforceable principle of fairness between market participants.

In 1997, the Supreme Court adopted and applied the misappropriation theory in *United States v. O'Hagan* 521 US 642 (1997). Hagan was a partner in a law firm representing a company making a tender offer for Pillsbury Company. Hagan acquired options in Pillsbury and sold them following the tender offer for profit. The Court held O'Hagan liable for fraud under Rule 10b-5 based on the misappropriation theory. Justice Ginsberg, delivering the opinion of the Court, indicated [at 652–653] that the:

> classical theory targets a corporate insider's breach of duty to shareholders with whom the insider transacts; the misappropriation theory outlaws trading on the basis of non-public information by a corporate 'outsider' in breach of a duty owed not to a trading party, but to the source of the information. The misappropriation theory is designed to protect the integrity of the securities markets against abuses by 'outsiders' to a corporation who have access to confidential information that will affect the corporations' security price when revealed, but who owe no fiduciary or other duty to that corporation's shareholders.

In 2000 the SEC codified the fiduciary duty and misappropriation theories in Rule 10b5-1. Rule 10b5-1 states that the insider trading prohibition under Rule 10b-5 is breached whenever someone trades on the basis of material non-public information.[90] The release accompanying this rule indicates that:

> this language incorporates all theories of insider trading liability under the case law – classical insider trading, temporary insider theory, tippee liability, and trading by someone who misappropriated the inside information.

This move by the SEC to publicly confirm the scope of the insider trading prohibition, including all of the insider trading circumstances encompassed within successful insider trading prosecutions, may have been initiated as a broad deterrent to financial market participants.

90. Rule 10b5-1(a) states: '*General.* The "manipulative and deceptive devices" prohibited by s. 10(b) of the Act ... and [rule] 10b-5 ... include among other things, the purchase or sale of a security of any issuer, on the basis of material non-public information about that security or issuer, in breach of a duty of trust or confidence that is owed directly, indirectly, or derivatively, to the issuer of that security or the shareholders of that issuers, or to any other person who is the source of the material non-public information.' The release accompanying this rule states that 'This language incorporates all theories of insider trading liability under the case law – classical insider trading, temporary insider theory, tippee liability, and trading by someone who misappropriated the inside information.'

Insider trading law in the US was clarified and arguably narrowed in a landmark decision by the US Court of Appeals for the Second Circuit in *United States v. Newman* 773 F.3d 438 (2d Cir. 2014), reh'g denied, Nos 13-1837, 13-1917 (2d Cir. Apr. 3, 2015). The defendants Newman and Chiasson, both portfolio managers of hedge funds, had been convicted in the United States District Court for the Southern District of New York of securities fraud and conspiracy to commit securities fraud under sections 10(b) and 32 of the Exchange Act, for trading in the securities of Dell and NVIDIA based on non-public information about the company's earnings before public release. The non-public information was originally obtained from insiders employed by Dell and NVIDIA and passed down a chain of three to four levels of tippees to Newman and Chiasson. The 2nd Circuit reversed the convictions and dismissed the charges against the defendants due to insufficient evidence. It stated that it must be proven beyond a reasonable doubt that the person who received the tip knew that an insider disclosed confidential information and that he or she did so in exchange for a personal benefit.[91] It confirmed that insider trading liability is based on breaches of fiduciary duty, and not informational asymmetries, and that a tippee's liability derives from the tipper's breach of a fiduciary duty.[92] Further, the test for determining whether a corporate insider has breached his or her fiduciary duty is whether the insider benefits directly or indirectly from the disclosure.[93]

The 2nd Circuit indicated that a friendship of a casual or social nature is not sufficient to satisfy the personal benefit requirement.[94] It noted that it had not found another case in which tippees as remote as Newman and Chiasson had been held criminally liable for insider trading.[95] It confirmed that Newman and Chiasson received four updates on Dell's earnings numbers in the weeks leading up to its August 2008 earnings announcements, and multiple updates on NVIDIA's earnings numbers prior to its earnings announcement. Nonetheless, it held that this was not sufficiently suspicious to warrant material inferences that Newman and Chiasson 'must have known, or deliberately avoided knowing, that the information originated with corporate insiders and that those insiders disclosed the information in exchange for a personal benefit.'[96] This finding was influenced by evidence that showed that insiders at Dell and NVIDIA regularly communicated with analysts and selectively disclosed the same type of information as the alleged 'inside' information.[97] The evidence referenced by the court concerning selective disclosure is critically important when considering effective company disclosure regulation and practice and is discussed more fully in Chapters 4 and 13.

To summarise, the Supreme Court has indicated that insider trading regulation in the US is not based on a 'parity of information' rationale because such a duty is too far removed from the established doctrine that a duty to disclose only arises from a specific

91. *United States v. Newman No. 13-1837 cr (L)* (2d Cir. 10 December 2014) 4, 18.
92. *United States v. Newman No. 13-1837 cr (L)* (2d Cir. 10 December 2014) 13, 16.
93. *United States v. Newman No. 13-1837 cr (L)* (2d Cir. 10 December 2014) 11.
94. *United States v. Newman No. 13-1837 cr (L)* (2d Cir. 10 December 2014) 21.
95. *United States v. Newman No. 13-1837 cr (L)* (2d Cir. 10 December 2014) 14--15.
96. *United States v. Newman No. 13-1837 cr (L)* (2d Cir. 10 December 2014) 25–26.
97. *United States v. Newman No. 13-1837 cr (L)* (2d Cir. 10 December 2014) 26–27.

relationship between parties. The Court's alternative rationales for the regulation seem to rest on the alleged price efficiency gains from the activities of analysts and other professionals within financial markets, and the need to balance this with any exploitation of informational advantages that comes from the possession of non-public information.[98] These efficiency arguments are founded to some extent on the Manne efficiency theory. Some reliance on property law concepts may also arise, but the nature of these property principles and rights have not been clearly delineated. The judicial reasoning may be that boards retain all rights to information produced within their company, including when, how and to whom material information will be distributed. If so, this judicial interpretation of the policy intentions underpinning Rule 10-b is more consistent with a voluntary disclosure environment than a mandatory disclosure framework.

Notably, Manne's market efficiency theory and arguments are reflected in case law outside of the US. For example, in *R v. Firns* (2001) 38 ACSR, Firns was convicted in the New South Wales District Court of Australia of two insider trading charges under section 1002G of the *Corporations Law*. In a subsequent appeal to the New South Wales Court of Criminal Appeal, President Mason, speaking for the majority, concluded that the equal access and efficiency rationales underpinning the Australian insider trading regime are incompatible,[99] and that convergence of these incompatible policy goals has produced 'legislated astigmatism.'[100] This reasoning derived from the Manne price efficiency theory,[101] which Mason P described as the proposition that insider trading enhances market efficiency by providing signals to the market that help move the price of securities towards their real value.[102]

This author suggests that Mason P selected an incorrect efficiency goal for consideration. The efficiency theories of Manne and Fama differ markedly with respect to the ultimate economic objective, the underlying assumptions, and the capacity for external researchers to empirically test the theories. The appropriate efficiency rationale to apply to company disclosure and insider trading law is long-term economic efficiency, and this efficiency goal is largely compatible with an equal access goal. Insider trading and company disclosure policy and case law that focuses on short-term price efficiency as the primary goal is flawed, because this approach returns to the efficiency theory that Manne developed to support insider trading in markets without regulatory interference.[103] Consequently, insider trading and company disclosure frameworks that purport to promote equality of access to information, but which

98. See *Dirks v. SEC.* 463 US 646 (1983) 658. For further detail, see Ch. 4.
99. *R v .Firns* (2001) 38 ACSR 223.
100. *R v. Firns* (2001) 38 ACSR 223, 232.
101. See Gill North, 'A Re-examination of the Manne Efficiency Theory and the Insider Trading and Company Disclosure Efficiency Rationales' (2011) 25 *Australian Journal of Corporate Law* 209.
102. *R v. Firns* (2001) 38 ACSR 223, 230.
103. The Manne market efficiency arguments were considered and rejected by both the Anisman and Griffiths reviews of insider trading law in Australia in the 1980s: Philip Anisman, *Insider Trading Legislation: An Outline of the Issues and Alternatives* (1986) 8–9; Standing Committee on Legal and Constitutional Affairs, House of Representatives, *Fair Shares for All: Insider Trading in Australia* (1989) ('Griffiths Report').

simultaneously permit trading on private information in order to enhance short-term price efficiency, are easily undermined.

The GFC has shown in stark terms that the debates concerning efficiency and fairness in financial markets are still evolving. Policy makers, regulators and scholars are fundamentally re-examining the efficiency and economic models applicable to financial markets and systems,[104] including Fama's efficient market theory, in the wake of the GFC. The capacity of markets to respond to issues such as information asymmetry, conflicts of interests and risk anomalies are primary areas of focus. For example, Lord Turner suggests the GFC:

> poses for regulators the challenge of complexity, because it involves rejecting an intellectually elegant but also profoundly mistaken faith in ever perfect and self-equilibrating markets, ever rational human behaviours; but it leaves us with no simple alternative philosophy ....[105]

Stiglitz suggests that most financial market and efficiency debates are not concerned with how to best allocate scarce national resources to productive investment, but are instead focused on rearranging the profits made on existing investments to ensure some community participants gain at the expense of others.[106] This argument is highly relevant to the mandatory disclosure and insider trading theoretical debates, and to real world disclosure practices, because insider trading often concerns rearrangements of secondary trading profits from uninformed traders to those 'in the know', rather than economic efficiency enhancements through improved allocation of new capital.

§3.06 EMPIRICAL RESEARCH

Some scholars and practitioners suggest that the debate on insider trading regulation ought to be determined empirically.[107] Insider trading studies are inevitably restricted in scope due to the inherent secrecy involved in such trading. Nevertheless, empirical

104. See, e.g., Tony D'Aloisio, Chairman ASIC, 'Developments in the Global Regulatory System' (Speech Delivered at the Financial Services Council Annual Conference, Melbourne, 12 August 2010) 7.
105. Adair Turner, Chairman, Financial Services Authority (Speech to the City Banquet, The Mansion House, London, 22 September 2009).
106. Commission of Experts of the President of the UN General Assembly on Reform of the International Monetary and Financial System, Principles for a New Financial Architecture (Commission), 21 September 2009, http://www.un.org/ga/president/63/commission/financial_commission.shtml viewed 13 October 2014. Stiglitz was the Chair of this Commission and has been awarded a Nobel prize in economics. He argues that '[f]inancial markets are not an end in themselves, but a means: they are supposed to perform certain vital functions which enable the real economy to be more productive such as mobilising savings, allocating capital, and managing risk'. See also Joseph Stiglitz, 'Using Tax Policy to Curb Speculative Short-Term Trading' (1989) 3 *Journal of Financial Services Research* 101, 109.
107. James Cox, 'Insider Trading and Contracting: A Critical Response to the "Chicago School"' (1986) 4 *Duke Law Journal* 628, 644–645; Laura Beny, 'Insider Trading Law and Stock Markets Around the World: An Empirical Contribution to Theoretical Law and Economics Debate' (2007) 32 *Journal of Corporation Law* 237, 239; Frank Easterbrook and Daniel Fischel, 'Mandatory Disclosure and the Protection of Investors' (1984) 70 *Virginia Law Review* 6695;

research suggests that regulation which prohibits insider trading is likely to enhance long-term economic efficiency.[108]

There are several bodies of empirical research that examine the effects and regulation of insider trading. One body of work examines whether private information held by corporate insiders enables abnormal returns over a period compared to benchmark market returns. These studies generally find that insiders are either able to make abnormal gains or reduce their losses. Seyhun found that corporate insiders were able to make excess returns, particularly when the insiders were chairmen or officer directors.[109] Elliott, Morse and Richardson found that the use of private information by insiders consistently resulted in profit.[110] Eyssell, Seyhun and Bradley found that insiders, especially top executives and officers, were involved in significant sale trades prior to bankruptcy filings, thereby avoiding significant capital losses based on non-public information.[111] Fidrmuc et al. found that the proportion of share ownership by directors compared to share ownership by outside shareholders had an impact on the abnormal returns achieved by insiders. The abnormal returns made by directors as insiders were significantly lower when the company was controlled by other companies or individuals unrelated to the directors, than when the dominant shareholders were institutional investors.[112] Skaife et al. found that the profitability of insider trading by top executives was significantly greater for companies with weak internal controls due to the potential for greater noise and bias in financial statements.[113] Chang et al. suggested that gains made by Australian directors from purchase transactions increased with the level of director ownership and the size of the trade.[114]

Another group of studies suggest the long-term impacts of allowing insider trading are a reduction in market liquidity and an increase in bid / ask spreads, two

---

Christopher Saari, 'The Efficient Capital Markets Hypothesis, Economic Theory and the Regulation of the Securities Industry' (1977) 29 *Stanford Law Review* 1031, 1056.

108. See, e.g., Lawrence Ausubel, 'Insider Trading In a Rational Expectations Economy' (1990) 80 *American Economic Review* 1022, 1022, 1038; Hayne Leland, 'Insider Trading: Should It Be Prohibited?' (1992) 100 *Journal of Political Economy* 859, 884.
109. H Nejat Seyhun, 'Insider's Profits, Costs of Trading and Market Efficiency' (1986) 16 *Journal of Financial Economics* 189, 210; H Nejat Seyhun, 'The Effectiveness of the Insider Trading Sanctions' (1992) 35 *Journal of Law and Economics* 149, 176. See also Michael Rozeff and Mir Zaman, 'Market Efficiency and Insider Trading: New Evidence' (1988) 61 *Journal of Business* 25, 45; Stephen Penman, 'Insider Trading and the Dissemination of Firm's Forecast Information' (1982) 55 *Journal of Business* 479.
110. John Elliott, Dale Morse and Gordon Richardson, 'The Association Between Insider Trading and Information Announcements' (1984) 15 *RAND Journal of Economics* 521, 535.
111. Thomas Eyssell, 'Corporate Insiders and the Death of the Firm: Evidence on the Incidence of Insider Trading in Corporate Dissolutions' (1991) 26 *Financial Review* 517, 517, 531; H Nejat Seyhun and Michael Bradley, 'Corporate Bankruptcy and Insider Trading' (1997) 70 *Journal of Business* 189, 214.
112. Jana Fidrmuc, Marc Goergen and Luc Renneboog, 'Insider Trading, News Releases, and Ownership Concentration' (2006) 61 *Journal of Finance* 2931, 2933.
113. Hollis Skaife, David Veenman and Daniel Wangerin, 'Internal Control Over Financial Reporting and Managerial Rent Extraction: Evidence From The Profitability of Insider Trading' (2013) 55 *Journal of Accounting and Economics* 91.
114. Millicent Chang, Richard Hillman and Iain Watson, 'Are Corporate Governance Mechanisms Effective in Reducing Insider Trading Profits?' (2005) 23 *Company and Securities Law Journal* 165, 178.

recognised measures of market efficiency. Cornell and Sirri found that short-term liquidity improved when insiders were active in the market prior to the announcement of a takeover bid due to higher trading volumes.[115] The market makers and insiders were able to exploit the uninformed in such cases, and as Cornell and Sirri suggest, the likely long run impact of such incidents is an increase in spreads.[116] A model by Fishe and Robe found that insider trading had a negative impact on market liquidity because market makers adjusted the depth and spread to compensate for the risk from informed traders.[117] Further, a study by Masson and Madhavan found that insider trading lowered company valuations.[118]

Another body of work examines selected variables across global securities markets. This research suggests that countries with insider trading laws have more liquid markets, more accurate pricing and a lower cost of capital. A study by Du and Wei found that countries with more prevalent insider trading have more volatile markets after controlling for the liquidity, maturity and fundamentals of the relevant markets. It found the 'effect of insider trading is quantitatively significant when compared with the effect of economic fundamentals.'[119] A study by Beny found that countries with insider trading laws generated positive market externalities due to associations with more liquid stock markets and more informative stock prices. The study found that enhanced liquidity and price accuracy resulted in lower costs of equity and improved capital allocation.[120] An initial study by Bhattacharya and Daouk found that countries which enforce their insider trading law have a significantly lower cost of capital.[121] In a subsequent study, they found 'the cost of equity *rises* when an emerging market introduces an insider trading law but does not enforce it.'[122] Fernandes and Ferreira found that enforcement of insider trading laws improves price informativeness in developed markets but has a lesser effect in emerging markets with weak legal

115. Bradford Cornell and Erik Sirri, 'The Reaction of Investors and Stock Prices to Insider Trading' (1992) 47 *Journal of Finance* 1031.
116. Bradford Cornell and Erik Sirri, 'The Reaction of Investors and Stock Prices to Insider Trading' (1992) 47 *Journal of Finance* 1031, 1055.
117. Raymond Fishe and Michael Robe, 'The Impact of Illegal Insider Trading in Dealer and Specialist Markets: Evidence From a Natural Experiment' (2004) 71 *Journal of Financial Economics* 461, 461-462, 481.
118. Robert Masson and Ananth Madhavan, 'Insider Trading and the Value Of the Firm' (1991) 39 *Journal of Industrial Economics* 333, 333.
119. Julian Du and Shang-jin Wei, 'Does Insider Trading Raise Market Volatility?' (2004) 114 *Economic Journal* 916, 916, 940. Du and Wei point out that a certain degree of market volatility is unavoidable; however excessive volatility not related to economic fundamentals diminishes the signalling function and impedes resource allocation.
120. Laura Beny, 'Do Insider Trading Laws Matter? Some Preliminary Comparative Evidence' (2005) 7 *American Law and Economics Review* 144. See also Laura Beny, 'Insider Trading Law and Stock Markets Around the World: An Empirical Contribution to Theoretical Law and Economics Debate' (2007) 32 *Journal of Corporation Law* 237; Laura Beny, 'Do Investors in Controlled Firms Value Insider Trading Laws? International Evidence' (2008) 4 *Journal of Law, Economics & Policy* 267.
121. Utpal Bhattacharya and Hazem Daouk, 'The World Price of Insider Trading' (2002) 62 *Journal of Finance* 75.
122. Utpal Bhattacharya and Hazem Daouk, 'When No Law is Better Than a Good Law' (2009) 13 *Review of Finance* 577, 580.

institutions.[123] Durnev and Amrita found that while insider trading regulation reduces insider trading levels, this effect is more limited when the insiders hold or control more of the company and investor protection levels are low.[124]

Interestingly, a study by Thevenot found that the frequency of insider trading in the US increases as the level of financial benefit from insider trading increases, but decreases as the perceived risk of class action litigation and regulatory enforcement rises.[125] Moreover, Cohen et al. found that the most informed insider traders in the US are locals from geographically concentrated and poorly governed companies.[126] Importantly, Jagolinzer et al. found that while trading during restricted periods is generally 'informed', general counsel can limit such trading.[127]

The empirical research as a whole suggests that countries which establish insider trading regulation achieve superior economic efficiency outcomes in the form of lower costs of capital and more efficient capital allocations, and these identified economic benefits are enhanced when legal institutions and enforcement are strong and when minority investors are well protected.

§3.07 SUMMARY

Manne's work has had a profound impact on the scholarly legal literature and judicial commentary on insider trading law, and more broadly on the scholarly debates concerning the benefits of company disclosure frameworks and efficiency in financial markets. The most significant influence of Manne's work has been to promote debate on the efficiency of insider trading and mandatory disclosure regulation, with many scholars remaining reluctant to argue for such regulation on grounds other than efficiency. Nevertheless, resolution through efficiency analysis has not eventuated. After many decades of vigorous debate, there are scholars who suggest it is still unclear whether insider trading enhances or impedes efficiency, whether anyone is harmed by insider trading, and whether mandatory disclosure regulation is efficient and beneficial.[128]

---

123. Nuno Fernandes and Miguel Ferreira, 'Insider Trading Laws and Stock Price Informativeness' (2009) 22 *Review of Financial Studies* 1845.
124. Art Durnev and S Nain Amrita, 'Does Insider Trading Regulation Deter Private Information Trading? International Evidence' (2007) 15 *Pacific Basin Financial Journal* 409.
125. Maya Thevenot, 'The Factors Affecting Illegal Insider Trading In Firms With Violations of GAAP' (2011) 53 *Journal of Accounting and Economics* 375.
126. Lauren Cohen, Christopher Malloy and Lukasz Pomorski, 'Decoding Inside Information' (2012) 57 *Journal of Finance* 1009.
127. Alan Jagolinzer, David Larcker and Daniel Taylor, 'Corporate Governance and the Information Content of Insider Trades' (2011) 49 *Journal of Accounting Research* 1249. See also Nadia Massoud, Deborah Nandy, Anthony Saunders and Keke Song, 'Do Hedge Funds Trade on Private Information? Evidence From Syndicated Lending and Short-Selling' (2011) 99 *Journal of Financial Economics* 477. Massound et al. found evidence consistent with short selling by hedge funds prior to public announcements of loan originations and loan amendments.
128. Frank Easterbrook and Daniel Fischel, *The Economic Structure of Corporate Law* (Harvard University Press, 1996) 254–255, 261–262. See also Dennis Carlton and Daniel Fischel, 'The Regulation of Insider Trading' (1983) 35 *Stanford Law Review* 857, 861–872; Edmund Kitch, 'Proposals for Reform of Securities Regulation: An Overview' (2001) 41 *Virginia Journal of*

Manne's theories are underpinned by a series of assumptions including: insider trading is routine and unstoppable; there are long delays until the public release of inside information; full disclosure is not a credible alternative to permitting insider trading; the public is unsophisticated and incapable of ensuring company information is accurately absorbed into share prices; and there is no visible evidence that investors lose confidence in markets that allow systemic insider trading. Most of these assumptions can be vigorously challenged on both theoretical and empirical grounds. Manne's economic analysis of the effects of insider trading is incomplete because he does not discuss the processes by which insider trading enhances the allocation of real capital and resources or the connections between individual and social utility. Further, he excludes the significant costs that arise in financial markets which permit company insiders and outsiders to trade on confidential company information, such as information asymmetry, misaligned incentives, agency issues, and weakened corporate governance processes. His analysis also ignores or dismisses the longer-term effects of permitting insider trading, including damage to investor confidence, restricted market participation, and adverse impacts on capital costs.

Most of the academic community dismisses fairness-based arguments supporting insider trading regulation.[129] Some scholars argue that public opposition to insider trading is irrational and emotive,[130] but interdisciplinary research suggests otherwise. Empirical studies that examine specific markets suggest that possible short-term efficiencies arising from insider trading are significantly outweighed by adverse long-term effects on investor confidence, volatility, liquidity, price accuracy and capital costs. These studies suggest that investment in a financial market that permits trading by company insiders with access to valuable confidential information is inherently high risk for most participants. Insiders are often well-positioned to control the release of information and manipulate their trades to enhance, or even to guarantee, potential trading profits. In such circumstances, an uninformed investor's skill or diligence cannot counteract an insider's actions. The rational response of such investors is to withdraw from the market.

Empirical research that compares a range of variables across a series of global financial markets find that countries with enforced insider trading laws gain economic benefits through enhanced liquidity, more informative stock prices, and lower costs of capital. This evidence suggests that the detrimental effects of insider trading on investors, markets and the broader public are significant, while the potential benefits,

---

International Law 629, 708, 719; Kimberly Krawiec, 'Fairness, Efficiency and Insider Trading: Deconstructing the Coin of the Realm in the Information Age' (2001) 95 *North Western University Law Review* 443, 495. Krawiec suggests that regulation requiring issuers to disclose all material information would optimise informational efficiency and informational equality' but such an approach is not practicable for commercial or competitive reasons. He concludes that informational efficiency may be enhanced by the transmission of information to the market without full disclosure.

129. See Donald Langevoort, 'Investment Analysts and the Law of Insider Trading' (1990) 76 *Virginia Law Review* 1023, 1048.

130. See, e.g., Frank Easterbrook and Daniel Fischel, 'Corporate Control Transactions' (1982) 91 *Yale Law Journal* 698, 703; Kenneth Scott, 'Insider Trading: Rule 10b-5, Disclosure and Corporate Privacy' (1980) 9 *Journal of Legal Studies* 801, 805.

if any, are minimal. These findings appear to have influenced policy developments around the world. All developed nations and many emerging economies have enacted insider trading regulation over the last twenty to thirty years.[131]

Importantly, the SEC in the US suggests that the most significant trading problems and losses arise from systemic professional insider trading on either a transactional or longer-term basis.[132] It notes that individuals engaged in misconduct are increasingly securities professionals, and gatekeepers, and that recidivist insider trading cases and serial illegal trading have become more common.[133] In such cases, trading can be carried out by a number of defendants, involving multiple trades over a number of months, using sophisticated approaches.[134] The next chapter builds on the insider trading debate by reviewing the theoretical frameworks relating to trading on selectively disclosed information by outsiders.

131. Utpal Bhattacharya and Hazem Daouk, 'The World Price of Insider Trading' (2002) 62 *Journal of Finance* 75, 104.
132. Linda Thomsen, Director Division of Enforcement, United States Securities and Exchange Commission, 'Insider Trading' (Testimony Before the US Senate Committee on the Judiciary, 26 September 2006).
133. Linda Thomsen, Director Division of Enforcement, United States Securities and Exchange Commission, 'Insider Trading' (Testimony Before the US Senate Committee on the Judiciary, 26 September 2006).
134. Linda Thomsen, Director Division of Enforcement, United States Securities and Exchange Commission, 'Insider Trading' (Testimony Before the US Senate Committee on the Judiciary, 26 September 2006). See also, Margaret Cole, Director of Enforcement, Financial Services Authority, 'Insider Dealing in the City' (Speech delivered at the London School of Economics, London, 17 March 2007).

CHAPTER 4
Selective Disclosure

> Selective disclosure is inimical to a belief that a level playing field exists, as well as to its existence in fact.[1]

§4.01 OVERVIEW[2]

Selective disclosure is the release of information by companies to some investors, such as sell-side brokers and analysts and buy-side asset managers and analysts, without simultaneous public disclosure. At the heart of the selective disclosure debates is the assumed role of financial intermediaries, with many theoretical models assuming a privileged position for these market participants. The theoretical debates in the US provide a rich spectrum of views on the role of financial intermediaries and selective disclosure issues. These debates were especially vigorous during the 1990s when Regulation Fair Disclosure (Reg FD) was proposed.[3] The Reg FD debates are discussed in this chapter because they provide valuable insight on effective company disclosure regulation and practice.

§4.02 PRICE EFFICIENCY

Many of the selective disclosure theories and models overlap with those applicable to the mandatory disclosure and insider trading debates. Some commentators argue that trading on selectively disclosed information provides price signals to the market,

---

1. *Australian Securities and Investments Commission v. Southcorp Limited (No. 2)* (2003) 130 FCR 406, [36].
2. Some of the material in this Chapter was included in a published article: Gill North, 'A Theoretical Basis for Selective Disclosure Regulation' (2009) 32 *University of New South Wales Law Journal* 143.
3. United States Securities and Exchange Commission, *Proposed Rule: Selective Disclosure and Insider Trading* (2000).

thereby increasing share price accuracy and market efficiency.[4] These price efficiency theories are the same as those expounded by Manne in defence of insider trading, except that the participants trading on the private information are outsiders. The counter arguments are also similar. When such trading is permitted, noise and uncertain signals may result in increased speculative trading activity, leading to a reduction in share price accuracy and increased price volatility. In any event, when information revealed through outsider trading becomes public soon after the trading occurs, any price efficiency gains are restricted to a few hours or days, with little, if any, positive impact on capital allocations and economic outcomes. The primary effect of trading in these circumstances is a shift in wealth from uninformed to informed participants. That is, participants with information advantages benefit systematically at the expense of participants without such advantages.

Brudney points out that the history of securities legislation in the US suggests that Congress has long sought to protect public investors from exploitation of institutional informational advantages that cannot be lawfully overcome or offset.[5] However, some scholars argue that uninformed or unsophisticated investors do not require protection from selective disclosure because they are protected by, or can rely on, market efficiency.[6] As discussed in Chapters 2 and 3, these arguments require further explanation to be credible, because uninformed investors are not protected when trading against counterparties with valuable private information unless the relevant financial market is strong form efficient under Fama's ECMH. Other commentators suggest that individual investors can gain access to private information by buying the information from an intermediary or investing with a fund manager.[7] This argument assumes that individuals should only invest with the assistance of professional advice

4. Stephen Choi, 'Selective Disclosure in the Public Capital Markets' (2002) 35 *UC Davis Law Review* 533, 535, 541; Ian Ayres and Stephen Choi, 'Internalizing Outsider Trading' (2002) 101 *Michigan Law Review* 313; John Barry, 'The Economics of Outside Information and Rule 10b-5' (1981) 129 *University of Pennsylvania Law Review* 1307, 1330; Merritt Fox, 'Required Disclosure and Corporate Governance' (1996) 62 *Law and Contemporary Problems* 113, 115–116. See also Paul Brountas Jr, 'Rule 10b-5 and Voluntary Corporate Disclosures to Securities Analysts' (1992) 92 *Columbia Law Review* 1517, 1533; Christopher Donald, 'A Critique of Arguments for Mandatory Continuous Disclosure' (1999) 62 *Saskatchewan Law Review* 85, 112–115.
5. Victor Brudney, 'Insiders, Outsiders, and Informational Advantages Under the Federal Securities Laws' (1979) 93 *Harvard Law Review* 322, 357, 360.
6. Christopher Saari, 'The Efficient Capital Markets Hypothesis, Economic Theory and the Regulation of the Securities Industry' (1977) 29 *Stanford Law Review* 1031, 1076; Frank Easterbrook and Daniel Fischel, 'Mandatory Disclosure and the Protection of Investors' (1984) 70 *Virginia Law Review* 669, 693–694; Roberta Romano, 'Empowering Investors: A Market Approach to Securities Regulation' (1998) 107 *Yale Law Journal* 2359, 2378; Christopher Donald, 'A Critique of Arguments for Mandatory Continuous Disclosure' (1999) 62 *Saskatchewan Law Review* 85, 112–115; Daniel Fischel, 'Symposium on Insider Trading: Insider Trading and Investment Analysts: An Economic Analysis of *Dirks v. Securities and Exchange Commission*' (1984) 13 *Hofstra Law Review* 127, 146.
7. See, e.g., Daniel Fischel, 'Symposium on Insider Trading: Insider Trading and Investment Analysts: An Economic Analysis of *Dirks v. Securities and Exchange Commission*' (1984) 13 *Hofstra Law Review* 127, 146; Christopher Saari, 'The Efficient Capital Markets Hypothesis, Economic Theory and the Regulation of the Securities Industry' (1977) 29 *Stanford Law Review* 1031.

or management, and is a paternalistic argument that closely aligns with an intermediated model of financial markets.

§4.03 INTERMEDIARY, ANALYST AND RESEARCH INCENTIVES

Most selective disclosure theories are centred on intermediary, analyst, and research incentives. These theories assume that intermediaries play a critical role within financial markets and therefore require privileged information. Traditional scholarly literature suggests that analysts require the right to obtain and use private company information in return for enhancing market efficiency by the provision of independent analysis and research.[8] It is assumed that analysts undertake all necessary discovery of security related information because they have the required education, experience, resources, and economies of scale to collect, analyse and produce information efficiently.[9] They are portrayed as 'crucial players in the mechanisms of market place efficiency that lead to optimal allocation of capital resources.'[10] The broader public are assumed to benefit from the work of analysts because the information discovered by analysts leads to more accurate or efficient security prices.[11]

Some commentators claim that selective disclosure is needed as an incentive for financial analysts to enter or remain in the market.[12] Barry indicates that stock trading based on selective disclosures prior to the publishing of research 'provides a just return for legitimate industry and encourages economically efficient behaviour.'[13] Fischel suggests the primary reason clients use an analyst is to obtain superior information and to thereby obtain higher returns.[14] He claims that '[n]obody will pay an analyst for

8. Jill Fisch and Hillary Sale, 'The Securities Analysts as Agent: Rethinking the Regulation of Analysts' (2003) 88 *Iowa Law Review* 1035.
9. See, e.g., Zohar Goshen and Gideon Parchomovsky, 'The Essential Role Of Securities Regulation' (2006) 55 *Duke Law Journal* 711, 722–725; Dennis Corgill, 'Insider Trading, Price Signals and Noisy Information' (1996) 71 *Indiana Law Journal* 355, 397.
10. Donald Langevoort, 'Investment Analysts and the Law of Insider Trading' (1990) 76 *Virginia Law Review* 1023, 1024.
11. Scott Russell, 'Regulation Fair Disclosure: The Death of the Efficient Capital Market Hypothesis and the Birth of Herd Behaviour' (2002) 82 *Boston University Law Review* 527, 550.
12. John Barry, 'The Economics of Outside Information and Rule 10b-5' (1981) 129 *University of Pennsylvania Law Review* 1307, 1353, 1387–1388; Dennis Corgill, 'Insider Trading, Price Signals and Noisy Information' (1996) 71 *Indiana Law Journal* 355, 397–398; Stephen Choi and Eric Talley, 'Playing Favorites With Shareholders' (2002) 75 *Southern California Law Review* 271, 310; Stephen Choi, 'Selective Disclosure in the Public Capital Markets' (2002) 35 *UC Davis Law Review* 533, 545; Paul Brountas Jr, 'Rule 10b-5 and Voluntary Corporate Disclosures to Securities Analysts' (1992) 92 *Columbia Law Review* 1517, 1540; Bruce Kobayashi and Larry Ribstein, 'Outsider Trading as an Incentive Device' (2006) 40 *UC Davis Law Review* 21, 31.
13. John Barry, 'The Economics of Outside Information and Rule 10b-5' (1981) 129 *University of Pennsylvania Law Review* 1307, 1388. See also Dennis Corgill, 'Insider Trading, Price Signals and Noisy Information' (1996) 71 *Indiana Law Journal* 355, 397–398, 416–1417.
14. Daniel Fischel, 'Symposium on Insider Trading: Insider Trading and Investment Analysts: An Economic Analysis of *Dirks v. Securities and Exchange Commission*' (1984) 13 *Hofstra Law Review* 127, 144.

information that he must publicly disclose before selling it to his clients.'[15] Choi and Barry argue that giving possessors of outside information a right to trade without disclosure preserves the necessary incentives for private analysis.[16] Brountas advocates the use of analysts as a filter to provide credibility to the information so it enters the public arena in a format that is more easily understandable by other investors.[17] Some scholars extend these arguments and suggest that trading profits from selective disclosure provide compensation for professional research efforts, but not at the expense of uninformed or unsophisticated investors.[18] However, secondary trading within financial markets is zero sum. It is, therefore, incorrect to claim that trading on selectively disclosed information will produce a gain for the trading party, while other uninformed investors will not make a corresponding loss.

Many of the traditional intermediary assumptions are no longer relevant or credible in modern financial markets. First, no compelling evidence has been found to support the theory that selective disclosure is required to incentivise analysts to produce research, which in turn is required to enhance market efficiency. As Lee notes, 'the argument for the necessity of speculative profits rests on untested, debatable assumptions about the absence of other incentives for investment in information.'[19] The relationships or links between access to company information, selective disclosure, research production and efficiency are weak and ill-defined, and the impacts of specific analyst research strategies on market and economic efficiency are still poorly understood.[20] In particular, the extent (and incremental value) of third party research on listed companies, such as sell-side analyst research and information, remains unclear.[21] To be of value, such research needs to provide genuinely independent information and analysis and critique of publicly available information, rather than a mere regurgitation of information received privately from company managers.

Second, the arguments that categorise participants entitled to receive private company information as 'analysts' or 'research providers' require further explanation.

---

15. Daniel Fischel, 'Symposium on Insider Trading: Insider Trading and Investment Analysts: An Economic Analysis of *Dirks v. Securities and Exchange Commission*' (1984) 13 *Hofstra Law Review* 127, 145.
16. Stephen Choi, 'Selective Disclosure in the Public Capital Markets' (2002) 35 *UC Davis Law Review* 533, 544–545; John Barry, 'The Economics of Outside Information and Rule 10b-5' (1981) 129 *University of Pennsylvania Law Review* 1307, 1353.
17. Paul Brountas Jr, 'Rule 10b-5 and Voluntary Corporate Disclosures to Securities Analysts' (1992) 92 *Columbia Law Review* 1517, 1540.
18. See, e.g., Daniel Fischel, 'Symposium on Insider Trading: Insider Trading and Investment Analysts: An Economic Analysis of *Dirks v. Securities and Exchange Commission*' (1984) 13 *Hofstra Law Review* 127, 146; Homer Kripke, *The SEC And Corporate Disclosure: Regulation In Search Of A Purpose* (Harcourt Brace Jovanovich Publishers, New York, 1979) 14–16, 284–286.
19. Ian Lee, 'Fairness and Insider Trading' (2002) 1 *Columbia Business Law Review* 119, 175.
20. Jeffrey Gordon and Lewis Kornhauser, 'Efficient Markets, Costly Information and Securities Research' (1985) 60 *New York University Law Review* 761, 792. See also Frank Easterbrook, 'Insider Trading, Secret Agents, Evidentiary Privileges, and the Production of Information' (1981) *Supreme Court Review* 309, 364; James Boyle, 'A Theory of Law and Information: Copyright, Spleens, Blackmail, and Insider Trading' (1992) 80 *California Law Review* 1413, 1452.
21. See, e.g., Ian Ayres and Stephen Choi, 'Internalizing Outsider Trading' (2002) 101 *Michigan Law Review* 313.

Company managers do not formally determine which participants are provided with access to private company information based on analytical skills or research production. Investors operate in a competitive market and the incentives to discover valuable information are powerful across all participant groups and not merely those labelled 'analysts'. The groups of investors that senior company executives typically meet with include sell-side brokers and analysts, buy-side analysts and asset managers, and wealthy families and individuals. Although sell-side brokers and analysts produce research reports for other participants, buy-side analysts and asset managers and individuals do not. Buy-side analysts and asset managers who meet with senior executives generally want to ensure their actual or potential investment in a company is sound and likely to produce optimal returns. Put simply, their primary purpose for attending private briefings is to obtain information to enhance portfolio returns. As most investors operate using this *modus operandi*, the theoretical (and practical) rationales for providing only some of these participants with private access remain uncertain.

Third, no compelling evidence has been found suggesting the security prices of companies not covered by analysts are inefficient primarily because of a lack of sell-side analyst coverage.[22] Many listed companies assume analyst coverage is necessary to build a market profile, encourage investor interest, and successfully raise new capital. While potential commissions or investment banking business options are sometimes insufficient for institutions to justify initiating or maintaining sell-side analyst coverage, particularly for smaller companies, these companies now have many communication options to convey their 'story' directly to potential institutional and retail investors. There are specialist funds that invest in companies with smaller market capitalisations in all major markets, and there are retail investors who are well-informed about these particular companies and securities. Searches for mis-valued stocks and informational advantages in contemporary markets are fiercely competitive, so investment opportunities that represent reasonable value will generally attract investor interest and capital, regardless of analyst coverage and size of company.

Finally, some companies argue that they need to disseminate information privately as incentive for analysts to produce research.[23] Kripke suggests that forcing companies to publicly disclose information may increase information production costs, making it more difficult to reduce information disparities.[24] Similar theories and arguments were discussed in Chapter 2. In reality, the cost of publicly disclosing comprehensive information using digital technologies is generally much less than the cost of privately disclosing similar information at a series of meetings with individual participants.

22. While there are empirical studies that measure the incremental impact of analyst initiation, the causal effects are not clear.
23. Donald Langevoort, 'Investment Analysts and the Law of Insider Trading' (1990) 76 *Virginia Law Review* 1023, 1029–1031; Paul Brountas Jr, 'Rule 10b-5 and Voluntary Corporate Disclosures to Securities Analysts' (1992) 92 *Columbia Law Review* 1517, 1540.
24. Daniel Fischel, 'Symposium on Insider Trading: Insider Trading and Investment Analysts: An Economic Analysis of *Dirks v. Securities and Exchange Commission*' (1984) 13 *Hofstra Law Review* 127, 145.

Some commentators argue that selective disclosure is necessary to compensate analysts for their continuous monitoring of a company. As discussed in Chapter 2, some commentators suggest analysts act as unbiased market gatekeepers, resulting in lower agency costs and therefore enhanced market efficiency.[25] Fischel argues that the fact that companies 'voluntarily transmit information to analysts suggests the use of analysts is an efficient method of communicating information.'[26] Other scholars question these agency and analyst efficiency claims. In voluntary disclosure environments, managers may limit disclosure to a select group of shareholders in order to optimise the short-term profits of the recipients and managers, rather than the long-term company performance.[27]

There are many conflicts of interest that exist when information is selectively disclosed to analysts or investors. This is because company managers and institutional participants have powerful incentives to engage in selective disclosure. When managers receive a large proportion of their remuneration as bonuses or stock options, selective disclosure may be used to artificially maintain or increase share prices.[28] Companies can also restrict the provision of information to analysts most likely to publish positive research recommendations,[29] or to those likely to provide the company with new capital,[30] and may blacklist or 'freeze out' analysts who issue negative recommendations or criticise the company.[31] If the relationships between managers and analysts and other favoured investors become too close, management may feel

25. Stephen Thurber, 'The Insider Trading Compensation Contract as an Inducement to Monitoring by the Institutional Investor' (1994) 1 *George Mason University Law Review* 119, 134; Cf John Coffee Jnr, 'What Caused Enron? A Capsule Of Social and Economic History of the 1990s' (2003) 89 *Cornell Law Review* 269 286–289.
26. Daniel Fischel, 'Symposium on Insider Trading: Insider Trading and Investment Analysts: An Economic Analysis of *Dirks v. Securities and Exchange Commission*' (1984) 13 *Hofstra Law Review* 127, 144.
27. See, e.g., Jill Fisch and Hillary Sale, 'The Securities Analysts as Agent: Rethinking the Regulation of Analysts' (2003) *88 Iowa Law Review* 1035, 1053–1056; Ronald Gilson and Reinier Kraakman, 'The Mechanisms of Market Efficiency Twenty Years Later: The Hindsight Bias' (2003) 28 *Journal of Corporation Law* 715, 736–737.
28. Jill Fisch and Hillary Sale, 'The Securities Analysts as Agent: Rethinking the Regulation of Analysts' (2003) 88 *Iowa Law Review* 1035, 1090; Victor Brudney, 'Insiders, Outsiders, and Informational Advantages Under the Federal Securities Laws' (1979) 93 *Harvard Law Review* 322, 335.
29. See, e.g., Bin Ke and Yong Yu, 'The Effect Of Issuing Biased Earnings Forecasts On Analysts' Access To Management And Survival' (2006) 44 *Journal of Accounting Research* 965; Donald Langevoort, 'Investment Analysts and the Law of Insider Trading' (1990) 76 *Virginia Law Review* 1023, 1041; Jill Fisch and Hillary Sale, 'The Securities Analysts as Agent: Rethinking the Regulation of Analysts' (2003) 88 *Iowa Law Review* 1035, 1054.
30. Jill Fisch and Hillary Sale, 'The Securities Analysts as Agent: Rethinking the Regulation of Analysts' (2003) 88 *Iowa Law Review* 1035, 1056.
31. Donald Langevoort, 'Investment Analysts and the Law of Insider Trading' (1990) 76 *Virginia Law Review* 1023, 1042; Jill Fisch and Hillary Sale, 'The Securities Analysts as Agent: Rethinking the Regulation of Analysts' (2003) 88 *Iowa Law Review* 1035, 1054. John Olsen the Merrill Lynch energy market securities analyst was fired when he downgraded Enron's stock. Similarly, analysts who criticized HIH Insurance were blacklisted.

pressured to manipulate or massage the company results, or even to adjust the corporate strategy, in order to satisfy analyst expectations.[32]

The recipients of selective disclosures also face a variety of potential conflicts. First, those who are privy to material private information can choose to profitably trade on disclosed information.[33] For example, participants that are selectively forewarned of bad news from a company can sell securities in advance of other investors.[34] Asset managers often prefer to exit when companies are in trouble rather than demanding governance changes from management.[35] Second, when sell-side analyst access to private information is dependent on a favoured relationship with company managers, this can encourage biased research.[36] Third, when sell-side analysts publish research including information obtained from a company privately, the content may be disseminated to their clients on a preferential basis.[37] Fourth, when commissions paid to buy-side analysts or fund managers are tied to brokerage levels or investment banking revenue within the same institution, this can pressure analysts to produce particular recommendations in order to increase their salaries or bonuses.[38] Gilson and Kraakman suggest that when they first published on the mechanisms of market efficiency, they should have been more sceptical of market institutions, incentives, and performance.[39] They note that they failed to appreciate the scale of the incentive problems in financial institutions that produce information about listed corporations.[40] They admit they were

32. Jill Fisch and Hillary Sale, 'The Securities Analysts as Agent: Rethinking the Regulation of Analysts' (2003) 88 *Iowa Law Review* 1035, 1056.
33. Donald Langevoort, 'Investment Analysts and the Law of Insider Trading' (1990) 76 *Virginia Law Review* 1023, 1042; Jill Fisch and Hillary Sale, 'The Securities Analysts as Agent: Rethinking the Regulation of Analysts' (2003) 88 *Iowa Law Review* 1035, 1044.
34. Jill Fisch and Hillary Sale, 'The Securities Analysts as Agent: Rethinking the Regulation of Analysts' (2003) 88 *Iowa Law Review* 1035, 1090; Stephen Choi, 'Selective Disclosure in the Public Capital Markets' (2002) 35 *UC Davis Law Review* 533, 549.
35. John Coffee, 'Liquidity versus Control: The Institutional Investor as Corporate Monitor' (1991) 91 *Columbia Law Review* 1277, 1288; Jill Fisch and Hillary Sale, 'The Securities Analysts as Agent: Rethinking the Regulation of Analysts' (2003) 88 *Iowa Law Review* 1035, 1088; Stephen Choi, 'Selective Disclosure in the Public Capital Markets' (2002) 35 *UC Davis Law Review* 533, 549, 555; Ian Ayres and Stephen Choi, 'Internalizing Outsider Trading' (2002) 101 *Michigan Law Review* 313.
36. Merritt Fox, 'Regulation FD and Foreign Issuers: Globalisation's Strains and Opportunities' (2001) 41 *Virginia Journal of International Law* 653, 657, 677; Stephen Choi, 'Selective Disclosure in the Public Capital Markets' (2002) 35 *UC Davis Law Review* 533, 548.
37. Paul Brountas Jr, 'Rule 10b-5 and Voluntary Corporate Disclosures to Securities Analysts' (1992) 92 *Columbia Law Review* 1517, 1546.
38. See, e.g., Jill Fisch and Hillary Sale, 'The Securities Analysts as Agent: Rethinking the Regulation of Analysts' (2003) 88 *Iowa Law Review* 1035, 1045–1046; Hsiou-Wei Lin and Maureen McNichols, 'Underwriting Relationships, Analysts Earning Forecasts And Investment Recommendations' (1998) 25 *Journal of Accounting & Economics* 101, 124–125; Harrison Hong and Jeremy Kubik 'Analysing The Analysts: Career Concerns and Biased Earnings Forecasts' (2003) 58 *Journal of Finance* 313.
39. Ronald Gilson and Reinier Kraakman, 'The Mechanisms of Market Efficiency Twenty Years Later: The Hindsight Bias' (2003) 28 *Journal of Corporation Law* 715, 736–737.
40. Ronald Gilson and Reinier Kraakman, 'The Mechanisms of Market Efficiency Twenty Years Later: The Hindsight Bias' (2003) 28 *Journal of Corporation Law* 715, 736.

naïve about the role of security analysts, particularly those on the sell-side of the market.[41]

All of the outlined conflicts of interest and biases have the potential to increase agency costs and to thereby interfere with an efficient allocation of capital.[42]

§4.04 JUDICIAL COMMENTARY

The courts in the US have generally accepted a series of traditional assumptions concerning the role of analysts. For instance, in *Securities and Exchange Commission v. Bausch & Lomb Inc,* Ward J of the District Court held that Bausch & Lomb had not disclosed material non-public information to securities analysts during interviews. Although the Chairman released an earnings estimate to securities analysts and did disclose material, non-public corporate information, the act was held to be an 'uncharacteristic and inadvertent' slip and not accompanied by the requisite intent. Ward J indicated [at 123] that:

> [a]nalysts provide a needed service in culling and sifting available data, viewing it in light of their own knowledge of a particular industry and ultimately furnishing a distilled product in the form of reports. These analyses can then be used by both the ordinary investor and by the professional investment advisor as a basis for the decision to buy or sell a given stock. The data available to the analyst - his raw material - comes in part from published sources but must also come from communication with management.[43]

This commentary indicates that Ward J assumed that analysts are entitled to obtain private information from managers directly, and that ordinary investors require information that has been filtered by analysts. These assumptions continue to be important elements of selective disclosure debates and policy developments around the world.

The liability of analysts to insider trading was left ambiguous in *Dirks v. SEC.* 463 US 646 (1983). Justice Powell J speaking for the majority indicated [at 658] that:

> [i]mposing a duty to disclose or abstain solely because a person knowingly receives material non-public information from an insider and trades on it could have an inhibiting influence on the role of market analysts, which the SEC itself recognizes is necessary to the preservation of a healthy market. It is commonplace for analysts to 'ferret out and analyze information'.

41. Ronald Gilson and Reinier Kraakman, 'The Mechanisms of Market Efficiency Twenty Years Later: The Hindsight Bias' (2003) 28 *Journal of Corporation Law* 715, 737.
42. Donald Langevoort, 'Investment Analysts and the Law of Insider Trading' (1990) 76 *Virginia Law Review* 1023, 1025; Jill Fisch and Hillary Sale, 'The Securities Analysts as Agent: Rethinking the Regulation of Analysts' (2003) *88 Iowa Law Review* 1035, 1079, 1097-1098. A conflict of interest exists when a party to a transaction can gain by taking actions that are detrimental to its counterparty.
43. *SEC v. Bausch & Lomb, Inc* 420 F. Supp. 1226 (1976) 1230.

Powell J further noted [at 659] that the nature of non-public information received by analysts from corporate officers and insiders at briefings is such that this information cannot be made simultaneously available to all of the corporation's stock holders or the public generally … Unless the parties have some guidance as to where the line is between permissible and impermissible disclosures and uses; neither corporate insiders nor analysts can be sure when the line is crossed.[44]

Thus Powell J assumed that the mosaic of information provided to financial intermediaries and analysts is, and should be, different from publicly released information because companies cannot provide the same information to all participants simultaneously.

Assumed differences between market participant groups are reflected in case law in other jurisdictions. For instance, in Australia, the case *Forrest v. Australian Securities and Investments Commission; Fortescue Metals Group Ltd v. Australian Securities and Investments Commission* [2012] HCA 39 (Fortescue) involved alleged misleading or deceptive conduct. Misleading and deceptive conduct requires identifying the relevant audience that was, or potentially could have been, misled or deceived. Heydon J of the High Court of Australia characterised the audience of the public disclosures of Fortescue Metals Group Limited, a large iron ore company, as comprised of 'superannuation funds, other large institutions, other wealthy investors, stock brokers and other financial advisers, specialised financial journalists, as well as smaller investors reliant on advice.'[45] In doing so, His Honour effectively placed investors into two classes; the first comprised of astute, sophisticated and well-informed large investors, and the other comprised of inexperienced and unsophisticated smaller investors[46] reliant on intermediary advice. These assumed links between institutions, wealth, sophistication, commercial knowledge, and large shareholdings, and between smaller investors and a requirement for intermediary advice, were not explained by Heydon J or supported by evidence.

The accuracy of assumptions about the role of analysts and the financial skill and knowledge of various investor groups is highly debatable in the context of modern financial markets. Rapid advances in digital technologies have fundamentally altered the substance of debates concerning access to listed company information and the need for intermediaries to control and filter company information and to broker the trading of company securities. In digital environments, listed companies can easily and cheaply disseminate information simultaneously to interested participants through security exchanges or information repositories. Online trading services that allow clients to invest and trade for fees without research cost loadings are also well-established. The SEC was an early responder in this new environment.

44. *Dirks v. Securities and Exchange* 463 US 646, 659 (1983).
45. *Forrest v. Australian Securities and Investments Commission; Fortescue Metals Group Ltd v. Australian Securities and Investments Commission* [2012] HCA 39, [105].
46. The phrase 'smaller investor' is not explained. It may mean investors that have made a small investment in a particular security or investors that have small investment portfolios.

§4.05 SECURITIES AND EXCHANGE COMMISSION

Public policy that actively encourages regular, informal and private contact between managers and selected participants raises major issues because it potentially results in a massive shift of wealth to those with privileged access to private company information.[47] As Maug notes, when trading based on selective disclosure is not regulated, 'managers and large shareholders ... form a "cozy cartel" at the expense of small shareholders.'[48] Ultimately this was the key issue leading up to the introduction of Reg FD in the US.

In 1981 the SEC stated *In the Matter of Raymond L Dirks*[49] that:

> [t]he value to the entire market of [analysts'] efforts cannot be gainsaid; market efficiency in pricing is significantly enhanced by [their] initiatives to ferret out and analyze information, and thus the analysts' work redounds to the benefit of all investors.[50]

However the SEC subsequently modified its position. In 2000, it confirmed that analysts serve a screening function for technical financial information and that analysts' work may benefit the market.[51] Nevertheless, it indicated that selective disclosure:

- impacts on the principles of integrity and transparency, and undermines the fundamental principle of fairness;[52]
- can lead to potential conflicts of interest which further impact the confidence of investors; and
- can undermine the independence of analyst reporting leading to incentives to delay public disclosure and to manipulate earnings and expectations.[53]

The SEC argued that advances in technology had reduced the importance of analysts as information intermediaries and made it easier and less costly for issuers to disseminate information directly to the public.[54]

---

47. Donald Langevoort, 'Investment Analysts and the Law of Insider Trading' (1990) 76 *Virginia Law Review* 1023, 1045, 1048–1049.
48. Ernst Maug, 'Insider Trading Legislation and Corporate Governance' (2002) 46 *European Economic Review* 1569, 1588.
49. United States Securities and Exchange Commission Lexis 2213 (1981).
50. United States Securities and Exchange Commission Lexis 2213 (1981). This paragraph is cited by Justice Powell in *Dirks v. Securities and Exchange Commission*, 463 US 646, 659 (1983).
51. United States Securities and Exchange Commission, *Proposed Rule: Selective Disclosure and Insider Trading* (2000).
52. Arthur Levitt, 'Audit Committee Oversight, Selective Disclosure and Insider Trading' (Statement delivered at the Open Commission Meeting, United States Securities and Exchange Commission, 15 December 1999) < http://www.sec.gov/news/extra/alsdisc.htm > at 26 April 2009; United States Securities and Exchange Commission (SEC), 'Final Rule', *Selective Disclosure and Insider Trading* (2000).
53. United States Securities and Exchange Commission, 'Final Rule', *Selective Disclosure and Insider Trading* (2000).
54. United States Securities and Exchange Commission, 'Final Rule', *Selective Disclosure and Insider Trading* (2000).

In 2000, the SEC proposed Reg FD to remove the information advantages that analysts enjoyed relative to other investors, ensure equal access to information for all investors, and deter selective disclosure of company information.[55] The SEC posited that Reg FD would result in:

- more open disclosure practices and increased investor confidence in the integrity of the market, with a consequential lowering of capital costs;
- an increase in the information provided by companies directly to the marketplace and improved analyst performance;
- genuine competition among analysts, with performance measured on ability and effort rather than favoured access to company management; and
- independent analyst reporting without adverse consequences on access to company information.[56]

The SEC suggested that while the New York Stock Exchange and National Association of Securities Dealers required listed companies to promptly disclose material information, companies still retained significant control over the release, timing, audience, and forum of many important disclosures.[57]

The SEC received six thousand public submissions or responses to the Reg FD proposals. Retail investors responded enthusiastically, with many expressing a strong desire to fairly compete directly with institutional investors and an unwillingness to invest through intermediaries.[58] For instance, a submission from Beyers stated that:

> I've never picked a stock on the basis of an analyst recommendation or report ... I take serious offence with the notion that I can't make an intelligent investment choice without first contacting a professional ... Let analysts make their money as 'analysts' - interpreters of data - rather than as gatekeepers of [data] as they mostly do today.[59]

Similarly, Connolly indicated that:

> [a]nalysts usually issue upgrades (downgrades) after good news (bad news) has been announced and is reflected in the companies' stock prices. I have been the

55. United States Securities and Exchange Commission, 'Final Rule', *Selective Disclosure and Insider Trading* (2000).
56. Arthur Levitt, 'Audit Committee Oversight, Selective Disclosure and Insider Trading' (Statement delivered at the Open Commission Meeting, United States Securities and Exchange Commission, 15 December 1999) <http://www.sec.gov/news/extra/alsdisc.htm> at 26 April 2009.
57. United States Securities and Exchange Commission, 'Final Rule', *Selective Disclosure and Insider Trading* (2000).
58. United States Securities and Exchange Commission, *Comments of 50 Individuals Received* (2000). <http://www.sec.gov/rules/proposed/s73199/0420b01w.html> at 26 April 2009.
59. United States Securities and Exchange Commission, *Comments of 50 Individuals Received* (2000). <http://www.sec.gov/rules/proposed/s73199/0420b01w.html> submission from Beyers.

> chief accountant at a mid-sized publicly held company where I have seen certain analysts being 'schmoozed' by top management.[60]

Dieckelman suggested that the majority of analysts probably have the same level of education as most retail investors.[61] Corbin argued that '[t]oday's investing marketplace is quite different from what we previously had ... The practice of companies disclosing information to select analysts in closed meetings is an anathema to the open flow of information.'[62]

As might be expected, the financial services industry response to the proposed regulation was generally negative. Brokers submitted that a decrease in information flow would result in more dramatic stock price movements upon the public release of earnings or earnings related news, and a shorter-term focus by investors.[63] Some parties suggested that efficient markets would be replaced by herd behaviour in which irrational individual investors would either speculate madly or free ride on the back of informed investors.[64] Lawyers pointed out companies would have to make difficult decisions on what information is material on a real-time basis.[65] The Securities Industry Association suggested that 'analysts should be able to ferret out information on behalf of investors'[66] and that individual analysts would no longer be able to distinguish themselves.[67]

A number of scholarly commentators suggested the only evidence provided by the SEC was anecdotal.[68] They argued the regulation would lead to a reduction in

60. United States Securities and Exchange Commission, *Comments of 50 Individuals Received* (2000). <http://www.sec.gov/rules/proposed/s73199/0420b01w.html> submission from Connolly.
61. United States Securities and Exchange Commission, *Comments of 50 Individuals Received* (2000). <http://www.sec.gov/rules/proposed/s73199/0420b01w.html> submission from Dieckelman.
62. United States Securities and Exchange Commission, *Comments of 50 Individuals Received* (2000). <http://www.sec.gov/rules/proposed/s73199/0420b01w.html> submission from Corbin.
63. Scott Russell, 'Regulation Fair Disclosure: The Death of the Efficient Capital Market Hypothesis and the Birth of Herd Behaviour' (2002) 82 *Boston University Law Review* 527, 542; Linda Yi, 'Road Shows On The Internet: Taking Individual Investors For A Ride On The Information Highway' (2002) 52 *Duke Law Journal* 243, 257–258.
64. Scott Russell, 'Regulation Fair Disclosure: The Death of the Efficient Capital Market Hypothesis and the Birth of Herd Behaviour' (2002) 82 *Boston University Law Review* 527, 551.
65. Scott Russell, 'Regulation Fair Disclosure: The Death of the Efficient Capital Market Hypothesis and the Birth of Herd Behaviour' (2002) 82 *Boston University Law Review* 527, 539.
66. See, e.g., T Andrew Eckstein, 'The SEC's New Regulation FD: A Return to the Parity Theory' (2001) 69 *University of Cincinnati Law Review* 1289, 1300–1301.
67. T Andrew Eckstein, 'The SEC's New Regulation FD: A Return to the Parity Theory' (2001) 69 *University of Cincinnati Law Review* 1289, 1301.
68. Scott Russell, 'Regulation Fair Disclosure: The Death of the Efficient Capital Market Hypothesis and the Birth of Herd Behaviour' (2002) 82 *Boston University Law Review* 527, 536; Brian Barry, 'The Securities and Exchange Commission's Regulation Fair Disclosure: Parity of Information or Parody of Information?' (2002) 56 *University of Miami Law Review* 645, 650, 661. The United States Securities and Exchange Commission cited a 1998 study by the National Investor

information flow from companies and increased price volatility.[69] Others argued that companies would hold public meetings or conference calls with watered down or scripted disclosures.[70] Some suggested that private meetings are required for nuanced communication and for the airing of difficult or confidential topics and questions.[71] They contended that without such meetings, companies would not be able to monitor and control market expectations and as a result, analyst forecasts would be less accurate and more dispersed.[72] As discussed later in this chapter, these arguments have been largely negated by academic empirical research that examines the impacts of Reg FD.

Following this extensive public consultation process, the SEC board voted three to one in favour of Reg FD, and the new law took effect on 23 October 2000. Reg FD prohibits companies, or those acting on a company's behalf, from selectively disclosing material non-public information to securities industry professionals, institutional investors, and specified other persons. Reg FD applies to closed-door meetings, conference calls with analysts,[73] and indeed any situation where material information is communicated, verbally or in writing.[74] The final rule was substantially modified in response to the many submissions received.[75] It only applies to communications to securities market professionals and any holder of the issuer's securities under circumstances in which it is reasonably foreseeable that the security holder will trade on the basis of the information. The issuer personnel subject to Reg FD are senior officials and persons who regularly communicate with securities market professionals or security holders.[76]

Relations Institute, which indicated that 26% of responding companies confirmed that they engage in some type of selective disclosure practices.

69. Scott Russell, 'Regulation Fair Disclosure: The Death of the Efficient Capital Market Hypothesis and the Birth of Herd Behaviour' (2002) 82 *Boston University Law Review* 527, 536; Linda Yi, 'Road Shows On The Internet: Taking Individual Investors For A Ride On The Information Highway' (2002) 52 *Duke Law Journal* 243, 263–268; Brian Barry, 'The Securities and Exchange Commission's Regulation Fair Disclosure: Parity of Information or Parody of Information?' (2002) 56 *University of Miami Law Review* 645, 662.
70. Linda Yi, 'Road Shows On The Internet: Taking Individual Investors For A Ride On The Information Highway' (2002) 52 *Duke Law Journal* 243, 268–270.
71. Scott Russell, 'Regulation Fair Disclosure: The Death of the Efficient Capital Market Hypothesis and the Birth of Herd Behaviour' (2002) 82 *Boston University Law Review* 527, 542.
72. Brian Barry, 'The Securities and Exchange Commission's Regulation Fair Disclosure: Parity of Information or Parody of Information?' (2002) 56 *University of Miami Law Review* 645, 662.
73. The courts in the United States have ruled that conference calls with analysts that have been recorded and transcribed are admissible as evidence: *Wenger v. Lumisys, Inc,* 2 F Supp.2d 1231 (ND Cal, 1998).
74. *Liability under Regulation Fair Disclosure (Reg FD) only arises when an issuer's personnel either knows, or is reckless in not knowing that the information he or she is communicating is both material and non-public.*
75. Regulation FD (Reg FD) does not establish a duty under Rule 10b-5's insider trading laws. A violation of Reg FD does not result in an issuer's loss of eligibility to use short-form registration for a securities offering. Communications made in connection with most securities offerings registered under the Securities Exchange Act are exempt from the scope of Reg FD. Foreign governments and foreign private issuers are also outside of the scope of Reg FD.
76. Failures by issuers to comply with Regulation Fair Disclosure may be subject to an SEC enforcement action under the regulation and s. 13(a) or 15(d) of the *Securities Exchange Act*. The SEC may bring an administrative action seeking a cause-and-desist action, or a civil action

Commissioner Unger of the SEC voted against Reg FD because she thought it interfered with 'the longstanding relationship between issuers and their analysts – a liaison that has never been particularly easy.'[77] She highlighted the benefits of analysts discovering and analysing information and then providing reports to investors to explain the information after it has been digested and put into context.[78] She suggested that 'investors will now be forced to perform the role previously played by analysts.'[79] Unger agreed that trading by analysts or institutional investors on selectively disclosed information is offensive or even illegal, but she thought that Reg FD went too far in requiring all material information disclosed to analysts to be made public.[80] She was concerned that companies would reduce both their level and quality of disclosure and that investors would not be able to process the information disclosed during webcasts or conference calls.[81]

§4.06 KAY REVIEW OF UK EQUITY MARKETS

Similar arguments to those submitted during the SEC Reg FD debate have been made in other countries. For example, the Kay Review was asked by the UK Government to 'examine the mechanisms of corporate control and accountability by UK equity markets and their impact on the long-term competitive performance of UK businesses, and to make recommendations.'[82] More specifically, it was asked to examine:

- the time horizons of company boards and managers, institutional shareholders, and fund managers and their beneficiaries;
- whether Government policies and equity market functions encourage company boards and institutional shareholders to adopt long-term time horizons;
- the quality of engagement between listed companies and shareholders;
- whether the activities of, and relationships between, companies, financial intermediaries and their clients are sufficiently transparent;
- how to ensure shareholders consider the competitive position of individual companies in which they invest; and

seeking an injunction and/or civil penalties. It may also bring an enforcement action against an individual or the issuer responsible for the violation, either as a 'cause of' the violation on a cease and desist proceeding or as an aider and abetter of the violation in an injunction action.

77. Laura Unger, Commissioner SEC, 'Fallout from Regulation FD: Has the SEC Finally Cut the Tightrope?' (Speech delivered at the Glassier LegalWorks Conference, 27 October 2000), citing *Dirks v. SEC* 463 US 646 (1983). Unger referred to the court's description of the relationship between companies and analysts as a 'fencing match conducted on a tightrope' in *SEC v. Bausch & Lomb Inc*, 565 F 2d 8 (2nd Cir, 1977).
78. Laura Unger, Commissioner SEC, 'Fallout from Regulation FD: Has the SEC Finally Cut the Tightrope?' (Speech delivered at the Glassier LegalWorks Conference, 27 October 2000).
79. Laura Unger, Commissioner SEC, 'Fallout from Regulation FD: Has the SEC Finally Cut the Tightrope?' (Speech delivered at the Glassier LegalWorks Conference, 27 October 2000).
80. Laura Unger, Commissioner SEC, 'Fallout from Regulation FD: Has the SEC Finally Cut the Tightrope?' (Speech delivered at the Glassier LegalWorks Conference, 27 October 2000).
81. Laura Unger, Commissioner SEC, 'Fallout from Regulation FD: Has the SEC Finally Cut the Tightrope?' (Speech delivered at the Glassier LegalWorks Conference, 27 October 2000).
82. United Kingdom Department for Business Innovation & Skills, *The Kay Review: Terms of Reference* (June 2011) URN 11/1015.

- the expected long-term impact of international investment and regulatory trends on UK equity markets and business.[83]

The Kay Review issued two reports, an interim and a final report. The Kay Review is discussed in detail in this chapter and later chapters, because the views expressed within its commentary on the role of financial intermediaries and direct investors, selective disclosure, and on company disclosure principles more generally, are expressed regularly by scholars, justices and others. The Kay Review reports assume a privileged role for financial intermediaries and in doing so, discount the role, rights and needs of direct investors. The Kay Review commentary also challenges the primary rationales for disclosure regulation and many of the fundamental tenants of best practice corporate disclosure frameworks, including the regularity, completeness, clarity, comparability and timeliness of information provided in listed company periodic reports and continuous disclosures. As such, detailed response is warranted.

The Kay Review Interim Report (Kay Interim Report) confirmed that good market practice in the UK encompasses the principle that all shareholders should have the same rights.[84] It indicated that individual investors generally have long average security holding periods. It further noted that these investors do not contribute significantly to high-levels of short-term trading and that 'many ... have a real interest in the long term stability and growth of the companies they invest in.'[85] Similarly the Kay Review Final Report (Kay Final Report) begins with a clearly stated aspiration for regulation directed to the interests of companies and savers (rather than the concerns of market intermediaries). It states that:

> the Review's principal concern has been to ask how well equity markets are achieving their core purpose[s]: to enhance the performance of UK companies and to enable savers to benefit from the activity of these businesses through returns to direct and indirect ownership of shares in UK companies.[86]

However, the only recommendation it contains to encourage and enable well-informed investment decisions by individual shareholders is a proposal to explore the most cost-effective means for retail investors to hold shares directly on an electronic register.[87] Although an investors' forum is proposed, the supporting discussion refers only to institutional and corporate representatives.[88]

---

83. United Kingdom Department for Business Innovation & Skills, *The Kay Review: Terms of Reference* (June 2011) URN 11/1015.
84. *The Kay Review of UK Equity Markets and Long-Term Decision Making: Interim Report* (February 2012) 15.
85. *The Kay Review of UK Equity Markets and Long-Term Decision Making: Interim Report* (February 2012) 15, 18.
86. *The Kay Review of UK Equity Markets and Long-Term Decision Making: Final Report* (July 2012) 9.
87. *The Kay Review of UK Equity Markets and Long-Term Decision Making: Final Report* (July 2012) 13.
88. *The Kay Review of UK Equity Markets and Long-Term Decision Making: Final Report* (July 2012) 18, 51. The Interim Report highlights at [18] that individuals who hold shares directly often hold them through Individual Savings Accounts (ISAs) and the tax rules require shares held in ISAs to be held though nominee accounts. The practice of holding through nominee accounts means

The rights of individual or direct investors appear to have been discounted in the Kay Review reports based on incomplete data suggesting the proportion of UK equities held by individuals as beneficial owners has declined over the last decade.[89] Similar arguments within the scholarly literature also belittle retail investors based on trading and investment trends and these arguments inevitably raise the proverbial 'chicken and egg' conundrum. One can argue that there has been a fundamental shift in financial markets towards intermediated services and that retail investors have specifically elected to have their savings portfolios professionally managed. Alternatively, one can argue that retail investors have considered the structure and operation of financial markets, and have gradually withdrawn from direct investment in response to ongoing power shifts and imbalances in access to listed company information.

The Kay Final Report indicates that '[g]overnment policies should not have the object of, or as far as possible, the effect of imposing particular choices on either companies or savers.'[90] It acknowledges that the rapid growth in intermediation has led to increased costs, greater potential for misalignments and 'a tendency to view market effectiveness through the eyes of intermediaries rather than companies or end investors.'[91] But at the same time, it suggests that most savers want to, and should, use intermediaries for investment.[92] Many readers may agree that most savers should use intermediaries. However, financial market structures and policies that facilitate and encourage individuals to assume at least partial control over their personal savings and retirement plans are become increasingly important within global communities.

This author suggests that it is difficult to overstate the importance of a continued presence of direct investors in financial markets. These participants assist to keep financial markets competitive, responsive and dispersed. They also form a critical

---

the individuals are not on the share register, they do not receive information directly from the company and they do not have voting rights.

89. *The Kay Review of UK Equity Markets and Long-Term Decision Making: Final Report* (July 2012) 31, 38. A detailed understanding of the investment trends in the UK is essential foundational material to consider possible reforms. Table 1 [at 31] reflects a declining share of UK equities held by individuals as beneficial owners over the last decade. In 2010 the level of individual ownership was 11.5% compared to ownership by pension funds and insurance companies of 5.1% and 8.6% respectively. Figure 7 [at 32] indicates that individuals represent 11% of the beneficial ownership of FTSE 100 companies. The decreases in the proportion of shares held by individuals, pension funds and insurance companies appear to arise from higher foreign ownership. The data in Tables 1 and 7 is vague, the definitions used in the table categories are not provided, and there are large unexplained categories in the charts. More substantive information is needed concerning the absolute equity investment trends for each investor group; the investment timeframes of each class of investor; the portion of investment in each category that is retirement related; the share of the total UK equity investment portfolio representing short-term trading; and the source, timeframe and purpose of foreign investment in UK equities.

90. *The Kay Review of UK Equity Markets and Long-Term Decision Making: Final Report* (July 2012) 84. The Kay Review Interim Report (Kay Interim Report) confirmed that good market practice in the UK encompasses the principle that all shareholders should have the same rights [at 15].

91. *The Kay Review of UK Equity Markets and Long-Term Decision Making: Final Report* (July 2012) 10.

92. *The Kay Review of UK Equity Markets and Long-Term Decision Making: Final Report* (July 2012) 83.

section of the market that genuinely competes with asset managers[93] and other financial intermediaries, thereby ensuring that these intermediaries provide client options that are competitive and effective. It is vital that all end savers are provided with meaningful choices including direct and indirect investment options, and readily obtainable quality information to make well-informed decisions.[94] Populations in developed nations are ageing rapidly and public debt levels are high in many countries, so many governments will not have sufficient capacity to provide pensions to all constituencies in future and an increasing number of people will have to independently fund their retirement. All governments should therefore ensure there are efficient, fair and transparent processes and mechanisms to enable people to manage their own savings and retirement plans when they elect or are required to do so. Notably though, savers can only engage with, and achieve a degree of control over, their financial and retirement decision when timely, relevant and complete information is provided at all levels of the relevant investment chain.[95]

Most of the Kay Final Report recommendations are founded on building levels of trust between companies and asset managers, At the heart of its vision and recommendations is a world in which 'the central figure is the asset manager, who develops trust relationships with the - narrower than today - range of companies in which he or she chooses to invest.'[96] It characterises the ideal asset manager as a mentor to company managers who provides 'reaction and advice' and who competes for funds 'by persuading savers and asset holders of the long-term merits of a distinctive investment approach,'[97] rather than competing on the basis of short-term performance figures. This model of asset managers is misconceived. The primary goal of most investors is to optimise returns by any legal means. While actions by asset managers may assist to improve a company's performance and competiveness, this is undoubtedly only a secondary objective of investors or traders, regardless of their status.[98] The Oxford dictionary defines a mentor as 'an experienced and trusted adviser'.[99] While the role of asset managers (and of other investors and stakeholders) should encompass frank exchanges with executives relating to performance, the relationship should not be

93. See, e.g., Ron Kaniel, Shuming Liu, Gideon Saar and Sheridan Titman, 'Individual Investor Trading and Return Patterns Around Earnings Announcements' (2012) 57 *Journal of Finance* 639; Joshua Coval, David Hirshleifer and Tyler Shumway, 'Can Individual Investors Beat the Market?' (Working Paper 04-025, Harvard University, September 2005).
94. As the Kay Final Report notes, financial intermediaries can, for many reasons, act as a herd.
95. Within listed company security markets, listed companies sit at the apex of the investment chain and provide the most important primary source of information used by both financial intermediaries and direct investors.
96. *The Kay Review of UK Equity Markets and Long-Term Decision Making: Final Report* (July 2012) 88.
97. *The Kay Review of UK Equity Markets and Long-Term Decision Making: Final Report* (July 2012) 88.
98. Indeed, if the equity ownership tables included in the Kay Final Report are accurate, foreign institutions now hold the largest share of UK equities and most of these institutions likely have global mandates with variable country specific allocations. Accordingly the long term competitive position of UK corporations may not be a high priority in their decision making processes, particularly for those primarily interested in short-term trading.
99. Oxford Dictionaries, 'definition of mentor' (Oxford University Press, 2013) http://oxforddictionaries.com/definition/english/mentor Viewed 10 April 2013.

perceived or understood as one of a trusted adviser. The proposed framework within the Kay Final Report confuses the roles of non-executive directors and asset managers. Non-executive directors are required by law to act in the long-term best interests of the corporation.[100] This duty necessitates decision making and actions that enhance the long-term competitive performance of the company. In contrast, the incentives and interests of asset managers (and of other institutional and retail investors) are rarely entirely equivalent to the long-term best interests of corporations.

The Kay Final Report paints a vision of asset managers that seems far removed from reality. The notion that optimal financial market structures and outcomes can be achieved through private relationships between company managers and asset managers founded on trust seems idealistic at best, given the enormous power imbalances, conflicts of interest, and money flows involved. Levels of trust between companies and their investors and stakeholders have to be earned and built over time. Further, trust within professional relationships involving large sums of money requires higher than normal degrees of openness and accountability. The Kay Final Report states that the most 'powerful mechanism for establishing a culture of trust and respect is for intermediaries and market participants to impose it on each other.'[101] This author respectfully disagrees. The most powerful mechanism for establishing a culture of trust and respect in financial markets is through public disclosure, transparency and accountability. Many listed companies acknowledge it is in their long-term interests to operate as entities with high-levels of public transparency, disclosure and community interaction. Some are fully embracing digital technologies to enhance the flow of information and the breadth and depth of investor and stakeholder engagement. Others would be well-advised to adopt these models when considering effective disclosure and communication policies and practices.

---

100. See, e.g., *Companies Act 2006* (UK) s 172. Section 172 provides that:

> (1) A director of a company must act in the way he considers, in good faith, would be most likely to promote the success of the company for the benefit of its members as a whole, and in doing so have regard (amongst other matters) to:
> (a) the likely consequences of any decision in the long term;
> (b) the interests of the company's employees;
> (c) the need to foster the company's business relationships with suppliers, customers and others,
> (d) the impact of the company's operations on the community and the environment;
> (e) the desirability of the company maintaining a reputation for high standards of business conduct; and
> (f) the need to act fairly as between members of the company.
>
> (2) Where or to the extent that the purposes of the company consist of or include purposes other than the benefit of its members, subsection (1) has effect as if the reference to promoting the success of the company for the benefit of its members were to achieving those purposes.
>
> (3) The duty imposed by this section has effect subject to any enactment or rule of law requiring directors, in certain circumstances, to consider or act in the interests of creditors of the company.

101. *The Kay Review of UK Equity Markets and Long-Term Decision Making: Final Report* (July 2012) 47.

As outlined in later chapters, the assumptions in the Kay Interim Report and Kay Final Report about the role of financial intermediaries and their relationships with company managers impact their commentary and recommendations on company disclosure principles and practices. For example, the Kay Final Report recommends abolishing quarterly reporting obligations and suggests this information should be discussed privately. This proposal is discussed more fully in Chapter 13.

§4.07 SELECTIVE DISCLOSURE EMPIRICAL RESEARCH

Fox suggests that policy makers should determine whether a ban on selective disclosure is desirable based on market efficiency evidence.[102] Langevoort suggests that empirical research on selective disclosure and private contacts using a cost-benefit analysis is difficult, if not impossible.[103] While it is not possible to accurately measure the extent of selective disclosure occurrences across markets or the net benefits of selective disclosure regulation, empirical studies provide valuable indicators. There are various bodies of research that examine selective disclosure issues. One body of work comprises qualitative surveys and interviews following the implementation of Reg FD. Another provides econometric studies that examine the short and longer-term effects of Reg FD. Broader empirical research considers the role and efficacy of intermediaries in financial markets.

[A] Regulation Fair Disclosure

In April 2001 a roundtable review of Reg FD was held. Analysts indicated that the quality of corporate information had reduced dramatically, and some argued that pricing had become more volatile. In 2002, the National Investor Relations Institute and PricewaterhouseCoopers surveyed companies and about half of the respondents indicated that Reg FD had not impacted their disclosure practices or share price volatility, with the remaining companies split almost evenly between increases and decreases in disclosure post-Reg FD.[104]

There are many accounting and finance studies that examine the impact of Reg FD on the quantity and quality of publicly disclosed information.[105] Gomes et al.

102. Merritt Fox, 'Regulation FD and Foreign Issuers: Globalisation's Strains and Opportunities' (2001) 41 *Virginia Journal of International Law* 653, 657.
103. Donald Langevoort, 'Investment Analysts and the Law of Insider Trading' (1990) 76 *Virginia Law Review* 1023, 1054.
104. National Investor Relation Institute, 'National Investor Relation Institute Releases Survey Result on the Impact of SEC Regulation Fair Disclosure' (Press Release, 2 July 2001); Jennifer Francis, Dhananjay Nanda and Xin Wang, 'Re-Examining the Effects of Regulation Fair Disclosure Using Foreign Listed Forms to Control for Concurrent Shocks' (2006) 41 *Journal of Accounting and Economics* 271, 275 footnote 6.
105. See, e.g., Stephen Brown, Stephen Hillegeist and Kin Lo, 'Conference Calls And Information Asymmetry' (2004) 37 *Journal of Accounting and Economics* 343, 345–346; Frank Heflin, Kenneth Subramanyam and Yuan Zhang, 'Regulation FD and the Financial Information Environment: Early Evidence' (2003) 78 *Accounting Review* 1; Warren Bailey, Haitao Li, Connie Mao and Rui Zhong, 'Regulation Fair Disclosure and Earnings Information: Market, Analyst,

suggest there is consensus in the academic literature that the quantity of company disclosures increased after Reg FD.[106] Most studies suggest that public disclosure improved and that institutional participants adjusted their behaviour and trading, without significant adverse effects on markets or companies. Kross and Suk found the speed and frequency of analysts' forecast revisions following public earnings announcements increased dramatically following the introduction of Reg FD. In addition, the magnitude of analyst forecast revisions increased following public disclosures, consistent with the hypothesis that Reg FD levelled the playing field between analysts and individual investors.[107] Agapova et al. found the frequency of guidance issuance increased and the precision of managerial forecasts improved after 2000, suggesting the quality of public guidance information did not deteriorate following Reg FD.[108] Sinha and Gadarowski found evidence suggesting many companies changed the way they provided information to the market, with a shift from private to public disclosure. The findings were consistent with the aim of the regulation to level the playing field and a reduction in the 'leakage' of information by larger companies (but not by smaller firms).[109] Lee et al. found a significant reduction in short-term security price continuation following analyst forecast revisions and earnings announcements, with the most pronounced effect among more opaque companies. Analyst forecast accuracy also improved for these companies, consistent with an improved information environment following the introduction of Reg FD and other regulation governing analyst reporting and conduct.[110]

Conference calls between company managers and participants are an important source of company information in the US, with a similar role to analyst/investor briefings in other jurisdictions. Lee et al. found the quantity of information post-Reg FD, measured by the total number of open access public conference calls and the number of companies hosting them, dramatically increased with no significant increase in volatility.[111] Kross and Suk also found the number of conference calls with

---

and Corporate Responses' (2003) 58 *Journal of Finance* 2487; Chun Lee, Leonard Rosenthal and Kimberly Gleason, 'Effect of Regulation FD on Asymmetric Information' (2004) 60 *Financial Analysts Journal* 79; Praveen Sinha and Christopher Gadarowski, 'The Efficacy of Regulation Fair Disclosure' (2010) 45 *Financial Review* 331; William Kross and Inho Suk, 'Does Regulation FD Work? Evidence from Analysts' Reliance on Public Disclosure' (2012) 53 *Journal of Accounting and Economics* 225; Anna Agapova, Jeff Madura and Zhanel Mailibayeva, 'Does Regulation Fair Disclosure Reduce Information Quality of Managerial Guidance?' (2012) 47 *Financial Review* 273.

106. Armando Gomes, Gary Gorton and Leonardo Madureira, 'SEC Regulation Fair Disclosure, Information and the Cost Of Capital' (2007) 13 *Journal of Corporate Finance* 300, 3.

107. William Kross and Inho Suk, 'Does Regulation FD Work? Evidence from Analysts' Reliance on Public Disclosure' (2012) 53 *Journal of Accounting and Economics* 225.

108. Anna Agapova, Jeff Madura and Zhanel Mailibayeva, 'Does Regulation Fair Disclosure Reduce Information Quality of Managerial Guidance?' (2012) 47 *Financial Review* 273.

109. Praveen Sinha and Christopher Gadarowski, 'The Efficacy of Regulation Fair Disclosure' (2010) 45 *Financial Review* 331, 353.

110. Edward Lee, Norman Strong and Zhenmei (Judy) Zhu, 'Did Regulation Fair Disclosure, SOX, and Other Analyst Regulations Reduce Security Mispricing?' (2014) 52 *Journal of Accounting Research* 733.

111. Chun Lee, Leonard Rosenthal and Kimberly Gleason, 'Effect of Regulation FD on Asymmetric Information' (2004) 60 *Financial Analysts Journal* 79, 87.

public access facilities increased dramatically following the introduction of Reg FD.[112] Kimbrough found an initiation of result-related conference calls was associated with a reduction in post-earnings announcement drift and more timely market response to earnings announcements.[113] Matsumoto et al. suggest that conference call presentations allow analysts to uncover information on the performance and quality of the earnings signal, resulting in a richer information environment than would otherwise exist.[114] Bowen et al. suggest the conference calls present a selective disclosure problem when the public is not privy because they increase the total information available about a company.[115] Brown et al. found link between regular open access conference calls and sustained reductions in information asymmetry. Further, they suggest these companies have lower costs of capital.[116]

[B] Financial Intermediaries

Empirical evidence of conflicts of interest arising from private relationships between company managers and intermediaries is generally consistent across jurisdictions. Analysts from a leading broker in Australia admitted that they 'seek to curry favour with management in order to preserve their information networks.'[117] In a survey by Reuters in the US, 88% of sell-side analysts indicated that publishing a 'sell' recommendation had resulted in exclusion from stock offerings and merger deals, and 54% indicated that it had resulted in exclusion from company briefings.[118] Analysts and others who criticise or raise the alarm about managerial misconduct are often frozen out from company communication channels, particularly when companies are facing adverse conditions or financial pressures.[119] For instance, John Olsen, the Merrill

112. William Kross and Inho Suk, 'Does Regulation FD Work? Evidence from Analysts' Reliance on Public Disclosure' (2012) 53 *Journal of Accounting and Economics* 225.
113. Michael Kimbrough, 'The Effect Of Conference Calls On Analyst And Market Underreaction To Earnings Announcements' (2005) 80 *Accounting Review* 189.
114. Dawn Matsumoto, Maarten Pronk and Erik Roelofsen, 'Managerial Disclosure vs Analyst Inquiry: An Empirical Investigation of the Presentation and Discussion Portions of Earnings-Related Conference Calls' (Working Paper, 1 November 2006) 32. Matsumoto et al. note that the conference calls do not provide merely boiler plate content. See also Richard Frankel, Marilyn Johnson and Douglas Skinner, 'An Empirical Examination of Conference Calls as a Voluntary Disclosure Medium' (1999) 37 *Journal of Accounting Research* 133.
115. Robert Bowen, Angela Davis and Dawn Matsumoto, 'Do Conference Calls Affect Analysts' Forecasts?' (2002) 77 *Accounting Review* 285, 313. See also William Mayew, 'Evidence of Management Discrimination Among Analysts During Earnings Conference Calls' (2008) 46 *Journal of Accounting Research* 627.
116. Stephen Brown, Stephen Hillegeist and Kin Lo, 'Conference Calls And Information Asymmetry' (2004) 37 *Journal of Accounting and Economics* 343, 345–346.
117. Alan Kohler, *Secrets and Lies* (2 December 2008) Business Spectator < http://www.businessspectator.com.au/bs.nsf/Article/Secrets-and-lies-LWRDP?OpenDocument&src=srch > at 3 December 2008.
118. Scott Findlay and Prem Mathew, 'An Examination of the Differential Impact of Regulation FD on Analyst's Forecast Accuracy' (2006) 41 *Financial Review* 9, 10 footnote 2.
119. See, e.g., Robert Rhee, 'The Madoff Scandal, Market Regulatory Failure and the Business Education of Lawyers' (2009) 35 *Journal of Corporation Law* 363, 365; Bin Ke and Yong Yu, 'The Effect Of Issuing Biased Earnings Forecasts On Analysts' Access To Management And Survival' (2006) 44 *Journal of Accounting Research* 965; Donald Langevoort, 'Investment

Lynch energy market securities analyst, was fired when he downgraded Enron's stock,[120] the handful of analysts who publicly criticised the HIH Group in Australia or placed a sell recommendation on the stock were frozen out or blacklisted from further contact with the company,[121] and David Einhorn, the President of Greenlight Capital, was blacklisted or excluded from Allied Capital briefings after criticising the company's accounting practices.[122]

A study by Ertimur et al. found evidence that managers delay disclosures of bad news to enable influential shareholders to sell their shares at favourable prices. These delays were more pronounced when the influential investors owned more shares and when the trading environment was more uncertain.[123] A global study by Maffett found that institutional investors were able to more profitably trade on private company information in opaque information environments at both company and country levels. In other words, more profit was gained from trading on private information when the availability and quality of financial reporting of a company was poor and the relevant country had lower quality governance, financial reporting and disclosure regulation.[124] These combined findings highlight the strong incentives institutional investors have to garner private information and to lobby for reduced or limited public disclosure by listed companies.

Independent investigations conducted from 2001 to 2003 found that individual investors in the US were being systematically harmed by tainted broker research.[125] De Franco et al. estimated that the losses resulting from misleading analyst behaviour

---

Analysts and the Law of Insider Trading' (1990) 76 *Virginia Law Review* 1023; Jill Fisch and Hillary Sale, 'The Securities Analysts as Agent: Rethinking the Regulation of Analysts' (2003) 88 *Iowa Law Review* 1035.

120. See John Coffee Jnr, 'What Caused Enron? A Capsule Of Social and Economic History of the 1990s' (2003) 89 *Cornell Law Review* 269.
121. Commonwealth of Australia, HIH Royal Commission, *The Failure of HIH Insurance* (2003) Vol. 1 xviii, 72-73.
122. David Einhorn, *Fooling Some of the People All of the Time: A Long Short Story* (John Wiley & Sons, 2008). See also House of Commons Treasury Committee, 'Banking Crisis: Reforming Corporate Governance and Pay in the City: Ninth Report of Session 2008 - 2009' (15 May 2009) 59-63. The Report outlines endeavours by institutional shareholders who tried unsuccessfully to engage with UK banks about their high risk management strategies.
123. Yonca Ertimur, Ewa Sletten and Jayanthi Sunder, 'Large Shareholders and Disclosure Strategies: Evidence from IPO Lockup Expirations' (2014) 58 *Journal of Accounting and Economics* 79.
124. Mark Maffett, 'Financial Reporting Opacity and Informed Trading By International Institutional Investors' (2012) *54 Journal of Accounting and Economics* 201.
125. Laura Unger, 'Conflicts of Interest Faced by Brokerage Firms and Their Research Analysts' (Written testimony to the Committee on Financial Services, United States House of Representatives, Washington DC, 31 July 2001). See also Paul Mahoney, 'Manager-Investor Conflicts In Mutual Funds' (2004) 18 *Journal of Economic Perspectives* 161; Unger indicated that:

    - The line between research and investment banking was badly blurred.
    - Analysts' relationships with the companies followed was cozy.
    - Booster shot' research reports were used close to the expiration of lock-up periods.
    - Sell-side analysts and other employees of the brokerage firms with stock ownership in companies covered sold their personal stock while maintaining a 'buy' rating.

were primarily borne by retail investors.[126] McNichols and Trueman found that analysts typically publicly disclosed their forecasts only after privately revealing them to the company's favoured clients.[127] A study by Fong et al. also found that brokers passed their best and most timely information to their largest clients first in order to generate higher returns for fund managers who were active enough to rank as a broker's 'best client'.[128] Chan et al. found evidence consistent with leakage of broker recommendations to some clients prior to their 'official' release.[129]

Mounting evidence of brokers' conflicts of interest eventually prompted the introduction of new regulation governing sell-side broker research in the US around the same period as the introduction of Reg FD.[130] The long-term efficacy of this regulation

126. Gus De Franco, Hai Lu and Florin Vasvari, 'Wealth Transfer Effects of Analysts Misleading Behavior' (2007) 45 *Journal of Accounting Research* 71, 104. De Franco et al. estimated that actively trading individual investors lost USD 2.2 billion, about two and half times the amount lost by institutions.
127. Maureen McNichols and Brett Trueman, 'Public Disclosure, Private Information Collection, And Short-Term Trading' (1994) 17 *Journal of Accounting and Economics* 69, 89.
128. Kingsley Fong, David Gallagher, Peter Gardner and Peter Swan, 'A Closer Examination Of Investment Manager Herding Behaviour' (Working Paper, University of New South Wales, 25 February 2004).
129. Howard Chan, Rob Brown and Yew Kee Ho, 'Initiation Of Analyst Coverage: Does It Add Value?' (Working Paper, Monash University, University of Melbourne, 20 May 2003) 14.
130. The major regulatory actions in the US included:

    (1) Section 501 in the *Sarbanes-Oxley Act* 2002 governing analysts conflict of interest.
    (2) New analyst independence rules by the National Association of Securities Dealers (NASD) and the New York Stock Exchange (NYSE).
    (3) Enactment of Regulation Analyst Certification (Reg AC).
    (4) A global settlement with leading investment banks.

    s. 501 of the *Sarbanes-Oxley Act*, codified as s. 15D of the *Securities Exchange Act* of 1934, required the SEC to adopt rules, directly or indirectly, to address analyst conflicts of interest. The NYSE and the NASD are self-regulated organizations that are subject to oversight by the SEC. As such, they were required to adopt new analyst independence rules. The NASD and NYSE adopted rules that require analyst compensation to be determined on criteria without any consideration given to service or contribution to an investment banking division. Investment banking staff may not: influence or control analyst compensation; review or discuss pending research reports; tie analyst compensation to investment banking business; or influence analyst coverage decisions: NASD Rules 2711(b)(1)(2), 2711(d)(1)(2); NYSE Rules 472(b)(1)(2) (1)(2), 472(h)(1)(2). In addition, analysts may not solicit investment banking business, participate in road shows and offer favourable research in return for business. Measures also included a ban on initial public offering spinning and preferential access to stock allocations; the appointment of independent monitors; and investor education programmes. Companies may not retaliate against analysts who issue unfavourable research or ratings: NASD Rules 2711(c)(4), 2711(e)(j); NYSE Rule 472(b)(5), 472(g)(1)(2). Reg AC requires certification by an analyst of a research report of the views expressed. That is, analysts must certify that they agree with their own recommendations: Securities Act Release 33-8193 (27 February 2003). A global settlement in 2003 required ten investment banks to pay a collective USD 1.3875 billion. The settlement also required specified research reports by investment banks to be made public within ninety days after the end of a quarter, allowing public analysis of such research. In addition, ten investment banks paid a collective USD 1.3875 billion under a global settlement: Securities Exchange Commission, 'Ten of Nation's Top Investment Firms Settle Enforcement Actions Involving Conflicts of Interest Between Research and Investment Banking' (Media Release 2003–2015).

has been challenged in various ways. First, there is continuing empirical evidence of herding behaviour by sell-side analysts.[131] Second, a study by Firth et al. found that sell-side analyst recommendations on company securities held by mutual fund clients of the brokerage firm were significantly higher than the market-wide analyst consensus figures. The optimistic bias in the recommendations increased with the weight of stock holdings in client portfolios and the commission revenue generated from these clients. It also found that analysts were less likely to downgrade stocks held by mutual fund clients following announcements of bad news.[132] Finally, this scholarly evidence is supported by regulatory action. In December 2014, the US Financial Industry Regulatory Authority imposed total fines of USD 43.5 million across ten financial institutions for offering favourable sell-side analyst research in connection with the planned initial public offering of Toys'R'Us and for allowing these analysts to solicit investment banking business.[133]

§4.08 SUMMARY

Theoretical models or arguments that expressly or impliedly suggest that retail investors are protected from selective disclosure because of market efficiency, or that these investors can free ride on the back of institutional investors, are not empirically credible. More complex arguments centred on the relationship between analyst incentives, research production, and efficiencies are also tenuous. Most of these theories fail to differentiate between intermediaries who produce research for third parties and those who engage in research solely for the purpose of enhancing institutional or personal profits. Further, these efficiency arguments largely ignore or dismiss the many conflicts that arise when unfettered selective disclosure is permitted in financial markets.

Participant incentives to obtain informational or timing advantages in financial markets are powerful and consuming because such advantages often lead to reliable trading gains (or reduced losses) without the need for diligent and sophisticated analysis. Institutional participants compete to obtain private meetings with company managers in order to gain the earliest and most substantive updates between reporting periods, and this battle for superior access continues on a daily basis across the full spectrum of market participants (and not simply between institutional and individual investors). The associated power games are typically based on perceived or actual wealth and political influence, so the financial institutions that control the largest funds or trading portfolios hold most sway given their voting power and greater ability to pay or manoeuvre for private access. This intense gamesmanship to gain private company

131. See, e.g., Jared Williams, 'Financial Analysts and the False Consensus Effect' (2013) 51 *Journal of Accounting Research* 855.
132. Michael Firth, Chen Lin, Ping Liu ad Yuhai Xuan, 'The Client is King: Do Mutual Fund Relationships Bias Analyst Recommendations?' (2013) 51 *Journal of Accounting Research* 165.
133. United States Financial Industry Regulatory Authority, 'FINRA Fines 10 Firms a Total of $43.5 Million for Allowing Equity Research Analysts to Solicit Investment Banking Business and for Offering Favorable Research Coverage in Connection With Toys'R'Us IPO' (Media Release 11 December 2014).

information adversely impacts conduct, competition and outcomes across national and global financial markets.

Processes involving regular informal contacts between companies and analysts and other privileged investors create a series of moral hazard problems.[134] The conflicts that can arise when company managers control the timing, content and recipients of their disclosures are real, significant and well documented.[135] First, regular feeding of private company information to selected investors discourages rigorous independent research and analysis and promotes institutional herd behaviour. Second, when sell-side analysts who criticise companies in research reports, media articles or other public forums can be removed from a company's invitation list without repercussion, the potential gatekeeper role of analysts and the governance benefits of public scrutiny are significantly undermined. Third, studies that examine sell-side broker research practices suggest it is difficult for retail investors to use traditional broker services to trade profitably. Traditional sell-side broking entities naturally favour large participants who trade in high volumes, such as asset managers and buy-side analysts. Most retail investors do not have sufficient financial power to maintain equivalent relationships, because the trading commissions they generate may not adequately compensate for the provision of high quality research and intermediated access to corporate managers.

In today's financial markets, company information should be directly accessible and not filtered through other participants with vested interests in preserving the status quo.[136] It is vital that all corporate stakeholders are able to scrutinise and criticise company management, sell a company's securities, and write independent research, without fear of losing access to company information. Otherwise, all forms of efficiency are weakened and corporate governance processes are severely undermined. Informational advantages among traders can and should be gained through insightful analysis of public information.[137] Equality of access does not prevent anyone from ferreting out, processing, disseminating or trading on publicly available or legally obtainable information.[138] Furthermore, information does not need to be private for analysts to make money. Analyst services will continue to be required and compensated when they provide independent analysis of publicly disclosed information that is insightful and useful.[139] Competition among participants should be based on superior analytical skills, rather than on who can curry sufficient favour to get the best access to company

134. Donald Langevoort, 'Investment Analysts and the Law of Insider Trading' (1990) 76 *Virginia Law Review* 1023, 1044.
135. Jill Fisch and Hillary Sale, 'The Securities Analysts as Agent: Rethinking the Regulation of Analysts' (2003) *88 Iowa Law Review* 1035, 1053–1056; John L Orcutt, 'Investor Skepticism v Investor Confidence: Why the New Research Analyst Reforms will Harm Investors' (2003) 81 *Denver University Law Review* 1, 26–28; Commonwealth of Australia, HIH Royal Commission, *The Failure of HIH Insurance* (2003) Vol. 1 xviii, 72–73.
136. Arthur Zeikel, 'On the Threat of Change' (November/December 1975) *Financial Analysts Journal* 17, 19.
137. Zohar Goshen and Gideon Parchomovsky, 'The Essential Role Of Securities Regulation' (2006) 55 *Duke Law Journal* 711, 714, 721, 725, 729–730, 738.
138. Marc Steinberg and Jason Myers, 'Lurking in the Shadows: The Hidden Issues of the Securities and Exchange Commission's Regulation FD' (2002) 27 *Journal of Corporation Law* 173, 185.
139. Ian Lee, 'Fairness and Insider Trading' (2002) 1 *Columbia Business Law Review* 119, 185.

management and private information.[140] Once company information is publicly released, all interested persons can choose whether to purchase supplemental information provided by outsiders such as brokers, when these services are required and of value.

Regulation governing access to company information has enormous financial consequences. All other things being equal, participants who can obtain superior or timelier information from company executives than other participants will profit to the detriment of those who are less informed. This is so whether the informational advantage is gained through private or public channels.[141] Some investors gain an informational edge — and use that edge to profit at the expense of the uninformed.[142] In financial markets without any regulation prohibiting trading on inside information, large institutional participants are likely to systematically lose to better informed company insiders, but systematically gain at the expense of less informed investors.[143] In markets that prohibit insider trading but permit trading on selectively disclosed information, it is generally the recipients of selective disclosures that capture most of the trading gains.[144] Accordingly, enactment of insider trading regulation without supporting regulation prohibiting selective disclosure merely shifts potential gains from insiders to outsiders, as the recipients of selective disclosures.

As discussed in prior chapters, economic efficiency outcomes need to be considered holistically over long periods. The fundamental questions that need to be addressed concern the extent to which identified short-term efficiencies from selective disclosure serve the long-term national interest, and whether select disclosure results in better long-term national outcomes than public disclosure frameworks. It is not possible to design an empirical model to conclusively resolve these questions; however, permitting selective or privileged access to company information based on favoured relationships in financial markets is unlikely to be the best approach to achieve the rationales for disclosure regulation. Selective disclosure results in investor participation that is limited to institutions and individuals of sufficient size and influence to negotiate mutually beneficial relationships with managers of listed companies.

Selective disclosure models and theories change significantly when the efficiency benchmark applied is long-term economic efficiency. For readers that are teachers, an imperfect analogy may assist. Many students ask teachers for hints on the likely content of forthcoming exams, and if given the opportunity, might even seek advance

140. Laura Unger, 'Corporate Communications Without Violations' (1999) 51 *Administrative Law Review* 1119, 1122-1124; Camilia Lopez-Fernandini, 'Regulation FD of the SEC's Selective Disclosure and Insider Trading Rule: Finally, Full And Fair Disclosure' (2001) 53 *Administrative Law Review* 1353, 1373.
141. United States Securities and Exchange Commission, *Proposed Rule: Selective Disclosure and Insider Trading* (2000).
142. United States Securities and Exchange Commission, *Proposed Rule: Selective Disclosure and Insider Trading* (2000).
143. Donald Langevoort, 'Investment Analysts and the Law of Insider Trading' (1990) 76 *Virginia Law Review* 1023, 1046.
144. Jonathan Macey, 'Ethics, Economics and Insider Trading: Ayn Rand Meets the Theory of the Firm' (1988) 11 *Harvard Journal of Law & Public Policy* 785, 803.

notice of the exam questions. It could be argued from the students' perspectives that this is efficient because it allows more focused exam revision. But consider what the likely outcomes would be if all teachers provided this information only to students with blue eyes within a class of students of similar skill and diligence. It would advantage the blue-eyed students and may, in the short-term, increase enrolments from blue-eyed students. Over the long run however, it would harm the blue-eyed students' abilities to learn, research and think critically, it would create increasing resentment among, and withdrawal from courses by, students with eyes that are not blue, and it would severely damage the credibility and reputation of the university. So it is in financial markets. Some company managers and large participants have strong incentives to oppose additional disclosures on a timely basis even when such disclosure is essentially costless.[145] These groups do not use personal profit arguments in disclosure policy submission documents, as such approaches are likely to be perceived as greedy and self-interested. Instead, institutional arguments are often framed in vague efficiency terms. For example, the efficiency arguments made by critics of Reg FD prior to its introduction were that:

- retail investors would be overwhelmed by the information provided;
- trading activities and volatility would be significantly altered;
- companies would have practical difficulties in determining what information to release;
- companies would no longer be able to provide a nuanced presentation of information;
- companies would reduce the amount and quality of information provided; and
- the traditional role and function of analysts would be threatened.

These arguments seem to have been largely unfounded. None of the many empirical studies reviewed by the author found evidence consistent with a 'chilling' in the quantity or quality of information provided in the post-Reg FD environment.[146] Instead, most studies have found that listed companies adjusted their disclosure processes by increasing the amount of publicly disclosed information, and that institutional investors responded to this increased public disclosure by trading after, rather than prior to, earnings releases.[147] Studies also confirm that the number of US listed companies providing public access to conference calls increased leading up to, and following, the introduction of Reg FD.[148] Most of these studies suggest that Reg FD

145. Nils Hakansson, 'On the Politics of Accounting Disclosure and Measurement: An Analysis of Economic Incentives' (1981) 19 *Journal of Accounting Research* 1, 27.
146. Brian Bushee and Theodore Goodman, 'Which Institutional Investors Trade Based on Private Information About Earnings and Returns?' (2007) 45 *Journal of Accounting Research* 289; Chun Lee, Leonard Rosenthal and Kimberly Gleason, 'Effect of Regulation FD on Asymmetric Information' (2004) 60 *Financial Analysts Journal* 79, 87.
147. Frank Heflin, Kenneth Subramanyam and Yuan Zhang, 'Regulation FD and the Financial Information Environment: Early Evidence' (2003) 78 *Accounting Review* 1; Warren Bailey, Haitao Li, Connie Mao and Rui Zhong, 'Regulation Fair Disclosure and Earnings Information: Market, Analyst, and Corporate Responses' (2003) 58 *Journal of Finance* 2487, 2487, 2512.
148. National Investor Relations Institute, 'Most Corporate Conference Calls Are Now Open to Individual Investors and the Media' (Press Release, 29 February 2000); Brian Bushee and

resulted in an improvement in the amount and quality of information provided during these conference calls.[149] These various changes in behaviour suggest that Reg FD has resulted in more equitable access to company information without significant adverse impacts on price, market or economic efficiency.

Theodore Goodman, 'Which Institutional Investors Trade Based on Private Information About Earnings and Returns?' (2007) 45 *Journal of Accounting Research* 289; Chun Lee, Leonard Rosenthal and Kimberly Gleason, 'Effect of Regulation FD on Asymmetric Information' (2004) 60 *Financial Analysts Journal* 79, 87.

149. Stephen Brown, Stephen Hillegeist and Kin Lo, 'Conference Calls And Information Asymmetry' (2004) 37 *Journal of Accounting and Economics* 343, 345–346; Richard Frankel, Marilyn Johnson and Douglas Skinner, 'An Empirical Examination of Conference Calls as a Voluntary Disclosure Medium' (1999) 37 *Journal of Accounting Research* 133, 149; Robert Bowen, Angela Davis and Dawn Matsumoto, 'Do Conference Calls Affect Analysts' Forecasts?' (2002) 77 *Accounting Review* 285, 313.

Part III
Company Disclosure Regulation: Country Profiles

> Financial markets are not an end in themselves, but a means: they are supposed to perform certain vital functions which enable the real economy to be more productive such as mobilising savings, allocating capital, and managing risk.[1]

INTRODUCTION

Part III provides national profiles for the US, Canada, Germany, the UK, Japan, Hong Kong, Australia and Singapore. This group of countries spans North America, Europe and the Asia Pacific and includes nations that have had company disclosure regulation in place for many decades, countries with more recently established disclosure frameworks, some of the largest exchange markets in the developed world, and markets that are expected to become more prominent during the twenty-first century.[2]

The national profiles include a summary outline of the periodic and continuous disclosure regulation and the overarching supervisory and enforcement framework. Empirical evidence of disclosure practices and issues is also provided. National regulators in some of the selected countries maintain company disclosure review programmes. Some also publish reports that outline the review programme methodology, the identified disclosure issues and findings, and policy guidance concerning appropriate disclosure standards and practices. Where available, series of these disclosure reports are summarised throughout Part III to highlight disclosure issues and regulatory concerns that commonly arise across jurisdictions, and to provide feedback

1. Commission of Experts of the President of the UN General Assembly on Reform of the International Monetary and Financial System, Principles for a New Financial Architecture (Commission), 21 September 2009, http://www.un.org/ga/president/63/commission/financial_commission.shtml viewed 13 October 2014.
2. Some of the content in Part III is included in a published article: Gill North, 'National Company Disclosure Regulator Frameworks: Superficially Similar but Substantively Different' (Summer 2015) 3 *Global Markets Law Journal*.

and insights on structures and steps to improve company disclosure standards and quality. To supplement these regulatory reviews, the author examines the disclosures of two large companies listed on the leading exchange in the selected countries for a period of three years, including the information available from the company website and the documents submitted to the relevant exchange and or information depositary. The purposes of these reviews are to highlight and discuss common disclosure practices and issues, and to identify excellent and innovative practices for inclusion within a best practice framework. To ensure this process is as constructive as possible, the best features of each company's disclosures are highlighted in Part III while most of the negative findings are discussed only in general terms within Part IV. The case study review process and the website pages and documents reviewed from each company are outlined in the Appendix.

CHAPTER 5
United States

> Our aim is not to do away with corporations; on the contrary, these big aggregations are an inevitable development of modern industrialism, and the effort to destroy them would be futile unless accomplished in ways that would work the utmost mischief to the entire body politic. We can do nothing of good in the way of regulating and supervising these corporations until we fix clearly in our minds that we are not attacking the corporations, but endeavoring to do away with any evil in them. We are not hostile to them; we are merely determined that they shall be so handled as to subserve the public good. We draw the line against misconduct, not against wealth.[1]

§5.01 OVERVIEW

The SEC is an independent federal regulatory agency that was established in 1934 following the Great Depression.[2] Section 2 of the Exchange Act states that:

> transactions in securities as commonly conducted upon securities exchanges ... are effected with a national public interest, which makes it necessary to provide for regulation and control of such transactions and of practices and matters related thereto, including ... to require appropriate reports ...

The SEC has primary responsibility for enforcing federal securities laws and regulation. It can issue rules pursuant to specific provisions to ensure they are effective, and can sanction, fine and otherwise discipline market participants that violate federal securities laws.

---

1. Theodore Roosevelt, State of the Union Address, 2 December 1902.
2. The United States Securities Exchange Commission was established under s. 4 of the *Securities Exchange Act of 1934* (codified as 15 U.S.C s 78d.).

Securities exchanges in the US operate largely as self-regulatory organisations, but must be registered with the SEC.[3] A registered stock exchange is required to comply with the rules and regulations under the Exchange Act. It must also be able to ensure that its members comply with its rules and any relevant statutory provisions. Thus, an exchange is responsible for ensuring that its members satisfy the listing criteria and continue to comply with the exchange rules, including the disclosure obligations. The largest securities exchange in the US (and in the world) by market capitalisation and trade value is the Intercontinental Exchange (NYSE). Most of the largest companies and many medium-sized companies in the US are listed on the NYSE. Other global companies are listed on the NYSE as foreign issuers.

Within the NYSE group, a subsidiary called NYSE Regulation, Inc (NYSER) operates as an independent not-for-profit corporation. The majority of its directors are not affiliated with any other NYSE board.[4] An Issuer Oversight area monitors and enforces listed company compliance with the original listing criteria and the continued listing standards.[5] It provides hyperlinks to pages that outline non-compliant issuers and delistings. The non-compliant issuer web page lists the name of the issuer, its symbol, a non-compliant indicator, the deficiency, the notification date, and the relevant market.[6] The non-compliant indicators include a '.BC', 'LF' and 'BC-FC'. These terms are not explained on the web page, but the deficiency explanations suggest that the BC indicates a breach of the continuing listing standards and LF applies where companies have not filed required quarterly or annual reports with the SEC on time.[7] The delistings web page outlines issuers that have been removed from listings.[8] These issuers are searchable by removals from listing initiated by the exchange for cause and voluntary delistings initiated by companies. At the time of review, all of the delistings on this page were voluntary.[9]

The NYSE regulatory home page states that the NYSER conducts 'limited real-time monitoring of trading activity on the facilities of U.S. securities as well as market Watch functions to determine whether to halt a listed security'.[10] The extent to which this real-time monitoring may lead to formal disciplinary actions against issuers, including actions involving breaches of the disclosure listing rules, is unclear. At the

---

3. The Intercontinental Exchange (NYSE) and NASDAQ OMX are respectively the largest and second largest stock exchanges in the world by market capitalisation: See Insider Monkey, 'The 8 Largest Stock Exchanges in the World', viewed 23 April 2015, http://www.insidermonkey.com/blog/largest-stock-exchanges-237624/.
4. NYSE, 'NYSE Regulation, Inc.' viewed 27 June 2015, https://www.nyse.com/regulation.
5. NYSE, 'NYSE Regulation, Inc.' viewed 27 June 2015, https://www.nyse.com/regulation.
6. NYSE, 'Noncompliant Issuers', viewed 27 June 2015, https://www.nyse.com/regulation/noncompliant-issuers.
7. The meaning of BC-FC is unclear.
8. NYSE, 'Removal From Listings', viewed 27 June 2015, https://www.nyse.com/regulation/delistings.
9. NYSE, 'Removal From Listings', viewed 27 June 2015, https://www.nyse.com/regulation/delistings.
10. NYSE, 'NYSE Regulation, Inc.' viewed 27 June 2015, https://www.nyse.com/regulation.

time of review, all of the actions listed on the 'NYSE Disciplinary Action' page involved the conduct of financial intermediaries.[11]

§5.02 PERIODIC REPORTS

A company defined as a 'reporting company' or one that registers its securities in the US is subject to the periodic and reporting requirements of sections 13(a) and 15(d) of the Exchange Act.[12] The reporting obligations include a requirement to file annually using Form 10-K, to file quarterly using Form 10-Q, and to file specified events using Form 8-K.[13] The type of events that may trigger an obligation to report on Form 8-K include major changes to the company's business and operations; material financial matters; events relating to corporate governance and management, asset backed securities and securities trading; and Reg FD disclosures.[14]

Public companies in the US must prepare two full year reports, one for the SEC and another for shareholders. Form 10-K is the full year report provided by listed companies to the SEC and federal regulation governs its form and content. Form 10-K reports must contain detailed financial and operating information, and discuss the company's performance, position and prospects. The content of these reports is provided within a standard template and includes financial and non-financial information. The reports are formatted in three parts under standard item headings. Part one provides an overview that includes a description of the business and an outline of any legal proceedings. Part two presents the financial statements, notes, management discussion and analysis (MD&A), quantitative and qualitative disclosures about market risk, an outline of controls and procedures, and any disclosure changes or disagreements with the auditors. It also includes a link to the company website where additional information can be found. Part three covers director, executive and professional advisor matters.

The deadline for filing a 10-K report depends on the size of the company and whether it is classified as a large accelerated filer, an accelerated filer, a non-accelerated filer, or a smaller reporting company. These classifications are determined according to the size of the company's public float. Large accelerator companies with a public float of USD 700 million or more are required to file a 10-K within sixty days

11. NYSE, 'NYSE Disciplinary Actions', viewed 27 May 2015, http://www.nyse.com/regulation/nyse/1022221394131.html. All of the disciplinary actions involve financial intermediaries. Suspicious activity may be referred to the Financial Industry Regulatory Authority (FINRA) for further investigation. FINRA is an independent regulator with responsibility for writing and enforcing rules that govern the activities of nearly 4,400 securities firms that encompass approximately 630,000 brokers: see Financial Industry Regulatory Authority home page at http://www.finra.org/.
12. A company may register its securities under s. 12(b) or 12(g) of the *Securities Exchange Act of 1934*. Companies with more than USD 10 million in assets whose securities are held by more than 500 shareholders must file annual and other periodic reports.
13. United States Securities Exchange Commission, 'Form 8-K', viewed 27 June 2015, http://www.sec.gov/answers/form8k.htm.
14. United States Securities Exchange Commission, 'Form 8-K', viewed 27 June 2015, http://www.sec.gov/answers/form8k.htm.

of the end of the fiscal year, accelerated companies with a float of more than USD 75 million but less than USD 700 million have seventy-five days to file, and all other companies (including a non-accelerated filer or smaller reporting company) with a float below USD 75 million have ninety days.[15]

Listed companies previously had some discretion over the content of annual reports provided to shareholders. However, the SEC has gradually standardised the disclosure framework and there are now only minimal differences between the two types of full year report. The annual reports must contain certified financial statements and specified items. The certified financial statements include audited balance sheets for two years and audited statements of income and cash flow for three years. The annual reports must also provide five-year summary financial data, including net sales or operating revenues, income or loss from continuing operations, total assets, long-term obligations, and cash dividends declared and paid.

Listed companies in the US have been required to provide comprehensive quarterly reports (Form 10-Q) since 1970. The Form 10-Qs are formatted in two parts; part one contains financial information and part two contains other information. The financial information includes condensed financial statements, MD&A of the financial conditions and results, and disclosures on market risks. The deadline for filing the 10-Q reports also depends on the size of the company. Companies with a public float of USD 75 million or more are required to file the 10-Q within forty days of the end of the financial year, and companies with a float below USD 75 million have forty-five days.[16] Foreign private issuers that have listed equity shares on exchanges in the United States must also report to the SEC. For example, Form 20-F reports must be submitted within six months of the end of the company's fiscal year, or if the fiscal year-end date changes,[17] and 6-K forms are required when material information arises between periodic reporting periods. The purposes of the 6-K notifications are to ensure that US investors have the same access to information that investors in the foreign company's home market receive.

Non-financial disclosures, such as MD&A, have been recognised as an important component of company reporting in the US for many years. Item 303 of Regulation S-K requires listed companies to include extensive MD&A in the full year (10-K) and quarterly reports (10-Q).[18] The mandated MD&A includes commentary on the company's financial condition and operational results and a description of the business, including the main products and services. The reports must include outlines of the

15. United States Securities Exchange Commission, 'Form 10-K', viewed 27 June 2015, http://www.sec.gov/answers/form10k.htm.
16. United States Securities Exchange Commission, 'Form10-Q', viewed 14 March 2014, http://www.sec.gov/answers/form10q.htm.
17. The reporting and eligibility requirements for Form 20-F are mandated in the *Securities Exchange Act of 1934*. The information requirements are generally not as onerous as for domestic companies listed in the United States.
18. Regulation S-K Item 303, *Management's Discussion and Analysis of Financial Condition and Results of Operations* (2005); United States Securities Exchange Commission, Securities Release 33-8350 (29 December 2003) Financial Reporting Release 72, *Interpretation: Commission Guidance Regarding Management's Discussion and Analysis of Financial Conditions and Results of Operations.*

critical accounting policies,[19] and information on liquidity, capital resources,[20] operational results,[21] favourable or unfavourable industry trends, significant events or uncertainties, off-balance sheet arrangements,[22] and contractual obligations. Forward-looking disclosures are also required for 'known trends, demands, commitments, events or uncertainties' in relation to these matters.[23] The stated objectives of these MD&A requirements are:

(1) to provide a narrative explanation of a company's financial statements that enables investors to see the company through the eyes of management;
(2) to enhance the overall financial disclosure and provide the context within which financial information should be analysed; and
(3) to provide information about the quality of, and potential variability of a company's earnings and cash flow, so that investors can ascertain the likelihood that past performance is indicative of future performance.[24]

The SEC operates a centralised depositary system for listed company documents provided under federal law. Companies must file the mandated reports and disclosures with the SEC using its Electronic Data Gathering, Analysis, and Retrieval System (EDGAR). The EDGAR website enables public access to filed company documents.[25] The documents available from the EDGAR website include the full year reports (10-K and annual), quarterly reports (10-Q), prospectuses, event disclosures (Form 8-K), and press releases submitted to the SEC. The EDGAR website also includes the various foreign issuer reports.

The SEC proactively supports the disclosure framework by providing companies with guidance on how to meet their disclosure requirements and satisfy the MD&A rules and objectives.[26] It also actively monitors and supervises the disclosure processes. Section 408 of the *Sarbanes-Oxley Act of 2002* requires the SEC to review a

19. United States Securities Exchange Commission, Securities Act Release 33-8040 (12 December 2001) Financial Reporting Release No. 60, *Cautionary Advice Regarding Disclosure About Critical Accounting Policies.*
20. United States Securities Exchange Commission, Securities Act Release 33-8056 (22 January 2002) Financial Reporting Release 61, *Disclosure Relating to Liquidity and Capital Resources, Off-Balance Sheet Arrangements, Trading Activities and Related Party Transactions.*
21. United States Securities Exchange Commission, Securities Act Release No. 33-6835 (18 May 1989) Financial Reporting Release No. 36, Final Rule: *Disclosure in Management's Discussion and Analysis of Financial Condition and Results of Operations; Certain Investment Company Disclosures.*
22. United States Securities Exchange Commission, Securities Act Release No. 33-8182 (28 January 2003) Financial Reporting Release No. 67, Final Rule: *Disclosure in Management's Discussion and Analysis About Off-Balance Sheet Arrangements and Aggregate Contractual Obligations.*
23. See Cathy Cole and Christopher Jones, 'Management Discussion and Analysis: A Review and Implications for Future Research' (2005) 24 *Journal of Accounting Literature* 135, 138–139.
24. United States Securities Exchange Commission, *Report on Review of Disclosure Requirements in Regulation S-K* (December 2013) 42 available at http://www.sec.gov/News/PressRelease/Detail/PressRelease/1370540530982.
25. United States Securities Exchange Commission, 'EDGAR Company filings', viewed 15 March 2014, https://www.sec.gov/edgar/searchedgar/companysearch.html.
26. United States Securities Exchange Commission, Interpretation: Commission Guidance Regarding Management's Discussion and Analysis of Financial Condition and Results of Operations 17

company's periodic reports at least once every three years.[27] The SEC may elect to do a full cover-to-cover review, a financial statement review, or a targeted issue review. When the SEC believes a company can improve its disclosure, it issues a 'comment letter'.[28] The company may respond by a 'response letter' or, if appropriate, may amend its filings. SEC comments and company responses are made available on the EDGAR website after the review is complete. When required, the SEC uses its enforcement powers. It has a track record of successful enforcement actions across the full spectrum of periodic disclosure rules, including those pertaining to preliminary full year reporting (10-K) and quarterly reporting (10-Q),[29] and the MD&A content within these periodic reports.[30]

Regulation S-K was created in 1982 to provide an 'integrated disclosure system' of the registration statement disclosure requirements under the Securities Act and the periodic reporting disclosure rules under the Exchange Act.[31] This regulation is now under review in the US. The SEC was mandated by Congress in the 2012 *Jumpstart Our Business Startups (JOBS) Act*[32] to report on its disclosure rules for US public companies, as a means to 'modernize and simplify disclosure requirements and reduce compliance costs for emerging growth companies.'[33] To achieve these aims, the SEC issued a Staff Report entitled *Report on Review of Disclosure Requirements in Regulation S-K* that documents the developments of Regulation S-K. The Staff Report concludes that Regulation S-K should be comprehensively reviewed.[34]

§5.03 CONTINUOUS DISCLOSURE

Continuous disclosure obligations in the US are imposed on listed companies under exchange listing rules. As the NYSE is the largest and most prominent global securities

CFR Parts 211, 231 and 241 [Release Nos. 33-8350; 34-48960; FR-72]. See also United States Securities Exchange Commission Sample Letters Sent to Public Companies on MD&A Disclosure.

27. Section 408 of *Sarbanes-Oxley Act.*
28. United States Securities Exchange Commission, 'Comment Letters', viewed 27 May 2015, http://www.sec.gov/answers/commentletters.htm
29. United States Securities Exchange Commission, Accounting and Auditing Enforcement Releases, 14 March 2014, < http://www.sec.gov/divisions/enforce/friactions.shtml >. This website provides details on many actions taken by the SEC relating to the content of quarterly reports (10-Q) and preliminary full year reports (10-K).
30. See, e.g., In the Matter of Bank of America Corporation, Release No 72888 (21 August 2014) https://www.sec.gov/litigation/admin/2014/34-72888.pdf; *In the Matter of Sony Corporation and Sumio Sano:* Release No. 40305 (5 August 1998) < http://www.sec.gov/litigation/admin/3440305.txt >; *In the Matter of Bank of Boston Corporation,* Administrative Proceeding File No. 3-8270 (1995) 14 March 2014, < http://www.sec.gov/litigation/aljdec/id81bpm.txt >.
31. United States Securities Exchange Commission, *Report on Review of Disclosure Requirements in Regulation S-K* (December 2013) 8.
32. Pub. L. No. 112-106, [126 Stat. 306] (2012); JOBS Act s. 101; Securities Act of 1933 s. 2(a)(19)[15 USC 77b(a)(19)]L. The specific mandate is to analyse the 'registration requirements' of Regulation S-K.
33. United States Securities and Exchange Commission, 'SEC Issues Staff Report on Public Company Disclosure' (Press Release 2013-269, 20 December 2013).
34. United States Securities and Exchange Commission, *Report on Review of Disclosure Requirements in Regulation S-K* (December 2013).

exchange, its rules are outlined in more detail than the rules of other exchanges outlined in subsequent country profiles.

Section 2 of the NYSE Listed Company Manual governs the disclosure and reporting of material information. It states that the listing agreement generally seeks to achieve the following objectives:

- Ensure timely disclosure of information that may affect security values or influence investment decisions, and in which shareholders, the public and the Exchange have a warrantable interest.
- Ensure frequent, regular and timely publication of financial reports prepared in accordance with generally accepted accounting principles.
- Provide the Exchange with timely information to enable it to efficiently perform its function of maintaining an orderly market for the company's securities, to enable it to maintain necessary records and to allow it the opportunity to make comment as to certain matters before they become established facts.
- Preclude certain business practices not generally considered sound.[35]

More specifically, NYSE Listing Rule 202.05 requires timely disclosure of material news developments. It provides that:

> A listed company is expected to release quickly to the public any news or information which might reasonably be expected to materially affect the market for its securities ... A listed company should also act promptly to dispel unfounded rumors which result in unusual market activity or price variations.

The Listing Rule 202.05 commentary confirms that '[t]his is one of the most important and fundamental purposes of the listing agreement which the company enters into with the Exchange.' Importantly, the wording of Listing Rule 202.05 and the introduction to section 2 of the NYSE Listed Company Manual indicate that the audience of listed company disclosures includes 'the public', thereby acknowledging the breadth of persons with a warrantable interest.

NYSE Listing Rule 202.06 notes that:

> Unfavorable news should be reported as promptly and candidly as favorable news. Reluctance or unwillingness to release a negative story or an attempt to disguise unfavorable news endangers management's reputation for integrity. Changes in accounting methods to mask such occurrences can have a similar impact.

The explicit wording of Listing Rule 202.06 indicates that the NYSE is fully aware of the practical challenges and difficulties in obtaining balanced and frank public disclosure of negative corporate developments. Listing Rule 202.06 discourages the use of financial measures within company reports and disclosures that exclude negative components in an attempt to present events or results in a positive light. In practice,

35. New York Stock Exchange, 'New York Stock Exchange Listed Company Manual 201 Introduction', viewed 15 August 2015, http://nysemanual.nyse.com/LCMTools/PlatformViewer.asp?selectednode=chp%5F1%5F3%5F2%5F6&manual=%2Flcm%2Fsections%2Flcm%2Dsections%2F.

this exhortation generally refers to the use of financial measures that are not prepared in accordance with relevant accounting standards.

NYSE Listing Rule 202.02 governs the relationship between company officials and outsiders. It states that:

> Security analysts play an increasingly important role in the evaluation and interpretation of the financial affairs of listed companies. Annual reports, quarterly reports, and interim releases cannot by their nature provide all of the financial and statistical data that should be available to the investing public. The Exchange recommends that companies observe an 'open door' policy in their relations with security analysts, financial writers, shareholders, and others who have legitimate investment interest in the company's affairs.
>
> A company should not give information to one inquirer which it would not give to another, nor should it reveal information it would not willingly give or has not given to the press for publication. Thus, for companies to give advance earnings, dividend, stock split, merger, or tender information to analysts, whether representing an institution, brokerage house, investment advisor, large shareholder, or anyone else, would clearly violate Exchange policy. On the other hand, it should not withhold information in which analysts or other members of the investment public have a warrantable interest.
>
> If during the course of a discussion with analysts substantive material not previously published is disclosed, that material should be simultaneously released to the public.

Listing Rule 202.02 clearly reflects the nature of the ongoing tensions that arise in corporate disclosure spheres when companies that are obliged to report publicly also meet with analysts, investors and other stakeholders privately on a regular basis. While the rule states that information should not be given to one inquirer that is not given to another, it also indicates that mandated reports and disclosures cannot provide all of the data that should be available to the investing public. The nature of the additional data that should be publically available, but which is not presently included in mandated reports and disclosures, is not identified or discussed within the NYSE Listed Company Manual. While these ambiguities are potentially problematic, the continuous disclosure obligations in the US are supported by Regulation Fair Disclosure (Reg FD).[36] Under Reg FD, a listed company that chooses to disclose material information to one group of investors must also disclose this information publicly. Reg FD applies to closed-door meetings, conference calls with analysts, and any situation where material information is communicated, verbally or in writing.[37] Companies, or those acting on a company's behalf, are prohibited from selectively disclosing material non-public information to securities industry professionals, institutional investors, and specified other persons.[38]

---

36. United States Securities Exchange Commission, Final Rule: *Selective Disclosure and Insider Trading* (2000).
37. United States Securities Exchange Commission, Final Rule: *Selective Disclosure and Insider Trading* (2000).
38. United States Securities Exchange Commission, Final Rule: *Selective Disclosure and Insider Trading* (2000).

Finally, the corporate governance requirements imposed on companies listed on the NYSE are generally stricter than in other jurisdictions.[39] Section 303A of the NYSE Listed Company Manual contains the corporate governance rules, and many of these rules are mandatory. For example, Listing Rule 303A.01 requires companies to have a majority of independent directors unless an exception applies,[40] and a nominating/corporate governance committee[41] and a compensation committee must be composed entirely on independent directors.[42] Listed companies must also adopt and disclose a code of business conduct and ethics for directors, officers and employees.[43] Further, they must have and maintain a publicly accessible website.[44]

§5.04 EMPIRICAL EVIDENCE

[A] Case Studies

The public disclosures of two large listed companies were reviewed to illustrate the nature and scope of public corporate information provided in the US. As software and financial services are two of the most prominent industries, the companies chosen for review were Microsoft Corporation and Citigroup Inc.

[1] Microsoft Corporation

Microsoft Corporation (Microsoft) is a large global software company. The Microsoft website is an excellent example of how companies can use their websites to present their 'story'.[45] The content for investors is extensive and includes long-term financial performance data and trends for periods of more than twenty years. All of the financial reports and earnings material are easy to find and quick to download. This data is provided in pre-populated spreadsheets, allowing everybody that wishes to engage in detailed fundamental analysis to work from equivalent sets of numbers. These numbers and trends are usefully summarised in charts and graphs and are supported by long-term KPI numbers and unit volumes.

39. See New York Stock Exchange Listed Company Manual, 'Section 3 Corporate Responsibility', viewed 15 August 2015 http://nysemanual.nyse.com/LCMTools/PlatformViewer.asp?selectednode=chp%5F1%5F4%5F3&manual=%2Flcm%2Fsections%2Flcm%2Dsections%2F.
40. The definition of independence is outlined in Listing Rule 303A.02 of the New York Stock Exchange Listed Company Manual. The exceptions to this rule are outlined in the introduction to Listing Rule 303A.
41. Listing Rule 303A.04 of the New York Stock Exchange Listed Company Manual. The exceptions to this rule are outlined in the introduction to Listing Rule 303A.
42. Listing Rule 303A.05 of the New York Stock Exchange Listed Company Manual. The exceptions to this rule are outlined in the introduction to Listing Rule 303A.
43. Listing Rule 303A.10 of the New York Stock Exchange Listed Company Manual. The exceptions to this rule are outlined in the introduction to Listing Rule 303A.
44. Listing Rule 307.00 of the New York Stock Exchange Listed Company Manual.
45. Microsoft Corporation, 'Microsoft Investor Relations', viewed 20 May 2015, http://www.microsoft.com/investor/default.aspx.

The periodic reports of Microsoft are also well presented and focused. These reports seek to present the group's financial position and prospects and are squarely aimed at shareholders. The MD&A provided in the full year and quarterly reports is methodical and coherent, and is framed around the financial statements, with detailed notes and explanation of the reported numbers. There are no pictures in these reports and the form, headings and content are similar from year to year. The commentary is carefully tailored and framed, and this author found it readable, informative and engaging.

The quarterly result material on the website for the third quarter of 2015 includes an outlook section.[46] This section provides a clearly labelled table with the projected revenue growth by segment, gross margin and cost levels, likely restructuring costs, tax rate, and expected capital expenditure and unearned revenue for the final quarter of 2015. This is the type of detailed information that analysts often seek from companies privately, so its public disclosure reduces potential instances of selective disclosure.

[2] Citigroup Inc

Citigroup Inc (Citigroup) is a large global financial group. The information in the Ctigroup's 10-K reports is extensive and logically presented. The initial pages contain an executive summary with some five year financial data. The pages dealing with risk management are clear and they encompass specific global developments and issues. The financial results are explained in detail. Further, the report on the EDGAR website has interactive data, allowing the report components to be downloaded as Excel spread sheets.

The Citigroup 2012 global citizenship report includes a key performance indicator table with metrics across the focus areas for periods up to eight years.[47] Long-term performance data and trends are essential for CSR and sustainability reports to provide useful information to stakeholders, given the long-term nature of many of the goals and plans involved.

46. Microsoft Corporation, 'Earnings Release FY15 Q3', viewed 20 May 2015, http://www.microsoft.com/investor/EarningsAndFinancials/Earnings/PressReleaseAndWebcast/FY15/Q3/default.aspx.
47. Citigroup Inc, *2012 Global Citizenship Report* 4-11.

CHAPTER 6
Canada

> Confidence in the capital markets requires confidence in the accuracy of the information that companies disclose about their business activities. Timely, accurate and complete financial statements are the core of good disclosure practice. In disclosure cases, the victims are typically company shareholders. Continuous disclosure programmes undertaken by ... [Canadian regulators] aim to ensure that investors have accurate and timely information about public companies on which to base their investment decisions.[1]

§6.01 OVERVIEW

Canada does not have a federal securities regulatory authority. While there is broad consensus among policy makers, practitioners and scholars on the benefits of a national securities scheme, endeavours to find a valid constitutional basis for such a scheme are still to be resolved.[2] Each province and territory has a securities commission or equivalent authority, and these ten provincial and three territorial governments work together to coordinate and harmonise regulation of the Canadian capital markets through the Canadian Securities Administrators (CSA).[3]

Most of the securities commissions operate under a passport system that allows for mutual recognition of decisions in the other provinces and territories. The passport

1. Canadian Securities Administrators, *Canadian Securities Administrators 2012 Enforcement Report* 25.
2. On 22 December 2011 the Supreme Court of Canada held that a draft proposed Canadian Securities Act would not be valid under the federal trade and commerce power under s. 91(2) of the Constitution: re Securities Act, 2011 SCC 66, [2011] 3 S.C.R. 837. The Supreme Court noted that it had not been asked for its opinion on the extent of Parliament's legislative authority under other heads of federal power, including the interprovincial and international trade branch of s. 91(2). It concluded that a cooperative legislative approach through which the federal and provincial governments exercise their powers collaboratively may be possible. Following this decision, the Canadian government announced that it was exploring how it might establish a national securities regulator with the cooperation of the provinces and territories.
3. See Canadian Securities Administrators, home page, viewed 19 May 2015, http://www.securities-administrators.ca/.

system covers prospectus filings and registration of companies and individuals.[4] Ontario Securities Commission (OSC) is the largest of the provincial regulators.[5] The regulation discussed in this chapter applies to companies listed on the Toronto Stock Exchange (TSX), as Toronto is the largest city in Canada and the provincial capital of Ontario.[6] The TSX is owned by, and operated as a subsidiary of, the TMX Group Ltd (TMX) for the trading of senior equities.[7] On 14 May 2011 Maple Group Acquisition Corp[8] lodged a successful bid to acquire the TMX. This bid encompassed the merger of the TMX with Alpha Group, an alternative trading system founded by a group of Canadian banks and the Canadian Pension Plan Investment Board.[9]

§6.02 PERIODIC REPORTS

Periodic and continuous disclosure obligations in Ontario are governed by state securities legislation. Listed companies must file annual and interim financial statements with the OSC. Non-venture companies must file an annual report within ninety days of the financial year-end and venture companies must file within 120 days.[10] A reporting issuer must also file interim financial statements for each three month period during a reporting year. The interim statements are due within forty-five days of the end of the interim period for non-venture companies and within sixty days for venture companies.[11] While the national instrument governing this reporting is entitled 'Continuous Disclosure Obligations', the type of disclosure this instrument prescribes is periodic reporting. The rules require summary financial data for three years within the annual report, including the following line items: revenue; income or loss before discontinued operations and extraordinary items; net income or loss, in total and on a per share and diluted per share basis; total assets; total long-term financial liabilities;

4. Ontario Securities Commission decides on a case-by-case basis whether to accept the decisions of the other provincial regulators.
5. See Ontario Securities Commission, home page, viewed 19 May 2015, http://www.osc.gov.on.ca/en/home.htm. The Ontario Securities Commission (OSC) is an independent Crown corporation that is responsible for regulating the capital markets in Ontario. Its statutory mandate is to 'provide protection to investors from unfair, improper or fraudulent practices and to foster fair and efficient capital markets and confidence in capital markets'.
6. TMG Group Limited, 'Toronto Stock Exchange', viewed 19 May 2015, http://www.tsx.com/?lang=en.
7. Companies may list on either the TSX or the TSX venture exchange (TSXV).
8. The Maple group included four of Canada's largest banks – Toronto Dominion Bank, National Bank of Canada, Canadian Imperial Bank of Commerce and Bank of Nova Scotia, and pension funds from the provinces of Ontario, Quebec and Alberta.
9. See, e.g., Pav Jordan and Claire Sibonney, 'Canada Banks Propose TMX Deal To Rival LSE Bid', *Reuters.com* 14 May 2011; Tom Steinert-Threlkeld, 'LSE Faces Counterbid for TMX Group', *Securitiestechnologymonitor.com* (16 May 2011). On 1 August 2012, TMX Group Limited completed the acquisitions of CDS and Alpha Trading Systems Inc and Alpha Trading Systems Limited Partnership (collectively, Alpha). On 14 September, TMX Group Limited completed the acquisition of TMX Group Inc (collectively the Maple Transaction): TMX Group Limited, *2014 Annual Report* 11.
10. National Instrument 51-102 *Continuous Disclosure Obligations* 4.2. Venture issuers must file within 120 days of year-end.
11. National Instrument 51-102 *Continuous Disclosure Obligations* 4.4. Venture issuers must file within sixty days of the period end.

and cash dividends per share.[12] There are also specialist disclosure requirements for venture companies,[13] companies with mineral projects[14] and companies with oil and gas activities.[15] Similarly, the TSX listing rules include tailored periodic disclosure requirements and standards for listed companies engaged in mineral exploration, development and/or production.[16]

The MD&A in the annual reports must provide 'analysis of a company's financial condition, results of operations and cash flows.'[17] At a minimum, the analysis must address the following areas: operating segments, industry and economic factors affecting company performance, why changes in financial conditions or results occurred or did not occur, and the effects of discontinued operations.[18] It must discuss the business segment revenue drivers, significant factors, cost of sales, factors causing changes in the gross and net margins, commitments, risks and uncertainties, inflationary impacts, use of working capital and unusual or infrequent events or transactions. It must also provide analysis of the company's liquidity, capital resources, off-balance sheet arrangements, transactions with related parties, proposed transactions, critical accounting estimates, and financial instruments.[19] The required MD&A in the interim reports is more limited. Companies must provide analysis of the current quarter and year-to-date operations and cash flows, changes in results not related to ongoing business operations, and seasonal aspects affecting the results, operations or cash flow.[20]

Public companies and investment funds in Canada are required to file all public securities documents and information with CSA using the System for Electronic Document Analysis and Retrieval (SEDAR).[21] The periodic reports of listed companies are therefore stored and retrievable from an independent central facility.

§6.03 CONTINUOUS DISCLOSURE

A company listed on the TSX is required to immediately disclose material information concerning its business and affairs when management becomes aware of it or when it becomes apparent that the information is material.[22] Section 406 of the TSX Company Manual states that it is:

12. Form 51-102F1 Management's Discussion and Analysis 1.3.
13. See, e.g., Form 51-102F1 Management's Discussion and Analysis 5.3.
14. Form 51-102F2 Annual Information Form 5.5.
15. Form 51-102F2 Annual Information Form 5.4.
16. Toronto Stock Exchange, *TSX Company Manual* Appendix B.
17. National Instrument 51-102 *Continuous Disclosure Obligations* Part 5; Form 51-102F1 Management's Discussion and Analysis.
18. National Instrument 51-102 *Continuous Disclosure Obligations* Part 5; Form 51-102F1 Management's Discussion and Analysis.
19. Form 51-102F1 Management's Discussion and Analysis 1.4-1.14.
20. Form 51-102F1 Management's Discussion and Analysis 2.2.
21. SEDAR, home page, viewed 19 May 2015, http://www.sedar.com/homepage_en.htm.
22. Toronto Stock Exchange, *TSX Company Manual*, s. 408, viewed 19 May 2015, http://tmx.complinet.com/en/display/display_main.html?rbid=2072&element_id=1. Section 408 initially uses the 'forthwith' but in the next sentence explains that 'immediate' release of

> a cornerstone policy of the Exchange that all persons investing in securities listed on the Exchange have equal access to information that may affect their investment decisions. Public confidence in the integrity of the Exchange as a securities market requires timely disclosure of material information concerning the business and affairs of companies listed on the Exchange, thereby placing all participants in the market on an equal footing.[23]

Section 407 of the TSX Company Manual indicates that each listed company is responsible for determining what information is material and would result in, or would reasonably be expected to result in, a significant change in the market price or value of any of the company's listed securities. Section 407 does not include a reasonable person test. Instead, it notes that the 'company itself is in the best position to apply the definition of material information to its own unique circumstances.'

Company announcements must be provided to CNW Group, a newswire service provider endorsed by the TSX for news release distribution, and these announcements are made available from the TSX website.[24] The public announcements must be factual and balanced and they must contain sufficient detail to enable media personnel and investors to appreciate 'the true substance and importance of the information so that investors may make informed investment decisions.'[25] Suggested examples of developments likely to require disclosure include '[f]irm evidence of significant increases or decreases in near-term earnings prospects.'[26] The TSX policy statement on timely disclosure indicates that forecasts of earnings are not required but 'where a significant increase or decrease in earnings is indicated in the near future, such as in the next fiscal quarter, this fact must be disclosed.'[27] Further, when forecasts are disclosed, they must be disclosed to the public and not provided on a selective basis to some investors.[28]

The TSX indicates in its policy statement on timely disclosure that it enforces its own rules,[29] but its enforcement powers are limited to suspension or delisting of a company's securities.[30] The market surveillance section of the TMX maintains a continuous stockwatch programme which is designed to identify unusual market activity, such as unusual price and volume changes in a stock relative to its historical pattern of trading.[31] At the time of writing, details of enforcement actions involving company disclosure matters could not be found on the TSX or TMX websites.

The TSX continuous disclosure rules are supported by various statutory disclosure obligations.[32] Section 75 of the *Securities Act 1990 (Ontario)* requires a company

---

information is necessary. Section 413 states that the 'overriding rule is that significant announcements are required to be released immediately.'

23. Toronto Stock Exchange, *TSX Company Manual*, s. 406.
24. Toronto Stock Exchange, Company Releases, viewed 19 May 2015, http://www.tmxmoney.com/en/news/company_releases/index.html.
25. Toronto Stock Exchange, *TSX Company Manual*, s. 418.
26. Toronto Stock Exchange, *TSX Company Manual*, s. 410.
27. Toronto Stock Exchange, *Policy Statement on Timely Disclosure* 3.
28. Toronto Stock Exchange, *Policy Statement on Timely Disclosure* 3.
29. Toronto Stock Exchange, *Policy Statement on Timely Disclosure* 3.
30. Toronto Stock Exchange, *Continued Listing Committee – Terms of Reference.*
31. Toronto Stock Exchange, *Policy Statement on Timely Disclosure* 4.
32. See, e.g., National Policy 51-201 *Disclosure Standards;* National Instrument 71-102 Continuous Disclosure and Other Exemptions Relating to Foreign Issuers; National Instrument 55-102

to file a report with the OSC when a 'material change' occurs in its affairs 'as soon as practicable and in any event within ten days of the date on which the change occurs.' The specific purposes of the section 75 notifications are not clear, as a reporting timeframe of ten days does not allow informed decision making on a timely basis in modern financial markets.

§6.04 EMPIRICAL EVIDENCE

[A] Regulatory Reviews

The Corporate Finance Branches of the OSC and CSA have well-established company disclosure review and report programmes. The annual review categories used by the OSC and CSA include: no action required; prospective changes; education and awareness; refilings; referral to the Enforcement Branch; the company being added to a default list; and or issuance of a cease trade order.[33] A company may fall within more than one category. The OSC and CSA take a proactive approach by contacting companies to discuss potential filing issues before the companies file their reports. After the filing, the company's disclosure is reviewed to assess whether the issue of concern was disclosed appropriately. The education and awareness category was created in 2008 to help issuers to provide complete, transparent and timely disclosure to their investors. Companies at risk of a specific disclosure issue are contacted to discuss the issue in advance of their next filing. Companies with minor issues are asked to make changes to their disclosures in upcoming filings. Disclosure deficiencies that are considered sufficiently significant to require a refiling result in the company name, the date of refiling, and a description of the deficiency being posted on the relevant website for three years as a deterrent measure.

The review categories reflect a carefully layered regulatory approach. These processes include proactive monitoring and supervisory functions that encompass education, guidance, industry feedback, and identification and discussion of specific risks. Further, the supporting enforcement framework addresses a spectrum of actions, including those requiring only minor regulatory follow-up, and serious offences requiring proper enforcement. This systematic regulatory framework is a reasonable and balanced approach to improve disclosure standards over time. It provides consistent monitoring, feedback and enforcement, and results in an accumulating pool of knowledge and understanding of disclosure content, quality and issues. The annual review reports provide considerable detail on specific disclosure issues identified, including graphs showing outcome trends over the prior three years. This is best illustrated by considering the reviews over a defined period.

The 2009 OCS review examined 436 continuous disclosures and 462 prospectuses and rights offering circulars, with a particular focus on issues arising from the severe

System for Electronic Disclosure By Insiders; National Instrument 62-103 *The Early Warning System and Related Take-Over Bid and Insider Reporting Issues.*

33. Ontario Securities Commission, *Corporate Finance Branch Report* (2009) 7.

market downturn.[34] Of the continuous disclosures reviewed, 46% led to agreed changes to disclosures in upcoming filings. Most of these changes involved correcting deficiencies in the required MD&A. The report highlighted that MD&A should not merely repeat information from the financial statements and that the analysis must be balanced, with negative information presented as clearly as positive news.[35]

In 2009, no action was required on 17% of the continuous disclosures,[36] and 26% of the disclosures were included within the ongoing education and awareness category. More seriously, 9% involved significant deficiencies that required the issuer to restate and refile documents, and 2% resulted in the company being added to the default list, the issuance of a cease trade order, or a referral to the Enforcement Branch.

Across the reviews of the prospectuses and rights offerings, 25% of the documents required no action,[37] while 46% required material disclosure changes to comply with an accounting, legal or other regulatory requirement. A further 10% of the disclosures required correction and refiling of documents or filing a required document not previously filed. Two percent of the reviews resulted in the company changing the structure of the offering. Seventeen percent involved exemptive relief or procedural enhancements as a result of the review. The primary areas of deficiency identified were MD&A, use of proceeds, and risk factor disclosure.

In 2011, the CSA established an annual review programme that examines the disclosures of a sample of listed companies across Canada.[38] The review programme for the 2011 fiscal year used a risk-based screening process to select the companies for review, and to decide whether to review the company in full or to limit the review to specific disclosure issues. A full review examined all of a company's disclosures, including its periodic reports, MD&A, press releases, company website, technical disclosures and material contracts. Nine hundred and nineteen companies were selected for issue-oriented reviews. The specific issues reviewed included: international financial reporting standards (IFRS) transition disclosure; matters requiring CFO and CEO certification; oil and gas technical disclosure; corporate governance disclosure; material contract disclosure; mining technical disclosure; and issues highlighted in complaints to the OSC from investors and other external stakeholders.

The reviews primarily focused on companies that were identified in advance as having a high risk of non-compliance, or company reporting that involved accounting or disclosure issues identified as areas requiring improvement. As a consequence, 70% of the companies reviewed were required to take some form of action.[39] To assist companies with their disclosure obligations, the CSA report includes appendices with specific examples of common deficiencies and guidance on how to improve disclosures. Appendix A highlights deficiencies in the MD&A, including issues relating to the

34. Ontario Securities Commission, *Corporate Finance Branch Report* (2009).
35. Ontario Securities Commission, *Corporate Finance Branch Report* (2009) 14.
36. Ontario Securities Commission, *Corporate Finance Branch Report* (2009) 7–8.
37. Ontario Securities Commission, *Corporate Finance Branch Report* (2009) 9–10.
38. Canadian Securities Administrators, CSA Staff Notice 51-334: *Continuous Disclosure Review Program Activities for the Fiscal Year Ended March 31, 2011* (15 July 2011).
39. Canadian Securities Administrators, CSA Staff Notice 51-334: *Continuous Disclosure Review Program Activities for the Fiscal Year Ended March 31, 2011* (15 July 2011) 2.

use of financial measures that are not calculated in accordance with accounting standards (non-compliant financial measures), the provision of forward-looking information, discussion of operations, liquidity or solvency outlines, quarterly discussion and mining project disclosure. Appendix B provides guidance on the presentation of inventory and related party transactions in financial statements. Appendix C provides specific examples of appropriate disclosure within executive compensation statements.

Appendix A indicates that the MD&A was often boilerplate disclosure that did not change from period-to-period. It suggests discussion of the financial results lacked analysis to enable investors to assess the current position and future prospects of the company.[40] It notes that companies often provide performance discussion in the continuous disclosures that is not compliant with accounting standards, without explanation of why these measures are meaningful, without clear quantitative reconciliation to the numbers in the financial statements, and with items described as non-recurring even when the items had occurred in the last two years or were likely to recur within the next two years.[41] Appendix A emphasises that forward-looking information should be clearly identified and that disclosure of both the material facts and assumptions, including the risk factors, must be provided.[42] It indicates that discussion of operations should analyse and quantify all material variances from the prior year. It highlights that disclosure of liquidity variability is especially important when companies have negative cash flows and advises companies that they should disclose any defaults or risk of defaults on debt covenants.[43]

The CSA review programme for the 2012 fiscal year included a targeted review focused on the first IFRS half year financial reports.[44] While compliance was better than expected, approximately 5% of companies were required to refile their financial statements due to basic IFRS transition issues.[45] More generally, issuers were required to take action to improve disclosure in 56% of the outcomes;[46] 9% were included in the education and awareness category; 28% were classified as requiring prospective changes; 17% were required to refile, and 2% were referred to the enforcement area or included on the default list.[47] The most common MD&A deficiency was a lack of clear

40. Canadian Securities Administrators, CSA Staff Notice 51-334: *Continuous Disclosure Review Program Activities for the Fiscal Year Ended March 31, 2011* (15 July 2011) 8 Appendix A MD&A Deficiencies.
41. Canadian Securities Administrators, CSA Staff Notice 51-334: *Continuous Disclosure Review Program Activities for the Fiscal Year Ended March 31, 2011* (15 July 2011) 8–9.
42. Canadian Securities Administrators, CSA Staff Notice 51-334: *Continuous Disclosure Review Program Activities for the Fiscal Year Ended March 31, 2011* (15 July 2011) 9.
43. Canadian Securities Administrators, CSA Staff Notice 51-334: *Continuous Disclosure Review Program Activities for the Fiscal Year Ended March 31, 2011* (15 July 2011) 10.
44. Canadian Securities Administrators, CSA Staff Notice 51-337: *Continuous Disclosure Review Program Activities for the Fiscal Year Ended March 31, 2012* (19 July 2012).
45. Canadian Securities Administrators, CSA Staff Notice 51-337: *Continuous Disclosure Review Program Activities for the Fiscal Year Ended March 31, 2012* (19 July 2012) 1.
46. Canadian Securities Administrators, CSA Staff Notice 51-337: *Continuous Disclosure Review Program Activities for the Fiscal Year Ended March 31, 2012* (19 July 2012) 2.
47. Canadian Securities Administrators, CSA Staff Notice 51-337: *Continuous Disclosure Review Program Activities for the Fiscal Year Ended March 31, 2012* (19 July 2012) 2–3.

labelling and identification of accounting principles.[48] Appendix B highlights the issues of boilerplate disclosure repeated from period-to-period and commentary that replicates disclosure from the financial statements without including proper analysis. It calls for analysis and quantification of all material variances.[49] More specific issues identified include incomplete or inadequate disclosure of required mineral project information,[50] incomplete executive compensation statements,[51] and inadequate disclosure of corporate governance practices.[52]

The CSA review programme for the 2013 fiscal year included 368 full reviews and 968 issue-oriented reviews.[53] Issues detailed and discussed in the appendices include deficiencies in the financial statements and MD&A. Appendix A outlines examples and discusses disclosure of management judgments, impairment of goodwill, and going concern statements.[54] One of the entity-specific examples considers the production stage of a mine. An impairment of goodwill example involves allocation of goodwill across business units, descriptions of the key assumptions supporting the cash flow projections, and the management's approach to determining the values assigned to each unit. The issues highlighted in Appendix A with respect to going concern assumptions discuss the need for managers to explain how they plan to resolve issues when the entity's ability to continue as a going concern are in doubt.[55] Appendix B highlights deficiencies in the disclosure areas of liquidity, operations, and related party transactions. The CSA points out that the MD&A should explain how a company will meet its obligations as they become due, how any deficiencies will be addressed, the factors that contribute to changes in its operations, and details of any related party transactions.[56] Appendix C focuses on disclosure regarding mineral projects, oil and

48. Canadian Securities Administrators, CSA Staff Notice 51-337: *Continuous Disclosure Review Program Activities for the Fiscal Year Ended March 31, 2012* (19 July 2012) 4.
49. Canadian Securities Administrators, CSA Staff Notice 51-337: *Continuous Disclosure Review Program Activities for the Fiscal Year Ended March 31, 2012* (19 July 2012) 12 Appendix B.
50. Canadian Securities Administrators, CSA Staff Notice 51-337: *Continuous Disclosure Review Program Activities for the Fiscal Year Ended March 31, 2012* (19 July 2012) 15 Appendix C; National Instrument 43-101, *Standards of Disclosure for Mineral Projects* (NI 43-101).
51. Canadian Securities Administrators, CSA Staff Notice 51-337: *Continuous Disclosure Review Program Activities for the Fiscal Year Ended March 31, 2012* (19 July 2012) 15–16 Appendix C; Form 51-102F6, *Statement of Executive Compensation* (Form 51-102F6).
52. Canadian Securities Administrators, CSA Staff Notice 51-337: *Continuous Disclosure Review Program Activities for the Fiscal Year Ended March 31, 2012* (19 July 2012) 18 Appendix C; Form 58-101F1, *Corporate Governance Disclosure*; Form 58-101F2, *Corporate Governance Disclosure (Venture Issuer)*.
53. Canadian Securities Administrators, CSA Staff Notice 51-339: *Continuous Disclosure Review Program Activities for the Fiscal Year Ended March 31, 2013* (18 July 2013).
54. Canadian Securities Administrators, CSA Staff Notice 51-339: *Continuous Disclosure Review Program Activities for the Fiscal Year Ended March 31, 2013* (18 July 2013) 6–10.
55. Canadian Securities Administrators, CSA Staff Notice 51-339: *Continuous Disclosure Review Program Activities for the Fiscal Year Ended March 31, 2013* (18 July 2013) 6–10.
56. Canadian Securities Administrators, CSA Staff Notice 51-339: *Continuous Disclosure Review Program Activities for the Fiscal Year Ended March 31, 2013* (18 July 2013) 11–13.

gas activities, and ventures. The deficiencies highlighted include incomplete, inadequate and non-compliant disclosure of mandated items under the disclosure standards for mineral projects and oil and gas activities.[57]

The CSA review programme for the 2014 fiscal year included 221 full reviews and 770 issue-oriented reviews.[58] While the number of companies reviewed was lower than in prior years, the reviews of the selected companies were more comprehensive. The aim of the 2013 review was 'to monitor quality of disclosure, observe trends and conduct research,'[59] with an objective to obtain 'more substantive outcomes.'[60] These more detailed reviews resulted in a much higher level of outcomes, requiring an issuer to take action to improve the disclosure, a referral to enforcement, or placement on the default list. The proportion of company reviews requiring some form of future action was 76% in 2014 compared to 47% in 2013. The largest review outcome in 2014 was the 'prospective changes' category requiring the issuer to make amendments when it next files. The primary areas of observed deficiencies included:

- financial statement measurement and disclosure (such as going concern, accounting policies, critical judgments, sources of estimation uncertainty and fair value measurement);
- compliance with executive compensation disclosure rules, particularly the compensation discussion and analysis;
- business acquisition reports; and
- the recurring issue of compliance with the MD&A rules (such as financial measures not in accordance with accounting standards, forward-looking information, and discussion of operations, liquidity, related party transactions, etc).[61]

Appendix A provides examples of good disclosure of interests in other entities, revenue recognition, and impairment of assets. Appendix B highlights MD&A deficiencies. It notes that 'MD&A should help current and prospective investors to understand what the financial statements show and do not show.'[62] It highlights that financial measures that do not comply with accounting standards are often found in public documents, including in MD&A, announcements, company websites and marketing material. It notes that even commonly used non-compliant financial measures, such as earnings before interest, tax, depreciation and amortisation (EBITDA), are often

57. Canadian Securities Administrators, CSA Staff Notice 51-339: *Continuous Disclosure Review Program Activities for the Fiscal Year Ended March 31, 2013* (18 July 2013) 15–16.
58. Canadian Securities Administrators, CSA Staff Notice 51-341: *Continuous Disclosure Review Program Activities for the Fiscal Year Ended March 31, 2014* (17 July 2014). This report is not paginated.
59. Canadian Securities Administrators, CSA Staff Notice 51-341: *Continuous Disclosure Review Program Activities for the Fiscal Year Ended March 31, 2014* (17 July 2014) 6663.
60. Canadian Securities Administrators, CSA Staff Notice 51-341: *Continuous Disclosure Review Program Activities for the Fiscal Year Ended March 31, 2014* (17 July 2014) 6663.
61. Canadian Securities Administrators, CSA Staff Notice 51-341: *Continuous Disclosure Review Program Activities for the Fiscal Year Ended March 31, 2014* (17 July 2014) 6663.
62. Canadian Securities Administrators, CSA Staff Notice 51-341: *Continuous Disclosure Review Program Activities for the Fiscal Year Ended March 31, 2014* (17 July 2014) 6663 Appendix B.

inconsistent and that adjustments are often made 'to make the metric look more positive.'[63] An example is provided of an EBITDA measure that excludes impairment, restructuring and foreign exchange changes.[64]

Appendix C highlights concerns regarding the disclosure of mineral projects and executive compensation, and the filing of news releases and material change reports. It notes that news releases and announcements of material changes should be factual, balanced and timely. It advises that issuers 'should avoid including unnecessary details, exaggerated reports or promotional commentary.'[65] It indicates that too many issuers file news 'when the timing may be inappropriate and or the content of the report is inadequate.'[66] It reminds issuers that disclosures should contain enough information for readers to understand the substance and importance of changes.[67]

The CSA review of annual disclosures is supported by state-based reviews. For example, the OSC reviewed disclosures of forward-looking information in 2012.[68] The review defined 'forward-looking information' as 'disclosure about events, conditions or financial performance that is based on assumptions about future economic conditions and courses of action.'[69] The review report notes that while disclosure of forward-looking information is not mandatory, investors increasingly want 'transparent and clear disclosure about present and future corporate operations and performance.'[70] The review identified four areas for improvement:

(1) clear identification of forward-looking information;
(2) disclosure of the underlying material factors or assumptions;
(3) updates to forward-looking information; and
(4) discussion of actual results following disclosure of forward-looking information or estimates.[71]

The report indicates that assumptions should be 'reasonable, supportable and entity specific' and it suggests that, where possible, the assumptions should be

63. Canadian Securities Administrators, CSA Staff Notice 51-341: *Continuous Disclosure Review Program Activities for the Fiscal Year Ended March 31, 2014* (17 July 2014) 6663 Appendix B.
64. Canadian Securities Administrators, CSA Staff Notice 51-341: *Continuous Disclosure Review Program Activities for the Fiscal Year Ended March 31, 2014* (17 July 2014) 6663 Appendix B.
65. Canadian Securities Administrators, CSA Staff Notice 51-341: *Continuous Disclosure Review Program Activities for the Fiscal Year Ended March 31, 2014* (17 July 2014) 6663 Appendix B.
66. Canadian Securities Administrators, CSA Staff Notice 51-341: *Continuous Disclosure Review Program Activities for the Fiscal Year Ended March 31, 2014* (17 July 2014) 6663 Appendix B.
67. Canadian Securities Administrators, CSA Staff Notice 51-341: *Continuous Disclosure Review Program Activities for the Fiscal Year Ended March 31, 2014* (17 July 2014) 6663 Appendix B.
68. Ontario Securities Commission, *Forward-Looking Information Disclosure* (OSC Staff Notice 51-721, 13 June 2013).
69. Ontario Securities Commission, *Forward-Looking Information Disclosure* (OSC Staff Notice 51-721, 13 June 2013) 6.
70. Ontario Securities Commission, *Forward-Looking Information Disclosure* (OSC Staff Notice 51-721, 13 June 2013) 4, 7.
71. Ontario Securities Commission, *Forward-Looking Information Disclosure* (OSC Staff Notice 51-721, 13 June 2013) 3.

quantified.[72] It outlines a range of examples of boilerplate disclosure and preferred entity-specific disclosure. The report indicates that only a third of companies reviewed provided an assessment of actual results compared to previously-disclosed prospective information and guidance. It notes that comparative analysis is 'important for investors in their assessment of the effectiveness of management and of the current and future business performance.'[73] It promotes timely updating of ongoing progress as compared to previously disclosed guidance and the use of financial and non-financial KPIs. It suggests that companies present forward-looking information in reports in a separate section, including a table that sets out the company's objectives, specific assumptions and risks.[74]

[B] Case Studies

Two of the largest industry sectors traded on the TSX are financial services and resources, so the companies selected for review were the Royal Bank of Canada and Teck Resources Limited.

[1] Royal Bank of Canada

The Royal Bank of Canada (RBC) is Canada's largest bank measured by market capitalisation and assets. RBC is listed on the TSX and has a foreign issuer listing on the NYSE. The investor material on the RBC website and in the periodic reports is well organised and layered to some extent. For example, a short executive summary titled 'RBC at a Glance' highlights the group's results for the quarter, including overviews of the company and business segments, the group's key strategic goals, financial highlights including segmental and geographical results, and the shareholder performance trends for the prior five quarters.[75] The MD&A section in the 2012 annual report is clearly presented and the use of headings, sections and bold type enhances readability. Key events during the year are outlined and the results are explained and compared to defined financial performance targets. A performance overview is provided, including segmental and geographic reporting. Reporting of the business segments includes outlook and priority commentary. The assumptions used in the management-reporting framework are explained, including the relevant performance measures and calculation methodologies. The section on risk management is extensive, including the main risk categories and risk processes. The RBC 2014 annual report includes a ten year financial performance table with balance sheet and income statement items, profitability measures, key ratios, share information and capital measures.

72. Ontario Securities Commission, *Forward-Looking Information Disclosure* (OSC Staff Notice 51-721, 13 June 2013) 11.
73. Ontario Securities Commission, *Forward-Looking Information Disclosure* (OSC Staff Notice 51-721, 13 June 2013) 18.
74. Ontario Securities Commission, *Forward-Looking Information Disclosure* (OSC Staff Notice 51-721, 13 June 2013) 20.
75. Royal Bank of Canada, 'Quarterly Information', viewed 24 May 2015, http://www.rbc.com/investorrelations/quarterly-financial-statements.html.

The broader RBC website is also well presented. Novel content includes economics pages that provide research on the economy, financial markets, Canadian housing, key indicators, forecasts and special reports.[76] This information provides valuable context for assessing the performance and prospects of the company, and of the banking sector, and may be of interest to various groups including investors, regulators, employees, and researchers. The corporate responsibility reporting (CRR) is readable and engaging. Useful content includes a summary CRR document, reports for specific stakeholders including an environmental report card, a carbon disclosure statement, a diversity progress report, and a public accountability statement. Interestingly, the 2012 CRR explains the purpose and intended audience of the bank's reporting and communication framework. It notes that the content in the CRR is not provided elsewhere and is intended for a wide audience, including socially responsible investors, employees, non-governmental organisations (NGOs), regulators, government officials and corporate responsibility practitioners.[77] It indicates that the group website is intended to meet the day-to-day information needs of 'the majority of consumers, employees, clients, NGOs, community partners, students, and corporate responsibility practitioners.'[78] It suggests that the intended audience of the annual and quarterly reports, the annual information form, and the management proxy circular is much narrower, with the target groups limited to investors, analysts and regulators.[79] This was the only material found by the author that discussed or explained a company's reporting structure, its aims and intended audience.

[2] Teck Resources Limited

Teck Resources Ltd (Teck) is a diversified resource company headquartered in Vancouver. Teck is listed on the TSX and has a foreign issuer listing on the NYSE. The Teck 2012 annual report includes tonnages, the five-year production record and expected share of production for 2013, and the average commodity prices and exchange rates. It also provides estimated production tonnages and exchange rate sensitivity analysis. Similarly, the outlook statement in the 2014 annual report includes production estimates and a sensitivity table showing the estimated effect of changes in commodity prices and the US dollar exchange rate. Historical and forecast production data and sensitivity tables are needed for outsiders to assess the likely impact of key factors on the company's businesses.

The report for the first quarter of 2015 includes informative MD&A that explains the impact of various factors on the results, including segmental, product, volume, pricing and expense details. It includes commentary on the use of non-compliant

76. Royal Bank of Canada, 'Economics', viewed 24 May 2015, http://www.rbc.com/economics/index.html.
77. Royal Bank of Canada, *2012 Corporate Responsibility Report and Public Accountability Statement* 22.
78. Royal Bank of Canada, *2012 Corporate Responsibility Report and Public Accountability Statement* 22.
79. Royal Bank of Canada, *2012 Corporate Responsibility Report and Public Accountability Statement* 22.

financial measures, reasons why the company uses these measures and why they are useful to investors, and tables that reconcile these measures to the reported numbers. Further, it provides an outlook statement that discusses the external environment and the likely impact of key factors. This type of content is important to assess the company's position and prospects.

The Teck 2012 sustainability report usefully categorises the company's community investment beyond the scope of normal business operations as philanthropic investment, community and infrastructure development, or commercial initiative.[80] It also indicates that the company had established medium-term sustainability goals through to 2015 and longer-term goals until 2030.[81] Long-term sustainability goals and plans are critical features of business and reporting frameworks that seek to determine and capture the creation of 'value' holistically, especially for resource companies with long project cycles.

80. Teck Resources Ltd, *Teck 2012 Sustainability Report* 35–36. The group's stated aim is to donate 1% of annual pre-tax earnings to community investments, on a rolling average basis.
81. Teck Resources Ltd, *Teck 2012 Sustainability Report* 15.

CHAPTER 7
Germany

> The European and German legislators are continuing their efforts towards strengthening the integrity of the capital market. The focus is on investor confidence in functioning capital markets. This confidence can be achieved through strong investor protection, notably through greater transparency on the part of capital market participants. In this connection, market participants have to be able to rely on ad hoc ... notifications being clear, informative and accurate as well as accounting standards being observed.[1]

§7.01 OVERVIEW

[A] The European Union

Market Abuse and Transparency Directives were adopted and implemented by the European Commission (EC) in 2004.[2] The Transparency Directive (TD), which includes the primary disclosure obligations, applies to listed companies trading on a regulated market.[3] The EC began a review of the TD in 2009.[4] After a curious series of twists and turns, the TD was amended in October 2013.[5] The prior TD was a 'minimum harmonisation directive' that allowed EU Member States to impose additional requirements. However, the amended TD prohibits Member States from imposing a requirement in their national legislation to publish periodic financial information more

1. Bafin, *Issuer Guideline* (14 May 2009) 21, viewed 7 April 2015, http://www.bafin.de/SharedDocs/Downloads/EN/Leitfaden/dl_Emittentenleitfaden_2009_en.html.
2. Directive 2004/109/EC. See Europa.eu, 'Transparency of Information about Issuers of Securities', http://europa.eu/legislation_summaries/internal_market/single_market_services/financial_services_transactions_in_securities/l22022_en.htm#.
3. European Parliament Directive 2013/50/EU amending European Transparency Directive 2004/109/EC and European Commission Directive 2003/71/EC.
4. See European Commission, Report from the Commission Staff Working Paper Impact Assessment (SEC (2011) 1280 final). See also Mazars, *Transparency Directive Assessment Report 90*, viewed 17 April 2013. http://www.mazars.co.uk/Home/News/Our-publications/General-publications/Transparency-Directive-Assessment-Report.
5. European Parliament, Directive 2013/50/EU amending 2004/109/EC and Directive 2003/71/EC.

frequently than on a half yearly basis. Member States are only permitted to require companies to publish additional financial information if this is not financially burdensome and the information is proportionate to factors influencing investment decision making.[6]

The TD amendments came into force on 26 November 2013 and Member States have two years to implement the changes.[7] The amendments to the TD abolish the requirement to publish interim management statements (IMSs) or quarterly reports, and extend the deadline for publishing half yearly reports to three months after the end of the reporting period. The stated rationale for these amendments is to 'make regulated markets more attractive to small and medium issuers raising capital in the Union.'[8] It is claimed that the obligations to publish IMSs encourage short-term performance and discourage long-term investment, thereby representing 'an important burden ... without being necessary for investor protection.'[9]

Regulated information must be disseminated using processes that ensure the information is accessible to as wide an audience as possible, with the timing of release across Europe as close to simultaneous as possible.[10] The Amending Directive notes that access to financial information on listed companies is difficult because interested parties must go through twenty-seven national databases. Although there is no centralised public repository of listed company disclosures in Europe presently,[11] the Amending Directive indicates that the EC proposes to develop technical standards to enable a pan-European access point to regulated information.[12]

[B] Germany

Frankfurter Wertpapierbörse (FWB® or the Frankfurt Stock Exchange) is the largest of Germany's seven stock exchanges, with a turnover share of more than 85%.[13] The FWB is operated by Deutsche Börse AG, a German public company.[14] The FWB operates a tiered market, and companies that wish to list on a European regulated

6. European Parliament, Directive 2013/50/EU amending 2004/109/EC and Directive 2003/71/EC, [5-6]. See also Official Journal of the European Union Volume 56, 6 November 2013 L294/14.
7. Official Journal of the European Union Volume 56, 6 November 2013 L294. See also Linklaters, *UK Corporate Update*, viewed 19 May 2015, http://www.linklaters.com/Insights/Publication1005Newsletter/Index/Pages/Transparency-Directive-amendments.aspx
8. European Parliament, Directive 2013/50/EU amending 2004/109/EC and Directive 2003/71/EC, [2].
9. European Parliament, Directive 2013/50/EU amending 2004/109/EC and Directive 2003/71/EC, [4].
10. Directive 2004/109/EC Art. 21(1); Implementation of certain provisions of Directive 2004/109/EC, Art. 12(2), visited 7 April 2015, http://eur-lex.europa.eu/legal-content/EN/TXT/?uri=CELEX:32007L0014.
11. European Commission, Revised Directive on Transparency Requirements for Listed Companies (Transparency Directive) - Frequently Asked Questions, Memo/13/544 4.
12. European Commission, COM (2011) 683 final 2011/0307(COD) Amending Directive 2004/109/EC& 2007/14/EC, 8.
13. Deutsche Borse Group, *Corporate Report 2013* 16, available at http://deutsche-boerse.com/dbg/dispatch/en/binary/gdb_content_pool/imported_files/public_files/10_downloads/12_db_annual_reports/2013/Annual_Report_2013.pdf.
14. See Deutsche Borse Group, *Annual Report 2013*.

market can elect to list on the main board under either a General or Prime Standard, or may raise capital under an exchange regulated unofficial market with an entry standard listing.[15]

The Trading Surveillance Office (TSO) is an independent supervisory body of the FWB responsible for monitoring market activity, including suspicious trading.[16] The TSO notifies the supervisory bodies and management boards of the exchange of any irregularities. The Sanctions Committee of the FWB may impose fines and or exclude participants from the exchange for up to thirty days.[17] The Exchange Supervisory Authorities (ESAs) are responsible at state level for supervision of the Exchange Act (Borsengesetz) including 'pricing processes, the supervision of the proper conduct of trading as well as the investigations of violations of the Exchange Act.'[18] The ESAs may impose sanctions on market participants in addition to those imposed by a disciplinary committee or the management boards of an exchange including the FWB.[19]

The Federal Financial Supervisory Authority (BaFin) monitors listed company compliance with the Securities Trading Act (Wertpapierhandelsgesetz - WpHG) and is responsible for monitoring and enforcing the rules governing insider trading, market manipulation, ad hoc notifications, and financial reporting.[20] The annual financial statements are monitored for compliance with the law by the German Financial Reporting Panel (Deutsche Prufstelle fur Rechnungslegung DPR e.V) on a random sample basis or at the request of BaFin.[21] The condensed financial statements and IMSs are subject to examination with cause. Any supervisory or enforcement measures are initiated by BaFin.[22]

---

15. The entry standard is intended to provide small-to-medium sized companies with an easy, fast and cost-effective way to list their shares for exchange trading.
16. Deutsche Borse Group, 'The Proper Conduct of Trading Within the Exchanges is Monitored by Market Surveillance', viewed 19 March 2014, https://deutsche-boerse.com/dbg/dispatch/en/kir/dbg_nav/about_us/20_FWB_Frankfurt_Stock_Exchange/40_Supervisory_Bodies.
17. Deutsche Borse Group, 'The Proper Conduct of Trading Within the Exchanges is Monitored by Market Surveillance', viewed 19 March 2014, https://deutsche-boerse.com/dbg/dispatch/en/kir/dbg_nav/about_us/20_FWB_Frankfurt_Stock_Exchange/40_Supervisory_Bodies.
18. Deutsche Borse Group Supervisory Bodies, 'The Proper Conduct of Trading Within the Exchanges is Monitored by Market Surveillance', viewed 19 March 2014, https://deutsche-boerse.com/dbg/dispatch/en/kir/dbg_nav/about_us/20_FWB_Frankfurt_Stock_Exchange/40_Supervisory_Bodies.
19. Deutsche Borse Group, 'The Proper Conduct of Trading Within the Exchanges is Monitored by Market Surveillance', viewed 7 April 2015, https://deutsche-boerse.com/dbg/dispatch/en/kir/dbg_nav/about_us/20_FWB_Frankfurt_Stock_Exchange/40_Supervisory_Bodies.
20. Deutsche Borse Group, 'The Proper Conduct of Trading Within the Exchanges is Monitored by Market Surveillance', viewed 19 March 2014, https://deutsche-boerse.com/dbg/dispatch/en/kir/dbg_nav/about_us/20_FWB_Frankfurt_Stock_Exchange/40_Supervisory_Bodies.
21. BaFin, 'Financial Reporting Enforcement', viewed 7 April 2015, http://www.bafin.de/EN/Supervision/StockExchangesMarkets/FinancialReportingEnforcement/financialreportingenforcement_node.html.
22. BaFin, 'Financial Reporting Enforcement', viewed 7 April 2015, http://www.bafin.de/EN/Supervision/StockExchangesMarkets/FinancialReportingEnforcement/financialreportingenforcement_node.html.

§7.02 PERIODIC REPORTS

The periodic reporting provisions of the TD are legislated in section 37v–37z of the WpHG. Pursuant to these provisions, the annual report must include audited financial statements, a management report, a responsibility statement, and an auditor certificate of registration.[23] The annual report must be made available to the public within four months of the financial year-end.[24] Companies are required to provide a corporate governance report that indicates whether they have complied with the corporate governance code.[25] Companies may deviate from the code recommendations but any deviations must be explained in the report.[26]

The half year report must be made available to the public within two months of the relevant reporting period.[27] This report must contain a condensed set of financial statements, an interim management report, and a responsibility statement.[28] The condensed financial statements must include a condensed balance sheet, a condensed profit and loss account, and notes.[29] The IMS must contain information on how the company has performed during the period, including an explanation of material events and transactions and their impact on the financial position, and a descriptive outline of the company's financial position and performance during the period covered.[30]

The statutory periodic reporting obligations applying to listed companies are enhanced by the exchange disclosure listing rules. A company listed on the FWB under the Prime Standard is generally required to produce half year and quarterly financial statements in German and English in accordance with international accounting standards. These reports must be provided to the Management Board electronically within two months of the end of the reporting period.[31] These companies must provide an updated financial calendar on their Internet websites in German and English, including the dates of the annual general meeting, the press conferences and analysts meetings.[32] These companies are also required to conduct an analysts meeting at least once a year in order to 'announce the figures from the annual accounts.'[33]

---

23. Wertpapierhandelsgesetz [WpH] [German Securities Trading Act], 26 July 1994, Federal Law Gazette at § 37v(2).
24. Wertpapierhandelsgesetz s. 37v(1).
25. Government Commission, German Corporate Governance Code (as amended 5 May 2015)).
26. Government Commission, German Corporate Governance Code (as amended 5 May 2015) 2–3.
27. Wertpapierhandelsgesetz s. 37w(1).
28. Bafin, *Issuer Guideline* (14 May 2009) 7, viewed 7 April 2015, http://www.bafin.de/SharedDocs /Downloads/EN/Leitfaden/dl_Emittentenleitfaden_2009_en.html.
29. Wertpapierhandelsgesetz s. 37w(2).
30. Wertpapierhandelsgesetz s. 37x(2). The provisions relating to interim management statements were still in force when the legislation was viewed on 7 April 2015.
31. Frankfurter Wertpapierborse, *Exchange Rules for the Frankfurter Wertpapier Borse* (16 December 2013) s. 51. An issuer that has its offices in a non-EU country or outside a contractual country of the Treaty on the European Economic Area must submit the half year and quarterly financial statements to the Management Board in electronic form within three months after end of the respective reporting period.
32. Frankfurter Wertpapierborse, *Exchange Rules for the Frankfurter Wertpapier Borse* (16 December 2014) s. 52.
33. Frankfurter Wertpapierborse, *Exchange Rules for the Frankfurter Wertpapier Borse* (16 December 2014) s. 53.

§7.03 CONTINUOUS DISCLOSURE

Directive 2003/124/EC of the European Parliament was introduced in Europe in 2003 to deter market abuse, including the use of company information that is not publicly available.[34] BaFin notes that the ad hoc disclosure requirements in the EC are intended to provide all participants with access to key information and to prevent insider trading.[35] In Germany, these obligations are enacted in section 15 of the WpHG, which requires companies that are listed on a regulated market to publish inside materially price-sensitive information without undue delay.[36] These notifications must be released through an electronic information dissemination system and the media.[37] Information is considered to be inside information when it would likely have a significant effect on securities prices. Materiality assessments are conducted from a reasonable investor perspective and consider the likelihood that such an investor would use the information when making investment decisions.[38] This reasonable person test is appraised on the *ex ante* available information.[39] It takes into consideration 'the anticipated impact of the information in light of the totality of the related issuer's activity, the reliability of the source of information and any other market variables likely to affect the related financial instrument.'[40] The listing rules of an exchange in Germany may impose higher continuous disclosure standards than those in the WpHG. For example, a company listed on the FWB under the Prime Standard must provide ad hoc disclosures in both German and English.[41]

§7.04 EMPIRICAL EVIDENCE

[A] Case Studies

The FWB includes companies with diverse industrial interests, so the companies selected for review were Siemens AG, a global industrial company, and Deutsche Bank, the largest financial institution in Germany.

[1] Siemens AG

Siemens AG (Siemens) describes itself as an integrated technology company. Siemens is listed on the FWB and on the NYSE as a foreign issuer. The Siemens website provides

34. 'Europa Summaries of Legislation', 'Market Abuse', viewed 19 May 2015, http://europa.eu/legislation_summaries/internal_market/single_market_services/financial_services_transactions_in_securities/l24035_en.htm.
35. Bafin, *Issuer Guideline* (14 May 2009) 45.
36. Bafin, *Issuer Guideline* (14 May 2009) 45.
37. Bafin, *Issuer Guideline* (14 May 2009) 74.
38. Official Journal of the European Union, Implementing Directive 2003/6/EC, L339/70. Art. 1 Directive 2003/6/EC.
39. Official Journal of the European Union, Implementing Directive 2003/6/EC, L339/70.
40. Official Journal of the European Union, Implementing Directive 2003/6/EC, L339/70.
41. Frankfurter Wertpapierborse, *Exchange Rules for the Frankfurter Wertpapier Borse* (16 December 2014) s. 54.

consensus figures that include estimated orders by segment, revenue, profits, restructure charges, reconciliation items, and consolidated net income and earnings per share figures for the next quarter and for the fiscal 2015 and 2016 years.[42] The structure of this prospective information is noteworthy because listed company public guidance rarely includes estimated orders and forecast restructuring charges and reconciliation items.

[2] Deutsche Bank AG

The Deutsche Bank share information web pages provide the name of analysts covering the company and a consensus document. At the time of review, a consensus document dated 12 May 2015 included forecast income statements, balance sheets, ratios and per share data for the next quarter and for 2015, 2016 and 2017. The minimum, maximum and average figures and the number of forecasts included in the consensus figures are also provided for each line item.[43] Once again, this integrated prospective information is well structured for detailed financial analysis of the company.

42. Siemens, 'Siemens Global Website Investor Relations', viewed 25 May 2015, http://www.siemens.com/entry/cc/en/. These pages are in English, but links to equivalent websites in German are provided.
43. Deutsche Bank, 'Analysts and Earnings Estimates', viewed 26 May 2015, https://www.db.com/ir/en/content/analysts.htm.

CHAPTER 8
The United Kingdom

> Some basic safeguards that help reduce investment risk include confidence that the board and management will: (1) release timely and reliable information about the company, so as to allow shareholders to react to changing circumstances; (2) deliver on stated strategy and performance targets; (3) take decisions in the interests of all investors .... It follows that well-governed, transparent companies that can demonstrate the above safeguards present a lower risk proposition for investors, and will therefore benefit from lower cost of capital and a more loyal shareholder base.[1]

§8.01 OVERVIEW

The London Stock Exchange (LSE) operates a tiered public market structure. The Main Market exists for more established and larger companies, the Alternative Investment Market (AIM) operates for small and medium sized companies,[2] and the Depositary Receipt Scheme enables international companies outside of the European Union to list and raise capital.[3] The disclosure requirements of AIM listed companies are less onerous than those that apply to the Main Market.[4]

The Financial Conduct Authority (FCA) is empowered to act as the UK Listing Authority (UKLA).[5] As such, the FCA supervises and enforces the LSE listing rules, including the reporting and disclosure rules.[6] The FCA Handbook includes a block entitled 'Listing, Prospectus and Disclosure United Kingdom Listing Authority rules'.[7]

---

1. London Stock Exchange, *Corporate Governance For Main Market and Aim Companies* 47.
2. London Stock Exchange, *A Guide to Aim* (2010) 4.
3. London Stock Exchange, *Guide To Listing Depositary Receipts* 6.
4. London Stock Exchange, *A Guide to Aim* (2010) 60–64.
5. Financial Conduct Authority, Listing Rules (March 2015) 1.1.1. The prior Financial Services Authority was split into the Financial Conduct Authority and the Prudential Regulation Authority on 1 April 2013: see Financial Conduct Authority, 'History of the FCA', viewed 28 January 2015, http://www.fca.org.uk/about/history#.
6. Financial Conduct Authority, Listing Rules (March 2015) 1.1.1.
7. Financial Conduct Authority, The Full Handbook, viewed 21 July 2015, http://www.fshandbook.info/FS/html/FCA.

The 'Disclosure Rules and Transparency Rules' (DTR) are provided in seven chapters. Chapter 2 governs disclosure and control of inside information by issuers, Chapter 4 details the periodic reporting rules, Chapter 6 deals with continuing obligations and access to information and Chapter 7 outlines the corporate governance rules.[8]

The FCA has broad powers with respect to potential or actual breaches of the listing rules. It may suspend the listing of a company's securities if required for the smooth operation of the market or if 'necessary to protect investors.'[9] When a company that has issued securities fails to comply with its obligations under Part 6 of the *Financial Services and Markets Act 2000* (UK), the company, or persons connected with the company, may be subject to an appropriate penalty.[10] At the time of writing, there were no suspensions or delistings for violations of the disclosure listing rules on the FCA website.[11] The only action on the website concerning listed company disclosure matters involved a failure to notify the market of share dealings by persons discharging managerial responsibilities.[12]

§8.02 PERIODIC REPORTS

The periodic reports in the UK include an annual financial report that must be made public within four months following the end of a financial year.[13] This report includes audited financial statements, a management report, and a responsibility statement.[14] DTRs 4.1.8 and 4.1.9 state that the management report must provide balanced and comprehensive analysis of the company's business developments and position.[15] Further, the review must provide performance analysis using key financial performance indicators and an explanation of the amounts included in the financial statements to enable readers to understand company developments, performance and position.[16] However, the type and scope of performance analysis and financial explanation are not prescribed and there is no requirement to provide historical performance data for years earlier than the reporting period and the prior year. Listed companies must include a corporate governance statement in the directors' report or as a separate report,[17] and this statement must detail any departure from the corporate governance code and explain the reason/s behind the departure.[18]

---

8. Financial Conduct Authority, Disclosure Rules and Transparency Rules (DTR), viewed 21 July 2015, http://www.fshandbook.info/FS/html/FCA/DTR.
9. Financial Conduct Authority, Listing Rules, s. 5.1.1; *Financial Services and Markets Act 2000* (UK) s 77(2).
10. *Financial Services and Markets Act 2000* (UK) s. 91.
11. Financial Conduct Authority, 'Enforcement', viewed 31 January 2015, http://www.fca.org.uk/firms/being-regulated/enforcement.
12. Financial Conduct Authority, 'Search Results', viewed 7 April 2015, http://www.fca.org.uk/your-fca/list?ttypes = Final + Notice&ssearch = listing + rules&yyear = . The UK Listing Authority imposed a financial penalty of UKP 539,800 on Reckitt Benckiser Group Plc.
13. DTR 4.1.3.
14. DTR 4.1.5.
15. DTR 4.1.8 and DTR 4.1.9.
16. DTR 4.1.9.
17. DTR 7.2.1; DTR 7.2.9.
18. DTR 7.2.3.

The DTRs and Listing Rules do not require companies to release preliminary full year statements prior to the release of the annual report.[19] When companies elect to do so, the statement must be published as soon as possible after it has been approved by the board; the statement must be agreed with the company's auditors; the figures in the financial accounts must be in a form consistent with the presentation to be used in the annual accounts; and the statement must highlight any expected auditor issues.[20] The content of the preliminary final statement must include 'any significant additional information necessary for the purpose of assessing the results being announced,' but the manner in which this information is included is discretionary.[21] Listed companies are required to operate a company website, but there are no rules requiring listed companies to provide public access to briefings or to release copies of briefing presentations or slides.

Listed companies must publish a half year financial report within two months of the end of the period.[22] The half year reports must include a condensed set of financial statements, an interim management report, and responsibility statements.[23] The content of the half yearly management reports must provide a summary outline of important events and their impact on the financial statements. They must also outline the principal risks and uncertainties.[24] The headings must be consistent with those presented in the most recent annual financial statements,[25] and additional line items are required where their omission would give a misleading view. Comparable figures are required for the prior year.[26]

§8.03 CONTINUOUS DISCLOSURE

The disclosure obligations that apply between reporting periods are contained in Chapter 2 of the FCA Handbook entitled 'Disclosure and control of insider information by issuers'. DTR 2.2.1 provides that 'An issuer must notify a Regulatory Information Service (RIS) as soon as possible of any inside information which directly concerns the issuer unless DTR 2.5.1 applies.' DTR 2.2.4 notes that companies should apply the reasonable investor test to determine whether information is inside information. This requires assessing whether the relevant information would be used by a reasonable investor when making investment decisions and would be likely to have a significant effect on the price of the company's securities. DTR 2.2.6 indicates that such an assessment should consider the expected impact of the information taking into account the totality of the company's activities and circumstances. It notes that information that is likely to be relevant to a reasonable investor's decision includes information that affects 'the performance, or the expectation of the performance' of the company's

19. DTR 9.7A.
20. DTR 9.7A.
21. DTR 9.7A.
22. DTR 4.2.2.
23. DTR 4.2.3.
24. DTR 4.2.7.
25. DTR 4.2.5.
26. DTR 4.2.5.

business. DTR 2.5.6 requires an issuer that intentionally discloses any inside information to a third person to simultaneously make complete and effective public disclosure of that information.

The exception in DTR 2.5.1 allows a delay in the public disclosure of inside information when omission would not be likely to mislead the public, any person receiving the information owes a duty of confidentiality to the relevant issuer, and the issuer is able to ensure its confidentiality. DTR 2.5.3 notes that it is legitimate to delay public disclosure where the outcome of negotiations would likely be affected. In particular, public disclosure can be delayed if it might undermine negotiations aimed at ensuring a company's long-term viability. However, DTR 2.5.4 states that 'an issuer [cannot] delay public disclosure of the fact that it is in financial difficulties or of its worsening financial condition.' The permitted delay is limited to the fact or substance of negotiations.

§8.04 EMPIRICAL EVIDENCE

[A] Case Studies

Oil, financial services and retailing are important sectors represented on the LSE. Accordingly, the two companies selected for review were BP Plc and Sainsbury Plc.

[1] BP Plc

BP Plc (BP) is a large global oil company, with a primary listing on the LSE and a listing on the NYSE as a foreign issuer. One of the quick links from the home page of BP provides access to a trading conditions page. This page explains that the 'trading conditions update is produced in order to provide disclosure to investors and potential investors of current trading conditions, and to ensure that they all receive equal access to the same information, at the same time.'[27] This is a novel practice that should be emulated by other companies and warrants praise.

The BP 2014 sustainability report is coherently structured and is reasonably engaging. A five year performance table outlines the key indicators across the areas of safety, the environment, people and performance. The focus area commentary outlines 'what we said we would do', 'where we are today' and 'what we plan to do next', with varying degrees of specificity. These headings and outlines within the performance commentary are clear and focused. Performance sections within all listed company financial reports, corporate social responsibility reports and sustainability reports should adopt a similar approach.

27. BP, 'Trading Conditions Update', viewed 26 May 2015, http://www.bp.com/extendedsection genericarticle.do?categoryId = 9016864&contentId = 7030494.

[2] J Sainsbury Plc

J Sainsbury Plc (Sainsbury) is a major UK retailer that provides a range of ancillary services, including financial services. The Sainsbury website was reviewed in 2013 and again in 2015. During this period, the content and presentation of the sustainability pages improved significantly. These web pages provide case studies, fact sheets and general information on the company's approach, values and progress, and the organisations with which it engages.[28] The 'our approach' pages explain how the group manages its sustainability commitments and provide a business case for sustainability. They explain how the governance structures at board and operating levels assist to direct and implement their sustainability plan. The 2014 sustainability report lists twenty specific goals across the focus areas to be achieved by 2020. These goals are well connected to the group businesses and likely stakeholder sustainability concerns.[29] The report structure and content are clear and informative.[30] Progress achieved is summarised in a performance table that outlines the specific commitments and progress during each of the last three years. The remainder of the report explains these achievements in more detail.

The Sainsbury 'analyst consensus' page indicates that the company seeks to keep the figures updated and consistent, but notes that it is under no obligation to do so.[31] It also notes that the company has not commented on any of the individual forecasts and that it does not intend to do so in future. These explicit statements on the company's approach to sell-side analyst estimates should be followed as standard practice on listed company websites.

28. J Sainsbury plc, 'Responsibility', viewed 28 May 2015, http://www.j-sainsbury.co.uk/responsibility/.
29. Importantly, the sustainability targets are sufficiently clear and specific for all stakeholders to assess the priorities and performance of the company.
30. Sainsbury, *Our 20 Sustainability Commitments To Help Us All Live Well For Less – An Update On Our Progress So Far*, 1 June 2015, available at http://www.j-sainsbury.co.uk/investor-centre/reports/2014/20x20-sustainability-plan-2014-update/.
31. J Sainsbury plc, 'Analyst Consensus', viewed 31 May 2015, http://www.j-sainsbury.co.uk/investor-centre/analyst-consensus/.

CHAPTER 9
Japan

> A financial instruments market functions to contribute to the development of the national economy through the proper and efficient connection of asset management via securities by the public and stable, long-term fund-raising via the issue of securities by companies. In order for a market to fulfil this role, it is vital to maintain investors' confidence in the fairness and soundness of the market, as well as provide appropriate information on securities required for investment decisions.[1]

§9.01 OVERVIEW

Japan has six stock exchanges.[2] These six organisations are self-regulatory with oversight from the Securities and Exchange Surveillance Commission (SESC).[3] The SESC operates within the Financial Services Agency, an external organ of the Cabinet Office.[4] It describes itself as the 'Guardian of the Market' with a 'primary role in maintaining fair, equitable, transparent, and sound markets through exerting its authority of daily market surveillance, inspection of financial instruments business operators, investigation of market misconduct, disclosure statements inspection and criminal investigation.'[5] One of the specific responsibilities of the SESC is to inspect

1. Japan Exchange Group, 'Timely Disclosure', viewed 28 June 2015, http://www.jpx.co.jp/english/equities/listing/disclosure/.
2. There are stock exchanges in Tokyo, Osaka, Nagoya, Fukuoka and Sapporo, as well as the Jasdaq Securities Exchange.
3. Securities and Exchange Surveillance Commission, 'English home page', viewed 29 June 2015, http://www.fsa.go.jp/sesc/english/index.htm.
4. Securities and Exchange Surveillance Commission, 'History of the SESC', viewed 29 June 2015, http://www.fsa.go.jp/sesc/english/aboutsesc/01.pdf.
5. Securities and Exchange Surveillance Commission, 'The SESC's Efforts', viewed 29 June 2015, http://www.fsa.go.jp/sesc/english/aboutsesc/actions.htm.

company reports and disclosure statements.[6] It may recommend to the FSA commissioner to issue an order to impose administrative monetary penalties.[7] The SESC is also responsible for ensuring the exchanges comply with their obligations, including their supervisory and enforcement roles. It supports the supervisory and enforcement roles of the exchanges by independently monitoring market trends. Suspicious transactions are identified and investigated for possible misconduct including insider trading, market manipulation, and false statements.[8]

On 1 January 2013, Japan Exchange Group, Inc. (JPX) was established via a business combination between the Tokyo Stock Exchange Group and the Osaka Securities Exchange.[9] The Tokyo Stock Exchange, Inc (TSE) is a cash equities market and Osaka Exchange, Inc is a derivatives market.[10] JPX is responsible for monitoring its members and ensuring compliance with the listing rules and relevant legislation.[11] The self-regulatory operations at JPX are divided into two main areas: issuer compliance and member compliance. The issuer compliance area investigates and examines the suitability of existing and potential listed issuers and products. The issuer compliance area is subdivided into two further areas: listing eligibility and listed company compliance.[12] The member compliance area supervises trading and ensures proper conduct in the market.[13]

The Listed Company Compliance Department (Compliance Department) is responsible for examining listed company compliance with the disclosure regulation.[14] The Compliance Department conducts examinations regarding violations of the timely disclosure rules and deficiencies in the internal management systems of listed companies.[15] When these examinations find evidence that a company's systems for handling information are not adequate or are non-compliant with the rules, the JPX may warn the company, put its securities on alert or require the company to submit an improvement report. It may also impose a listing agreement violation penalty.[16] If the company does not make improvements within the specified period, it may be

6. Securities and Exchange Surveillance Commission, 'The SESC's Efforts', viewed 29 June 2015, http://www.fsa.go.jp/sesc/english/aboutsesc/actions.htm.
7. Securities and Exchange Surveillance Commission, 'The SESC's Efforts', viewed 29 June 2015, http://www.fsa.go.jp/sesc/english/aboutsesc/actions.htm.
8. Securities and Exchange Surveillance Commission, 'The SESC's Efforts', viewed 29 June 2015, http://www.fsa.go.jp/sesc/english/aboutsesc/actions.htm.
9. Japan Exchange Group, 'About JPX', viewed 7 April 2015, http://www.jpx.co.jp/english/corporate/about-jpx/about-jpx/index.html.
10. Japan Exchange Group, 'About JPX', viewed 7 April 2015, http://www.jpx.co.jp/english/corporate/about-jpx/about-jpx/index.html.
11. Japan Exchange Regulation, 'About JPX-R', viewed 31 January 2015, http://www.jpx.or.jp/en/about/index.html.
12. Japan Exchange Group, 'Ensuring Sound Market Operations', viewed 7 April 2015, http://www.jpx.co.jp/english/regulation/ensuring/index.html.
13. Japan Exchange Group, 'Outline of Self-Regulatory Corporation Activities', viewed 7 April 2015, http://www.jpx.co.jp/english/regulation/outline/index.html.
14. Japan Exchange Group, 'Listed Company Compliance', viewed 7 April 2015, http://www.jpx.co.jp/english/regulation/ensuring/listing/compliance/index.html.
15. Japan Exchange Group, 'Listed Company Compliance', viewed 7 April 2015, http://www.jpx.co.jp/english/regulation/ensuring/listing/compliance/index.html.
16. Japan Exchange Group, 'Listed Company Compliance', viewed 7 April 2015, http://www.jpx.co.jp/english/regulation/ensuring/listing/compliance/index.html.

delisted.[17] Investigation findings may also be reported to the SESC.[18] When companies are disciplined for non-compliant conduct, the details are outlined on the exchange website to enhance corporate disclosure standards and market transparency more generally.[19] At the time of writing, ten companies were listed on the JPX website as having violated their listing agreement.[20] The public announcements web page lists the reminders issued by the JPX to listed companies for inappropriate disclosure during the period from 2003 to the present.[21] It also includes twenty-five public announcement actions during the period January 2011 until April 2015, with many of these actions involving misstatements of financial items.[22]

§9.02 PERIODIC REPORTS

Company reporting in Japan is governed by two legal codes: the *Companies Act* and the *Financial Instruments and Exchange Act* (FIEA). The *Companies Act* applies to all companies, while the FIEA is limited to public companies.[23] The Financial Services Authority (FSA) is responsible for disclosures under the FIEA, and the Ministry of Justice regulates disclosures under the *Companies Act*. Listed companies must file financial statements with the FSA, including an annual report with an internal control report and a statement of cash flow, and quarterly reports with financial statements that have been reviewed by a certified public accountant or an audit corporation.[24] The Commissioner of the FSA may impose a penalty and or require the submission of amended financial statements.[25]

A securities exchange may impose additional disclosure requirements on its listed issuers. For example, the TSE requires companies to issue preliminary full year reports to ensure timely periodic disclosure, but does not mandate the content and form of these reports.

17. Japan Exchange Group, 'Listed Company Compliance', viewed 7 April 2015, http://www.jpx.co.jp/english/regulation/ensuring/listing/compliance/index.html.
18. The Financial Supervisory Agency and the SESC were split off from the Ministry of Finance in June 1998: Securities and Exchange Surveillance Commission, *SESC Brochure* (October 2012) 2.
19. See Tokyo Stock Exchange, 'Listed Company Information', viewed 31 January 2015, http://www.tse.or.jp/english/listing/index.html.
20. See Japan Exchange Group, 'Public Announcement Measure', viewed 7 April 2015, http://www.jpx.co.jp/english/listing/stocks/public-announce/01.html.
21. See Japan Exchange Group, 'Public Announcement Measure', viewed 7 April 2015, http://www.jpx.co.jp/english/listing/stocks/public-announce/01.html.
22. See Japan Exchange Group, 'Public Announcement Measure', viewed 7 April 2015, http://www.jpx.co.jp/english/listing/stocks/public-announce/01.html.
23. Companies Act, No. 86 of 2005, Art. 435(2) (Japan) requires all companies to provide a business report and non-consolidated financial statements. Larger companies are also required to prepare consolidated financial statements. While there are differences between the two sets of regulation, the requirements have converged following a series of revisions. See Japanese Institute of Certified Public Accountants, *Corporate Disclosure in Japan Overview* (6th ed., 2010) 13.
24. See Japanese Institute of Certified Public Accountants, *Corporate Disclosure in Japan Overview* (6th ed., 2010) 6, 13–14. Page 3 notes that a quarterly reporting system was introduced in in order to enhance its disclosure.
25. Japanese Institute of Certified Public Accountants, *Corporate Disclosure in Japan Overview* (6th ed., 2010) 6, 13–14.

§9.03 CONTINUOUS DISCLOSURE

The continuous disclosure rules (referred to as the 'timely disclosure rules') are governed by the Securities Listing Regulations (SLR) of the TSE.[26] Rule 402 of the SLR requires companies to disclose details of specified items immediately. The items requiring disclosure include decisions by listed companies, various factors or events, earnings information, amendments to performance estimates, dividend estimates or amendments to such estimates, and equivalent information relating to subsidiaries.[27] Compliance guidelines published by the TSE state that disclosure of corporate information is examined for its timeliness, accuracy, completeness, balance, and appropriateness.[28]

A company announcements service in English was established in 2011 to enhance communications between listed companies and overseas investors, with announcements posted on the English website of the TSE for thirty-one days.[29] Use of this service by listed companies is voluntary.

§9.04 EMPIRICAL EVIDENCE

[A] Case Studies

Two of the largest sectors represented on the TSE are banks and electrical appliances, so the two companies chosen for review were Sumitomo Mitsui Financial Group and Sony Corporation.

[1] Sumitomo Mitsui Financial Group

Sumitomo Mitsui Financial (Sumitomo) is the largest financial services group in Japan. Sumitomo has a primary listing on the TSE and is listed on the NYSE as an American Depositary Receipt. The preliminary final report for the year to 31 March 2012 includes five-year consolidated and non-consolidated financial statements with notes. The management pages include targeted indices for the core Tier one ratio, profitability metrics, an overseas banking ratio, a high-level strategic statement, and issues to be addressed. Further, the operating and financial review includes an earnings forecast and outlook statement for the next year. This combined long-term performance data, specific KPIs, and prospective information provides a set of information that should be included within all best practice disclosure frameworks. This reporting is supported by additional performance analysis on the company website. The profile pages on the

26. Japan Exchange Group, Securities Listing Regulations (1 July 2014), viewed 7 April 2015, http://www.jpx.co.jp/english/rules-participants/rules/regulations/index.html.
27. Japan Exchange Group, 'Corporate Information Required for Timely Disclosure', viewed 7 April 2015, http://www.jpx.co.jp/english/rules-participants/rules/regulations/index.html.
28. Tokyo Stock Exchange Inc, *Guidelines Governing Listed Company Compliance* (16 July 2013) 1.
29. Japan Exchange Group, 'Company Announcements', visited 7 April 2015, http://www.jpx.co.jp/english/listing/disclosure/index.html.

Sumitomo website include a message from top management with an update and progress on achievement of key financial metrics.[30]

[2] Sony Corporation

Sony Corporation (Sony) has a primary listing on the TSE and is listed on the NYSE as an American Depositary Receipt. The Sony quarterly reports for 2012 refer to the annual earnings forecast, and explain whether it remains unchanged or has been revised. For example, the report for the third quarter of 2012 noted that the forecast remained unchanged, but an announcement on 25 April 2013 (clearly labelled as a 'forecast revision') indicated that the annual forecast had been revised upwards.[31] Similarly, the result material for the third quarter of 2014 includes an outlook statement with specific forecasts and this forecast is updated in a forecast revision announcement. Sony also provides regular earnings guidance and updates. These reporting processes are commendable, as they provide clear and unambiguous forecasts and regular updates on a consistent basis.

As discussed further in Chapter 13, empirical studies across major developed financial markets consistently confirm that listed companies regularly seek to avoid, delay or disguise public disclosure of negative news. Yet, it is during periods of stress that investors and stakeholders most need clear and balanced public disclosure and communication. The Sony website includes a statement from the President and CEO during a corporate strategy meeting on 18 February 2015.[32] This statement provides an admirably frank appraisal of the performance over the first three years of the restructuring plan, why the performance targets were not achieved, and the revised vision, specific plans and financial targets for the next three years.

30. Sumitomo Mitsui Financial Group, 'Message from Top Management', viewed 1 June 2015, http://www.smfg.co.jp/english/aboutus/message.html.
31. Sony Group, 'Investor Relations', viewed 29 June 2013, http://www.sony.net/SonyInfo/IR/financial/fr/index.html.
32. Sony Corporation, 'Corporate Strategy Meeting', viewed 1 June 2015, http://www.sony.net/SonyInfo/IR/info/strategy/.

CHAPTER 10
Hong Kong

> Developments that strengthen our markets and make them more effective and efficient are to be welcomed. But those that can intensify systemic risk or disadvantage a certain segment of investors to the benefit of others raise concerns ... perhaps it is time to return to basics and remind ourselves of the true function of financial markets. Computer-generated liquidity is already affecting real liquidity and altering trading activity. We run the risk of having it all just being a mathematical playground for the few to the detriment of many. A piecemeal approach seems inadequate to these vast changes. Perhaps a more fundamental reassessment of how to achieve the right balance between humans and technology in the financial field is called for. We need to focus on what really adds economic value and how to ensure market integrity and fairness.[1]

§10.01 OVERVIEW

The principal regulator of securities markets in Hong Kong is the Securities and Futures Commission (SFC).[2] The SFC is an independent statutory body that was established in 1989 by the *Securities and Futures Commission Ordinance* (SFCO).[3] The SFC comprises four operational divisions; the Corporate Finance Division, the Intermediaries and Investment Products Division, the Enforcement Division, and the Supervision of Markets Division.[4] The Enforcement Division of the SFCO conducts market surveillance to identify possible market misconduct. The SFCO is also responsible for misconduct by licensed intermediaries.

---

1. Ronald Arculli, Chairman Hong Kong Exchange, 'The Role of Exchanges in the New Economic Order', World Federation of Exchanges, viewed 27 June 2015, http://webcache.googleusercontent.com/search?q=cache:http://www.world-exchanges.org/insight/views/role-exchanges-new-economic-order. This website is no longer available but a cached version can still be accessed.
2. Hong Kong Exchange, Introduction to Regulatory Framework, 29 April 2014, https://www.hkex.com.hk/eng/rulesreg/regintro/introreg.htm.
3. Hong Kong Exchange, Introduction to Regulatory Framework, 29 April 2014, https://www.hkex.com.hk/eng/rulesreg/regintro/introreg.htm.
4. Hong Kong Exchange, Introduction to Regulatory Framework, viewed 29 April 2014.

The Hong Kong Exchange (HKEx) owns and operates the only stock exchange in Hong Kong, the Stock Exchange of Hong Kong Limited (HKSE).[5] HKEx is a listed company and the SFC is responsible for regulating the HKEx in relation to conflicts of interest and compliance with the listing rules.[6] The HKSE operates a Main Board and a Growth Enterprise Market (GEM).

The HKSE has a duty under section 21 of the SFCO to ensure, so far as reasonably practicable, an orderly, informed and fair market. The role of the HKSE is closely tied to the development and growth of securities markets in China.[7] The stated mission of HKEx is to 'aim to be the global exchange of choice for our China clients and our international clients seeking China exposure.'[8] Companies that are incorporated in the People's Republic of China are listed on the HKSE as H-share companies.

§10.02 PERIODIC REPORTS

Companies listed on the HKSE Main Board must comply with its disclosure listing rules. They must publish annual reports within four months of the end of a financial year and half year reports must be released within three months of the end of a period.[9] They must also comply with corporate governance standards and practices, or explain why an individual corporate governance standard has not been followed.[10]

Under the HKSE listing rules, the preliminary full year results must be published within three months of the end of a financial year.[11] The required content of these reports is governed by Chapter 4 and Appendix 16 of the Main Board Listing Rules. Companies must include a business review section that includes a fair review of business developments, details of important events, an indication of likely future developments, and any supplemental information necessary for a reasonable appreciation of the results.[12] Additional MD&A is required in the annual report, including segmental information, a risk management outline, and a corporate governance

5. Hong Kong Exchange, Introduction to Regulatory Framework, 29 April 2014, https://www.hkex.com.hk/eng/rulesreg/regintro/introreg.htm. The Stock Exchange of Hong Kong Limited (HKEx) is a wholly owned subsidiary of Hong Kong Exchange.
6. The Securities and Futures Commission imposes obligations on the HKEx under ch. 38 of the Main Board Listing Rules and ch. 36 of the GEM Listing Rules. There is also a Memorandum of Understanding between the SFC, HKEx and the HKSE: Securities and Futures Commission and the Stock Exchange of Hong Kong Limited, *Memorandum of Understanding Governing Listing Matters* (28 January 2003).
7. See Fanpeng Meng, 'A History of Chinese Companies Listing in Hong Kong and Its Implications for the Future' (2011) 11 *Journal of Corporate Law Studies* 243, 265.
8. Hong Kong Exchange, *HKEX Group Strategic Plan 2013-2015* 1.1 available at https://www.hkex.com.hk/eng/exchange/corpinfo/mission/Documents/HKEx_Group_Strategic_Plan.pdf.
9. Hong Kong Stock Exchange Main Board Listing Rules 13.47 and 13.48. Notably companies listed on the Growth Enterprise Market must publish annual and half year reports more quickly than companies on the Main Board and they must publish quarterly reports.
10. Hong Kong Stock Exchange Main Board Listing Rules *Disclosure of Financial Information* Appendix 16 p 31. The Main Board Listing Rules are available at http://www.hkex.com.hk/eng/rulesreg/listrules/mbrules/listrules.htm.
11. Hong Kong Stock Exchange Main Board Listing Rule 13.49.
12. Hong Kong Stock Exchange Main Board Listing Rules, *Disclosure of Financial Information* Appendix 16 ss 45(3)-(4).

report.[13] The financial statements in the annual report must be drawn up in conformity with one of the following three standards: Hong Kong Financial Reporting Standards, International Financial Reporting Standards, or China Accounting Standards for Business Enterprises.[14] Hong Kong Exchanges and Clearing Ltd (HKEC) has an established annual programme that reviews and reports on company disclosures. Its disclosure review reports provide detailed feedback and policy guidance in order to promote high quality disclosure standards.[15]

§10.03 CONTINUOUS DISCLOSURE

Listed companies have continuing disclosure obligations that are intended 'to ensure that all users of the market have simultaneous access to the same information.'[16] Chapter 13 of the HKSE Main Board Listing Rules outlines the circumstances in which a company must disclose information to the public. Price-sensitive information must be publicly announced where there is, or there is likely to be, a false market in the company's securities.[17] The HKSE operates an enquiry system that monitors and picks up unusual movements in security prices or trading volumes.[18] When the system is triggered, the relevant company is asked to confirm whether it is in compliance with its disclosure obligations.

The HKSE operates a disciplinary committee that adjudicates on breaches of some listing rule matters.[19] These disciplinary processes and associated schedule of penalties do not appear to encompass failures to comply with the periodic reporting and continuous disclosure listing rules. At the time of writing, none of the actions shown on the enforcement news page of the exchange involved periodic reporting or continuous disclosure matters.[20] The continuous disclosure listing rules are supported by statutory obligations imposed on listed companies and their directors to disclose inside information as soon as reasonably practical after they become aware of the information.[21] Disclosure is deemed to have been made when the information is

13. *Companies Ordinance 2014* (Hong Kong).
14. Hong Kong Stock Exchange Main Board Listing Rule 4.11 (Accounting Standards). See also Hong Kong Stock Exchange Main Board Listing Rules Appendix 13.
15. See, e.g., Hong Kong Exchanges and Clearing Limited, *Financial Statements Review Programme Report 2009*; Hong Kong Exchanges and Clearing Limited, *Financial Statements Review Programme Report 2010* (August 2010); Hong Kong Exchanges and Clearing Limited, *Financial Statements Review Programme Report 2012* (January 2013).
16. Hong Kong Stock Exchange Main Board Listing Rule 13.03.
17. Hong Kong Stock Exchange Main Board Listing Rule 13.09.
18. Hong Kong Stock Exchange Main Board Listing Rule 13.10.
19. Hong Kong Stock Exchange, 'Disciplinary Procedures', viewed 11 March 2015, http://www.hkex.com.hk/eng/rulesreg/listrules/listdisciplinarypro/disproced.htm.
20. These obligations are monitored and enforced by the Securities and Futures Commission. See Securities and Futures Commission, 'Enforcement News', viewed 21 July 2015, http://www.sfc.hk/edistributionWeb/gateway/EN/news-and-announcements/news/enforcement-news/.
21. Section 307B of the *Securities and Futures Ordinance* provides that:

> A listed corporation must, as soon as reasonably practicable after any inside information has come to its knowledge, disclose the information to the public.

released through the electronic publication system of the exchange.[22] Exceptions to the disclosure requirements include inside information that remains confidential.[23]

§10.04 EMPIRICAL EVIDENCE

[A] Regulatory Reviews

HKEC reviews the company reports on a sample basis each year for compliance with the listing rules and relevant accounting standards. The companies reviewed are selected using a risk-based approach based on impact and probability criteria. A general accounting theme and an industry theme are reviewed each year. The reports of companies within the selected industry are reviewed and the selected accounting issues are examined across the sample companies. The outcomes and key issues identified in the annual reviews are outlined in a public report.[24] The reports for the period 2008–2014 indicate that there were no significant breaches of the listing or accounting rules, but a small number of companies were asked to rectify disclosure items in future reports or their reports were referred to the Financial Reporting Council and or the Hong Kong Institute of Certified Public Accountants for further consideration.[25]

The annual disclosure review reports provide valuable insight on significant and recurring disclosure issues. The general accounting theme for the 2008 review was business combinations and investments in associates and joint ventures and the industry theme was toll road infrastructure projects. The major recommendations included: clearer disclosure of the accounting policies and consolidation method for associates and joint ventures; disclosure of factors resulting in recognition of goodwill; better disclosure of impairment provisioning; more disclosure concerning fair value assessments and financial instrument risks; and more detailed MD&A and clearer descriptions of the approach used to amortise infrastructure assets.[26] The report notes that some companies tended to repeat information from the financial statements in

(2) For the purposes of subsection (1), inside information has come to the knowledge of a listed corporation if—
   (a) information has, or ought reasonably to have, come to the knowledge of an officer of the corporation in the course of performing functions as an officer of the corporation; and
   (b) a reasonable person, acting as an officer of the corporation, would consider that the information is inside information in relation to the corporation.

22. *Securities and Futures Ordinance 2003* (Hong Kong) s 307C(2).
23. *Securities and Futures Ordinance 2003* (Hong Kong) s 307D.
24. Hong Kong Stock Exchange. 'Financial Reporting Matters', viewed 25 February 2013, http://www.hkex.com.hk/eng/rulesreg/listrules/listguid/guidance5.htm.
25. See, e.g., Hong Kong Exchanges and Clearing Limited, *Financial Statements Review Programme Report 2012* (January 2013) 2. The final outcomes of the issues referred to the Financial Reporting Council and/or the Hong Kong Institute of Certified Public Accountants are not detailed.
26. Hong Kong Exchanges and Clearing Limited, *Financial Statements Review Programme Report 2009* 2–3.

narrative form in the MD&A without further explanation or analysis of significant events affecting past and future operations.[27]

The general accounting theme in the 2010 review concerned accounting for financial instruments and the industry theme was companies with a major or principal business of mining activities. The main recommendations were for greater explanation of performance indicators; robust asset impairment review processes; disclosures of the amortisation/depreciation method adopted for mining assets; and disclosure of financial instrument fair value assumptions and methodologies.[28] The report notes that some companies with substantial fluctuations in turnover, operating results and net asset value provided little explanation or discussion. While some companies provided useful performance indicators in the MD&A and five year financial summaries, there was increasing use of financial measures such as EBITDA and adjusted EBITDA without the inclusion of definitions and inconsistent use of such measures.[29] The report recommends that companies expand their MD&A to explain how the reported and prospective financial positions, liquidity and operations have been, or will be, affected. It points out that if performance indicators are presented, the title must be clearly stated, the purpose and usefulness of the indicator must be demonstrated, a definition and calculation formula must be provided, the figures must be reconciled to the financial statement, and any changes in definition or calculation from the prior year must be explained and justified.

The industry theme in the 2011 review was companies whose major or principal business involved property construction or investment in properties. The general accounting theme was segment disclosure. The major recommendations included: additional information to improve understanding of the nature and impact of significant events or material balances and transactions; discussion in the MD&A that is consistent with the financial statements and that provides additional useful narrative; improvements in connected and related party disclosure, disclosure of investment property fair value assumptions and methodologies; and balanced and consistent segment information.

The 2012 review examined the annual, half year and quarterly reports of 120 companies. The industry theme was businesses involved in telecommunications and internet services and the general accounting theme was accounting for goodwill and intangible assets. Major issues identified included the omission of disclosures required in Appendix 16 of the Listing Rules, inadequate explanation of significant events and transactions in the annual and half yearly reports, and less than optimal presentation of financial information not in accordance with accounting standards.[30] The report indicates that some companies failed to disclose the group's liquidity and

27. Hong Kong Exchanges and Clearing Limited, *Financial Statements Review Programme Report 2009* 7.
28. Hong Kong Exchanges and Clearing Limited, *Financial Statements Review Programme Report 2010* (August 2010) 2-3.
29. Hong Kong Exchanges and Clearing Limited, *Financial Statements Review Programme Report 2010* (August 2010) 8-9.
30. Hong Kong Exchanges and Clearing Limited, *Financial Statements Review Programme Report 2012* (January 2013) 2-3.

financial resources and the debt maturity profile. In addition, some omitted explanation or commentary relating to changes in turnover, operating results, net asset values and segment results.[31] Once again, some companies provided a narrative version of the financial statements in the MD&A without providing additional analysis or explanation.[32]

The report notes that only a few of the companies that disclosed financial information not in accordance with accounting standards provided an explanation or a reason for doing so.[33] It recommends that when such financial information is used, it must be clearly distinguished from financial information prepared in accordance with accounting standards, the purpose and usefulness of the information must be explained, a definition and the calculation formula must be provided, there must be a clear quantitative reconciliation with reasons given for adjustments made, any changes in definitions from prior years must be explained, and users must be warned that the information may not be comparable to similarly titled measures.[34] The report emphasises that financial information prepared in accordance with accounting standards is the most important section of the financial reports.[35]

The 2013 review examined the annual, interim and quarterly reports of 120 companies.[36] The selected accounting and industry themes were accounting for impairment of assets and companies with a major or principal business involving power and utilities services. Following the reviews, two cases were referred to the Financial Reporting Council for further investigation of possible accounting and auditing irregularities and one was considered for further enforcement action. Where disclosure issues were viewed as less significant or less material, companies were asked to confirm in writing that future financial reports would be rectified.[37]

The executive summary of the review report notes that issuers were still omitting required disclosures, particularly MD&A to provide a 'better understanding of the nature and impact of significant events or material balances and transactions.'[38] It also highlights issues in relation to proper accounting for complex or material transactions and compliance with rules that apply to impairment of assets. The main body of the review report states that the 'absence of information on significant events leading to

31. Hong Kong Exchanges and Clearing Limited, *Financial Statements Review Programme Report 2012* (January 2013) 11.
32. Hong Kong Exchanges and Clearing Limited, *Financial Statements Review Programme Report 2012* (January 2013) 11.
33. Hong Kong Exchanges and Clearing Limited, *Financial Statements Review Programme Report 2012* (January 2013) 28.
34. Hong Kong Exchanges and Clearing Limited, *Financial Statements Review Programme Report 2012* (January 2013) 29–30.
35. Hong Kong Exchanges and Clearing Limited, *Financial Statements Review Programme Report 2012* (January 2013) 29.
36. Hong Kong Exchanges and Clearing Limited, *Financial Statements Review Programme Report 2013* (February 2014) 2. The Report notes that the Financial Statements Review Programme is separate from the review of disclosures in issuer annual reports that monitor compliance with the Listing Rules.
37. Hong Kong Exchanges and Clearing Limited, *Financial Statements Review Programme Report 2013* (February 2014) 2.
38. Hong Kong Exchanges and Clearing Limited, *Financial Statements Review Programme Report 2013* (February 2014) 2.

material balances and transactions in periodic financial reports may be viewed as non-compliance with the relevant Listing rules or accounting standards.'[39] It notes that effective presentation of information is an essential element of high quality MD&A, including MD&A that is balanced, consistent with information disclosed in other parts of the reports (particular the financial statements) and adequate, particularly with respect to material transactions.[40]

The types of commonly omitted or incomplete disclosures that the report highlights include MD&A on treasury activities, the currencies in which borrowings are made, the levels of fixed interest rate borrowings, comments on segmental performance, employee remuneration details and the methodologies used to calculate gearing ratios.[41] The report discusses issues with the risk disclosures and suggests some companies are providing minimal or boilerplate disclosures on financial risk management.[42] It emphasises that investors and other users 'need to understand what management thinks are the key financial risks and why management thinks that they have [been] adequately managed.'[43] The report also reminds companies that they need to explain the events and circumstances that 'led to the recognition or reversal of impairment losses.'[44] It notes that of the eighteen companies that had suffered losses for three consecutive years or more, only seven explained the reasons for the continued losses and these explanations were brief.[45]

The 2013 review included a specifically designed programme to identify disclosure of financial information that did not comply with international or Hong Kong accounting standards (non-compliant financial information). It found that around 20% of the 120 companies reviewed presented non-compliant financial information in the financial review or MD&A section of their periodic reports. The most common non-compliant financial measures used were EBITDA, adjusted EBITDA, underlying profit and adjusted net income.[46] It found that most of these disclosures were clearly labelled and balanced and the calculation methodology was generally consistent from year to year. However, it noted that only a few companies explained the purpose or reason for using these measures and only half provided reconciliation between the

39. Hong Kong Exchanges and Clearing Limited, *Financial Statements Review Programme Report 2013* (February 2014) 8.
40. Hong Kong Exchanges and Clearing Limited, *Financial Statements Review Programme Report 2013* (February 2014) 8.
41. Hong Kong Exchanges and Clearing Limited, *Financial Statements Review Programme Report 2013* (February 2014) 7.
42. Hong Kong Exchanges and Clearing Limited, *Financial Statements Review Programme Report 2013* (February 2014) 19.
43. Hong Kong Exchanges and Clearing Limited, *Financial Statements Review Programme Report 2013* (February 2014) 19.
44. Hong Kong Exchanges and Clearing Limited, *Financial Statements Review Programme Report 2013* (February 2014) 28.
45. Hong Kong Exchanges and Clearing Limited, *Financial Statements Review Programme Report 2013* (February 2014) 37.
46. Hong Kong Exchanges and Clearing Limited, *Financial Statements Review Programme Report 2013* (February 2014) 40.

non-compliant financial measures presented and the reported figures, the calculation methodologies for specific measures varied across the companies.[47]

The report recommends that power and utilities companies should highlight any legal, regulatory or contractual obligations for decommissioning and site restoration.[48] It notes that operational data on quality of services is beneficial for readers of reports to evaluate the performance and outlook of individual companies. It provides examples of useful data including frequency of network failures, compliance issues, and risk factors in the areas of grid congestion, climate, industry, and competition.[49]

[B] Case Studies

The two companies selected for review were PetroChina Limited and China Mobile, two of the largest companies listed on the HKEx by market capitalisation.

[1] PetroChina Company Limited

PetroChina Company Limited (PetroChina) is a global oil and gas producer and distributor. PetroChina is incorporated in the People's Republic of China with A shares listed on the Shanghai Stock Exchange, H shares listed on the HKEx, and American Deposit Shares representing H shares listed on the NYSE. The PetroChina corporate governance web pages clearly explain the differences in the corporate governance standards and practices for the group and a company listed as a US domestic issuer under the NYSE corporate governance rules.[50] This commentary is important for investors with international equity portfolios and persons engaged in comparative analysis of corporations.

[2] China Mobile Limited

China Mobile Limited (China Mobile) is a Chinese state-owned telecommunication company that was incorporated in Hong Kong in 1997. China Mobile has a primary listing on the HKEx and is listed on the NYSE as a foreign issuer. The China Mobile corporate governance web pages provide well-written commentary on the role and function of directors, shareholder rights, shareholder value and communication, attention to other stakeholders, the board of directors, and the board committees with accompanying descriptions of each committee, its membership, responsibilities, and

47. Hong Kong Exchanges and Clearing Limited, *Financial Statements Review Programme Report 2013* (February 2014) 40–41.
48. Hong Kong Exchanges and Clearing Limited, *Financial Statements Review Programme Report 2013* (February 2014) 36.
49. Hong Kong Exchanges and Clearing Limited, *Financial Statements Review Programme Report 2013* (February 2014) 38. This author could not find any subsequent reports.
50. Petrochina Company Limited, 'Corporate Governance Structure', viewed 2 June 2015, http://www.petrochina.com.cn/ptr/gszljg/gszljg.shtml.

work done in 2014. They also explain the role of management and employees, the internal and external audit and control frameworks, and the differences between the company's corporate governance processes and those required by the NYSE.[51]

51. China Mobile, 'Corporate Governance', viewed 2 June 2015, http://www.chinamobileltd.com /en/about/cg.php.

CHAPTER 11
Australia

> [A] market where there is inequality of information is an unfair market and an inefficient market and a disorderly market ... Good corporate disclosure practices form part of a virtuous circle, in which greater market integrity builds investor confidence, which in turn builds market depth and liquidity; this in turn lowers the cost of capital raising which, in a competitive global market is the next best thing to an improved share price valuation.[1]

§11.01 OVERVIEW

Company disclosure law is supervised and enforced in Australia using a co-regulatory structure involving the Australian Securities and Investments Commission (ASIC) as the federal company and securities regulator, and the Australian Securities Exchange (ASX).[2] The partnership between ASIC and the ASX is underpinned by a memorandum of understanding.[3] Section 792D of the memorandum of understanding requires the ASX to provide ASIC with the assistance that it reasonably requires to perform its functions.

The ASX demutualised and listed on the exchange in 1998.[4] It is required as a market operator licensee to ensure a fair, orderly and transparent market. There must be adequate operating rules and procedures and market supervision arrangements, including arrangements to handle conflicts of interest, monitor the market and participant conduct, and enforce compliance with the market operating rules.[5] In July

1. Karen Hamilton, 'Launch of "Enhanced Disclosure"' (Speech delivered at the Committee for Economic Development of Australia, Sydney, 19 July 2002).
2. The Newcastle and Bendigo Stock Exchange represent a relatively insignificant proportion of listings and capital raisings in Australia.
3. Australian Securities Exchange, *Memorandum of Understanding Between Australian Securities and Investments Commission and Australian Stock Exchange Limited* (28 October 2011).
4. The stated objectives of the Australian Securities Exchange include 'providing a fair and well-informed market for financial securities and providing an internationally competitive market': Australian Securities Exchange, ASX Introduction to Listing Rules.
5. *Corporations Act 2001* (Cth) ss 792A, 796.

2006, the supervisory functions of the ASX were placed into a separate subsidiary company with external directors to improve the level of independence. The ASX is subject to external review. The directors of ASX Supervisory Review Pty Limited report directly to the ASX Board on compliance matters. In addition, ASIC is required to review the ASX as a licensee on an annual basis.[6] Change to the supervisory structure were made in August 2010 in preparation for the entry of new trading platforms but these did not change the regulatory framework governing company disclosure. The ASX remains responsible for enforcing the disclosure listing rules, while ASIC supervises and enforces statutory company disclosure law and the insider trading and other market misconduct regulation.

There is only one board on the ASX with approximately 2,000 companies listed. Thus, this exchange includes large companies with an established track record and many smaller less developed entities.[7] The same disclosure rules generally apply to all listed companies regardless of size, but there are additional tailored periodic reports for mining and resource entities. There are no formal disciplinary processes governing listed company disclosure within the ASX structure. The powers of the ASX are limited to suspension or cancellation of the listing of a company's securities, or referral of a possible breach of the continuous disclosure obligations to ASIC.[8]

§11.02 PERIODIC REPORTS

The periodic disclosure regulation for listed companies in Australia includes the statutory obligations under the *Corporations Act 2001* (Cth) and the reporting requirements under the ASX listing rules.[9] The *Corporations Act 2001* (Cth) requires companies to file annual and half year reports with ASIC. Companies must also file annual and half year reports with the ASX, but may file a preliminary final report in place of the

6. *Corporations Act 2001* (Cth) s. 794C.
7. A company may list on the Australian market under one of the following three tests;

    (1) AD 1 million net profit over the past three years + AD 400,000 net profit over the last twelve months; or
    (2) AD 2 million in net tangible assets; or
    (3) AD 10 million market capitalisation.

    Australian Securities Exchange *IPO: The Road to Growth and Opportunity* (2008) 14.
8. Listed companies are contractually bound to comply with the listing rules under the listing agreement with the ASX. This obligation is given statutory force under ss 792A, 793C and 1101B of the *Corporations Act 2001* (Cth). Where there is an infringement of a listing rule, ASIC, a licensee, ASX, or an aggrieved person may apply to the courts for an order directing compliance with the listing rules under ss 793C and 1101B. The Australian Securities Exchange 'has an absolute discretion concerning the admission of an entity to, or its removal from, the official list and the quotation or suspension of its securities. ASX also has discretion whether to require compliance with the Listing Rules in a particular case.' : Australian Securities Exchange Introduction to Listing Rules 1-2 http://www.asx.com.au/documents/rules/introduction.pdf at 15 August 2015.
9. See Gill North, 'Periodic Disclosure Regulation: Enhancements To Enable All Investors To Make Informed Decisions?' (2009) 27 *Company and Securities Law Journal* 23.

annual report if the annual report is not filed within the stipulated two month timeframe.

Listed Australian companies must produce an annual report, including an audited financial report and a directors' report.[10] Listed companies must lodge the annual report with ASIC within three months after the end of the financial year,[11] and it must be posted or available to members by the earlier of twenty-one days prior to the annual general meeting or four months after the end of the financial year.[12] Companies must provide a corporate governance statement at the same time as their annual report, indicating the extent to which the company has followed the ASX Corporate Governance Council best practice recommendations.[13] Where a recommendation was only partially complied with or not followed at all, a company must highlight and explain this. The ASX must be given a copy of a company's annual report when it differs from the preliminary final report.[14]

Listed Australian companies must report their full year results to the ASX within two months after the end of the accounting period.[15] A small number of companies release the annual report within the required two month time frame, but most report initially on a preliminary basis, with the annual report released a month later.[16] When companies report on a preliminary basis, it must be in accordance with Appendix 4E.[17] Appendix 4E includes fourteen prescribed items. Items 3–5 cover the required financial statements. These combined items require a full set of financial statements in compliance with Australian Accounting Standards. The balance sheet may be condensed but must report as line items each significant class of asset, liability, and equity element with appropriate sub-totals'. The numbers in the financial statements of the preliminary final reports generally accord with those in the annual reports, but significantly more detailed MD&A, financial notes and explanation is required in the annual report than in the preliminary final report.

The statutory half year reports include an audited financial report and a directors' report.[18] The reports must be lodged with ASIC within seventy-five days after the end

10. *Corporations Act 2001* (Cth) ss 295–301.
11. *Corporations Act 2001* (Cth) s. 319.
12. *Corporations Act 2001* (Cth) ss 314–315.
13. Australian Securities Exchange Listing Rule 4.10.3. See also Australian Securities Exchange Corporate Governance Council, *Corporate Governance Principles and Recommendations* (3rd ed., 2014).
14. Australian Securities Exchange Listing Rule 4.7.
15. Australian Securities Exchange Listing Rule 4.3B; Australian Securities Exchange Guidance Note 14 *Company Announcement Platform* 2.
16. When companies report on a preliminary basis, it must be in accordance with Appendix 4E. Appendix 4E includes fourteen prescribed items. Items 3-5 cover the required financial statements. Item 3 requires a statement of financial performance in compliance with Australian Accounting Standards Board (AASB) 1018. Item 4 requires a statement of financial position together with notes to the statement. This statement 'may be condensed but must report as line items each significant class of asset, liability, and equity element with appropriate sub-totals'. Item 5 requires a statement of cash flows in compliance with AASB 1026.
17. Australian Securities Exchange Listing Rule 4.3.
18. *Corporations Act 2001* (Cth) s. 302–306.

of the half year.[19] The financial report must include financial statements and accompanying notes in accordance with existing regulation and accounting standards, including information necessary to give a true and fair view of the financial position and performance of the entity. Listed companies other than listed mining exploration entities must report their half year results within two months after the end of the accounting period.[20] The half year report must comply with all relevant accounting standards but the presentation or form is not prescribed.[21] In practice, most companies release their half year results using the statutory report.

Most listed Australian companies are not required to report on a quarterly basis. Some must provide quarterly cash flow reports to provide comfort in relation to their solvency.[22] In addition, mining producing entities and mining exploration companies are required to provide specialised quarterly reports.[23] A mining entity must report its exploration results and a mining exploration company must provide a quarterly cash flow report that informs the market how the entity's activities have been financed for the past quarter and the effect on its cash position. These reports must comply with the Australasian Code for Reporting of Exploration Results, Minerals Resources and Ore Reserves (JORC Code),[24] and with the Valmin Code when providing technical assessments and valuation reports.

MD&A in the preliminary final reports must provide sufficient commentary 'for the user to be able to compare the information presented with equivalent information for previous periods.'[25] The commentary must include 'any ... significant information needed by an investor to make an informed assessment of the entity's activities and results' in relation to: the earnings per security and dilution; returns to shareholders including distributions and buybacks; operating performance; segmental results; performance trends; and other factors that affected the results.[26] The directors' report within the annual report must include: a review of operations; details of significant changes to the entity's position; details of any matters that have significantly affected, or may significantly affect, the entities operations or position; likely operational developments; environmental performance; and other information that company members would reasonably require to make an informed assessment of the entity's

19. *Corporations Act 2001* (Cth) s. 320.
20. Australian Securities Exchange Listing Rule 4.2B, 4.3B.
21. Australian Securities Exchange Listing Rules 4.2, 4.2A.3, 4.3A.
22. Australian Securities Exchange Listing Rule 4.7B. Companies are required to report under Listing Rule 4.7B(d) when required to comply with Listing Rule 1.3.2(b), or when the Australian Securities Exchange requests a cash flow statement. Australian Securities Exchange Listing Rule 1.3.2(b) applies the assets test such that when half or more of the company's total tangible assets are cash or in a cash equivalent form, the company must provide business objectives and a plan for use of the cash.
23. Australian Securities Exchange Listing Rules 5.1–5.18.
24. The Joint Ore Reserves Committee of the Australasian Institute of Mining and Metallurgy, Australian Institute of Geoscientists and Minerals Council of Australia (JORC), *Australasian Code For Reporting of Exploration Results, Mineral Resources and Ore Reserves - The JORC Code 2012 Edition.*
25. Australian Securities Exchange Appendix 4E, 2.
26. Australian Securities Exchange Appendix 4E, 2–3.

operations, financial position and future prospects.[27] The half year reports must include a directors' report, but the content is restricted to a review of the entity's operations during the half year period, the results of these operations, and the names of the entity's directors.[28]

§11.03 CONTINUOUS DISCLOSURES

The primary continuous disclosure obligation applying to listed companies in Australia is ASX Listing Rule 3.1. Listing Rule 3.1 was strengthened in 1994 by the introduction of statutory provisions. Under ASX Listing Rule 3.1, a listed Australian company must keep its security holders fully informed of any price-sensitive information of which it becomes aware.[29] Unless an exception applies, when a listed company:

> is or becomes aware of any information concerning it that a reasonable person would expect to have a material effect on the price or value of the ... securities, the ... [company] must immediately tell ASX that information.[30]

A company must also disclose the necessary information to the ASX to correct, or prevent, a false market in its securities.[31] This obligation arises when there is a 'reasonably specific rumour or media comment'[32] that is likely to have an impact on the security price.[33] An exception to ASX Listing Rule 3.1 may arise [i] when a reasonable person would not expect the information to be disclosed; [ii] the information is confidential; and [iii] one of more of the following applies:

- It would be a breach of a law to disclose the information.
- The information concerns an incomplete proposal or negotiation.
- The information comprises matters of supposition or is insufficiently definite to warrant disclosure.
- The information is generated for internal management purposes of the entity.
- The information is a trade secret.[34]

There are no rules in Australia governing the nature or content of MD&A provided in continuous disclosures.

The continuous disclosure statutory obligations are found in Chapter 6CA of the *Corporations Act 2001* (Cth). The main provision is section 674. Section 674 requires disclosure of information that a reasonable person would expect to have a material

27. *Corporations Act 2001* (Cth) ss 298–300.
28. *Corporations Act 2001* (Cth) s. 306.
29. Australian Securities Exchange Listing Rule 3.1; *Corporations Act 2001* (Cth) s. 674. Unlisted public companies and large proprietary companies in Australia may also be subject to continuous disclosure as 'disclosing entities': *Corporations Act 2001* (Cth) ss 675(1), 675(2)(a), 111AP, Pt 1.2A, Div 2.
30. Australian Securities Exchange Listing Rule 3.1.
31. Australian Securities Exchange Listing Rule 3.1B.
32. Australian Securities Exchange Listing Rule 3.1B Note.
33. Australian Securities Exchange Listing Rule 3.1B Note.
34. Australian Securities Exchange Listing Rule 3.1A.

effect on the price or value of securities. This obligation may be breached when a listing rule requires notification of information to the market operator and the undisclosed information is materially price-sensitive[35] and not generally available.[36]

§11.04 EMPIRICAL EVIDENCE

In December 2010, ASIC released a review of a selection of 30 June 2010 financial reports. It also provided commentary and guidance on a review of the financial reports, market announcements, investor and analyst presentations, and related media releases for 50 of the top 200 listed entities in relation to profit disclosures not calculated in accordance with accounting standards (referred to as 'alternative profits').[37] ASIC noted that of the thirty-one entities it reviewed that disclosed alternative profits:

- Fifteen did not provide a reconciliation between their alternative profit figure and statutory profit in order to enable users to understand the basis of the calculation.
- Twenty-one gave the alternative profit figure more prominence than the statutory profit figure.
- Eight included only positive adjustments to their statutory profit in calculating the alternative profit and appeared to be attempting to remove 'bad news'.
- Eight focused on a profit figure different from the prior year, and another five adopted an alternative profit that was not consistent with the prior year.

ASIC pointed out that profit figures prepared in accordance with accounting standards enable users of financial reports to make comparisons between entities and over time. It noted that some of the alternative profit calculations were not determined on a consistent basis and many entities excluded 'non-recurring' items such as impairment losses and restructuring costs, even when those items appeared in previous years.[38]

ASIC also reviewed the Operating & Financial Reviews (OFRs) within annual reports of 50 of the top 200 listed entities.[39] It found there were significant opportunities to improve the quality of the OFRs. Most of the companies provided minimal

35. *Corporations Act 2001* (Cth) ss 674(2)(c)(ii), 677.
36. *Corporations Act 2001* (Cth) ss 674(2)(c)(i), 676.
37. Australian Securities and Investments Commission, 'ASIC's Review of 30 June 2010 Financial Reports and Focuses for 31 December 2010' (22 December 2010) Media Release 10-282AD. The Australian Securities and Investments Commission defines the term 'alternative' profit disclosures to mean profits disclosed in a format not in accordance with International Financial Reporting Standards.
38. The Australian Securities and Investments Commission released Consultation Paper 150 concerning disclosure of financial information other than in accordance with accounting standards in March 2011. In December 2011 it released Regulatory Guide 230 on disclosing financial information not in accordance with International Financial Reporting Standards; Australian Securities and Investments Commission, Regulatory Guide 230: *Disclosing Non-IFRS Financial Information* (December 2011).
39. Australian Securities and Investments Commission, 'ASIC's Review of 30 June 2010 Financial Reports and Focuses for 31 December 2010' (22 December 2010) Media Release 10-282AD.

disclosures, and the disclosures did not appear to comply with the obligation to provide members with all of the information they reasonably require. The OFRs often lacked information and explanations that would provide users with an understanding of the drivers of an entity's performance. Most entities did not provide KPIs, production statistics or similar information and most did not present the OFR information in a single section of the financial report. About half of the entities reviewed did not disclose business strategies and prospects for future financial years to a level ASIC would ordinarily expect.[40]

ASIC released a regulatory guide to effective disclosure in an OFR in March 2013.[41] It indicates that an OFR should provide 'reasoned and meaningful description of the underlying drivers of, and reasons for, any entity's performance.'[42] It suggests that non-IFRS financial information may be included provided it is not presented in a misleading manner.[43] It notes that the required discussion relating to strategy and future prospects should include an outline of the main risks.[44]

In December 2011, ASIC released its review of financial reports for the year-ended 30 June 2011.[45] It also provided commentary on a review of financial reports, market announcements, investor and analyst presentations and related media releases for 120 listed entities in relation to profit disclosures. It indicated that over half of these entities disclosed a profit number not in accordance with IFRS.[46] ASIC released Regulatory Guide 230 on disclosing financial information other than in accordance with accounting standards.[47] Regulatory Guide 230 states that financial information that is presented other than in accordance with relevant accounting standards 'is being used increasingly in financial reports and other documents, such as transaction documents and market announcements.'[48] It notes that information that has not been prepared in accordance with IFRS 'will be misleading unless it is appropriately presented and explained.'[49] ASIC does not suggest that non-IFRS financial information should not be used, but it highlights important considerations to ensure the information is not misleading. It recommends that:

40. *Corporations Act 2001* (Cth) s. 299A(1)(c).
41. Australian Securities and Investments Commission, Regulatory Guide 247: *Effective Disclosure in an Operating and Financial Review* (March 2013).
42. Australian Securities and Investments Commission, Regulatory Guide 247: *Effective Disclosure in an Operating and Financial Review* (March 2013) 10.
43. Australian Securities and Investments Commission, Regulatory Guide 247: *Effective Disclosure in an Operating and Financial Review* (March 2013) 14.
44. Australian Securities and Investments Commission, Regulatory Guide 000: *Effective Disclosure in an Operating and Financial Review* (September 2012) 37–38.
45. Australian Securities and Investments Commission, 'Improved Financial Information for Investors and Others' (21 December 2011) Media Release 11-312MR.
46. Australian Securities and Investments Commission, 'Improved Financial Information for Investors and Others' (21 December 2011) Media Release 11-312MR.
47. Australian Securities and Investments Commission, Regulatory Guide 230: *Disclosing Non-IFRS Financial Information* (December 2011).
48. Australian Securities and Investments Commission, Regulatory Guide 230: *Disclosing Non-IFRS Financial Information* (December 2011) 4.
49. Australian Securities and Investments Commission, Regulatory Guide 230: *Disclosing Non-IFRS Financial Information* (December 2011) 17.

- IFRS financial information should be given equal or greater prominence compared to non-IFRS financial information, in particular IFRS profits; and
- Non-IFRS financial information should:
  - be explained and reconciled to the IFRS financial information;
  - be calculated consistently from period to period; and
  - be unbiased and not used to remove 'bad news'.[50]

ASIC carried out further reviews of financial reports during the period 2013–2014 but published commentary on these reviews is limited to summary media releases.[51] One of these media releases states that 'the quality of financial reporting is comparable with other major jurisdictions,' however no evidence is provided to support this claim.[52]

[A] Case Studies

The two largest sectors represented on the ASX by market value are resources and finance. Thus, the two companies selected for review were BHP Billiton and Commonwealth Bank.

[1] BHP Billiton Plc; BHP Billiton Limited

BHP Billiton Limited (BHP) is the largest resource group in the world by market value. BHP has dual listings on the ASX and LSE.[53] The BHP website home page includes headings for 'about us', business, and society.[54] The overviews of the company and strategy in the 'about us' pages are short but well-written. The business pages provide summaries of the coal, copper, iron ore and petroleum and potash businesses, including the division executives and primary assets.[55] The society pages provide information on 'our contribution', the environment, operating with integrity, community and sustainability reports, community and sustainability news, climate change, indigenous communities, and regulatory information.[56] The content on most of these pages is tailored and integrated, with links to specific project information and news.

50. Australian Securities and Investments Commission, Regulatory Guide 230: *Disclosing Non-IFRS Financial Information* (December 2011) 17.
51. See, e.g., Australian Securities and Investments Commission, 'Findings from 30 June 2013 Financial Reports' (Media Release 13-341, 16 December 2013); Australian Securities and Investments Commission, 'Findings from 31 December 2013 Financial Reports' (Media Release 14-141, 27 June 2014); ASIC, 'Findings from 30 June 2014 Financial Reports' (Media Release 14-332, 12 December 2014).
52. Australian Securities and Investments Commission, 'Findings from 30 June 2013 Financial Reports' (Media Release 13-341, 16 December 2013).
53. The review of this company was begun prior to the demerger of South 32, approved by BHP Billiton shareholders on 6 May 2015.
54. BHP Billiton, 'Resourcing the Future', viewed 2 June 2015, http://www.bhpbilliton.com/home/Pages/default.aspx.
55. BHP Billiton, 'Businesses', viewed 2 June 2015, http://www.bhpbilliton.com/home/businesses/Pages/default.aspx.
56. BHP Billiton, 'Society', viewed 2 June 2015, http://www.bhpbilliton.com/home/Society/Pages/default.aspx.

The regulatory information is arranged by project within the product groups.[57] For example, the Mt Arthur Coal pages include the environmental management plans, environmental monitoring information, annual environmental management reports, independent environmental audits, the annual *Environment Protection and Biodiversity Conservation Act 1999* (Cth) compliance documents, blast information, community information including complaints reports, the Mt Arthur coal community consultative committee meeting documents, coal transport information, environment protection licence pollution studies and reduction programmes, the Mt Arthur coal open cut mine modification project exhibition documents, project exhibitions, assessments and approvals, and the sustainable development policy.[58] The structuring and content of this diverse material is orderly and informative for a range of stakeholders.

The preliminary result slides for the year ended 30 June 2014 include a detailed sensitivity table that outlines the estimated impact of factors on net profit. This type of information is valuable when assessing the prospects of the company and potential earnings volatility due to external factors.

[2] Commonwealth Bank of Australia Limited

The Commonwealth Bank of Australia Limited (CBA) is the largest bank and financial group in Australia. As already highlighted, several of the companies examined, including CBA, provide pre-populated spreadsheets of the financial results. CBA goes further and provides Excel and pdf templates prior to the announcement of its financial results. This practice is especially helpful when people need to alter group financial models due to a change in the company's reporting format. CBA also provides sustainability performance data in downloadable Excel spreadsheets, allowing users to analyse long-term trends. This practice suggests the company is willing to openly disclose and engage with relevant stakeholders around its sustainability performance and specific metrics.

The form and presentation of the CBA periodic reports are similar to those in the US. They contain no pictures but provide charts and use colour to enhance readability. These reports include excellent initial executive summaries. These executive summaries include KPI tables and the company's market shares and credit ratings. The reports also include a comprehensive five year performance table including performance ratios, productivity indicators, and shareholder metrics.[59] The company reports on both a statutory and cash basis, but it explains why this is useful, and reconciliation tables are included.

---

57. BHP Billiton, 'Society', viewed 2 June 2015, http://www.bhpbilliton.com/home/Society/Pages/default.aspx.
58. BHP Billiton, 'Society', viewed 2 June 2015, http://www.bhpbilliton.com/home/Society/Pages/default.aspx.
59. Commonwealth Bank Limited, *Annual Report 2012* 92–93.

PART IV
Company Disclosure Regulation and Practice

> In the increasingly globalized securities markets, widely accepted international disclosure standards play an important role in facilitating cross-border capital raising. The International Organization of Securities Commissions … has recognized that disclosure of reliable, timely information that is readily accessible contributes to liquid and efficient markets by enabling investors to make investment decisions based on all the information that would be material to their decisions.[1]

INTRODUCTION

Part IV discusses the primary disclosure principles, practices and issues applicable to listed companies in the countries reviewed. The issues discussed are wide-ranging, with a particular focus on the efficacy of the integrated disclosure frameworks from a reasonable investor or stakeholder perspective. Some of the issues are those highlighted by national regulators, while others are identified by the author based on the empirical reviews in Part III and many years of experience using and analysing company disclosures both as a buy-side analyst and retail investor.

Part IV considers whether periodic reports and continuous disclosures in the jurisdictions reviewed are achieving their objectives. As noted in Chapter 2, IOSCO suggests the overarching objectives of corporate disclosure regimes are to protect investors, ensure that markets are fair, efficient and transparent, and to minimise systemic risk.[2] These IOSCO objectives are used as high-level benchmarks for considering the efficacy of existing company disclosure regulation and practice. IOSCO supports its broad disclosure objectives with a series of principles for periodic

---

1. International Organization of Securities Commissions, *Objectives and Principles of Securities Regulation* (June 2010) 3.
2. International Organization of Securities Commissions, *Objectives and Principles of Securities Regulation* (June 2010) 3.

disclosure by listed entities.[3] These principles are outlined and discussed in Chapter 13, and are considered when determining the essential components of best practice disclosure frameworks in Part V of the book.

Periodic and continuous disclosure regimes are intended to operate together to ensure that listed companies disclose and communicate their objectives, strategies, positions and performance effectively within public forums. Part IV concludes that company disclosure regimes only achieve the IOSCO objectives and principles when the publicly available information from listed companies is sufficiently regular, complete, and timely to enable meaningful decision making and engagement by all groups with a warrantable interest, including members of the public.

3. Technical Committee of the International Organization of Securities Commission, *Principles For Periodic Disclosure By Listed Entitles Final Report* (February 2010).

CHAPTER 12
Singapore

> The profit motive of a demutualised exchange creates a natural tension between its regulatory responsibilities and duty to the public, and its shareholders. This natural tension gives rise to ... conflict issues ... A mutual exchange needs to balance the interests of its 'member-owners' with the interests of the investing public in [its] decision making and rule-making.[1]

§12.01 OVERVIEW

The Singapore Exchange (SGX) is the only securities exchange in Singapore. The SGX listed on its own market in 2000,[2] and is a self-regulatory organisation with oversight from the government regulator, the Monetary Authority of Singapore (MAS). The processes to manage potential conflicts within the SGX include the Risk Management and Regulation Group, which bears frontline and operational responsibility for ensuring that SGX's regulatory functions are not compromised by its commercial function, and the Regulatory Conflicts Committee,[3] which supervises the management of conflicts on behalf of the SGX Board. More broadly, the MAS oversees the SGX and reinforces its management of conflicts by:

- Undertaking an annual assessment of the SGX in relation to compliance with its obligations under the *Securities & Futures Act 2002* (Singapore).
- Reviewing changes to the listing rules.

1. SGX Ltd, 'Rule Making and SRO', 7 June 2012, http://www.sgx.com/wps/wcm/connect/cp_en/site/regulation/rulemaking_and_sro/Rule-making+and+SRO+Page?presentationtemplate=design_lib/PT_Printer_Friendly. The website with this commentary is no longer available.
2. Singapore Exchange, *Annual Report 2010*, 6.
3. The Regulatory Conflicts Committee (RCC) is a specialised board committee comprised of directors who are independent from management and business relationships with SGX. The Committee was established in 2005 to ensure that the SGX Board gives due regard to SGX's public interest obligations, as well as its duty to SGX shareholders. The key responsibilities of the RCC include: overseeing the arrangements within SGX for managing SRO conflicts; assisting in decision making in specific cases of SRO conflicts; and monitoring the adequacy of financial, human and system resources that SGX allocates to support its regulatory function.

- Issuing directives to SGX if and when required.
- Regulating the SGX listing under the SGX Listing Manual and monitoring trading in SGX's shares.

The SGX includes a mainboard and Catalist.[4] Many parties expect Asia to be the primary focus for growth of new listings and securities trading over the next decade, with much of this growth coming from the listing of Chinese companies. The SGX listing requirements were made more onerous during 2012 in an attempt to establish Singapore as the financial centre for Asia and to attract higher quality companies and larger initial public capital raisings.[5] More than 40% of the listings on the SGX are foreign based.[6]

§12.02 PERIODIC REPORTS

The main periodic disclosure rules are contained in SGX Listing Rule 705 and Appendix 7.2 of the SGX Listing Manual. These SGX rules require full year, half yearly and quarterly reports.[7] Financial statements for a full financial year must be announced immediately after the figures are available, and not later than sixty days after the end of the period.[8] The financial statements for each of the first three quarters of a financial year must be announced once the figures are available and not later than forty-five days after the quarter end if the company's market capitalisation exceeds SGD 75 million.[9]

Appendix 7.2 outlines the individual items of information that must be included in the income statement, statement of financial position and cash flow statement. It also requires a review of the performance of the group, including discussion of the following:

(a) any significant factors that affected the turnover, costs, and earnings of the group for the current financial period reported on, including (where applicable) seasonal or cyclical factors; and
(b) any material factors that affected the cash flow, working capital, assets or liabilities of the group during the current financial period reported on.[10]

Commentary must be provided on the significant trends and competitive conditions of the industry in which the group operates and any known factors or events that may affect the group in the next reporting period and the next twelve months.[11] Further, where a forecast or prospect statement has been previously disclosed to

4. Catalist listed companies are directly supervised by their sponsors.
5. Jeremy Grant, 'Singapore Exchange Tightens Listing Rules', *FT.com* 19 July 2012. Companies must have minimum market capitalisation of SGD 150 million and they must have an operating record of three years, including a minimum pre-tax profit of SGD 30 million for the most recent year.
6. Jeremy Grant, 'Singapore Exchange Tightens Listing Rules', *FT.com* 19 July 2012.
7. SGX Listing Manual, Rule 705, Appendix 7.2.
8. SGX Listing Manual, Rule 705(1).
9. SGX Listing Manual, Rule 705(2).
10. SGX Listing Manual, Rule 705, Appendix 7.2.8.
11. SGX Listing Manual, Rule 705, Appendix 7.2.10.

shareholders, any variance between it and the actual results must be disclosed.[12] Additional information required in the full year announcement includes segmental results, a sales breakdown and commentary on the factors leading to any material changes in contributions to turnover and earnings by the business or geographical segments.[13] The quarterly or half yearly reports must contain a statement from the board of directors confirming that, to the best of their knowledge, nothing has come to their attention which may render the financial statements to be false or misleading in any material respect.[14] Life science companies and mineral, oil and gas companies that are unable to meet specified profit criteria must provide a quarterly announcement on the use of funds or cash for the quarter and a projection on the use of funds or cash for the next quarter.[15]

Listed companies must issue their annual report to shareholders and the SGX within four months of the end of the financial year and at least fourteen days prior to the annual general meeting.[16] The Chairman's statement in the annual report must provide a balanced and readable summary of the company's performance and prospects.[17] Singapore has a Code of Corporate Governance (SGX Code) that comes under the purview of the SGX and the MAS.[18] While compliance with the SGX Code is not mandatory, the listing rules require companies to disclose their corporate governance practices and to provide explanations in their annual report concerning any non-compliance with the SGX Code.[19]

§12.03 CONTINUOUS DISCLOSURE

The main continuous disclosure obligation is provided in SGX Listing Rule 703 and this rule has statutory support in section 203 of the *Securities & Futures Act 2002* (Singapore).[20] Under SGX Listing Rule 703, an issuer must disclose information that is (a) necessary to avoid the establishment of a false market in its securities, or (b) that would be likely to have a material effect on the price or value of its securities. All material information must be disclosed even when the information is already publicly available. The disclosures are released through the SGX website. Section 203(2) of the *Securities & Futures Act 2002* (Singapore)[21] provides that:

12. SGX Listing Manual, Rule 705, Appendix 7.2.9.
13. SGX Listing Manual, Rule 705(15)(16)(17).
14. SGX Listing Manual, Rule 705(5).
15. SGX Listing Manual, Rule 705(6).
16. SGX Listing Manual, Rule 707(1)(2).
17. SGX Listing Manual, Rule 708.
18. SGX, *Code of Corporate Governance 2012.*
19. SGX Listing Manual, Rule 710.
20. *Securities & Futures Act 2002* (Singapore) s. 203.
21. Section 203 of the *Securities & Futures Act 2002* (Singapore) states that:

    (1) This section shall, apply to:
        (a) a corporation which is admitted to the official list of a securities exchange; or
        (b) a responsible person of a collective investment scheme the units of which are quoted on a securities exchange, if the corporation or responsible person is required by the listing rules of the securities exchange to notify the securities exchange of information

> The corporations or responsible person must not intentionally, recklessly, or negligently fail to notify the securities exchange of such information as is required to be disclosed under the listing rules of the securities exchange.

The SGX Listing Manual indicates that a public announcement should be factual, clear and succinct, it must contain sufficient quantitative information to allow investors to evaluate its relative importance to the activities of the issuer, and it should be balanced and fair.[22]

The SGX is responsible for monitoring and enforcing the continuous disclosure obligations. The SGX has a 'Regulators Column' to keep market participants informed about regulatory philosophy, processes and practices, as well as emerging issues and market developments. The Market Surveillance and Enforcement Department (MSE Department) of the SGX uses a real-time market surveillance system to monitor unusual price and volume movements of a company's securities. When potentially questionable transactions are identified, the MSE Department may query the relevant company verbally or in writing.[23] There is a disciplinary tribunal within the SGX structure governing issuer matters. A disciplinary committee hears the charges and decides whether the member has violated any rules or requirements of the exchange and, if so, decides the appropriate penalty. An appeal can be made to either the Disciplinary Committee or Appeals Committee, both of which are independent of the SGX, and the decision of the Committee is final. A member charged may be reprimanded, fined, suspended and or expelled.[24] The exchange operates a website that lists 'past disciplinary actions' taken by the Disciplinary and Appeals Committees against offenders who have breached SGX rules. When viewed, some of these actions involved disclosure matters.[25]

§12.04 EMPIRICAL EVIDENCE

[A] Case Studies

The companies selected for review were Singapore Telecommunications Ltd and Keppel Corporation, two of the largest entities listed on the SGX.

---

on specified events or matters as they occur or arise for the purpose of the securities exchange making that information available to a securities market operated by the securities exchange.

(2) The corporations or responsible person must not intentionally, recklessly, or negligently fail to notify the securities exchange of such information as is required to be disclosed under the listing rules of the securities exchange.

(3) Notwithstanding s. 204, a contravention of subsection (2) shall not be an offence unless the failure to notify is intentional or reckless.

22. SGK Listing Manual A-9, A-15.
23. SGX-ST Listing Rules Practice Note 7.2 Queries Regarding Unusual Trading Activity 1-2.
24. A disciplinary committee hears the charges and decides whether the member has violated any rules and requirements of the exchange; and if so, decides the appropriate penalty. An appeal to a committee independent of the SGX is allowed and the decision of this Committee is final.
25. See SGX Ltd, 'Past Disciplinary Actions', viewed 19 May 2015, http://www.sgx.com/wps/portal/sgxweb/home/regulation/consult_pub/past_dis_action.

[1] Singapore Telecommunications Limited

Singapore Telecommunications Limited (Singtel) is the largest listed company on the Singapore Exchange. The result material for the final quarter and year ended 31 March 2015 is presented coherently and includes detailed information on the internal and external environments. Further, the news release and presentation contain an outlook section that includes guidance on capital expenditure, free cash flow, dividends, revenue and EBITDA.

[2] Keppel Corporation

The business segments of Keppel Corporation (Keppel) include offshore and marine, infrastructure, property and investments. The key financials for the first quarter of 2015 include the net order book and contracts secured for the last ten years. This is useful information for people wanting to comprehend the linkages and lead times between orders, contracts and the financial results, and the regularity and recurring nature (or otherwise) of the various businesses.

CHAPTER 13

Periodic Disclosure Regulation and Practice

> Periodic reports facilitate investor decision making and monitoring of the markets by making it possible for investors to compare the performance of the same company over regular intervals, and by enabling investors to make useful comparisons among different companies.[1]

§13.01 OVERVIEW

In 1998, IOSCO adopted a comprehensive set of Objectives and Principles of Securities Regulation (IOSCO Principles) that seek to facilitate cross-border cooperation, reduce global systemic risk, protect investors, and ensure fair, efficient and transparent financial markets. The Technical Committee of IOSCO acknowledges the need for, and importance of, regular reporting by public companies in addition to disclosure on an ad hoc basis throughout a financial year.[2] IOSCO confirms that financial information in periodic reports is the core information around which related information, such as MD&A of historical results and prospects, should be framed.[3]

§13.02 PERIODIC DISCLOSURE KEY PRINCIPLES

The IOSCO Principles for periodic disclosure naturally fit within two categories; namely, public access and review, and the form and content of disclosures. The IOSCO public access and review principles encompass the following:

- the reports should be provided to the public in a timely manner;

1. Technical Committee of the International Organization of Securities Commission, *Principles For Periodic Disclosure By Listed Entitles* Final Report (February 2010) 4.
2. Technical Committee of the International Organization of Securities Commission, *Principles For Periodic Disclosure By Listed Entitles* Final Report (February 2010) 4.
3. Technical Committee of the International Organization of Securities Commission, *Principles For Periodic Disclosure By Listed Entitles* Final Report (February 2010) 4.

- the reports should be stored in a central location that facilitates public access to the information;
- all investors should have equal access to the information contained in periodic reports;
- when a company is listed in more than one jurisdiction, material information should be released promptly to each relevant market; and
- the reports should be filed with the relevant regulator for review.[4]

The IOSCO disclosure form and content principles include the following:

- the periodic reports should contain relevant information;
- the reports should be presented in a format that facilitates ready analysis of the information;
- information should be presented in a clear and concise manner;
- the reports should not be misleading or deceptive, omit any material information or rely on boilerplate language;
- the persons responsible for the financial statements should be clearly identified and these individuals should be required to state that the financial information provided is fairly presented; and
- the financial reporting internal controls should be subject to ongoing review.[5]

IOSCO indicates that the content of periodic reports should include at a minimum:

- audited consolidated financial statements that conform with internationally accepted accounting standards;
- information relating to the financial position, performance and cash flows of a company to allow liquidity and solvency assessments;
- an audit report;
- an outline of any significant changes that have occurred since the end of the financial year; and
- MD&A of the reported financial position and performance, and of the factors and trends expected to have a material impact on the company's future operations and performance.[6]

Policy makers, regulators and listed corporations in the countries reviewed appear to broadly accept the IOSCO Principles. The areas involving the most differences and contention include the following:

(1) the clarity, completeness and accuracy of company information provided;
(2) the regularity of periodic reporting, most notably an obligation to report quarterly;

4. Technical Committee of the International Organization of Securities Commission, *Principles For Periodic Disclosure By Listed Entitles* Final Report (February 2010) 7–28.
5. Technical Committee of the International Organization of Securities Commission, *Principles For Periodic Disclosure By Listed Entitles* Final Report (February 2010) 7–28.
6. Technical Committee of the International Organization of Securities Commission, *Principles For Periodic Disclosure By Listed Entitles* Final Report (February 2010) 7–28.

(3) the nature and scope of required MD&A;
(4) the timeliness of disclosure of 'bad news';
(5) the use and referencing of numbers that have not been calculated in accordance with accounting standards;
(6) the presentation of financial and non-financial information using standard forms;
(7) the role and content of preliminary final reports and annual reports;
(8) the provision of long-term performance data and commentary, including specific key performance indicators;
(9) public access to company briefings; and
(10) the use of digital facilities and forums to enhance corporate communication.

The remainder of this chapter discusses these issues.

§13.03 THE CLARITY, COMPLETENESS AND ACCURACY OF COMPANY INFORMATION

The objective of financial reporting is to provide information about the financial position and prospects of a company that is useful to a wide-range of users in making economic and other decisions. In practice, the quality of listed company reporting and disclosure varies greatly across the globe. As highlighted in Part III, some companies report and communicate their story and performance in a concise and effective manner, but others provide lengthy disclosures conveying little. Many national regulators provide guidance on the appropriate form, balance and tone of company reports to enhance their quality and readability. These guidance principles often draw on principles developed by the plain English movement. The plain English movement has a long history across many professional areas and jurisdictions. Its primary aim is to encourage the presentation of complex information in an orderly and clear manner so that readers have the best possible chance of understanding it.[7]

The plain English movement has significantly influenced securities disclosure regulation and practice around the globe over the last thirty years. In the 1980s, Arthur Levitt, the Chair of the SEC, promoted the publication of a plain English handbook to improve the readability and comprehension of disclosure documents. He indicated that he could not always decipher what was being said in the filed documents of public companies. He suggested a range of possible explanations for the poor quality of company disclosures, including the following:

- The reader may not have the technical knowledge to grasp what the writer wishes to convey.
- The writer may not understand what he or she is talking about.

7. See, e.g., 'The principles of plain English' at http://www.plainenglish.com.au/princi.htm; 'What is Plain Language?' at 'http://www.plainlanguage.gov/whatisPL/.

- The ill-intentioned writer does not want the reader to understand the subject but disclosure on the matter is legally required.
- The well-intentioned and informed writer fails to get the message across to an intelligent and interested reader because of stilted jargon and complex construction.[8]

The plain English handbook developed by the SEC indicates that disclosure documents must impart complex information in a way that enables investors to make informed decisions. It describes writing documents in plain English as:

> analyzing and deciding what information investors need to make informed decisions, before words, sentences, or paragraphs are considered. A plain English document uses words economically and at a level the audience can understand. Its sentence structure is tight. Its tone is welcoming and direct. Its design is visually appealing. A plain English document is easy to read and looks like it's meant to be read.[9]

Warren Buffett assisted with the production of the handbook. In the preface he suggests that disclosures should be written with a specific person in mind. He states that:

> When writing Berkshire Hathaway's annual report, I pretend that I'm talking to my sisters. I have no trouble picturing them: Though highly intelligent, they are not experts in accounting or finance. They will understand plain English, but jargon may puzzle them. My goal is simply to give them the information I would wish them to supply me if our positions were reversed. To succeed, I don't need to be Shakespeare; I must, though, have a sincere desire to inform.[10]

The most common problems the SEC identifies in disclosure documents include long sentences, passive voice, weak verbs, superfluous words, legal and financial jargon, numerous defined terms, abstract words, unnecessary details, and unreadable design and layout.[11] Its plain English initiatives have been wide-ranging, encompassing policy guidance and testing disclosures in prospectuses, mutual fund documentation, and listed company reports. The plain English disclosure testing rules require companies to write the cover page, summary and risk factors sections using short sentences, definite, concrete and everyday language, the active voice, tabular presentation of complex information, no legal or business jargon, and no double negatives.[12] Specific disclosures were tested by presenting them in various alternative formats across a

8. See United States Securities Exchange Commission, *A Plain English Handbook: How to Create Clear SEC Disclosure Documents* (August 1988) Preface.
9. United States Securities and Exchange Commission, *A Plain English Handbook: How to Create Clear SEC Disclosure Documents* (August 1988) 5.
10. United States Securities and Exchange Commission, *A Plain English Handbook: How to Create Clear SEC Disclosure Documents* (August 1988) 2.
11. See United States Securities and Exchange Commission, *A Plain English Handbook: How to Create Clear SEC Disclosure Documents* (August 1988).
12. Cynthia A Glassman, United States Securities and Exchange Commissioner, 'Does the SEC Disclosure Eschew Obfuscation? Res Ipsa Loquitor' (Speech presented at the Plain Language Associations International's Fifth International Conference, Washington DC, 4 November 2005).

number of cities. The testing confirmed that to be effective, the format and placement of information in the disclosures are as important as the content and words used.[13]

In 2005, SEC Commissioner Cynthia Glassman suggested that:

> it is clear that there is a difference in goals of the disclosing parties and the recipients of those disclosures. Very simply put, it is my perception that disclosing parties and their lawyers – be they mutual funds, broker-dealers, investment advisors, or operating companies – view their disclosure obligations with an eye toward limiting their potential liability. Thus, the disclosures that they make, while often voluminous, do not necessarily provide information in a helpful informative manner. In contrast, the recipients want timely, complete, and useful information that is readily understandable.[14]

Glassman suggested the primary goal is the provision of clear, concise and accurate information to enable sound investment decisions.[15]

In 2007, Christopher Cox, the Chairman of SEC, argued that companies can best control their litigation risk by presenting material information in plain English,[16] but conceded that making investor communication easier to read and understand is a big job and requires changing ingrained practices.[17] He noted the tendency to use legal jargon and boilerplate language and suggested this discourages investors from reading the disclosures. He indicated that clear disclosure of the key figures and facts and meaningful analysis and explanation is required. His ultimate test of effective disclosure is whether the substance and presentation of the disclosed content matter is readable and useful to its readers.[18]

Disclosure principles outlined by other national corporate and securities regulators are broadly similar to those promoted by the SEC. For instance, a recurring feature of Australian securities regulation is a legislative requirement for disclosure documents to be 'clear, concise and effective'.[19] Clear, concise and effective documentation has been described by Belinda Gibson, a prior Commissioner of ASIC, as:

---

13. Cynthia A Glassman, United States Securities and Exchange Commissioner, 'Does the SEC Disclosure Eschew Obfuscation? Res Ipsa Loquitor' (Speech presented at the Plain Language Associations International's Fifth International Conference, Washington DC, 4 November 2005).
14. Cynthia A Glassman, United States Securities and Exchange Commissioner, 'Does the SEC Disclosure Eschew Obfuscation? Res Ipsa Loquitor' (Speech presented at the Plain Language Associations International's Fifth International Conference, Washington DC, 4 November 2005).
15. Cynthia A Glassman, United States Securities and Exchange Commissioner, 'Does the SEC Disclosure Eschew Obfuscation? Res Ipsa Loquitor' (Speech presented at the Plain Language Associations International's Fifth International Conference, Washington DC, 4 November 2005).
16. Christopher Cox, Chairman United States Securities and Exchange, 'Plain Language and Good Business' (Speech delivered to the Center for Plain Language symposium, Washington DC, 12 October 2007).
17. Christopher Cox, Chairman United States Securities and Exchange, 'Plain Language and Good Business' (Speech delivered to the Center for Plain Language symposium, Washington DC, 12 October 2007).
18. Christopher Cox, Chairman United States Securities and Exchange, 'Plain Language and Good Business' (Speech delivered to the Center for Plain Language symposium, Washington DC, 12 October 2007).
19. *Corporations Act 2001* (Cth) ss 249L, 715A, 719, 942B, 942C, 947B, 947C, 1012C, 1013C, 1019I, 1019J.

> [d]ocuments ... [that are] readable – if they are lengthy, there must be a clear road map to enable the readers to select the information they need to make a sensible investment decision. They must be understandable. The content must be clear and relevant to the investment decision at hand. The risk must be put up front and in one place.[20]

She indicates that the key elements of the Australian disclosure regime are:

- disclosure of price-sensitive information to the market in a timely fashion;
- announcements that are not false, misleading or deceptive; and
- announcements that are clear, accurate and complete.[21]

She defines 'clear announcements' as market releases containing information that is factual and expressed in an objective and clear manner; 'complete announcements' as documents that can be read as a whole without reference to other documents to locate price-sensitive information; and 'accurate announcements' as disclosures that contain factually correct and easily understandable information, and that grant due prominence to both positive and negative information.[22] As the Kay Final Report acknowledges, useful information 'is provided when the content of the information is driven by the needs of users.'[23]

A empirical study by Lawrence found that individuals generally invest more in companies with clear and concise financial disclosures because this approach leads to improved returns.[24] This finding is important because it highlights the direct benefits for retail investors of well-written reports and disclosures, and the likely indirect benefits for corporations that communicate effectively, including improved investor confidence and trust, a diverse investor base, and lower capital costs.

§13.04 REGULARITY OF PERIODIC REPORTING[25]

The regularity of periodic reports remains a highly contentious issue in some jurisdictions. Listed companies in the US have been required to provide mandatory comprehensive quarterly reports to the SEC since 1970. Quarterly regimes have also been adopted in other markets over the last decade. For example, the Singapore Exchange

20. Belinda Gibson, 'Working In a Regulated Environment' (Speech delivered at the Law Society of Western Australia Summer School, 26 February 2010) 5.
21. Belinda Gibson, 'Disclosure And The Role of ASX and ASIC' (Speech delivered at the Listed Companies Conference, 26 March 2008) 6.
22. Belinda Gibson, 'Disclosure And The Role of ASX and ASIC' (Speech delivered at the Listed Companies Conference, 26 March 2008) 6.
    Belinda Gibson, 'Disclosure And The Role of ASX and ASIC' (Speech delivered at the Listed Companies Conference, 26 March 2008) 11–12.
23. *The Kay Review of UK Equity Markets and Long-Term Decision Making: Final Report* (July 2012) 72 .
24. Alastair Lawrence, 'Individual Investors and Financial Disclosure' (2013) 56 *Journal of Accounting and Economics* 130.
25. Chapter 13 contains content that was included in a published article: Gill North, 'Listed Company Disclosure and Financial Market Transparency: Is this a Battle Worth Fighting or Merely Policy and Regulatory Mantra?' (2014) 6 *Journal of Business Law* 486.

has required quarterly reports that include financial statements since 2004,[26] and Japan introduced comprehensive quarterly reporting in 2008. Quarterly reporting proposals around the world have generally been welcomed by investors but opposed by business communities.[27] For instance, institutional investors in Europe called for comprehensive quarterly reporting in 2003,[28] but the European Parliament rejected this proposal following strong lobbying from businesses. In 2004, the European Commission (EC) opted for a compromise solution and the IMS obligations were introduced as part of the TD.[29] As a result, companies listed on the main exchanges in Europe were required to provide either quarterly reports or IMSs from 2007.[30] These IMSs included an outline of material events and transactions that had taken place during the quarter and their impact on the company's financial position, as well as a general description of the financial position and performance of the company.

As discussed in Chapter 7, the TD was reviewed in 2009 and the EC adopted successively changing positions.[31] In 2010, the EC recommended continuing IMS reporting,[32] but later reversed its position and sought to abolish the quarterly reporting obligation for all listed companies.[33] It also sought to prohibit individual countries from imposing stricter rules.[34] Both of these proposals were supported by the Kay Review Committee and the UK Government.[35]

[A] The Kay Review

The Kay Final Report recommended removal of the obligation to provide IMSs. The central argument underpinning this recommendation is that quarterly statements encourage listed companies and investors to focus unduly on short-term performance indicators. The Kay Interim Report cites an observation by the Institute of Directors that

26. Singapore Stock, *Listing Manual*, Ch. 7, 'Continuing Obligations' Rule 705, Appendix 7.2.
27. See, e.g., 'For and Against - Cost and Benefit Study Needed' (2003) 12 *Accountancy Age* 12; 'Europe Drops Quarterly Reporting' (2004) 23 *International Financial Law Review* 12; 'Quarterly Reporting System' (2008) 27 *International Financial Law Review* 8.
28. See, e.g., Chartered Financial Analysts Institute, *European Investment Professionals Back Quarterly Reporting* (20 November 2003).
29. European Commission (2004) Directive 2004/109/EC of the European Parliament and of the Council, Official Journal of the European Union, L 390.
30. The Transparency Directive was required to be transposed into national law by January 2007. Delays in implementation meant it was not adopted in some countries until 2009.
31. For a detailed outline of these processes, see Benedikt Link, 'The Struggle for a Common Interim Reporting Frequency Regime in Europe' (2012) 9 *Accounting In Europe* 191.
32. See European Commission, *Report from the Commission to the Council, the European Parliament, the European Economic and Social Committee and the Committee of the Regions* (27 May 2010a).
33. European Commission, *Proposal for a Directive of the European Parliament and the European Council* amending Directive 2004/109/E, (25 October 2011) http://ec.europa.eu/internal_market/securities/docs/transparency/modifying-proposal/20111025-provisional-proposal_en.pdf.
34. Securities exchanges in Germany and Austria previously required companies listed in their prime segment to provide quarterly reports. Sweden, Finland, Greece and Portugal also required quarterly reporting prior to the amendments to the Transparency Directive.
35. Department for Business Innovation & Skill United Kingdom, *Ensuring Equity Markets Support Long Term Growth: The Government Response to the Kay Review* (November 2012) 6.

'quoted companies can be subject to short termist pressure from equity markets. This may arise due to fluctuation in share prices or as a result of pressure from sell-side analysts or activist investors (e.g., hedge funds).'[36] The Kay Final Report highlights the short-term focus of financial markets. It recommends that companies should disengage from management of short-term earnings expectations.[37] Further, it suggests that frequent reporting of financial performance encourages investors to adopt a short-term focus.[38]

The argument that quarterly reporting leads to a greater focus by investors on short-term factors and that it encourages short-term earnings management presumes there are significant correlations or relationships between the following:

(1) the preparation and release of quarterly reports (or IMSs);
(2) a general investor focus on short-term factors; and
(3) short-term earnings management by listed company executives.

However, the Kay Final Report does not discuss these connections. Most critically, it does not explain how the removal of quarterly reporting (or the IMS obligations) will simultaneously alter short-term pressures from market participants (such as sell-side analysts and hedge funds) and executive engagement in short-term earnings management. Any links or correlations between quarterly reporting, short-termism and management of short-term earnings expectations are instead assumed. The Kay Final Report acknowledges that analysts predict likely earnings results and companies engage in this process by providing explicit or implied earnings guidance, but it does not include any concrete proposals to alter these entrenched patterns beyond removal of the IMS obligations.[39] Regardless of the length of the reporting period, sell-side analysts will continue to publish research reports with near term company earnings estimates and security price targets, and many listed companies will continue to seek to align these sell-side analyst forecasts with internal company forecasts. The Kay Final Report does not discuss the motivations driving, or resolve the conflicts involved with, short-term earnings management. Company boards and managers are not obliged to, and should not in fact, adjust their strategies or management because they report quarterly. Managerial concerns with meeting short-term earnings expectations encourage misconduct, absorb considerable scarce resources without producing any corresponding benefits for the company, and are potentially costly over long horizons.[40]

36. *The Kay Review of UK Equity Markets and Long-Term Decision Making: Interim Report* (February 2012) 8.
37. *The Kay Review of UK Equity Markets and Long-Term Decision Making: Final Report* (July 2012) 13.
38. *The Kay Review of UK Equity Markets and Long-Term Decision Making: Final Report* (July 2012) 10.
39. *The Kay Review of UK Equity Markets and Long-Term Decision Making: Final Report* (July 2012) 64.
40. See, e.g., Lynne Dallas, 'Short-Termism, the Financial Crisis, and Corporate Governance' (2012) 37 *Journal of Corporation Law* 265, 278–279.

The Kay Interim Report states that the general principle that 'more information is better has driven regulation of both corporate governance and securities markets in the past, and continues to do so.'[41] The Kay Final Report highlights the broad consensus among respondents that too much data (bad or useless information) is being produced and not enough information.[42] It links the provision of large quantities of data, which it asserts is of little value to users, to an exaggerated faith in Fama's efficient market hypothesis.[43] It extends this argument to a claim that providing mass data may drive 'damaging short-term decisions by investors, aggravated by well-documented cognitive biases.'[44] These comments infer that most irrational or biased trading and behaviour in equity markets is driven by the receipt of copious data. The report does not provide specific examples or evidence to support these comments, so it is unclear what the report authors consider constitutes 'copious data' and whether this is data provided by companies or financial intermediaries. The Kay report authors may consider that IMSs provide copious or useless data.[45] It is doubtful though that investors and stakeholders without ongoing private access to company executives would agree with this stance. In any event, IMSs typically provide summary high-level commentary on trading conditions, without the support of financial statements, so they provide minimal grist for persons focused on short-term numbers.

The Kay Final Report suggests the type of information contained in IMSs should be 'disclosed in negotiations between asset managers and companies'.[46] However, company directors and managers and asset managers are subject to the same personal failings and cognitive biases as everyone else and this recommendation ignores the issues and conflicts of interest that arise from discretionary private relationships between company managers and favoured investors. Institutional demands for private meetings with executives and for continuing updates on a company's performance and prospects could be expected to accelerate in the wake of the TD reforms. Further, the segments of the market that are most focused on short-term trading and near horizon

41. *The Kay Review of UK Equity Markets and Long-Term Decision Making: Interim Report* (February 2012) 21.
42. *The Kay Review of UK Equity Markets and Long-Term Decision Making: Interim Report* (February 2012) 21–22. It would be interesting to know the characteristics of the respondents that indicated during the consultations processes that too much data is being produced.
43. *The Kay Review of UK Equity Markets and Long-Term Decision Making: Final Report* (July 2012) 10.
44. *The Kay Review of UK Equity Markets and Long-Term Decision Making: Final Report* (July 2012) 10.
45. *The Kay Review of UK Equity Markets and Long-Term Decision Making: Interim Report* (February 2012) 21–22. An outline of the type of participants that gave these responses and an explanation of the reasons why the information in interim management statements is useless would be helpful to progress the debate.
46. *The Kay Review of UK Equity Markets and Long-Term Decision Making: Final Report* (July 2012) 74. If the basis on which asset managers and company managers are intended to 'negotiate' refers to bidding arrangements, this accords with current practices in the UK. The Financial Times in the UK reported in 2013 that asset managers were paying large sums of money to brokers and investment bankers for arranging meetings with chief executive officers. Analysis by the Financial Services Authority (FSA) found some large asset managers were making these payments using client commissions: Steve Johnson, 'FSA Crackdown on Cash For CEO Access', *FT.com*, 4 March 2013.

security price movement are, if anything, likely to expand,[47] as any information gleaned from private briefings will be more valuable due to the longer period until its public release. Hence, the removal of the obligation to report quarterly across the EC will provide company managers with greater control and discretion over disclosure processes, it will add fuel to the drivers motivating short-term earnings management, and it will increase the likelihood of selective disclosure.

[B] Europe: Policy Reviews of Quarterly Reporting

In February 2012, staff of the EC produced an impact assessment report (Impact Report) of the TD.[48] The Impact Report indicated that '[w]hilst there is a consensus that yearly and half yearly reports are necessary for investor protection, this is not the case for quarterly information.'[49] Somewhat ironically, it argued that annual and half yearly reports provide assurance to investors because they are prepared in accordance with accounting standards, are independently audited, and allow for comparability of information. It suggests that IMSs are not useful because they are not subject to audit and are not standardised, and are therefore unable to be used for comparative analysis. Additionally, the EC argued that all materially price-sensitive information has to be disclosed under the Market Abuse Directive. On this basis, it questioned whether other information needs to be disclosed quarterly and suggested the information that is disclosed quarterly could just as well be disclosed in yearly or half yearly financial statements.[50] It further claimed that quarterly information places a high administrative burden on companies.[51] Comments from various sources were cited suggesting quarterly reporting produces an excessive focus on short-term earnings rather than the long-term strategies of companies and other long-term metrics.[52]

Claims made by European companies that the preparation of online quarterly updates involves high costs should not be accepted without clear evidence, particularly given the response by companies across Europe suggesting compliance has not been onerous. In 2009, the EC commissioned the Mazars Group to carry out European-wide

47. The Kay Final Report does not propose any changes to short-term trading rules. Professor Kay is cited in a recent article in the *Financial Times* stating 'We have to move to a world that has less trading in it': David Oakley, 'John Kay: Professor pf Doom is "Waiting for the Next Crisis"', *FT.com*, 10 June 2013. The author agrees, but suggests this will only occur if policy makers are willing to alter (or reverse) some of the market policies that encourage short-term trading.
48. European Commission, Report from the Commission Staff Working Paper *Impact Assessment* (SEC(2011) 1280 final).
49. European Commission, Report from the Commission Staff Working Paper *Impact Assessment* (SEC(2011) 1280 final) 11.
50. European Commission, Report from the Commission Staff Working Paper *Impact Assessment* (SEC(2011) 1280 final) 12-13.
51. European Commission, Report from the Commission Staff Working Paper *Impact Assessment* (SEC(2011) 1280 final) 13. No direct evidence of these costs is outlined. Instead, the Impact Report provides varying estimates and quotes from company associations and company representatives.
52. European Commission, Report from the Commission Staff Working Paper *Impact Assessment* (SEC(2011) 1280 final) 15. It is suggested that investors 'do not have the time to consider the promising long-term stories that small companies may offer.'

consultation on the impact of the TD (Mazars Report). It sought feedback from a broad range of groups impacted by, or involved with, the TD. Across all of the company respondents, 34.1% thought the cost of compliance was too high, while 48.8% disagreed and 17.1% had no opinion. When these responses were sorted by company size, the percentage of issuers who did not think the cost was too high increased as the size of the company increased. That is, smaller companies were most vocal about the compliance costs. A slicing of the results by country found that companies that considered the compliance cost to be too high were from France, Spain and Slovakia, while companies in the UK, Hungary, Sweden, Romania, Austria and Germany did not consider the costs onerous.[53]

The costs to produce unaudited online quarterly reports or trading updates are marginal at most and should not be considered onerous. Listed company directors and managers are required to keep abreast of trading conditions and the company's financial and operational positions. To satisfy these obligations, companies have established structures, technologies, and processes to provide regular (usually monthly) financial reports to assist the directors and managers to monitor developments and performance. As noted earlier, it is more cost-efficient for companies to disclose publicly than to communicate similar information repeatedly with selected investors and stakeholders on an individual or small group basis, as this requires considerable managerial time. If, as is claimed, it *is* difficult and costly for managers to produce a short interim trading update, one might reasonably question the regularity and quality of information that is provided to the company board, particularly to the non-executive directors.

When the costs of disclosure regulation are debated, the costs included in such analysis are often limited to the direct costs borne by a company to produce and disseminate relevant reports or announcements. Such analysis is short-sighted and incomplete. Complete cost-benefit analysis must include the costs *and* long-term benefits derived from public disclosure frameworks. These costs and benefits should then be compared to the costs borne by companies, investors and the public when listed company information is not disclosed at all, is selectively released, or the public disclosure is not clear, concise and effective.

The argument that quarterly reporting is not necessary in addition to continuous disclosure and insider trading regimes is not new. Policy makers in other countries have also considered and rejected comprehensive quarterly regimes on this basis.[54] However, periodic reporting and continuous disclosure regimes have different roles and purposes. These frameworks are intended to operate together to enable investors and other stakeholders to remain well-informed at all times of the year. The main purpose of continuous disclosure regimes is to ensure all investors and other stakeholders are provided with materially price-sensitive information between reporting

53. Mazars, *Transparency Directive Assessment Report* 90, viewed 13 June 2015, http://www.mazars.co.uk/Home/News/Our-publications/General-publications/Transparency-Directive-Assessment-Report.
54. See, e.g., Companies and Securities Advisory Committee, Commonwealth of Australia, *Report on Continuous Disclosure* (1996) 6.

periods, but these regimes are inherently limited with respect to the nature, scope and consistency of information provided. The regular and relatively standardised periodic reports provide the comprehensive baseline information and the continuous disclosures are only meaningful when they are timely and sufficiently connected to the reported positions. For example, the months following the GFC provided a unique opportunity to examine global disclosure issues in a stressed environment. During this period, many listed companies made large write-offs, incurred losses, increased provisioning, and needed to restructure, refinance or raise capital. These patterns led to a strong market focus on the cash, debt and capital positions of listed companies and their ability to service or refinance debt. Few continuous disclosures across the jurisdictions reviewed encompass such information. Analysis of these factors generally requires the comprehensive information provided in a periodic report, including a full set of financial statements, notes and MD&A.

The Impact Report commentary presents an incomplete summary of the quarterly reporting developments in Europe. In 2003, the Association for Investment Management and Research (AIMR) surveyed investment professionals, including portfolio managers, research analysts, financial advisors and investment company chief executive officers, on the introduction of quarterly reporting in Europe. Eighty nine percent of the European respondents and 85% of the UK respondents indicated that mandatory comprehensive quarterly reporting, defined as unaudited financial statements with supporting notes and assumptions, would improve the quality of financial information to investors.[55] Only 26% of those surveyed saw the IMS option as a significant improvement. John Barrass, a spokesman for the AIMR pointed out that investors do not make investment decisions once or twice a year, so they 'need, and deserve, regular, comprehensive reporting of financial information by Europe's issuers.'[56] He suggested that 'quarterly financial statements, based on generally accepted accounting standards determined through an independent standard-setting process, are the perfect vehicle for reaching all investors large and small.'[57] He indicated that the proposals to introduce summary quarterly reporting were 'better than nothing' but noted that such reports should be seen as simply the first step towards more comprehensive and regular financial disclosure across Europe. Despite this plea on behalf of investors, the quarterly reporting obligations adopted in the TD in 2004 were limited to IMSs.

The Mazars Group asked European respondents about quarterly reporting as part of its commissioned review of the TD. Responses to a question asking whether the publication of quarterly financial information had enhanced the transparency and efficiency of the market were strongly positive, with 68.8% of respondents answering

55. PR Newswire, 'European Investment Professionals Back Quarterly Reporting', viewed 14 April 2015, http://www.prnewswire.co.uk/news-releases/european-investment-professionals-back-quarterly-reporting-153987615.html.
56. PR Newswire, 'European Investment Professionals Back Quarterly Reporting' http://www.prnewswire.co.uk/news-releases/european-investment-professionals-back-quarterly-reporting-153987615.html, last viewed 14 April 2015.
57. PR Newswire, 'European Investment Professionals Back Quarterly Reporting' http://www.prnewswire.co.uk/news-releases/european-investment-professionals-back-quarterly-reporting-153987615.html, last viewed 14 April 2015.

affirmatively and only 24.2% negatively. Most notably, 70.2% of the company respondents across Europe answered affirmatively, with the clear exception being the UK where 66.7% thought the quarterly information was not useful.[58] The Mazars Report concluded that:

> most stakeholders confirmed that they believe that quarterly information is useful and contributes to the transparency and efficiency of the market. They also generally supported the balanced approach of the Directive in requiring as a minimum only the information required in the IMS.[59]

However, the Impact Report summarily dismissed these views and findings, arguing the 'fact that quarterly financial information is considered as useful by a number of investors does not mean that it is necessary for investor protection.'[60] This report does not explain its use of the term 'investor protection', but it appears the staff believed investors are only 'unprotected' when companies disclose specific hard numbers to some investors. This narrow interpretation of investor protection is not fully credible to persons with a reasonable comprehension of company security analysis and investment practice. Nonetheless, as noted previously, the TD in Europe was amended in October 2013 to abolish the requirement to publish IMSs or quarterly reports, and the deadline for publication of half yearly reports was extended to three months after the end of the reporting period.[61]

The policy reviews of quarterly reporting in Europe, the policy position adopted in the 2004 TD which required only IMSs, and the removal of this minimal obligation in 2013, all highlight the continuing gap between the desired reporting scenarios of corporate managers and market participants. Quarterly reporting regimes ensure comprehensive corporate updates are regularly provided in the public sphere and they limit earnings surprises and trading on privately disclosed information to a relatively short period. In the absence of quarterly reporting, the six-month periods between half year and full year reports is a long time for those relying on public disclosures to assess companies without the receipt of comprehensive financial statements and management commentary and updates. This wait is particularly long when continuous disclosures are incomplete or irregular, or when the general business environment is less stable. The market participants who will ultimately derive most benefit from the recent amendments to the TD are the largest financial institutions with the most highly prized access to senior executives.

Serious transparency issues have arisen in Europe over the last decade, including incomplete or inappropriate disclosure from some Member States and financial institutions. Nevertheless, the amended Transparency Directive applicable to listed company disclosure can best be characterised as minimalist regulation. One can

58. Mazars, *Transparency Directive Assessment Report* 88. It is not clear whether users of the company reports provided the negative responses, as a breakdown of the UK respondents by type of stakeholder is not provided.
59. Mazars, *Transparency Directive Assessment Report* 90.
60. European Commission, Report from the Commission Staff Working Paper *Impact Assessment* (SEC(2011) 1280 final) 29.
61. European Parliament, Directive 2013/50/EU amending 2004/109/EC and Directive 2003/71/EC.

credibly argue that the amended directive fails to satisfy many of the IOSCO disclosure principles, including those that suggest that:

- the periodic reports should be provided to the public in a timely manner;
- the periodic reports should contain relevant information;
- the information should be presented in a clear and concise manner;
- the reports should be presented in a format that facilitates ready analysis of the information;
- all investors should have equal access to the information contained in periodic reports;
- the reports should be stored in a central location that facilitates public access to the information.[62]

When companies listed on exchanges across the EC satisfy only the minimum TD standards, the half year and annual reports across the EC will not be timely, they will not contain all relevant information because the MD&A will be limited in content and quality, the periodic reports and continuous disclosures will not be presented or formatted in a way that facilitates comparative analysis of the information, the disclosure structures will not provide all investors with equal access to reported information, and the reports and disclosures will not be stored in a central location that facilitates public access. The amended rules require corporations to release annual reports four months after the end of the financial year and half year reports within three months of the end of the relevant period. These reporting periods are long in modern financial markets, so the timeliness and materiality of the content of the reports is likely to be an issue. While the periodic reports (the statutory half year and annual reports) must include some MD&A and financial notes, companies may reference non-compliant financial measures in the MD&A sections of these reports. Long-term financial performance measures and commentary are not mandated in either of these reports and the presentation of these reports is not standardised. In addition, the LSE listing rules relating to the content and form of the preliminary full year reports remain largely discretionary. Hence, the informational asymmetries that arise because of the content and timing differences of the preliminary final report and subsequent annual report will be magnified by the longer periodic reporting period of six months.

The utility of such limited public disclosure frameworks is debatable, particularly when jurisdictions encourage regular private briefings between company managers and select participants without corresponding obligations to webcast the briefings, or effective monitoring and enforcement of the private exchanges. The TD amendments are intended to assist small and medium issuers raising capital in the Union. Yet any increases in cost of capital are likely to apply most harshly to smaller entities, as these companies are generally a riskier investment class than larger and more established companies. Therefore, the logical response by investors to the TD amendments is an upward adjustment in the return sought to compensate for the higher risk and lower

62. Technical Committee of the International Organization of Securities Commission, *Principles For Periodic Disclosure By Listed Entitles* Final Report (February 2010) 7–28.

transparency levels. The revised EC transparency policy does not entirely prevent Member States and security exchanges across Europe from establishing higher corporate disclosure standards. So it will be interesting to see if Member States that previously had relatively higher disclosure standards – including more regular, timely, and comprehensive reporting – maintain these obligations. The comparative cost of market-based capital across European financial markets should be closely monitored. It will be important to observe any movement in investment capital flows to corporations and markets across Europe, or to other jurisdictions that require or provide higher quality public disclosures from listed corporations.

The removal of the obligation to provide IMSs across the EC will mark a further shift from a public communication model to a private communication framework based on private exchanges with privileged participants. The author expects this move will be counterproductive over the long-term. The longer window of six months between the mandated periodic reports will make privately obtained company information potentially more valuable, it will increase information asymmetries across the market, and it may increase potential levels of market uncertainty, volatility and speculation. The empirical research discussed in this book suggests that reduced regularity and quality of public reporting is likely to lead to declining levels of investor and public trust in large corporations and financial markets. As public access to company information is further eroded, the decline in retail investor participation in equity markets will likely accelerate.

§13.05 NATURE AND SCOPE OF MANAGEMENT DISCUSSION AND ANALYSIS

Another area of contention within corporate reporting spheres concerns the form and content of MD&A in periodic reports and continuous disclosures. The information that listed companies publicly report includes quantitative and qualitative information. As discussed in earlier chapters, the qualitative information is commonly referred to as MD&A. MD&A is discussion and analysis by company management about the past, current and prospective positions of the company. MD&A is an 'integral component of financial reporting, [and] an essential companion to the financial statements.'[63] Company information provided without context can be misleading, rather than informative, because financial statements alone are often insufficient for an investor to judge the quality of a company's earnings and whether past results are indicative of likely future performance. Notes on the financial accounts, explanations of the financial results and other MD&A are important to evaluate the recurring and non-recurring components of results and to understand the historical and prospective positions of the company. IOSCO indicates that MD&A should include detailed information relating to:

63. Canadian Institute of Chartered Accountants, *Building a Better MD&A, A Guide for Smaller Issuers* (November 2007) 1.

- a company's historical and expected or forecast financial performance;
- its risks;
- its ownership;[64]
- any compensation awarded or paid to the directors and senior managers; and
- disclosure of possible conflicts between the interests of the company and its directors.[65]

Short and longer-term risk management is an essential component of a company's strategy. All companies should systematically identify foreseeable risks and estimate the likely consequences should these risks eventuate. They should also establish plans and controls to manage or mitigate these risks. These risk frameworks should then be effectively communicated throughout the company and to outsiders. Risk disclosures within MD&A are necessary for outsiders to make informed assessments of a company's financial position and prospects. IOSCO indicates that risk disclosures should include:

- an outline of the assumptions underpinning any management forecasts;
- disclosure of off-balance sheet transactions;
- information regarding the estimates, assumptions, methodologies and sensitivities encompassed within the adopted accounting policies; and
- detailed information about the company's exposure to financial market risks, and management of these risks, including: interest rate risks, foreign currency exchange rate risks, commodity price risks, liquidity risks and derivative instrument risks.

While some of these IOSCO risk disclosure categories have been broadly adopted, comprehensive risk disclosure is not always stipulated within the national reporting frameworks of the countries reviewed. For instance, Australia does not require comprehensive risk disclosures within periodic reports and continuous disclosures.

IOSCO includes disclosure of key corporate governance practices in its risk metrics, with recommended disclosure limbs including information on the:

- company's directors and senior management;
- independence of the directors;
- existence and operation of an audit committee;
- members of the compensation committee; and
- adoption of a code of ethics.[66]

As noted earlier, most major exchanges have corporate governance codes requiring listed companies to either comply with the relevant principles or provide an

64. IOSCO indicates that required information relating to company security ownership includes details relating to significant shareholders, details of the classes of securities, the number and nature of the voting securities, and management ownership.
65. Technical Committee of the International Organization of Securities Commission, *Principles For Periodic Disclosure By Listed Entitles* Final Report (February 2010) 7–28.
66. Technical Committee of the International Organization of Securities Commission, *Principles For Periodic Disclosure By Listed Entitles* Final Report (February 2010) 7–28.

explanation for why a recommendation has not been followed. These codes generally require disclosure of similar corporate governance matters as those recommended by IOSCO. Disclosure relating to executive compensation has received particular attention since the GFC. IOSCO suggests that information on compensation should include detailed disclosure about director and senior management compensation, including procedures used to determine remuneration, and explanations about the alignment of compensation with performance, investors' interests and shareholder returns. It also recommends companies to provide details of any equity compensation plans, including potential dilutive effects.[67] Related party transactions are another area acknowledged to be of increasing importance. IOSCO recommends disclosure of the nature and materiality of, and business rationales for, related party transactions.[68]

The SEC suggests that MD&A should include explanation and interpretation of publicly announced results and financial reports, as well as commentary on non-financial or qualitative issues such as strategy, growth opportunities, industry trends and issues, competitive advantages, business risks, and financial parameters and targets. It notes that the purpose of MD&A is to allow investors to see the company through the 'eyes of management.'[69] The SEC highlights the need for clear language and presentation, with an emphasis on material information. It advises that disclosures must address known material events and uncertainties and there must be genuine analysis of key material items rather than boilerplate discussion and explanation.[70] Countries outside of the US are also increasingly acknowledging the importance of high quality MD&A within well-integrated and effective company reporting structures.[71] Similar guidance to that provided by the SEC is provided by other national regulators, as outlined in Chapters 6 and 10. Regulators and expert commentators frequently emphasise the need for tailored reports that focus on material issues and communicate results effectively, rather than mechanically produced reports with long disclosures of immaterial matters.[72]

---

67. Technical Committee of the International Organization of Securities Commission, *Principles For Periodic Disclosure By Listed Entitles* Final Report (February 2010) 7–28.
68. Technical Committee of the International Organization of Securities Commission, *Principles For Periodic Disclosure By Listed Entitles* Final Report (February 2010) 7–28.
69. Regulation S-K Item 303, *Management's Discussion and Analysis of Financial Condition and Results of Operations* (2005).
70. Regulation S-K Item 303, *Management's Discussion and Analysis of Financial Condition and Results of Operations* (2005).
71. See, e.g., International Accounting Standards Board, *Exposure Draft: An Improved Conceptual Framework for Financial Reporting* (2008); Canadian Institute of Chartered Accountants (CICA), *Building a Better MD&A, Risk Disclosure* (March 2008); CICA, *Building a Better MD&A, A Guide for Smaller Issuers* (November 2007); CICA, *CFO Beyond-GAAP Briefing: Forward-Looking Information* (May 2008); CICA, *MD&A Guidance on Preparation And Disclosure* (July 2009). The CICA emphasise six general principles for MD&A disclosures: through the eyes of management; integration with financial statements; completeness and materiality; forward-looking orientation; strategic perspective; and usefulness.
72. Arthur Radin, 'Have We Created Financial Statement Overload?' (2007) 77 *CPA Journal* 6; David Jutuah, 'Box Ticking Isn't Enough for Investors, warns PwC' (27 September 2007) *Accountancy Age* 8; Carol Baker, 'Company Report- Written to Order' (2008) 29 *Credit Control* 6.

The Kay Final Report recommends that high quality and succinct narrative reporting should be strongly encouraged.[73] It indicates that good 'quality narrative reporting can put the financial results in context, highlight important factors and communicate strategy and risks in an understandable, engaging and concise format.'[74] This statement accords with the views of national regulators, as outlined in Part III. The form and content of MD&A, and the context within which it is presented, are all important to ensure the commentary and analysis is understandable and useful. MD&A that is disconnected from the reported financial statements can present a misleading picture of the company's result, and can make it difficult for readers to analyse and comprehend the company's performance and its relative position within the industry and across the market.

All of the jurisdictions reviewed in Part III require listed companies to publicly release financial statements at least twice annually. Further, they all require some financial notes and MD&A within periodic reports, but most do not prescribe the specific form or content of the MD&A sections of periodic reports or of the commentary provided in continuous disclosures and on company websites. The mandated MD&A content in half year and preliminary full year reports in most jurisdictions is minimal in comparison to the material required in preliminary full year (10-K) reports in the US, and is sometimes considerably less substantive than the MD&A provided in the quarterly (10-Q) reports. As a result, the quality of MD&A provided within listed company periodic reports and continuous disclosures varies greatly across the jurisdictions reviewed. As one regulator notes, MD&A in some reports is 'sometimes so formulaic that it communicates very little to the reader.'[75] While some national regulators have processes in place to monitor and promote improved MD&A reporting, evidence of formal enforcement of MD&A rules outside of the US is limited.

[A] Empirical Research

Empirical studies confirm the importance of MD&A in the assessment of a company's prospects and future earnings. A study by the American Association for Investment

73. *The Kay Review of UK Equity Markets and Long-Term Decision Making: Final Report* (July 2012) 74. There are proposals in the United Kingdom to improve the quality of MD&A provided in annual reports, but the author expects these reforms to have only a marginally beneficial effect. The proposed strategically focused MD&A is already provided at private briefings and during the preliminary final reporting period, so a short report with high-level commentary and tailored key performance metrics within the annual report (four months after the financial year end) will be of limited value to investors who need access to comprehensive information on a timely basis.
74. *The Kay Review of UK Equity Markets and Long-Term Decision Making: Final Report* (July 2012) 74.
75. Belinda Gibson, Australian Securities and Investments Commissioner, 'Facilitating Capital Raising for Corporate Australia' (Speech delivered at the Corporate Finance World Australia 2009 Conference, 10 November 2009) 8.

Management and Research found that investment professionals and financial statement users 'wanted companies to disclose more internal management information.'[76] A study by the American Institute of Certified Public Accountants concluded that 'the information that investors consider most useful in valuing a company's securities is essentially the same as the information that managers use within the firm.'[77] A research project by the Financial Accounting Standards Board in the US highlighted that 'sophisticated investors want access to the business operating information generated and used within the firm' and that all users value disclosure of non-financial information.[78]

Scholarly studies confirm these views. Bryan found that MD&A disclosures, particularly prospective disclosures, assist in assessing a company's future prospects over the following year.[79] Fox et al. concluded that share prices in the US are more informed as a result of enhanced MD&A disclosure requirements.[80] Vanstraelen et al. also found that continental European companies that provided higher levels of forward-looking non-financial disclosures were associated with lower dispersion and higher accuracy in analysts' earnings forecasts.[81] Importantly, a study that examined the effects of risk disclosures in 10-K reports in the US found that the disclosures meaningfully reflected the risks faced by companies and significantly reduced information asymmetry among shareholders.[82]

§13.06 DISCLOSURE OF BAD NEWS

As discussed in Chapter 2, company disclosure regimes are intended to overcome potential managerial conflicts of interest and promote timely disclosure of material company information in the public arena, especially of negative news. Some listed companies disclose in a straightforward manner when facing difficult environments or when there is negative news to report. Other companies ignore or gloss over bad news in reports and public announcements, or disclose in a manner that draws attention to positive aspects of the company's performance. Although positively framed corporate reports may be technically compliant in some jurisdictions, such disclosure adversely

76. Michael Guttentag, 'An Argument for Imposing Disclosure Requirements on Public Companies' (2004) 32 *Florida State University Law Review* 123, 173 citing a study entitled *Financial Reporting in the 1990's and Beyond.*
77. Michael Guttentag, 'An Argument for Imposing Disclosure Requirements on Public Companies' (2004) 32 *Florida State University Law Review* 123, 173.
78. Peter Clarkson, Jennifer Kao and Gordon Richardson, 'The Voluntary Inclusion of Forecasts in the MD&A Section of Annual Reports' (1994) 11 *Contemporary Accounting Research* 423.
79. Stephen Bryan, 'Incremental Information Content of Required Disclosures Contained in Management Discussion and Analysis' (1997) 72 *Accounting Review* 285, 285, 298.
80. Merritt Fox, Randall Morck, Bernard Yeung and Artyom Durnev, 'Law, Share Price Accuracy, and Economic Performance: The New Evidence' (2003) 102 *Michigan Law Review* 331, 368–379.
81. Ann Vanstraelen, Marilyn Zareski and Sean Robb, 'Corporate Nonfinancial Disclosure Practices and Financial Analyst Forecast Ability Across Three European Countries' (2003) 14 *Journal of International Financial Management and Accounting* 249.
82. John Campbell, Hsinchun Chen, Dan Dhakiwal, Hsin-min Lu and Logan Steele, 'The Information Content of Mandatory Risk Factor Disclosures in Corporate Filings' (2014) 19 *Review of Accounting Studies* 396.

impacts investors and stakeholders, particularly when companies are in financial difficulties.

Global empirical studies confirm that both the level and quality of disclosure from companies facing adverse news or performance trends are poor. Holland found that listed companies in the UK did not willingly release information about downside risks or negative news within public disclosures unless it 'involved a well-publicised problem, a profits warning, or they were faced by a clear regulatory requirement.'[83] He suggests that company disclosures are written in ways that reflect an optimistic bias and avoid discussion of downside risks where possible.[84] In the US, Pastena and Ronen found that company managers delayed the disclosure of negative information. Moreover, they disclosed primarily soft positive information rather than soft negative information, and disclosed negative information only after such information became hard.[85] Similarly, Lewellen et al. found evidence that companies chose to report against stock return benchmarks that showed the results in a favourable light. The degree of bias against disclosing downward risks was stronger for companies with relatively weaker earnings and share price performance.[86]

Interestingly, Rogers and Stocken found company managers' willingness to misrepresent forward-looking information was a function of the market's ability to detect the misrepresentation.[87] That is, managers were more likely to issue forecasts that were biased when it was more difficult for investors to detect the bias.[88] A study by Graham et al. comprising a combination of field interviews and a survey of more than 400 CFOs in the US confirmed these trends. Although profitable companies were inclined to release bad news quickly, unprofitable companies were more likely to delay bad news.[89] Some CFOs admitted they allow 'fuzziness' in bad news disclosures and several indicated that they delay the release of bad news 'in hopes that the firm's status improves before the next required information release, perhaps saving the company the need to ever release the bad information.'[90] Vyas examined the timeliness of write-downs by US financial institutions during the financial crisis of 2007-2008. He found that companies with higher financial leverage, more complex exposures, and

83. John Holland, *A Model of Corporate Financial Communications* (Institute of Chartered Accountants of Scotland, 2006) 132.
84. John Holland, *A Model of Corporate Financial Communications* (Institute of Chartered Accountants of Scotland, 2006) 157.
85. Victor Pastena and Joshua Ronen, 'Some Hypotheses on the Pattern of Management's Informal Disclosures' (1979) 17 *Journal of Accounting Research* 550, 563-564.
86. Wilbur Lewellen, Taewoo Park and Byung Ro, 'Self-serving Behaviour in Managers' Discretionary Information Disclosure' (1996) 21 *Journal of Accounting and Economics* 227. See also Donald Langevoort, 'Organized Illusions: A Behavioral Theory of Why Corporations Mislead Stock Market Investors (and Cause Other Social Harms)' (1997) 146 *University of Pennsylvania Law Review* 101.
87. Jonathan Rogers and Phillip Stocken, 'Credibility of Management Forecasts' (2005) 80 *Accounting Review* 1233.
88. Jonathan Rogers and Phillip Stocken, 'Credibility of Management Forecasts' (2005) 80 *Accounting Review* 1233.
89. John Graham, Campbell Harvey and Shiva Rajgopal, 'The Economic Implications of Corporate Financial Reporting' (2005) 40 *Journal of Accounting and Economics* 3.
90. John Graham, Campbell Harvey and Shiva Rajgopal, 'The Economic Implications of Corporate Financial Reporting' (2005) 40 *Journal of Accounting and Economics* 3, 65.

greater capital constraints were less timely in making required write-downs. Conversely, companies that reported better quality corporate governance indicators, faced greater litigation pressure, or were under investigation by the regulators, were timelier in their write-downs.[91]

Schrand and Zechman examined companies subject to accounting and auditing enforcement releases by the SEC for incidents of misreporting. Their analysis suggested that most instances of misreporting began with an optimistically biased misstatement by an overconfident executive (whether intentional or not). When the initial performance expectations could not be met, the executives made a conscious decision to continue misreporting on an escalating scale, in order to hide the initial reporting errors. They describe this process as the slippery slope of financial reporting misconduct.[92] Arlen and Carney reported that 91.3% of the fraud on the market cases in the US during the period 1970–1990 involved either the concealment of a decline in earnings or the concealment of bad news. These concealment cases had serious impacts, with overall stock prices falling more than 40% when the truth was revealed.[93]

The language and tone adopted by corporate managers in company reports have been shown to influence investor judgments. A body of empirical studies that examines the non-financial component of company reporting confirms the importance of MD&A and the significance of the tone used in oral and written disclosures.[94] A study by Tan et al. found that market participants react positively to optimistic language sentiment or tone embedded in financial disclosures, and that investors' reactions to negative news are more muted with poor disclosure readability. Notably, the study found that when readability is low, disclosure couched in positive language leads to high earnings judgments for less sophisticated investors, but lower earnings judgments for more

91. Dushyantkumar Vyas, 'The Timeliness of Accounting Write-Downs by US Financial Institutions During the Financial Crisis of 2007-2008' (2011) 49 *Journal of Accounting Research* 823.
92. Catherine Schrand and Sarah Zechman, 'Executive Overconfidence and the Slippery Slope to Financial Misreporting' (2012) 53 *Journal of Accounting and Economics* 311.
93. Jennifer Arlen and William Carney, 'Vicarious Liability for Fraud on Securities Markets: Theory and Evidence' (1992) *University of Illinois Law Review* 691. Arlen and Carney found that 8.7% of the cases involved attempts to understate the value of securities when there were conflicts of interest or the managers were attempting to buy out the shareholders at an unfairly low price. See also R Tillman and M Irgaard, *Control Overrides in Financial Statement Fraud: A Report to the Institute for Fraud Protection* (16 January 2007). Tillman and Indergaard highlight that the most expensive corporate frauds to date have involved alleged CEO and CFO involvement or collusion.
94. See, e.g., Jeffrey Hales, Xi Kuang and Shankar Venkataraman, 'Who Believes the Hype? An Experimental Examination of How Language Affects Investor Judgments' (2011) 49 *Journal of Accounting Research* 223; Feng Li, 'The Information Content of Forward-Looking Statements in Corporate Filings – A Naïve Baysian Machine Learning Approach' (2010) 48 *Journal of Accounting Research* 1049; Jun Han and Hun Tong Tan, 'Investors Reactions to Management Earnings Guidance: The Joint Effect of Investment Position, News Valance, and Guidance Form' (2010) 48 *Journal of Accounting Research* 123; Paul C Tetlock, Maytal Saar-Tsechansky and Sofus Macskassy, 'More than Words: Quantifying Language to Measure Firms' Fundamentals' (2008) 63 *Journal of Finance* 1437; Donald Langevoort, 'Half-Truths: Protecting Mistaken Inferences by Investors and Others' (1999) 52 *Stanford Law Review* 87.

sophisticated investors.[95] The study authors suggest that more sophisticated investors see through the 'strategic nature of management's use of positive language and low readability, and 'punish' management accordingly by discounting such disclosures.'[96] While company managers universally prefer to disclose news using optimistic framing and language, cultural differences can impact disclosure patterns. For example, Hooghiemstra found the tendency of CEOs to emphasise good news and portray the company in the best possible light in their letters to shareholders is more emphatic in the US than in Japan, while the practice of ascribing bad news to causes beyond managerial control is stronger in Japan.[97]

Behavioural economists contribute some interesting and valuable evidence with respect to misleading, deceptive and fraudulent behaviour. Ariely's experimental findings suggest that humans have conflicting motivations when engaging in dishonest behaviour because we naturally want to see ourselves as honourable and honest, but at the same time we seek to optimise personal benefits. To rationalise such conduct, we fool others and ourselves by means of 'cognitive flexibility' which allows us to perceive or believe that we are not cheating or getting away with anything.[98] Ariely notes that distance can be a significant factor. In other words, 'cheating becomes much simpler when there are more steps between us and the dishonest act.'[99] For example, we are more likely to do something dishonest that ultimately provides us with cash value than to steal cash directly. Importantly, Ariely finds that some of the worst conflicts of interest arise when there is a professional relationship of trust. In such scenarios, people are commonly unwilling or unable to acknowledge or recognise when dishonesty is occurring. He confirms that cheating can gain momentum, scale and acceptance in a group, making it important to respond early on. He suggests that we need to acknowledge our fallibilities so we can establish protective measures for others and ourselves.[100]

Some of Ariely's propositions are reflected in a study by Brown, which found that if a manager engages in a small level of earnings management, this causes the manager to begin to believe that earnings management is appropriate. Brown found that participants who choose to manage earnings are motivated to rationalise their behaviour. They compare their behaviour against more egregious examples and find their

95. Hun-Tong Tan, Elaine Ying Wang and Bo Zhou, 'When the Use of Positive Language Backfires: The Joint Effect of Tone, Readability, and Investor Sophistication on Earnings Judgements' (2014) 52 *Journal of Accounting Research* 273.
96. Hun-Tong Tan, Elaine Ying Wang and Bo Zhou, 'When the Use of Positive Language Backfires: The Joint Effect of Tone, Readability, and Investor Sophistication on Earnings Judgements' (2014) 52 *Journal of Accounting Research* 273, 275.
97. Reggy Hooghiemstra, 'Letters to the Shareholders: A Content Analysis Comparison of Letters Written by CEOs in the United States and Japan' (2010) 45 *The International Journal of Accounting* 275.
98. Dan Ariely, *The (Honest) Truth About Dishonesty: How We Lie to Everyone---Especially Ourselves* (HarperCollins, 2012). Dan Ariely is the James B. Duke Professor of Psychology and Behavioral Economics at Duke University.
99. Dan Ariely, *The (Honest) Truth About Dishonesty: How We Lie to Everyone---Especially Ourselves* (HarperCollins, 2012).
100. Dan Ariely, *The (Honest) Truth About Dishonesty: How We Lie to Everyone---Especially Ourselves* (HarperCollins, 2012).

conduct was relatively innocuous, and this sometimes encourages continued earnings management. He suggests that this behaviour may serve as a contributing factor to the slippery slope phenomenon of financial reporting misconduct.[101]

§13.07 REPORTING IN ACCORDANCE WITH ACCOUNTING STANDARDS

One of the common approaches used to disguise negative performance or bad news is the provision of MD&A that references non-compliant financial measures. As highlighted in Part III, company managers are able to provide consistently positive commentary and claim that profits are growing, when all of the bad news or poor performance is excluded as abnormal or significant items, non-recurring items, discontinued business, non-cash items, restructuring costs, integration costs, write-offs, impairments, provisioning, acquisition or sale related costs, amortisation and so forth. Regulators in most jurisdictions are aware that non-compliant financial measures are commonly used to frame negative news. BaFin indicates that 'the key figures used in publications must be those customarily used in business and must permit comparison with previously used key figures.'[102] Similarly, NYSE Listing rule 202.06 notes that:

> Reluctance or unwillingness to release a negative story or an attempt to disguise unfavorable news endangers management's reputation for integrity. Changes in accounting methods to mask such occurrences can have a similar impact.

While some countries continue to use nationally based accounting standards, most of the jurisdictions reviewed have moved, or are moving to, international accounting standards. The Financial Accounting Standards Board in the US suggests 'there is demand for international convergence, driven by investors' desire for high quality, internationally comparable financial information that is useful for decision making in our increasingly global capital markets.'[103] PricewaterhouseCoopers (PwC) suggests that convergence of accounting standards towards International Financial Reporting Standards (IFRS) will contribute to the flow of international investment and benefit all capital markets stakeholders because it:

- renders international investments more comparable for investors;
- reduces the cost of complying with accounting requirements for global businesses;
- potentially establishes a more transparent accounting system with greater accountability;

101. Timothy Brown, 'Advantageous Comparison and Rationalization of Earnings Management' (2014) 52 *Journal of Accounting Research* 849.
102. Bafin, *Issuer Guideline* (14 May 2009) 59, viewed 13 June 2015, http://www.bafin.de/SharedDocs/Downloads/EN/Leitfaden/dl_Emittentenleitfaden_2009_en.html.
103. International Accounting Standards Board, International Convergence of Accounting Standards - Overview, 14 February 2013 http://www.fasb.org/jsp/FASB/Page/SectionPage&cid=1176156245663.

- reduces 'operational challenges' for accounting firms; and
- gives standard-setters the opportunity to 'improve the reporting model'.[104]

There is some empirical evidence suggesting the adoption of IFRS can enhance the quality of disclosure. For example, Landsman et al. examined earnings announcements from sixteen countries that required adoption of IFRS and eleven countries that retained domestic accounting standards.[105] They found an improvement in the information content of company announcements following mandatory IFRS adoption.[106] Further, companies from countries with strong enforcement experienced a greater change in information content than those from countries with weak enforcement.[107] A study by Wang also found that international accounting standards facilitate transnational information transfers and better comparable analysis.[108]

Most countries mandate the content and form of financial statements within periodic reports and these numbers are required to be calculated in accordance with accounting standards. However, the rules relating to the use of non-compliant financial measures within the MD&A sections of periodic reports are generally less strict than those governing financial statements. As outlined in Part III, some countries require listed companies to provide some form of reconciliation between the reported numbers in the financial statements and non-compliant financial measures referenced in the MD&A sections of periodic reports. A few jurisdictions go further and oblige companies to provide a side-by-side reconciliation, an outline of the calculation methodology, and reasons why the non-compliant financial measures are useful. Notably, rules relating to the use of non-compliant financial measures within continuous disclosures are either minimal or do not exist at all. Many companies reference non-compliant financial measures in their continuous disclosures without adequate explanation, making it difficult for users to make essential connections between the content in periodic reports and continuous disclosures.

Some company managers argue that certain accounting standards do not allow them to present the company's position fairly. For example, in *QBE Insurance Group Ltd and Ors v. ASC*,[109] the managers of QBE Insurance thought that mark-to-market adjustments resulted in undue volatility in the reported financial statements. Lockhart J indicated that:

> if, in the opinions of the directors of a company, the accounts prepared in compliance with the accounting standards would not give a true and fair view of

104. PricewaterhouseCoopers, *ViewPoint* (April 2007).
105. Measured as the abnormal return volatility and abnormal trading volume.
106. Wayne Landsman, Edward Maydew and Jacob Thornock, 'The Information Content of Annual Earnings Announcements and Mandatory Adoption of IFRS' (2012) 53 *Journal of Accounting and Economics* 34.
107. Wayne Landsman, Edward Maydew and Jacob Thornock, 'The Information Content of Annual Earnings Announcements and Mandatory Adoption of IFRS' (2012) 53 *Journal of Accounting and Economics* 34.
108. Clare Wang, 'Accounting Standards Harmonization and Financial Statement Comparability: Evidence from Transnational Information Transfer' (2014) 52 *Journal of Accounting Research* 955, 989.
109. *QBE Insurance Group Ltd and Ors v. Australian Securities Commission* (1992) 8 ACSR 631.

the company's profit and loss for a financial year, the directors can add information or appropriate notes.[110]

This judicial response is accurate and reasonable. For disclosure regimes to achieve their objectives, it is vital that performance analysis over long periods can be done without the need for complex and ambiguous adjustments. Listed companies can add notes or commentary if necessary to convey useful information. When companies provide performance analysis, they should focus on achievements and progress that satisfy their long-term objectives. The effects of voluntary adjustments to reported numbers that comply with accounting standards are generally only relevant for short-term analysis, with the value of these adjustments diminishing over time. Consequently, the best way to communicate the effects of mark-to-market variations on a company's performance is to include a long-term performance table that includes the earnings results with and without these variations.

The Kay Final Report suggests that accounting standards emphasise comparability at the expense of relevance and this emphasis on comparability benefits large international accounting companies.[111] It would be interesting to discover what underpinned these conclusions and whether the Kay Report Review Committee sought evidence on this issue. Company financial statements that are calculated in accordance with generally accepted accounting standards are intended to enhance the utility, reliability and accuracy of company reporting.[112] Accounting standards are subject to ongoing review, with adjustments made as reporting environments develop and change. Scholars and other commentators naturally have differing views on the quality and relevance of individual accounting standards and the benefits of international convergence.[113] These ongoing debates are important and form an essential part of a professional standards framework.

Many companies outside of the US reference non-compliant financial measures in the commentary sections of periodic reports and within continuous disclosures and investor presentation material. Some companies reference the same non-compliant financial measures and performance indicators over long periods, while others regularly change the referenced non-compliant financial measures during a reporting period and from period-to-period without adequate or clear explanations. Issues that commonly arise when companies regularly change financial benchmarks include

110. *QBE Insurance Group Ltd and Ors v. Australian Securities Commission* (1992) 8 ACSR 631. Paragraph 23 of the Australian Accounting Standards Board required insurance companies to bring to account unrealised gains and losses on investments at balance date within the profit and loss statement. This requirement applied irrespective of the length to maturity of the investments and whether the gains or losses were real or permanent.

111. *The Kay Review of UK Equity Markets and Long-Term Decision Making: Final Report* (July 2012) 72.

112. The Australian Accounting Standards Board indicates that reporting frameworks encompassing accounting standards seek to 'present fairly the financial position, financial performance and cash flows of a company ... [and to assist third parties] in making and evaluating decisions about the allocation of scarce economic resources ...': Australian Accounting Standards Board, *Frequently Asked Questions* <http://www.aasb.com.au/About-the-AASB/Frequently-asked-questions.aspx#qa770> at 2 July 2010.

113. See, e.g., Ray Ball, 'International Financial Reporting Standards (IFRS): Pros and Cons for Investors' (2006) 36 (Special issue) *Accounting and Business Research* 5.

comprehension difficulties and a lack of managerial scrutiny and accountability, especially when the benchmarks emphasised are financial measures that show the company (and the managers) in the most favourable light. Many companies adopt and reference non-compliant financial measures that they hope or expect investors will use to assess their performance. For example, financial companies often emphasise cash or operational earnings (prior to, or excluding, provisioning and mark-to-market adjustments). Yet, as the GFC highlighted, the management of scarce capital is a critical component of financial entity operations and valuations. Reductions in the capital of financial institutions in the form of loan provisions and fair value reductions often have to be replenished, particularly when the external environment is under stress for sustained periods.

Some companies reference non-compliant financial measures that exclude most or all of the bad news so regularly that it becomes a standard feature of their reporting cycle. For some companies, writing off millions or billions of dollars from asset and capital values is portrayed in reports, disclosures and presentations as relatively insignificant, with large write-downs included as ancillary items with a one or two line explanation in the financial notes. In extreme cases, these processes can become such an ingrained part of a company's culture that its managers begin to view objectively poor performance as positive. When this occurs, negative factors tend to be glossed over even when significant issues are developing that should be dealt with as a matter of priority or urgency. Indeed, the most significant risks associated with reporting patterns based on non-compliant or 'underlying' financial measures are managerial complacency and inadequate response to poor performance and deteriorating financial positions.

It is important that listed companies comply with accounting standards in all of their reports and disclosures, including within financial statements, financial notes, MD&A, and continuous disclosures. While discussion of non-compliant financial measures can provide supplementary information, such discussion is only useful when carefully explained and justified. When companies disclose their results using or referencing unexplained non-compliant financial measures, interpreting periodic reports and disclosures can be time-consuming or even futile, particularly when these measures change on a regular basis. Investors and stakeholders with private access to senior executives can seek explanation or clarification of ambiguous reporting, but other participants do not have the means or time to query uncertain terminology used in public disclosures.

[A] Empirical Research

There are practical issues around the use of non-compliant financial measures in most jurisdictions. Bowen et al. found that US managers emphasised the set of numbers in press releases that portrayed company performance most favourably.[114] Marques

114. Robert Bowen, Angela Davis and Dawn Matsumoto, 'Do Firms Strategically Emphasize Performance Metrics in their Earnings Press Releases?' (2005) 80 *The Accounting Review* 1011.

found that managers emphasised non-compliant financial measures in order to satisfy strategic benchmarks.[115] Doyle et al. also found evidence consistent with managers opportunistically defining earnings using non-compliant financial measures in order to meet or beat analyst expectations.[116] They noted that companies were able to do this by including unexpected exclusions from the earnings measures. Similarly, Walker and Louvari concluded that companies adopted adjusted earnings per share measures in the UK when the compliant measure was a loss and the adjusted non-compliant financial measure enabled the firm to report a positive result.[117] Empirical research on Australian company disclosures revealed similar patterns. North found that MD&A in company reports, exchange announcements and media releases regularly referenced non-compliant financial measures in order to frame results positively.[118] This pattern was most prominent when the diluted earnings per share trends were negative or declining.[119]

§13.08 STANDARDISED REPORTING

[A] The Development of Standardised Reporting

The use of standard forms for corporate reporting is a discrete but connected issue to reporting in accordance with accounting standards. The importance of company reporting in a form that enables investment comparability is often stated in regulatory material across the jurisdictions reviewed. For example, IOSCO indicates that:

> periodic reports facilitate investor decision making and monitoring of the markets by making it possible for investors to compare the performance of the same company over regular intervals, and by enabling investors to make useful comparisons among different companies.[120]

Nonetheless, rules that require company disclosure in a form that assists users of company disclosures to engage in comparative analysis are usually limited to the calculation of financial items in the financial statements in accordance with accounting standards. Companies are also required to provide prior year comparisons in the

115. Ana Marques, 'Disclosure Strategies Among S&P Firms: Evidence on the Disclosure of Non-GAAP Financial Measures and Financial Statements in Earnings Press Releases' (2010) 42 *British Accounting Review* 119.
116. Jeffrey Doyle, Jared Jennings and Mark Soliman, 'Do Managers Define Non-GAAP Earnings To Meet Or Beat Analyst Forecasts?' (2013) 56 *Journal of Accounting and Economics* 40.
117. Martin Walker and Evagelia Louvari, 'The Determinants of Voluntary Disclosure of Adjusted Earnings Per Share Measures by UK Quoted Companies' (2003) 33 *Accounting and Business Research* 295.
118. Gill North, 'Continuous Disclosure in Australia: The Empirical Uncertainties' (2011) 29 *Company and Securities Law Journal* 394.
119. Gill North, 'Continuous Disclosure in Australia: The Empirical Uncertainties' (2011) 29 *Company and Securities Law Journal* 394.
120. Technical Committee of the International Organization of Securities Commission, *Principles For Periodic Disclosure By Listed Entitles* Final Report (February 2010) 4.

financial statements in all of the countries reviewed, but not for earlier periods, so when historical line items are not calculated on a comparable basis for periods extending back more than two years, longer-term trends can be difficult to determine.

The Kay Final Report notes that a core area of securities regulation developed in the US in the 1930s involved templates that prescribed the information companies needed to provide, with restrictions on the provision of information outside of these templates.[121] It indicates that other countries then adopted this practice. It links this practice of standardised reporting to an economic theory[122] that hypothesises that information asymmetry and misaligned incentive problems are resolved and optimal long-term decisions are made when markets are supplied with sufficient information, and participants trade using this information.[123] These statements overreach, as the information provided in standard templates is not intended to, and in practice cannot, mitigate all information asymmetry or incentive issues. In any event, none of the jurisdictions examined prohibit companies from providing the market with supplementary information.[124]

The Kay Final Report claims that '[d]isclosure and transparency have become mantras in policy and in regulation.'[125] It indicates that market participants are presented with a continuous flow of data on their screens and through other electronic means. It argues that '[m]uch of the information that is provided in standard templates is simply noise'[126] and that what is needed is knowledge and understanding.[127] It notes that 'annual returns and regulatory filings have steadily increased in length ... [and] [m]uch of the content of reports and filings is boiler plate – verbiage which is produced in almost identical form from year to year and by company after company.'[128] This combined commentary suggests that much of the information provided under mandatory disclosure regimes is not useful.[129] However, no specific recommendations or proposals are outlined to improve the quality of public disclosures.

121. *The Kay Review of UK Equity Markets and Long-Term Decision Making: Final Report* (July 2012) 27.
122. The economic theory that the Kay Final Report refers to is not named or explained.
123. *The Kay Review of UK Equity Markets and Long-Term Decision Making: Final Report* (July 2012) 27.
124. As previously discussed, most jurisdictions require listed companies to reconcile non-compliant financial measures with the reported numbers and to explain the reasons why these measures are useful.
125. *The Kay Review of UK Equity Markets and Long-Term Decision Making: Final Report* (July 2012) 70.
126. *The Kay Review of UK Equity Markets and Long-Term Decision Making: Final Report* (July 2012) 71.
127. *The Kay Review of UK Equity Markets and Long-Term Decision Making: Final Report* (July 2012) 73.
128. *The Kay Review of UK Equity Markets and Long-Term Decision Making: Final Report* (July 2012) 71.
129. This discussion is difficult to critique without an explanation or understanding of the distinction between information characterised as 'noise' and information that purportedly enables knowledge and understanding.

[B] Tailored Reporting and Disclosure

Some companies argue that standardised reporting is inappropriate for their specific circumstances and they need to report on a tailored basis. For example, the Kay Final Report states that the provision of information should be tailored to the needs of users because standard templates are seriously limited and they cannot fit the wide variety of companies that provide information or satisfy the needs of all users.[130] Companies that manage long dated assets or projects are cited as an example. It suggests the profitability of oil, mining, utilities, and pharmaceutical companies can only be meaningfully assessed over many years,[131] and that construction companies and banks should be judged over a complete economic cycle.[132] It acknowledges that ongoing assessment of these companies is necessary, but suggests these judgments are fine, qualitative and subjective.[133] It concludes that useful information can be given to asset managers and shareholders, but the nature of this information should be 'discursive rather than statistical and the appropriate form and frequency will be company specific.'[134] Thus, a consistent theme of the Kay Final Report is a preference for tailored non-financial commentary from company managers rather than quantitative information.

The Kay Interim Report states that:

> A company's accounts are a snapshot on a particular day. They must present a true and fair view of the affairs of the company and also contain information about the past, present and future. Not only will elements always be volatile, but subjectivity is also inevitable. It is not realistic to imagine that any prescribed body of quantitative data can fully meet all these purposes.[135]

These comments suggest the content of a company's financial statements is volatile and subjective and that no prescribed body of quantitative data can present a true and fair view of the affairs of a company. The argument seems to be that reported numbers lack objectivity and usefulness, in that they are products merely of opinion, and these numbers do not reflect the commercial realities of individual companies or the business community more generally. The Kay Interim Report claims that to interpret a company's numbers and adequately understand its position requires skill,

130. *The Kay Review of UK Equity Markets and Long-Term Decision Making: Final Report* (July 2012) 46.
131. *The Kay Review of UK Equity Markets and Long-Term Decision Making: Final Report* (July 2012) 73.
132. *The Kay Review of UK Equity Markets and Long-Term Decision Making: Final Report* (July 2012) 73.
133. *The Kay Review of UK Equity Markets and Long-Term Decision Making: Final Report* (July 2012) 73.
134. *The Kay Review of UK Equity Markets and Long-Term Decision Making: Final Report* (July 2012) 74.
135. *The Kay Review of UK Equity Markets and Long-Term Decision Making: Interim Report* (February 2012) 23.

judgment and experience, as well as supplementary specific knowledge of the company and its industry.[136] This discussion infers that company managers need to explain the results in fine nuanced terms and the complexities involved are such that only company managers and asset managers are capable of understanding the 'true' financial position and performance. This model elevates financial reporting and company analysis into an unwarranted sphere of complexity, subjectivity and specialism.

Many listed companies within resource, financial, property, real estate and infrastructure sectors manage long-dated assets. One can justifiably argue that short-term indicators are not appropriate to value these assets individually, and that a valuation methodology such as the application of a price earnings ratio is unlikely to provide a fair or meaningful valuation. The most common valuation approach for such assets is a discounted return or cash flow model, and this requires forecasts or assumptions to be made about future demand, cost and growth levels. Nevertheless, it is a large unexplained leap from an argument that a single long-term asset should be valued over its life, to the position that reporting by companies using standard templates is not useful. Few large listed companies manage a single long-dated asset. Most operate or manage a portfolio of assets with a spectrum of maturities, risks, and cash attributes, including some in a start-up and early development phase that require cash funding, as well as more mature assets that generate high-levels of cash. Additionally, most of the large securities exchanges, including the LSE,[137] operate tiered markets, with the most stringent disclosure obligations applying only to larger and more established companies. Large companies that are well-established and profitable generally have a mature and diversified portfolio of assets allowing a range of valuation models or methodologies to be applied. In these instances, reporting by means of standard templates is valid, comprehensible and useful.

[C] Comparative Analysis

The Kay Final Report describes the existing disclosure frameworks as founded on an assumption that information asymmetry can be overcome by the provision of 'sufficient, consistent, comparable and – in principle – equally available information.'[138] It asserts that policy makers 'may have emphasised comparability at the expense of relevance'[139] and that a search for comparability implies the user does not have specific knowledge of the companies in which funds are invested. Accordingly, it claims that persons who seek company information in forms that enable comparable analysis do not have specific knowledge of the companies in which they are investing and that those who use tailored figures provided by company managers are better informed. No

136. *The Kay Review of UK Equity Markets and Long-Term Decision Making: Interim Report* (February 2012) 23.
137. The London Stock Exchange includes AIM and the main market.
138. *The Kay Review of UK Equity Markets and Long-Term Decision Making: Final Report* (July 2012) 71.
139. *The Kay Review of UK Equity Markets and Long-Term Decision Making: Final Report* (July 2012) 71.

examples are provided, so it is not clear what the alleged benefits of tailored disclosures are for users (whether institutional or retail investors). As already discussed, companies need to use a common financial language to communicate effectively. Moreover, all investors, whether institutional or otherwise, need to ultimately compare available investment opportunities, and in doing so must adopt some form of standardisation. When companies use financial terms that are unexplained, ambiguous and inconsistent, comparative analysis is inefficient and time-consuming regardless of a user's skill. In this author's experience, any large company can present its results comprehensively and meaningfully using standard templates that include substantive notes and MD&A.[140]

When periodic results are reported in a standard template, investors can more readily compare performance trends and investment options for individual companies and across the market. The standard forms require companies to fill in and address all of the mandated sections,[141] making it difficult for management to unduly emphasise positive aspects of company performance. The standard form reports in the US do not contain pictures, an electronic table of contents is provided, specific information is easy to locate, the reports are formatted in self-contained online pages, and the quarterly and full year versions can be readily accessed and downloaded from the EDGAR website.[142] While some managers may prefer to report company results using tailored numbers and commentary, standardised reporting that readily enables comparative analysis is important to assess the performance of companies, and to drive competitive outcomes across markets and economies.

§13.09 FULL YEAR REPORTING

Company full year reporting frameworks require some fresh thinking. The full year reporting processes across all of the jurisdictions reviewed use two tier structures, including voluntary or mandated preliminary final reporting and a mandatory annual report. As outlined in Part III, with the exception of the US, it is the relevant exchange listing rules that determine whether preliminary final reports are mandated or voluntary and the nature, timing and content of these reports. When preliminary final reports are obligatory, the required timing of these reports is prior to the publication of the annual report. While the financial statements included in preliminary final reports and annual reports are generally the same, the mandated financial notes and MD&A content are generally significantly less in the preliminary final report than in the annual report.

---

140. The author is open to discuss specific instances of companies listed on the London Stock Exchange that may not be able to present their results usefully or fairly using the established reporting frameworks.
141. United States Securities and Exchange Commission, Securities Act Release 33-8039 (4 December 2001) Financial Reporting Release 59, *Cautionary Advice Regarding the Use of 'Pro-Forma' Financial Information in Earnings Releases.*
142. See United States Securities and Exchange Commission, *SEC Filings And Forms (EDGAR)* <http://www.sec.gov/edgar.shtml>.

As discussed in more detail in the section on company briefings, institutional participants do not wait until the release of annual reports to update their valuation models. Instead, they expect company executives to give them detailed commentary and analysis during the preliminary final reporting period. Company managers provide this commentary and analysis in various forms. They may release this information publicly through the relevant exchange and on the company website. Most companies also hold briefings in the days following the release of periodic results, including a group meeting and meetings with invited individuals. These briefings generally include presentations by the CEO and CFO (with support from other senior executives), and they typically also include lengthy and forthright question and answer sessions. The leadership team are 'on show' during these meetings, and know that large segments of the market will assess the company's performance based on the financial results, the accompanying explanations, and the responses to questions asked. They also know that all participants engaged in fundamental analysis, including sell-side and buy-side analysts, will ask for a high-level of detail to enable reliable inputs into valuation models that will be updated in a matter of hours following the meetings. The content discussed at these meetings is therefore broad ranging and extends well beyond the content typically included in the financial notes and MD&A of preliminary final reports and annual reports. Some companies enable public access to the general result briefings by means of webcasts or audio conference calls. However, such open access policies are discretionary in most jurisdictions, and when companies elect not to provide open access, the information provided publicly is sometimes sparse and sanitised in comparison to the information provided privately to select participants. Investors who rely on public disclosures may be limited in some jurisdictions to a preliminary final report with one or two pages of general MD&A, and an annual report with more detailed content that is dated and therefore no longer materially price-sensitive.

The author has been unable to locate material that details the history of, and rationales for, the existing full year reporting frameworks. It is likely that they developed in response to demands from institutional investors for timely information. The arguments that may be made to support these frameworks include the importance of timely reporting of full year results and the need to comply with continuous disclosure obligations. However, both of these lines of argument are circular. One cannot credibly argue that listed companies need three to four months to prepare the annual report when they are releasing equivalent detail (and more) during private sessions several weeks earlier. Similarly, an argument that companies are releasing information on a tiered basis in order to comply with continuous disclosure obligations is misconceived, when the same companies are providing additional content during the preliminary final reporting seasons at private sessions with no public access.

It is difficult to comprehend how the traditional full year reporting processes for listed companies have survived for so long. The tiered full year reporting structures severely undermine the public disclosure and communication models. They result in significant information asymmetry across the market and they do not promote any of the disclosure and transparency variables that the bodies of empirical research suggest are necessary to optimise long-term corporate and national outcomes. These reporting structures are consistent with an intermediated financial markets model because they provide financial intermediaries and institutions that have private access to senior executives with significant informational advantages.

The mandated form and content of annual reports have changed in most jurisdictions over the last twenty years. Modern content typically includes financial statements, MD&A, remuneration reports and corporate governance reports. Annual reports are often considered from a legal perspective to be the most important corporate disclosure document. However, many of these reports lack substantive commentary and analysis, and instead provide voluminous pictures that create noise and are cumbersome and costly to print. An emphasis on glossy pictures and high-level positive commentary makes some annual reports look and read like marketing documents prepared by public relations teams, rather than reports that are intended to inform readers interested in understanding the company's position, performance and prospects.

The role, purpose and content of preliminary final reports and annual reports should be reviewed as a matter of urgency in all countries. To determine their appropriate form and content, company executives and policy makers should reconsider the purposes of the reporting framework and the intended audience. All listed companies should provide one set of publicly disclosed full year accounts including comprehensive notes and MD&A. The SEC has elected to merge the required content in the preliminary final reports and annual reports so that differences in content in the two reports are minimal.[143] Similar reform is required in other jurisdictions.

§13.10 LONG-TERM PERFORMANCE TABLES

One of the most important classes of information lacking in modern company reports is long-term performance reporting and commentary. In the US, the full year reports submitted to the SEC (10-Ks) must report line items with three years of comparative data, commentary and analysis, and they must include a five year performance table. While some listed companies outside of the US voluntarily provide performance tables, commentary and key performance indicators in their periodic reports, the presentation and content of this material vary markedly. Some company periodic reports and websites provide concise and effective discussion of developments over the prior two years, but not many record or explain the company's 'story' over longer periods.

Interestingly, the structure, presentation and content of the corporate sustainability reports examined in Part III were often more focused, succinct and informative than the related annual reports. Many of the sustainability reports examined provided management commentary on performance and assessments against specified targets, including specific short, medium and long-term goals and targets. Some of these reports also provided vital statistics sections and or appendices with performance metrics for three to five year periods. Sustainability objectives and targets are an

143. While this means the annual reports in the US are somewhat redundant, the cost of producing and distributing the annual reports are likely to be minimal, particularly when the form and content is limited to functional matters.

integral part of corporate strategy, but these goals can usually only be attained when companies generate sufficient cash to pay their debts and make an adequate level of return on capital invested. Hence it is not clear why some corporations are publishing clear sustainability goals and metrics without supporting business and financial goals and metrics.

The Kay Review was primarily concerned with the long-term competitive performance of listed UK corporations. The author fully endorses the principles underpinning item 6 of the Good Practice Statement for Company Directors, which states that company directors should:

> provide information, in the context of corporate reporting and ongoing shareholder engagement, which supports shareholders' understanding of company strategy and likely long term creation of value, including by agreeing to a range of performance metric[s] relevant to the company.[144]

Curiously though, the Kay Final Report does not discuss how the long-term performance or competitiveness of a company ought to be measured, except for a broad statement that 'the performance of equity markets should ... be assessed by their effectiveness in allowing companies to make long term decisions appropriate to their business and in allowing savers to make financial plans appropriate to their objectives.'[145] It is company directors and senior managers who are required to balance a company's short and longer-term goals and the interests of its various stakeholders. To do so, they need to regularly stand back from day-to-day events and noise (including security price movement) to consider the company's longer-term objectives, strategies, plans and performance. Such reviews require the full board of directors to grapple with the company-specific and broader macro environments.

Admittedly, it can be difficult for diligent and capable directors and managers to keep abreast of all significant developments and to monitor long-term performance trends, including those of the company, its industry, its markets, and the real economy. An excellent way for boards and participants to efficiently review performance patterns and indicators is by means of comprehensive ten year performance tables prepared in accordance with accounting standards. This author recommends the introduction of mandatory ten year performance tables in a standard form in the front section of periodic reports and on company websites. This would enable company boards and outsiders to readily locate and consider a company's long-term performance trends, and to compare these against its competitors and market peers. Details of the author's proposal are outlined in Part V.

144. *The Kay Review of UK Equity Markets and Long-Term Decision Making: Final Report* (July 2012) 58.
145. *The Kay Review of UK Equity Markets and Long-Term Decision Making: Interim Report* (February 2012) 8.

§13.11 PUBLIC ACCESS TO COMPANY BRIEFINGS

Company briefings are an important means by which listed companies impart information to investors. A survey by Epstein and Palepu found that analysts rated private contacts and analyst meetings as the two primary sources of their information,[146] and this stance has been confirmed in subsequent studies.[147] Listed companies are generally prohibited in the jurisdictions reviewed from privately disclosing material price-sensitive information that has not been disclosed to the rest of the market.[148] At the same time, analysts and other select participants are invited by companies to obtain 'additional' information.

The most important listed company briefings are typically held on, or close to, the day on which financial results are announced. While these meetings are often referred to as 'analyst' briefings, the invitation list compiled by a company typically includes buy-side asset managers and analysts, sell-side brokers and analysts, and family entities and individuals. As discussed previously, at these briefings a company's CEO, CFO and other top executives generally give a presentation providing details and commentary on the company results and prospects, followed by a question and answer session. The presentation slides may be released through the relevant stock exchange or on the company website. Listed companies in most jurisdictions also hold private briefings with select individual participants. These meetings are typically held with the top executives of a company or with a representative from the company's investor relations area. The format of these meetings is normally a question and answer session.[149] Most institutional investors are also in regular contact with company executives by telephone and email. For example, the *Financial Times* in the UK reported in 2013 that asset managers were paying large sums of money to brokers and investment bankers for arranging meetings with chief executive officers. Analysis by the Financial Services Authority (FSA) found some large asset managers were making these payments using client commissions.[150] Daniel Godfrey, chief executive of the Investment Management Association, suggested that '[p]ayments for access to companies may be something you have to hold your nose to do, but maybe it is in the interests of your clients to do it.'[151] And an anonymous senior figure from a large UK asset manager confirmed that payments for corporate access were commonplace and that this was 'how ... the buyside have always operated.'[152]

While asset managers may consider payments for executive access as 'normal',[153] such conduct does not create a healthy investment environment that is likely

146. Marc Epstein and Khrishna Palepu, 'What Financial Analysts Want' (1999) 80 *Strategic Finance* 48, 50.
147. See, e.g., Eugene Soltes, 'Private Interaction Between Firm Management and Sell-side Analysts' (2014) 52 *Journal of Accounting Research* 245, 268.
148. See, e.g., Australian Securities Exchange, ASX Listing Rule 3.1.
149. The author has participated in many general analyst and individual briefings in many jurisdictions.
150. Steve Johnson, 'FSA Crackdown on Cash For CEO Access', *FT.com*, 4 March 2013.
151. Steve Johnson, 'FSA Crackdown on Cash For CEO Access', *FT.com*, 4 March 2013.
152. Steve Johnson, 'FSA Crackdown on Cash For CEO Access', *FT.com*, 4 March 2013.
153. Steve Johnson, 'FSA Crackdown on Cash For CEO Access', *FT.com*, 4 March 2013.

to enhance corporate performance and competitiveness. As outlined in the next section, empirical studies confirm that analysts are concerned with the need to stay in favour with companies in order to maintain private access to executives. Studies also confirm that analysts and others who criticise or raise the alarm about managerial misconduct are commonly frozen out from company communication channels, particularly when companies are facing adverse conditions or financial pressures. Given this evidence, it is not clear how the recommendation in the Kay Final Report that companies should privately discuss quarterly trading conditions with asset managers is intended to enhance the long-term corporate performance, stewardship or competitive position of UK companies.

Many large companies listed on the leading security exchanges enable public access to general result briefings by means of webcasts or audios and publicly released copies of presentation slides or briefing transcripts. These open access practices are less common among medium and smaller sized companies. In most of the jurisdictions reviewed, companies are not required to provide public access to company briefings or to publicly release information disclosed at general analyst or individual briefings. Moreover, listed companies rarely publicly disclose details of private briefings with individual participants. The company information required over a financial year is limited in some jurisdictions to a half year report with one or two pages of generic MD&A, a preliminary final report with one or two pages of general MD&, and an annual report with more detailed financial notes and MD&A. However, the notes and MD&A in annual reports are often dated because this content has already been disclosed, either publicly or privately, during the preliminary final reporting period. When the mandated content in the half year reports is limited or of poor quality, the adverse effects that arise from a lack of substantive information in the preliminary full year reports are magnified because the combined set of publicly available information is inadequate for a longer period. When companies do not allow public access to briefings, the legal burden to establish that material price-sensitive information may have been released at a private meeting is placed on regulators (or investors who believe they have suffered loss as a result of selective disclosure). This is a difficult task if there are no written or recorded notes of the meetings.

The arguments made during an Australian policy review of private briefings are typical of those made around the globe. These include the following:

- analyst briefings provide more information to the market than would otherwise be received if no briefings were held;[154]

154. Law Council of Australia, *Response to CAMAC's Issues Paper: Aspects of Market Integrity* (10 March 2009) 7. The Law Council did not explain how more information reaches the market as a result of closed rather than open analyst briefings. See also Representatives of the Australian Accounting Profession, *Aspects of Market Integrity* (31 March 2009) and Allens Arthur Robinson, *Submissions to the Corporations and Markets Advisory Committee in Response to its Issues Paper on Aspects of Market Integrity* (10 March 2009) 5. Allens Arthur Robinson argued that banning private briefings would have a negative effect on the market because it would reduce the amount and quality of informed opinion about Australian companies available to security holders and investors.

- making the information provided during analysts briefings available to the public will discourage analyst research;[155]
- only the largest of institutional investors have the resources to assess the true value of a company and its securities;[156] and
- webcasting and other forms of public disclosure are costly and burdensome.[157]

These, and similar arguments made by participants with privileged access to private company information, should be carefully assessed against the IOSCO securities regulation objectives and national interest benchmarks and criteria.

[A] Company Briefings Empirical Research

Holland conducted interviews in the 1990s with executives of thirty-three of the largest listed companies in the UK on disclosure of company information to financial institutions and the broader market.[158] The companies indicated to Holland that management cannot spend time with all shareholders, and they generally establish close relationships with twenty or thirty core institutions.[159] These companies suggested that the close private relationships allow an exchange of information on management quality, research and development, and innovation. They also allow the release of information to the major market influencers because this core set of financial institutions keeps the market informed through advisory or trading actions.[160]

The companies argued that the public and private channels for information dissemination were clearly differentiated.[161] They suggested that the numbers were reported publicly but the private discussion focused on questions concerning how and why the results were achieved.[162] The companies suggested that the financial report was becoming more obscure, complex and technical, and required explanation.[163] Companies therefore met with analysts and institutions privately in batches after earnings announcements. This ensured that the financial reports were adequately

155. Australian Financial Markets Association, *CAMAC Market Integrity Paper Responses* (10 March 2009) 12–13.
156. Securities & Derivatives Industry Association, *Submission on CAMAC Issues Paper – Aspects of Market Integrity* (11 March 2009) 6.
157. Business Council of Australia, *Aspects of Market Integrity* (3 March 2008). See also Chartered Secretaries Australia, *Market Integrity* (10 March 2009) 11.
158. John Holland, 'Private Voluntary Disclosure, Financial Intermediation And Market Efficiency' (1998) 25 *Journal of Business Finance & Accounting* 29.
159. John Holland, 'Private Voluntary Disclosure, Financial Intermediation And Market Efficiency' (1998) 25 *Journal of Business Finance & Accounting* 29, 39.
160. John Holland, 'Private Voluntary Disclosure, Financial Intermediation And Market Efficiency' (1998) 25 *Journal of Business Finance & Accounting* 29, 40.
161. John Holland, 'Private Voluntary Disclosure, Financial Intermediation And Market Efficiency' (1998) 25 *Journal of Business Finance & Accounting* 29, 42.
162. John Holland, 'Private Voluntary Disclosure, Financial Intermediation And Market Efficiency' (1998) 25 *Journal of Business Finance & Accounting* 29, 45.
163. John Holland, 'Private Voluntary Disclosure, Financial Intermediation And Market Efficiency' (1998) 25 *Journal of Business Finance & Accounting* 29, 51.

construed.[164] Several companies summarised the content of private meetings with institutions as being about the company's strategy for maximising returns, the execution of that strategy, the achievable returns, and what the company intended to do with the returns.[165] Others indicated that institutions use the private meetings to ensure face-to-face contact with the chairman and chief executives.[166] They pointed out that nuances and small behavioural traits and responses convey critical information to institutions.[167] All of the companies indicated that they prefer private meetings rather than public meetings because anything said in private remains deniable, the meetings allow two-way exchanges, and qualitative information can be discussed.[168]

Holland highlighted that the companies were aware of the fine line between these dialogues and continuous disclosure and insider trading laws.[169] The companies recognised that practices involving management or steering of earnings forecasts and assisting sell-side analysts to write their research reports are risky in the new regulatory climate.[170] While most companies argued that they stay within the legal limits, one suggested the approach of privately providing interpretation, explanation and commentary of the public facts was not well tested in law.[171] Holland concluded that the quality of private disclosure is much higher than public disclosure because it encompasses much deeper analysis and is conceptually richer.[172] He indicated that he was left with a sense that public disclosure is often intended to merely satisfy minimum regulatory standards and market pressures.[173] He argued that companies manage private meetings around public result announcements and presentation slides to be able to claim they are saying the same thing in private and public, when in practice, the content of public disclosures is significantly more limited than the information disclosed during private exchanges.[174] He suggested that the level and content of public disclosure are determined by generally accepted communication benchmarks across a market, liquidity requirements, legal obligations, and the need to provide a sufficient

164. John Holland, 'Private Voluntary Disclosure, Financial Intermediation And Market Efficiency' (1998) 25 *Journal of Business Finance & Accounting* 29, 55.
165. John Holland, 'Private Voluntary Disclosure, Financial Intermediation And Market Efficiency' (1998) 25 *Journal of Business Finance & Accounting* 29, 47.
166. John Holland, 'Private Voluntary Disclosure, Financial Intermediation And Market Efficiency' (1998) 25 *Journal of Business Finance & Accounting* 29, 48.
167. John Holland, 'Private Voluntary Disclosure, Financial Intermediation And Market Efficiency' (1998) 25 *Journal of Business Finance & Accounting* 29, 51.
168. John Holland, 'Private Voluntary Disclosure, Financial Intermediation And Market Efficiency' (1998) 25 *Journal of Business Finance & Accounting* 29, 52.
169. John Holland, 'Private Voluntary Disclosure, Financial Intermediation And Market Efficiency' (1998) 25 *Journal of Business Finance & Accounting* 29, 50.
170. John Holland, 'Private Voluntary Disclosure, Financial Intermediation And Market Efficiency' (1998) 25 *Journal of Business Finance & Accounting* 29, 56.
171. John Holland, 'Private Voluntary Disclosure, Financial Intermediation And Market Efficiency' (1998) 25 *Journal of Business Finance & Accounting* 29, 52.
172. John Holland, 'Private Voluntary Disclosure, Financial Intermediation And Market Efficiency' (1998) 25 *Journal of Business Finance & Accounting* 29, 49.
173. John Holland, 'Private Voluntary Disclosure, Financial Intermediation And Market Efficiency' (1998) 25 *Journal of Business Finance & Accounting* 29, 64.
174. John Holland, 'Private Voluntary Disclosure, Financial Intermediation And Market Efficiency' (1998) 25 *Journal of Business Finance & Accounting* 29, 49.

base of publicly disclosed information to justify the provision of additional detailed private information.[175]

Companies responding to an Australian Investor Relations Association snap poll on one-on-one meetings confirmed that private meetings were the most frequently used communication tool and very effective.[176] Some indicated that individual meetings were one of the best ways to ensure analysts understand the company properly and were a great way to build rapport with fund managers and brokers. They noted that investors like to get a sense of knowing management, which is difficult if they are restricted to group forums. Companies suggested that the content discussed at these meetings is generally focused on broad strategy, growth opportunities, and gaining a greater understanding of the nature of the industry and operations of the business.[177] They suggested that it was difficult for investors to get a complete understanding of these basics in other forums.[178] Interestingly though, one company indicated that individual meetings are of questionable value for domestic institutions and analysts who know the company well and who are frequently just looking to get a competitive edge in a market where all material information should be lodged with the exchange. Another executive suggested that if regulators really wanted to push the subject hard, the future of individual meetings might be short.[179]

A survey by Soltes provides useful insights on private interactions between executives and sell-side analysts in the US. Soltes examined three related questions. First, who interacts with management? Second, when do they interact? And third, why do they interact?[180] Soltes confirms that analysts interact privately with CEOs, CFOs and divisional executives throughout the year, with most of the private interactions occurring over the phone, and the remaining exchanges occurring at company offices and during conferences. Sell-side analysts confirmed that a significant portion of the value they provide to buy-side asset managers and analysts involves facilitating access to management, rather than providing better information about a company.[181] Soltes acknowledges that sell-side analysts seek opportunities to introduce buy-side clients to corporate managers in order to strengthen client relationships.[182] He suggests the purpose of private interactions is to provide analysts with additional context to

175. John Holland, 'Private Voluntary Disclosure, Financial Intermediation And Market Efficiency' (1998) 25 *Journal of Business Finance & Accounting* 29, 64.
176. Australian Investor Relations Association *Snap Poll: One-on-One Meetings with Analysts & Fund Managers* (15 June 2005).
177. Australian Investor Relations Association *Snap Poll: One-on-One Meetings with Analysts & Fund Managers* (15 June 2005).
178. Australian Investor Relations Association *Snap Poll: One-on-One Meetings with Analysts & Fund Managers* (15 June 2005).
179. Australian Investor Relations Association *Snap Poll: One-on-One Meetings with Analysts & Fund Managers* (15 June 2005).
180. Eugene Soltes, 'Private Interaction Between Firm Management and Sell-side Analysts' (2014) 52 *Journal of Accounting Research* 245, 246.
181. Eugene Soltes, 'Private Interaction Between Firm Management and Sell-side Analysts' (2014) 52 *Journal of Accounting Research* 245, 264.
182. Eugene Soltes, 'Private Interaction Between Firm Management and Sell-side Analysts' (2014) 52 *Journal of Accounting Research* 245, 247.

interpret news and to better understand a company's operations.[183] However, the responses from sell-side research directors and analysts paint a rather different picture. The research directors indicated that analysts seek private exchanges to '"triangulate their hypotheses," "bounce ideas," and "calibrate expectations of future performance and strategy".'[184] One research director noted that 'divisional managers are the best informational source because they know the details of the business and they are less polished when speaking with us.'[185] He or she indicated that these sources are valuable because they often provide 'deeper insights than they might be willing to share publicly, but you have to make sure you don't get them into trouble so we blend these insights in with other analysis.'[186] Several directors confirmed that sell-side analysts seek clarification or substantiation from management prior to publishing reports. Notably, all of the research directors suggested that analysts should not share their most valuable questions during public calls and should keep any insights private[187] in order to maintain a competitive advantage.

The published comments from research directors in Soltes' survey strongly suggest that the primary motivation for private meetings is to gain a competitive advantage through superior information gathering from management. The most troubling practice highlighted by the research directors is the habitual seeking of clarification or substantiation of the content included in sell-side analyst reports from company managers prior to publication. This practice provides a captive process for managing short-term earnings expectations and is a continuation of the traditional focus by companies on sell-side analyst reports as the benchmark for 'market expectations'. As discussed in more detail later in this chapter, these processes are an explicit form of selective disclosure that weaken the efficiency, fairness and transparency of financial markets and undermine the efficacy and benefits of public disclosure frameworks.

A study by Green et al. found that sell-side analysts that host conferences for listed companies to present to the firm's clients issued more informative, accurate and timely earnings forecasts than non-hosting analysts. Furthermore, recommendation changes in the three months following conferences provided incremental abnormal returns.[188] The study authors concluded that investor conferences serve as a general proxy for access to management.

183. Eugene Soltes, 'Private Interaction Between Firm Management and Sell-side Analysts' (2014) 52 *Journal of Accounting Research* 245, 257.
184. Eugene Soltes, 'Private Interaction Between Firm Management and Sell-side Analysts' (2014) 52 *Journal of Accounting Research* 245, 259.
185. Eugene Soltes, 'Private Interaction Between Firm Management and Sell-side Analysts' (2014) 52 *Journal of Accounting Research* 245, 268.
186. Eugene Soltes, 'Private Interaction Between Firm Management and Sell-side Analysts' (2014) 52 *Journal of Accounting Research* 245, 268.
187. Eugene Soltes, 'Private Interaction Between Firm Management and Sell-side Analysts' (2014) 52 *Journal of Accounting Research* 245, 265–266.
188. T Clifton Green, Russell Jame, Stanimir Markov and Musa Subasis, 'Access to Management and the Informativeness of Analyst Research' (2014) 114 *Journal of Financial Economics* 239.

[B] Company Briefings Summary

Most regulators and scholars argue or infer that the purpose of company briefings is merely to clarify publicly disclosed information, and that the content discussed at these briefings is restricted to immaterial background information.[189] Empirical evidence on briefings, reviews of publicly available briefing content, and the author's personal experience of briefings, suggests this argument is rather facile. Empirical research on briefings indicates that the content discussed at general analyst and individual briefings includes detailed incremental information to assist invitees to understand the historical performance of a company *and* its likely prospects. Company management confirm that they provide the following information at briefings:

- interpretation and explanation of publicly announced results and the financial reports;
- discussion on financial parameters and targets;[190]
- information around the management philosophy, the quality of management, and management succession;
- capital investment and technological change;
- corporate strategy, competitive advantages and risks and growth opportunities; and
- industry trends and issues.[191]

All of these classes of information are critical to an assessment of a company's position and prospects. Most, if not all, of the information exchanged during these briefings is therefore materially price-sensitive from a reasonable investor's perspective, especially for persons engaged in fundamental research and analysis of listed companies. Even when no inside information is disclosed at briefings, those present are typically given comprehensive background information by senior executives that enables a deeper understanding of the publicly released information. These participants also have the opportunity to ask questions and receive immediate responses from company managers.[192] As one regulator points out, '[T]here is not always a clear line between what is price sensitive and what is not ... A particular piece of information may, when fitted together with other information in the possession of those present at a private briefing, affect the company's share price.'[193]

189. See, e.g., Australian Securities and Investments Commission, *'Heard It On The Grapevine...' Draft ASIC Guidance And Discussion Paper. Disclosure Of Information To Investors And Compliance With Continuous Disclosure And Insider Trading Provisions* (November 1999) 20.
190. John Holland, 'Private Voluntary Disclosure, Financial Intermediation And Market Efficiency' (1998) 25 *Journal of Business Finance & Accounting* 29, 46.
191. John Holland, 'Private Voluntary Disclosure, Financial Intermediation And Market Efficiency' (1998) 25 *Journal of Business Finance & Accounting* 29, 46.
192. Australian Securities and Investments Commission, *'Heard It On The Grapevine...' Draft ASIC Guidance And Discussion Paper. Disclosure Of Information To Investors And Compliance With Continuous Disclosure And Insider Trading Provisions* (November 1999) 7.
193. Australian Securities and Investments Commission, *'Heard It On The Grapevine...' Draft ASIC Guidance And Discussion Paper. Disclosure Of Information To Investors And Compliance With Continuous Disclosure And Insider Trading Provisions* (November 1999) 13.

The information provided to participants with regular company briefing access is undoubtedly richer than the information publicly released to other investors and stakeholders, resulting in information asymmetry across the market. Moreover, the value of information privately obtained from company managers is enhanced by ambiguous or minimal periodic and continuous disclosure obligations, longer public reporting periods, and limited or cumbersome access to comparative information. That is, privately obtained company information is most valuable in jurisdictions where periodic reporting is less regular, mandated MD&A and financial notes are limited and or ambiguous, company information is not reported on a standardised basis and comparative data is difficult to construct from public disclosures, monitoring of private meetings is minimal or non-existent, and enforcement of selective disclosure events is unlikely. It is worth repeating here that a global study by Maffett found that institutional investors were able to more profitably trade on private company information in opaque information environments. Notably, they made larger profits from trading on private information when the availability and quality of financial reporting of a company was poor and the relevant country had lower quality governance, financial reporting and disclosure regulation.[194]

Listed companies, policy makers and scholars should reflect more deeply and critically on the benefits and risks associated with frameworks where demands from the most powerful participants and institutions for private meetings and information continue to grow. As one director notes:

> [I]institutional investors have unparalleled access to management through briefings, one-on-one meetings, broker conferences, site visits and strategy days throughout the year ... [W]here companies have issues, fund managers are not backward in seeking an audience with the chairman and managing director to ensure their views are heard.[195]

Despite an increasing use of private briefings as the primary form of communication and information exchange between company executives and financial market participants, the rationales for these private contacts remain unclear.[196] All of the major questions around private briefings remain unanswered within scholarly literature and policy documents. If, as is suggested, institutional investors and sell-side analysts require explanation of publicly released reports to be able to understand them, how are persons without private access to senior executives supposed to comprehend the publicly released information without the same explanations? And if information provided at briefings is not material, even on a composite basis, why are closed briefings beneficial or required? Those advocating continued use of private briefings should explain how they support the aims of disclosure regulation and improve

194. Mark Maffett, 'Financial Reporting Opacity and Informed Trading By International Institutional Investors' (2012) 54 *Journal of Accounting and Economics* 201.
195. Victoria Geddes, FIRST Advisers, 'Opinion Restoring the Relevance of AGMS' *Company Director* 1 August 2010.
196. Donald Langevoort, 'Investment Analysts and the Law of Insider Trading' (1990) 76 *Virginia Law Review* 1023, 1028, 1054.

long-term corporate and national outcomes.[197] Potential issues arising from regular private exchanges of listed company information with privileged invitees extend well beyond a battle between participants to gain informational advantages. When discussion of substantive company matters is confined to private exchanges, the conflicts and misaligned incentives that regulatory frameworks are intended to address are left unresolved. Further, when asset managers and others are buying access to corporate managers, the level and quality of market transparency is poor, the efficacy of the corporate disclosure regimes are severely undermined, and these environments are unlikely to serve the best interests of the corporations or the communities in which they operate.

As discussed in Chapter 2, agency problems within corporate law include potential conflicts between managers and shareholders, between controlling and non-controlling shareholders, and between controllers of the company and non-shareholder stakeholders.[198] Establishing measures and processes to deal with all three categories of agency problems simultaneously is notoriously difficult. While there are no perfect regulatory or practical solutions, public communication models that require regular and layered corporate disclosure are likely to best address the multilayered agency conflicts by maximising the levels of market transparency, accountability and competition. All corporate investors and stakeholders need regular and balanced discussion concerning a company's strategy, operations and positions in order to make well-informed decisions and respond appropriately, particularly as business, industry and economic conditions change.

§13.12 PERIODIC REPORTING DEVELOPMENTS

Most of the companies examined in Part III publish CSR or sustainability reports in compliance with the Global Reporting Initiative (GRI).[199] GRI was founded in Boston in the US. It developed from the Coalition for Environmentally Responsible Economies and the Tellus Institute, with support from the United Nations Environment Programme during its establishment. The GRI website suggests that sustainability reporting enables governments and businesses to understand and establish goals and measures to communicate their economic, environmental, social and governance performance. These processes are intended to assist bodies to manage their performance effectively, and to build trust with their stakeholders and the public through transparent reporting. A sustainability report is described as:

> a report published by a company or organization about the economic, environmental and social impacts caused by its everyday activities. A sustainability report

197. Donald Langevoort, 'Investment Analysts and the Law of Insider Trading' (1990) 76 *Virginia Law Review* 1023, 1028, 1054.
198. Paul Davies et al., 'European Company Law Experts' Response to the European Commission's Green Paper Green Paper "The EU Corporate Governance Framework"' (22 July 2011) 1 at http://papers.ssrn.com/sol3/papers.cfm?abstract_id=1912548 (last visited 14 June 2013).
199. Global Reporting Initiative, 'GRI Empowering Sustainable Decisions', viewed 29 June 2015, https://www.globalreporting.org/information/Pages/default.aspx.

> also presents the organization's values and governance model, and demonstrates the link between its strategy and its commitment to a sustainable global economy.[200]

The GRI website highlights that 82% of the world's largest 250 corporations report on their sustainability performance using GRI standards.[201] It suggests that sustainability reporting can be considered as synonymous with other terms for non-financial reporting, including triple bottom line reporting, and CSR reporting. It also notes that sustainability reporting is an intrinsic element of integrated reporting that combines the analysis of financial and non-financial performance.

The term 'integrated reporting', while open to varying meanings when discussing company reporting, is increasingly being used in relation to a global coalition of regulators, investors, companies, standard-setters, the accounting profession and non-governmental organisations that have established an International Integrated Reporting Council (IIRC).[202] The IIRC mission is to establish integrated reporting and thinking within mainstream business practice as the norm in the public and private sectors.[203] Its vision is to align capital allocation and corporate behaviour to wider goals of financial stability and sustainable development through the cycle of integrated reporting and thinking.[204] Integrated reporting is described as:

> a process founded on integrated thinking that results in a periodic integrated report by an organization about value creation over time and related communications regarding aspects of value creation ... An integrated report is a concise communication about how an organization's strategy, governance, performance and prospects, in the context of its external environment, lead to the creation of value in the short, medium and long term.[205]

In 2013, the IIRC released a consultation draft for an International Integrated Reporting framework. The consultation paper indicated that the proposed processes are intended to apply to an integrated report once a year and to other relevant reports and communications, including analyst briefings and the entity website.[206] It stated that the content of the integrated report is governed by guiding principles.[207] For example, the stakeholder responsiveness principle suggests that an 'integrated report

200. Global Reporting Initiative, 'GRI Empowering Sustainable Decisions', viewed 29 June 2015, https://www.globalreporting.org/information/Pages/default.aspx.
201. Global Reporting Initiative, 'GRI and Sustainability Reporting', viewed 29 June 2015, https://www.globalreporting.org/information/sustainability-reporting/Pages/gri-standards.aspx.
202. International Integrated Reporting Council, 'Integrated Reporting', viewed 29 June 2015, http://integratedreporting.org/.
203. International Integrated Reporting Council, 'The IIRC', viewed 29 June 2015, http://integratedreporting.org/the-iirc-2/.
204. International Integrated Reporting Council, 'The IIRC', viewed 29 June 2015, http://integratedreporting.org/the-iirc-2/.
205. International Integrated Reporting Council, 'Integrated Reporting', viewed 20 September 2014, http://www.theiirc.org/.
206. International Integrated Reporting Council, *Consultation Draft of the International Framework* (2013) 30.
207. The IIRC guiding principles underpinning the preparation of an integrated report include: strategic focus and future orientation; connectivity of information; stakeholder relationships; materiality; conciseness; reliability and completeness; and consistency and comparability.

should provide insight into the quality of the organization's relationship with key stakeholders and how and to what extent the organization understands, takes into account and responds to their legitimate needs, interests and expectations.'[208] The paper suggested that responsiveness 'is demonstrated through decisions, actions and performance, as well as ongoing communication with stakeholders.'[209] It noted that engagement with stakeholders may occur regularly on a day-to-day basis or may be undertaken for a particular purpose. The draft guidance states that information should only be included in the integrated report when it is of practical use to readers and the disclosure is specific to the circumstances of the reporting organisation.[210]

In December 2013, the IIRC released a report on the international framework.[211] This report suggests that integrated reporting will become the norm over time and will replace the 'numerous, disconnected and static communications' that exist presently. It notes that an integrated report aims to provide insight on the use of various forms of capital in the organisation, including financial, manufactured, intellectual, natural, and social and relationship capital.[212] The proposed elements of an integrated report include the following:

- Organisational overview and external environment: What does the organisation do and what are the circumstances under which it operates?
- Governance: How does the organisation's governance structure support its ability to create value in the short, medium and long term?
- Business model: What is the organisation's business model?
- Risks and opportunities: What are the specific risks and opportunities that affect the organisation's ability to create value over the short, medium and long term, and how is the organisation dealing with these?
- Strategy and resource allocation: Where does the organisation want to go and how does it intend to get there?
- Performance: To what extent has the organisation achieved its strategic objectives for the period and what are its outcomes in terms of effects on capital?
- Outlook: What challenges and uncertainties is the organisation likely to encounter in pursuing its strategy, and what are the potential implications for its business model and future performance?[213]

The international framework report notes that an integrated report should include all material matters, whether positive or negative, in a balanced way. An explanatory document explains that an integrated report is more than a summary of information in other communications, such as financial statements, sustainability reports, analysts' calls and websites.[214] It confirms that the purpose of integrated

208. International Integrated Reporting Council, *Consultation Draft of the International Framework* (2013) 6.
209. International Integrated Reporting Council, *Consultation Draft of the International Framework* (2013) 20.
210. International Integrated Reporting Council, *Consultation Draft of the International Framework* (2013) 18.
211. International Integrated Reporting Council, *The International Framework* (December 2013).
212. International Integrated Reporting Council, *The International Framework* (December 2013) 4.
213. International Integrated Reporting Council, *The International Framework* (December 2013) 21.
214. International Integrated Reporting Council, *Basis for Conclusions* (December 2013) 5.

reporting is to explicitly connect information in order to communicate how value is created over time.[215] It suggests that an integrated report could be prepared as a standalone document or its content could be included as part of an existing report or communication.[216] It does not propose specific forms of reporting.

The proposed IIRC framework is sound. Integrated reporting essentially requires companies to explain how value is being created over short, medium and long-term horizons. Such explanation forms a central tenet of effective corporate disclosure and communication frameworks. All persons with a warrantable interest in a corporation are entitled to ask, and should ask, the board and senior executives to explain their strategies and plans for creating value. They should ask company boards and executives to publicly disclose and explain the company's short, medium and long-term objectives and targets, and its risks and opportunities. Further, they should demand regular updates and explanations about the company's performance and prospects against these objectives and targets. Many of these constituent elements have been discussed throughout the book, including the importance of substantive MD&A that explains and analyses a company's strategy and plans, business model, performance, risks, outlook, and governance model and processes.

The proposed IIRC framework requires sophisticated analysis by company boards that synthesises and integrates the company's financial strategy and performance with its overarching business strategy and performance. This requires high-levels of business expertise and complex judgments and analyses on the use of human, environmental and financial capital as a means to create value. It also requires a willingness by company boards and executives to effectively communicate this analysis within public spheres. The review of company disclosures in Part III suggests that larger listed companies are embedding some social and sustainability responsibility matters within their strategy, planning, performance and reporting processes, and are publicly communicating this to some extent. Nevertheless, critical questions concerning the creation of value, particularly over longer periods, are often poorly explained or not addressed at all within many company reports and disclosures. Most substantive discussion concerning 'value creation' presently occurs during private forums between company executives and invited participants. Thus for the IIRC framework to progress, its advocates need to address the content and timing asymmetries between company information provided privately and publicly, the realities of an increasing shift towards private disclosure and communication models, and potential reforms that may be required.

The author fully endorses the IIRC aims, but suggests there is currently a large gulf between the stated aspirations of the proposed integrated reporting framework and the realities of modern corporate reporting and disclosure. As discussed throughout the book, the content and MD&A provided in many periodic reports and continuous disclosures are often surprisingly limited in quantity and quality. In particular, many listed companies fail to publicly explain the drivers (i.e., the 'how' and 'why') of their results and performance within the periodic reports. Secondly, there is often a distinct

215. International Integrated Reporting Council, *Basis for Conclusions* (December 2013) 5.
216. International Integrated Reporting Council, *Basis for Conclusions* (December 2013) 5.

lack of commentary explaining a company's strategies, plans, risks and opportunities, its financial and non-financial targets, and how it is faring against these plans and targets. Finally, very few listed companies discuss the explicit or indirect connections between the constituent factors that create value over time and the information outlined in the various reports and disclosures. Consequently, the proposed integrated reporting framework would require a momentous change in the reporting and disclosure culture of most companies, and an enormous improvement in the quality of public reporting.

CHAPTER 14
Continuous Disclosure Regulation and Practice

> It must be accepted that there will be differing opinions in particular instances about what requires disclosure and what does not. From the point of view of proper risk management against the possibility of contravention, a conservative approach which favours disclosure is to be preferred. Certainly those who play calculated risk games of non-disclosure in the shadow of the Rules cannot expect indulgence from the courts if their assessments are not accepted.[1]

§14.01 OVERVIEW

Continuous disclosure obligations (or ad hoc or episodic disclosure requirements) are intended to enhance the periodic reporting regimes by requiring companies to keep investors informed of any material price-sensitive information between reporting periods. The driving principle of these regimes is that all investors should have access to this information at the same time, so that trading in the relevant securities takes place by informed participants. The IOSCO commentary is limited to a statement that there is a need for regular reporting by public companies in addition to disclosure on a continuous basis throughout a financial year.[2] This limited focus by IOSCO on continuous disclosure regulation and principles is intriguing and may reflect the differences in the structure of, and emphasis on, continuous disclosure regimes around the world.

Major issues arise in the areas of continuous disclosure regulation and practice. Chapter 14 explores and discusses some of these issues, including:

- the nature of 'material' information;
- the timeliness of continuous disclosures;

1. *Australian Securities and Investments Commission v. Chemeq Ltd* [2006] FCA 936, [87].
2. Technical Committee of the International Organization of Securities Commission, *Principles For Periodic Disclosure By Listed Entitles* Final Report (February 2010) 4.

- the benefits and burdens of public earnings guidance;
- supervisory and enforcement issues; and
- integration of disclosure frameworks.

§14.02 MATERIALITY

Decisions on the materiality of information lie at the heart of continuous disclosure regimes. As the SEC noted during the Reg FD consideration period, listed company executives retain significant discretion under continuous disclosure rules in relation to what must be disclosed publicly and additional information that is permitted to be disclosed privately to some market participants. Some company executives may prefer to keep the spectrum of circumstances that are considered material as narrow as possible. Conversely, investors and others who rely on public disclosures prefer the most liberal interpretation of materiality to ensure they have access to the same information as other participants and can make well-informed decisions on a timely basis.

Materiality under most continuous disclosure rules is determined by a reasonable person test at the time of the relevant event. BaFin confirms that the test in Germany is whether a reasonable investor aware of all publicly available information would consider there is a 'reasonable likelihood of a significant impact on prices.'[3] It indicates that it is 'irrelevant whether the price of an insider security actually changes after the inside information has become publicly known.'[4] It notes that an assessment of whether information is materially price-sensitive involves two steps. The first step requires an *ex ante* assessment of whether the information in and of itself is reasonably likely to have a significant effect on prices at the time the decision is being made. The second step requires consideration of all the specific circumstances existing or foreseeable at the time the decision is being made.[5]

Similarly, the judiciary in Australia have noted that the materiality test within the continuous disclosure regime is objective and determined on an *ex ante* basis.[6] The Court of Appeal in New South Wales confirmed that 'the question is not an *ex post facto* one, whether the market did react to the disclosure of the information. The question is whether a reasonable person would expect the information to have a material effect on the market price.'[7] The ASX updated its guidance on continuous disclosure in 2013 to provide greater clarity to listed companies in relation to their disclosure obligations. It suggests that an officer of a listed entity who is faced with a decision on whether information needs to be disclosed under the continuous disclosure listing rules may find it helpful to ask two questions:

3. Bafin, *Issuer Guideline* (14 May 2009) 31.
4. Bafin, *Issuer Guideline* (14 May 2009) 31.
5. Bafin, *Issuer Guideline* (14 May 2009) 31.
6. See, e.g., *James Hardie Industries NV v. Australian Securities and Investments Commission* [2010] NSWCA 332, [546].
7. *Australian Securities and Investments Commission v. Macdonald (No. 11)* (2009) 71 ACSR 368, [1123].

(1) Would this information influence my decision to buy or sell securities in the entity at their current market price?
(2) Would I feel exposed to an action for insider trading if I were to buy or sell securities in the entity at their current market price, knowing this information had not been disclosed to the market?[8]

It notes that an affirmative answer to either of these questions may serve as an indicator that the information is material and should be disclosed.

Reasonable investors must holistically assess information about a company, so the materiality or price-sensitivity of single pieces of news should be considered in context rather than in isolation. The effect of single items of news depends on the quantity and quality of publicly available information and the specific environment within which the relevant entity is operating and trading. In the US, information is generally material if there is a 'substantial likelihood that the disclosure of the omitted fact would have been viewed by the reasonable investor as having significantly altered the "total mix" of information made available.'[9] This principle is expressed elsewhere as materiality through an accumulation of factors.[10]

Most jurisdictions do not provide explicit thresholds or guidance around what information is material and requires disclosure between reporting periods. Nevertheless, materiality guidance is provided implicitly across all of the countries reviewed, because materiality thresholds are a necessary input or variable within stockwatch programmes. Stockwatch programmes are used by the major security exchanges and national regulators to review trading patterns as a means to identify possible suspicious trading.[11] However, the materiality parameters used in these programmes are not published.

The types of information that are materially price-sensitive between reporting periods are wide ranging. Three of the most important classes of information concern:

(1) possible or agreed mergers and acquisitions;
(2) potential and proposed capital raisings; and
(3) news that feeds into a company's prospective earnings.

More than a decade ago, the FCA, and its predecessor the Financial Services Authority (FSA), identified the timely disclosure of takeover bids, capital raisings and price-sensitive announcements as high risk scenarios with a material impact on investors. In 2003, the FSA began commissioning independent annual empirical 'market cleanliness' studies to monitor the possible extent to which trading may be

8. Australian Securities Exchange Compliance, *Continuous Disclosure: An Abridged Guide* (March 2013) 4.
9. *TSC Industries, Inc. v. Northway, Inc., 426 U.S. 438* (1976).
10. See, e.g., *Australian Securities and Investments Commission v. Macdonald (No. 11)* (2009) 71 ACSR 368, [1117].
11. As outlined in Part III, day-to-day monitoring of company disclosures by exchanges and taxpayer-funded regulators is increasingly relying on automated stockwatch programmes that review trading patterns to identify possible suspicious trading.

occurring on the LSE on an informed basis prior to these high risk events.[12] However, publication of these study findings has narrowed over recent years. The FSA annual report for 2012/2013 highlights the studies that monitor possible informed trading prior to takeover announcements and a positive trend downwards in such trading from 2009 to 2012,[13] but no publicly available information is available on the other two classes of information. The reasons for this are unclear.

Determining the materiality of company information involving mergers or acquisitions or capital raisings is generally straightforward. In most instances, this type of news would be materially price-sensitive to a reasonable investor. Issues within these classes of information generally centre on the precise timing and content of the required disclosures. A disclosure obligation may arise due to either a leakage of confidential company information or private disclosure of the information. All of the continuous disclosure regimes examined require information within these two classes that has become known by the market (or segments of the market), or that appears to be known by the market as reflected in unusual security price movement or level of trading, to be disclosed publicly.

Determining the materiality of company information in the area of earnings related news involves more complex judgments, and these decisions are more critical than other classes of information due to the broader potential impacts on investors and stakeholders. Indeed, one's interpretation of what constitutes material earnings related news establishes the main parameters for the operation and effectiveness of continuous disclosure regimes. If company executives or regulators interpret the materiality of this class of information narrowly as news involving explicit historical or prospective earnings numbers, or as information that will result in significant immediate share price movement, this leaves a large pool of earnings related information that can legitimately be released and discussed privately with select participants. Regardless of one's position on these matters, the rationales and usefulness of continuous disclosure regimes are questionable when company earnings change significantly from one period to another, or when there are large share price movements, which are not supported by public disclosure and explanation.

§14.03 TIMELINESS OF CONTINUOUS DISCLOSURES

Some commentators criticise disclosure enforcement actions that involve what is perceived as 'short' delays in the announcement of agreed deals or transactions. They suggest that continuous disclosure rules that require 'immediate' disclosure are not practical or reasonable. They highlight particular difficulties faced by companies when

12. See, e.g., Ben Dubow and Nuno Monteiro, 'Measuring Market Cleanliness', *Financial Services Authority Occasional Paper Series 23* (March 2006); Nuno Monteiro, Qamar Zaman and Susanne Leitterstorf, 'Updated Measurement of Market Cleanliness', *Financial Services Authority Occasional Paper Series 25* (March 2007).
13. Financial Services Authority, *FSA Annual Report 2012/13* 37. See also Jim Goldman, Stefan Hunt, Paul Minter, Felix Suntheim and Qamar Zaman, 'Why Has the FCAs Market Cleanliness Statistic for Takeover Announcements Decreased Since 2009?' *Financial Conduct Authority Occasional Paper No. 4* (July 2014).

the details of a deal are still the subject of negotiation. For instance, in March 2007 ASIC issued a continuous disclosure infringement notice against Promina Group Limited (Promina) relating to a takeover bid by Suncorp Metway Limited. ASIC alleged that Promina had breached section 674(2) of the *Corporations Act 2001* (Cth) during the period from 12.03 pm on 11 October 2006 to 8.29 am the next day because reasonably specific details of the bid were released through the media on 11 October 2006 (including through the Dow Jones Newswire at 12.03 pm), but Promina waited until 8.29 am on 12 October to make an announcement through the ASX. On 11 October 2006, Promina's closing share price rose nearly 6% on the previous day close and nearly 11 million shares were traded.[14] A year later, ASIC issued an infringement notice against Rio Tinto Limited (Rio Tinto) in relation to a takeover bid for Alcan Inc (Alcan). ASIC alleged that Rio Tinto had contravened its continuous disclosure obligations by delaying a trading halt for twenty-two minutes between 2.30 pm and 3.42 pm. Rio Tinto was informed that it was the preferred bidder for Alcan at 8.07 am on 12 July 2007, subject to final agreement and documentation. Further, news of the bid had been aired in the media over the prior few days, and confirmation that the deal was nearing final stages was announced through the Dow Jones Newswire at 2.30 pm and 2.41 pm on 12 July 2007. At 3.42 pm on 12 July, Rio Tinto requested a trading halt. The facts alleged by ASIC in the infringement notice against Promina suggest that the key terms of the Suncorp Metway were agreed well before any ASX announcement was made. Similarly, the facts alleged by ASIC in the infringement notice against Rio Tinto suggest that the directors received confirmation that the company was the preferred bidder and they were aware of the media speculation during the prior few days and of the unusual trading volumes in the securities of the company, prior to the announcements made through the ASX.

Theories that suggest listed company managers have the capacity and wherewithal to withhold significant news from all market participants for several days are now largely illusory. For continuous disclosure regimes to be effective, material company information needs to be submitted to an exchange or regulatory information repository rapidly. Announcements of major events, such as a merger or acquisition or a capital raising, should be submitted to the relevant exchange within a few minutes of an agreement, so that all investors are alerted to the developments on a timely and simultaneous basis. When executives delay public disclosure of important news or updates, even for short periods, there is a high probability that the news will either be disclosed privately, or will leak to segments of the market, with large potential shifts of wealth to those with advance knowledge. While privately disclosed company news may be absorbed into a company's security prices more slowly than publicly disclosed information, news travels rapidly across financial markets, particularly among institutional segments. When participants are trading on confidential company information, the trading gains are effectively risk-free and any uninformed counterparties suffer losses (or the loss of the profit) of equivalent amounts.

14. Australian Securities and Investments Commission, 'Promina Pays $100,000 Fine' (Press Release, 20 March 2007) 07-69.

§14.04 PUBLIC GUIDANCE

When listed companies publicly disclose their expected financial performance and prospective earnings, this is commonly referred to as 'public guidance'. Public guidance may be provided for various time periods, but is most often for the next financial year. The form of public guidance may also vary, but is generally framed as a profit measure. The profit measure may be a specific number or an estimated earnings range.

Some critics describe public guidance or any form of earnings forecasts as 'internal' management data that should not be subject to regulation.[15] However, this argument only retains credibility if internal data and any prospective forecasts and related matters remain confidential and are not discussed privately (explicitly or implicitly) with any participants that may trade on the news. When companies share information about the company's position and prospects privately with participants who are not bound by confidentiality agreements or trading bans, and this information feeds into earnings forecasts directly or indirectly, this information can no longer be characterised as 'internal' or confidential.

Some national regulators explicitly state that companies do not need to provide public forecasts, while others encourage public guidance. Listed companies provide public earnings guidance for various reasons. Public guidance simultaneously provides all participants with updates about the company's ongoing and expected performance, limiting the need for managers to respond privately to ongoing earnings related questions from institutions and others that seek informational advantages between reporting periods. Empirical research discussed later in this chapter suggests the provision of public guidance enhances the efficiency, fairness and transparency of financial markets. Studies have also found that companies that voluntarily provide earnings guidance can enhance the liquidity of the company's securities, reduce the company's cost of capital, and earn a premium valuation.

[A] The United States

The SEC changed its view on the voluntary disclosure of management forecasts in the 1970s and released a policy statement encouraging the provision of public guidance.[16] Its policy material suggests that forward-looking information should provide cautionary statements that state that actual results may materially differ from public guidance and outline the important assumptions and factors that may result in material

15. See, e.g., Skadden, Arps, Slate, Meagher & Flom LLP, Corporate Finance Alert (September 2012).
16. See, e.g., John Burton, Chief Accountant United States Securities and Exchange Commission, 'FORECASTS: A Changing View From The Securities and Exchange Commission' (Speech delivered to Northwestern University Conference on Public Reporting of Corporate Financial Forecasts, 2 April 1973); AA Sommer Jnr, Commissioner United States Securities and Exchange Commission, 'Forecasting: A Look at the Future' (Speech delivered to Corporate Financial Forecast and Disclosure Conference, Drexel University, Philadelphia, 29 March 1974).

variations.[17] Companies are advised to disclose assumptions and limitations associated with any voluntary forecasts as specifically as possible.

A significant legal issue that arises for companies that provide public guidance is determining whether an obligation arises to update this guidance when circumstances change. Rule 10b-5 of the Exchange Act provides that companies and company directors and officers must not misstate or omit material facts if this results in misleading statements within periodic reports or continuous disclosures. Companies and their directors, officers and underwriters may also be liable under sections 11 and 12 of the *Securities Act of 1933* (Securities Act) for misstatements or omissions of facts that are misleading in a public offering. A safe harbour rule was introduced to shelter companies from liability under both the Exchange Act and Securities Act in relation to forecasts made in good faith and on a reasonable basis. The effect of this rule is that a company is only liable if a plaintiff can establish that a forecast was made with knowledge that it was false or misleading.

The SEC has indicated that companies should update the market when circumstances change sufficiently so that prior announcements left uncorrected become materially inaccurate or false or misleading. However, there is no federal securities law or regulation in the US that explicitly imposes a duty to update a forward-looking statement. There have been circumstances when the Courts have acknowledged that a duty may exist to update a forward-looking statement (e.g., disclosures provided during a hostile takeover bid), but such a duty has not been applied by the courts more generally to earnings guidance or forecasts.[18] Case law involving interpretation of Rule 10b-5 and section 10(b) suggests there is no general obligation to update forward-looking earnings statements when they become inaccurate or misleading. The US Court of Appeals for the Third Circuit addressed this issue in *In re Burlington Coat Factory* Sec.Litig.114 F.3d1410 (3rd Cir. 1997). In November 1993, the chief accounting officer of Burlington said he was comfortable with analyst projections of AUD 1.20–AUD 1.30 as a mid-range for earnings-per-share in fiscal 1994. When the 1994 earnings were lower than the analyst projections, the plaintiffs alleged that Burlington had an affirmative duty to update. The court stated that:

> Except for specific periodic reporting requirements (primarily the requirements to file quarterly and annual reports), there is no general duty on the part of a company to provide the public with all material information ... Thus, possession of material non public information alone does not create a duty to disclose it.
>
> Equally well settled is the principle that an accurate report of past successes does not contain an implicit representation that the trend is going to continue, and hence does not, in and of itself, obligate the company to update the public as to the state of the quarter in progress.
>
> Finally, the existing regulatory structure encourages companies to produce and disclose internal forecasts by protecting them from liability for disclosing internal forecasts that, although reasonable when made, turn out to be incorrect. However, where it comes to affirmative disclosure requirements, the current

17. *Private Securities Litigations Reform Act of 1995.*
18. See, e.g., *Weiner v. Quaker Oats*, 129 E3d 310 (3rd Cir 1993); *In re Time Warner Inc* Secs Litg, 9 F.3rd1112, 1117, 1125 (10th Cir 1997).

> regulatory scheme focuses on backward-looking 'hard' information, not forecasts. Increasing the obligations associated with disclosing reasonably made internal forecasts is likely to deter companies from providing this information, a result contrary to the SEC's goal of encouraging the voluntary disclosure of company forecasts.
>
> Based on features one and two, we do not think it can be said that an ordinary earnings projection contains an implicit representation on the part of the company that it will update the investing public with all material information that relates to that forecast ... We conclude that ordinary, run-of-the-mill forecasts contain no more than the implicit representation that the forecasts were made reasonably and in good faith ... In sum, under the existing disclosure apparatus, the voluntary disclosure of an ordinary earnings forecast does not trigger any duty to update.[19]

This judicial commentary was made prior to the introduction of Reg FD.[20] The SEC has indicated that Reg FD does not alter the law relating to public guidance, but has also confirmed that providing earnings guidance on a selective or private basis is prohibited.[21] For example, it bought an action against Office Depot in 2010 when employees from the investor relations area were instructed by the CEO and CFO to speak with analysts to highlight the impact of the slowing economy on the company operations. Similar statements were not publicly disclosed for six days, by which time the share price had fallen nearly 8%. The company reached a settlement with SEC relating to an alleged breach of Reg FD. It agreed to pay a USD 1 million penalty and the CEO and CFO each paid a further USD 50,000.[22]

More recently, the efficacy of the continuous disclosure listing rules and Reg FD has been challenged in the *Chiasson* case. The facts of this case were summarised in Chapter 3. The appellants Newman and Chiasson received updates on Dell's and NVIDIA earnings numbers prior to the public earnings announcement.[23] Goyal, an analyst at Neuberger Berman, received the earnings related information from Dell's investor relations department before it was publicly released. He gave this information to other analysts, who in turn, passed it along to the appellants at three and four levels removed from the inside tipper.[24] The NVIDIA tipping chain was initiated by Choi, a person within NVIDIA's finance unit, who tipped the information to Lim, who in turn passed the information to Kuo, an analyst at Whittier Trust. Kuo then circulated this information to other analysts, who passed the information to Newman and Chaisson

19. *Burlington Coat Factory Sec.*Litig.114 F.3d1410 (3rd Cir. 1997).
20. Notably, the judicial commentary in *Burlington Coat Factory Sec.*Litig.114 F.3d1410 (3rd Cir. 1997) characterises the periodic reporting framework in the US narrowly as providing only historical information.
21. United States Securities and Exchange Commission, *Regulation FD Compliance & Disclosure Interpretations* Question 101.02 (14 August 2009).
22. *In the Matter of Office Depot, Inc.*, Accounting and Auditing Enforcement Release No. 3198 (21 October 2010) http://www.sec.gov/litigation/admin/2010/34-63152.pdf; *In the Matter of Stephen A. Odland*, Exchange Act Release No. 63153 (21 October 2010) http://www.sec.gov/litigation/admin/2010/34-63153.pdf; *In the Matter of Patricia A. McKay*, Exchange Act. Release No. 63154 (21 October 2010) http://www.sec.gov/litigation/admin/2010/34-63154.pdf31.
23. *United States v. Newman No. 13-1837 cr (L)* (2d Cir. 10 December 2014) 25.
24. *United States v. Newman No. 13-1837 cr (L)* (2d Cir. 10 December 2014) 5–6.

four levels down from the original inside tipper.[25] Newman and Chiasson used the information received to execute trades in Dell and NVIDIA stock, earning profits for their respective funds totalling around USD 4 million and USD 68 million respectively.[26]

The appellants provided evidence to the court through cooperating witnesses and investor relations associates that 'analysts routinely solicited information from companies in order to check their assumptions in their models in advance of earnings announcements.'[27] Goyal testified that he would frequently ask the internal relations departments of companies whether his valuation assumptions were "too high or too low" or in the "ball park" in order to update his numbers prior to an earnings announcement. Similarly, a supervisor in the Dell investor relations department confirmed that they 'routinely assisted analysts with developing their models.'[28] Evidence was also established that the investor relations departments at NVIDIA and Dell often 'leaked' earnings information to analysts in advance of earnings announcements, including explicit guidance on prospective earnings matters, such as the operating and gross margins and the level of operating expenses.[29] Given this clear evidence of generalised selective disclosure and regular communication between corporate insiders and analysts, the Court held that no reasonable jury could have found beyond a reasonable doubt that the appellants knew, or deliberately avoided knowing, that the information originated with corporate insiders.[30]

The evidence in this case highlights the insidious practice of short-term earnings management by means of private exchanges between company executives, sell-side analysts, buy-side analysts and asset managers. Similar practices were also highlighted by US research directors in the Soltes study discussed in Chapter 13.[31] When large listed corporations are routinely sharing (or discussing or confirming) prospective earnings information with selected market participants between reporting periods, and company managers and analysts are willing to testify that this is 'normal practice' in open court and during independent scholarly studies, one can legitimately question the effectiveness of the continuous disclosure regimes (and of Reg FD) in the US. Moreover, as previously highlighted, issues concerning short-term earnings management and private exchanges between managers and analysts involving prospective earnings information arise in other jurisdictions.

[B] Australia

The framework around earnings guidance in Australia provides interesting comparative insights. As outlined in Chapter 11, the primary continuous disclosure obligation

25. *United States v. Newman No. 13-1837 cr (L)* (2d Cir. 10 December 2014) 6.
26. *United States v. Newman No. 13-1837 cr (L)* (2d Cir. 10 December 2014) 5.
27. *United States v. Newman No. 13-1837 cr (L)* (2d Cir. 10 December 2014) 26.
28. *United States v. Newman No. 13-1837 cr (L)* (2d Cir. 10 December 2014) 26.
29. *United States v. Newman No. 13-1837 cr (L)* (2d Cir. 10 December 2014) 26–27.
30. *United States v. Newman No. 13-1837 cr (L)* (2d Cir. 10 December 2014) 27.
31. Eugene Soltes, 'Private Interaction Between Firm Management and Sell-side Analysts' (2014) 52 *Journal of Accounting Research* 245.

in Australia is contained in ASX Listing Rule 3.1, which requires a listed company to keep its security holders fully informed of any price-sensitive information of which it becomes aware.[32] Listing Rule 3.1 is supported by statutory provisions, which require information that is materially price-sensitive and not generally available to be released through the ASX.[33] There is no specific regulation prohibiting selective disclosure in Australia, but potential liability for selective disclosure may arise under the continuous disclosure regime. For example, ASIC successfully initiated an action against Southcorp Limited for disclosing material information to analysts privately without simultaneously releasing it to other participants through the ASX. An executive general manager of corporate affairs at Southcorp sent an email to analysts disclosing that the group's profit for the 2003 year would be diminished by AUD 30 million due to the poor 2000 vintage, but this information was not simultaneously disclosed to the ASX. From the time the email was sent until a trading halt was called at 1.07 pm on 19 April 2002, the Southcorp share price fell 7%.[34] Southcorp subsequently admitted that it had contravened ASX Listing Rule 3.1 and section 674(2) of the *Corporations Act 2001* (Cth) because the information released to the analysts had not been announced through the ASX and was not generally available to the market.[35]

More recently, the Federal Court of Australia imposed a AUD 1.2 million penalty on Newcrest Mining Limited (Newcrest), a large Australian resource group, for contravening its continuous disclosure obligations.[36] The court found that Newcrest contravened its continuous disclosure obligations under section 674(2) of the *Corporations Act 2001* (Cth) in two instances.[37] First, by failing to notify the ASX that during the period from 12.05 pm on 28 May 2013 until 9.19 am on 7 June 2013, Newcrest management expected total gold production for the 2014 financial year to be approximately 2.2–2.3 million ounces. Secondly, by failing to notify the ASX that during the period from 5 June until 9.19 am on 7 June 2013, Newcrest management expected the capital expenditure figure for the 2014 financial year to be approximately AUD 1 billion. Middleton noted that for resources companies, 'which do not typically publish earnings guidance, production estimates are market sensitive.'[38] He further noted that '[s]elective disclosure to analysts can generate confusion and a loss of faith in market

32. Australian Securities Exchange Listing Rule 3.1; *Corporations Act 2001* (Cth) s. 674. Unlisted public companies and large proprietary companies in Australia may also be subject to continuous disclosure as 'disclosing entities': *Corporations Act 2001* (Cth) ss 675(1), 675(2)(a), 111AP, Pt 1.2A, Div 2.
33. The statutory provisions are found in Ch. 6CA of the Corporations Act 2001 (Cth). The main provision is s. 674, which applies when a listing rule requiring notification of information to the market operator is breached and the undisclosed information is materially price-sensitive but not 'generally available'.
34. *Australian Securities and Investments Commission v. Southcorp Limited (No. 2)* (2003) 130 FCR 406, 416. This equated to a reduction in the market capitalisation of Southcorp Limited of more than USD 332 million.
35. *Australian Securities and Investments Commission v. Southcorp Limited (No. 2)* (2003) 130 FCR 406, 406.
36. *Australian Securities and Investments Commission v. Newcrest Mining Ltd* (2014) 101 ACSR 46.
37. Newcrest admitted that it disclosed this market-sensitive information to analysts privately without simultaneous disclosure through the Australian Securities Exchange.
38. *Australian Securities and Investments Commission v. Newcrest Mining Ltd* (2014) 101 ACSR 46, 55.

integrity.'[39] The rules concerning public guidance in Australia were altered by the ASX in 2013. Prior to May 2013, Guidance Note 8 to Listing Rule 3.1 *Continuous Disclosure Listing Rule 3.1-3.1B* (Guidance Note 8) suggested the 'way to manage earnings expectations is ... to establish a range within which earnings are likely to fall,' with a public announcement of any change in expectations.[40] It further indicated that a variation in expected earnings in excess of 10–15% in comparison with a previously released earnings forecast or a previous corresponding period would generally be considered material.[41] This guidance provided a uniform, objective and measurable benchmark.[42] In March 2013, the ASX released amendments to Guidance Note 8 that took effect from 1 May 2013.[43] The amended version of Guidance Note 8 acknowledges that 'the market's expectations of its earnings ... will often be a material driver of the price or value of its securities.'[44] It indicates that if earnings guidance has been published, any variation in the expected earnings of 5–10% from the announced benchmark should be disclosed, and updated guidance should be provided.[45] Curiously though, it provides no earnings variation threshold levels that trigger an obligation to disclose for companies covered by sell-side analysts that have not provided public guidance. Instead, Guidance Note 8 suggests that listed entities covered by sell-side analysts should be monitoring the sell-side analyst forecasts for an understanding of the 'market's expectations'. It states that if an entity becomes aware that its earnings will materially differ from the consensus estimates of sell-side analysts or, where not covered by its sell-side analysts, its earnings for the prior corresponding period, there may be a legal obligation to disclose this under the continuous disclosure or misleading and deceptive conduct provisions. However, the ASX notes that in its opinion 'there needs to be a reasonable degree of certainty that there will be such a difference ... [and the company may not have this] degree of certainty until after the end of the reporting period, when it is preparing its financial statements.'[46]

Consequently, under the amended Guidance Note 8, companies that provide no public guidance are not required to update the market about changes in expected earnings until there is a reasonable degree of certainty about a variation, and this level of certainty may not be established until after the end of the reporting period.

---

39. *Australian Securities and Investments Commission v. Newcrest Mining Ltd* (2014) 101 ACSR 46, 59.
40. Australian Securities Exchange, Guidance Note 8 *Continuous Disclosure Listing Rule 3.1* (June 2005) 19. See also Australian Securities and Investments Commission, *Better Disclosure for Investors - Guidance Rules* (23 August 2000) 3.
41. Australian Securities Exchange, Guidance Note 8 *Continuous Disclosure Listing Rule 3.1* (June 2005) 19.
42. A series of empirical studies (including one by the author) suggested that compliance with the guidance on disclosure of changes in earnings expectations was poor.
43. Australian Securities Exchange, *ASX Listing Rules Guidance Note 8* (1 May 2013). Further amendments were made to Guidance Note 8 in July 2015. Discussion of these amendments was not possible within the book schedule.
44. Australian Securities Exchange, *ASX Listing Rules Guidance Note 8* (1 May 2013).
45. Companies providing such guidance are reminded that material assumptions and qualifications must be outlined: Australian Securities and Investments Commission, Regulatory Guide 170: *Prospective Financial Information.*
46. Australian Securities Exchange, *ASX Listing Rules Guidance Note 8* (1 May 2013).

Moreover, disclosure may not be required if the sell-side analyst forecast estimates referenced by the company have already altered to reflect the changes in expectations. In contrast, listed companies that elect to provide public guidance impose on themselves a continuing obligation to update the guidance for all step changes amounting to a 5–10% variation. These marked differences in the standards imposed on companies that have and have not provided public guidance are likely to lead to a decline in the number of listed companies that provide guidance. They are also likely to reduce the spectrum of circumstances involving failures to continuously disclose a change in prospective trading conditions that may potentially result in company or director liability.

The commentary in Guidance Note 8 concerning prospective earnings potentially allows companies not to make public disclosures even in the face of significant changes in trading conditions and or unusual movements in the prices of the company's securities. Non-disclosure may be justified on the following grounds. First, the executives responsible for determining whether to make a public disclosure may suggest the materiality threshold was not triggered. The amended ASX guidance appears to shift materiality determinations back to directors and managers of listed companies, despite confirmation from Australian courts that a 'company's deliberations and ultimate decision are not determinative of whether information is material.'[47] Second, a company may argue that the board of directors was not sufficiently certain about the financial impact to disclose anything. Finally, a company may allege that 'the market' (which for many companies is effectively defined as sell-side analysts) knew about the changes to trading conditions and the consensus estimates reflected this knowledge.

The compilation, dissemination and discussion of company earnings forecasts are major areas of difficulty within company disclosure spheres. The ASX suggests that investors can readily access consensus numbers through their sell-side brokers.[48] However, consensus figures within financial markets comprise a selection of estimates that are subject to continual adjustment, so there is no single data source for outsiders to reference as a reliable benchmark. In any event, many listed companies prefer to maintain their own set of consensus data, rather than rely on third party compilers, in order to ensure greater accuracy and reliability.[49] As a result, company outsiders have no means to determine which set of estimates management is referencing at any point in time, nor the timing or changes to these sets of forecasts.

The ASX suggests that managerial feedback on the facts and assumptions underlying sell-side analyst valuation models can be provided.[50] The ASX indicates in

47. *James Hardie Industries NV v. Australian Securities and Investments Commission* (2010) 274 ALR 85; [2010] NSWCA 332, [527]. Spigelman CJ and Beazley and Giles JJ highlighted at [522] that the statutory obligation to disclose involves an objective test.
48. Australian Securities Exchange, 'Review of ASX Listing Rules Guidance Note 8 Continuous Disclosure: Listing Rules 3.1-3.1B' (March 2013) 51.
49. Australasian Investor Relations Association, 'The What, When and Where of Consensus Estimates for Listed Entities in Australia' (Issues Paper, February 2010) 15.
50. See, e.g., Australian Securities Exchange, *ASX Listing Rules Guidance Note 8* (1 May 2013) 48.

Guidance Note 8 that it does not believe that a listed entity has an obligation to correct analysts' forecasts. Nevertheless, it suggests that:

> where an analyst's forecast differs materially from a listed entity's internal forecast, it is in the entity's interests for it to explore with the analyst why that might be so and, if it becomes apparent that the analyst may have made a factual or computational error, to point that out to the analyst. This may help to set market expectations about the entity's earnings at an appropriate level and avoid any later earnings surprises that could raise potential disclosure issues under Listing Rule 3.1.[51]

This commentary is misconceived. Listed companies that have not provided public earnings forecasts or updates should not be permitted to discuss the accuracy or underlying assumptions of analyst valuation models, as this constitutes selective disclosure of materially price-sensitive information.

AIRA confirms that some listed Australian companies distribute their consensus data to analysts who seek it on a regular or informal basis and to invitees at individual briefings. These processes are also flawed because, once again, they involve selective disclosure of materially price-sensitive information.[52] As reflected in both the Southcorp and Newcrest cases, the private disclosures between executives at Southcorp and Newcrest and their respective sell-side analysts were made specifically to align market expectations (as reflected in the sell-side analyst forecasts) to internal management estimates.

The revised ASX policy guidance, which recommends that sell-side analyst forecasts should be the primary benchmark for determining whether disclosure is required by most large listed entities, is a major step backwards in the journey towards quality listed company disclosure and fair, efficient and transparent financial markets. The judgment of 'the market' is the aggregated opinion of all participants[53] (including asset managers, buy-side analysts and other investors who engage in securities research and make independent portfolio decisions) and not simply the views of sell-side analysts.[54] As discussed, a benchmark based on an ambiguous set of forecasts is subjective, transient and extremely difficult to empirically examine. Moreover, the use of privately obtained sell-side analyst forecasts as the primary determinant of disclosure obligations encourages earnings management processes and selective disclosure, it promotes conflicted relationships and discourages outsider research based on in-depth independent analysis and scrutiny, and it results in opaque markets.

---

51. Australian Securities Exchange, ASX Listing Rules Guidance Note 8 *Continuous Disclosure: Listing Rules 3.1-3.1B* (1 May 2013) 48.
52. While the Australasian Investor Relations Association suggests listed companies could include broker and consensus estimates on their websites with the authors' permission, no Australian companies appear to be doing so. Some global companies include a table of analyst forecast numbers on their websites (with clear disclaimers attached), but this practice is not common. See, e.g., J Sainsbury Plc, 'Analyst Consensus' at http://www.j-sainsbury.co.uk/investor-centre/analyst-consensus/.
53. See *The Kay Review of UK Equity Markets and Long-Term Decision Making: Interim Report* (February 2012) 9.
54. See, e.g., Boris Groysberg, Paul Healy and David Maber, 'What Drives Financial Analyst Compensation at High-Status Banks?' (2011) 49 *Journal of Accounting Research* 969.

Policy reports commonly acknowledge that the focus on expected earnings results within financial markets is often intense. Indeed, when the SEC changed its view on the provision of management forecasts in the 1970s, it noted that an instrumental reason for doing so was the realisation that 'very often projections were the subject matter of selective disclosure, that is, the information was furnished to selected investors, such as institutions or favoured analysts, and was not made available to public investors.'[55] Company directors and managers are human, and they are subject to the same personal failings and cognitive biases as everyone else. As Ries, the Research Director of E.L&C Ballieu, noted on the ABC programme *Inside Business*:

> [m]ost companies are very smart these days in massaging analysts' expectations. You know they give you a nod and a wink and stamp their feet on the floor three times so most of the numbers will be pretty close to what the companies report.[56]

Even if the news and signals they provide during private briefings are not explicit, body language and disclosure omissions are often more informative than specific verbal responses.

The theories and arguments discussed in Chapters 2-4, which suggest that private exchanges between company executives and segments of the market concerning prospective company earnings are economically efficient, are not supported by empirical research and are barely credible when examined holistically. The amendments to Guidance Note 8 are likely to adversely impact market transparency and public disclosure standards across the Australian market. As noted previously, both the rationales for continuous disclosure regimes and confidence in the integrity of the market are severely undermined when company earnings change significantly from one period to another, or when there are large security price movements, that are not supported by public disclosure and explanation.

[C] Germany

The German framework provides a useful contrast to the Australian position. BaFin indicates that certain scenarios are likely to be materially price-sensitive and subject to ad hoc disclosure obligations. These include results that are expected to:

- significantly depart from the prior year's figures;
- represent a change in business performance (e.g., a turnaround after several quarters in loss, or a sharp drop in sales after a growth phase has been sustained over several quarters); or
- significantly depart from market expectations.[57]

55. For example, AA Sommer Jnr, Commissioner US SEC, Forecasting, Speech delivered to Corporate Financial Forecast and Disclosure Conference at Drexel University, Philadelphia: A Look at the Future (29 March 1974).
56. Australian Broadcasting Corporation Television, *Ivor Ries with a Reporting Season Forecast* (19 July 2009) Inside Business, viewed 13 June 2015, http://www.abc.net.au/insidebusiness/content/2009/s2629947.htm.
57. Bafin, *Issuer Guideline* (14 May 2009) 58.

It confirms that when a company has provided a public forecast and its results are trending in line with the forecast, no disclosure is required. However, when companies publish annual forecasts and it becomes clear during the year that the results will depart from those forecasts, notification may be required.[58] It notes that such disclosure obligations arise as soon as the board of management (or other person or corporate body responsible for disclosure pursuant to section 15 of the WpHG) has gained access to the information concerned.[59]

The German framework differs significantly from the ASX position because listed German companies that have not provided a forecast must publicly notify significant changes in earnings expectations. All listed companies have equivalent disclosure obligations regardless of whether they provide public guidance or not. More critically, all users of public disclosures are continuously updated without having to determine (or guess) the latest consensus earnings figure relied upon by a listed company.

[D] Empirical Research

There is a distinct body of scholarly research on the provision of management earnings forecasts. The accounting and finance literature suggest that company management provides earnings forecasts to ensure a successful capital raising,[60] enhance market valuations or reputation by releasing good news,[61] reduce selective or unequal access to private information,[62] correct or confirm analyst forecasts, move market expectations on prospective earnings,[63] or avoid litigation.[64] Conversely, managers may

58. Bafin, *Issuer Guideline* (14 May 2009) 58.
59. Bafin, *Issuer Guideline* (14 May 2009) 57.
60. Bipin Ajinkya, Sanjeev Bhojraj and Partha Sengupta, 'The Association Between Outside Directors, Institutional Investors and the Properties of Management Earnings Forecasts' (2005) 43 *Journal of Accounting Research* 343, 428; William Ruland, Samuel Tung and Nashwa George, 'Factors Associated with the Disclosure of Managers' Forecasts' (1990) 65 *Accounting Review* 710; Mark Lang and Russell Lundholm, 'Cross-Sectional Determinants of Analysts Ratings of Corporate Disclosures' (1993) 31 *Journal of Accounting* 246.
61. Stephen Penman, 'An Empirical Investigation of the Voluntary Disclosure of Corporate Earnings Forecasts' (1980) 18 *Journal of Accounting Research* 132; Bipin Ajinkya, Sanjeev Bhojraj and Partha Sengupta, 'The Association Between Outside Directors, Institutional Investors and the Properties of Management Earnings Forecasts' (2005) 43 *Journal of Accounting Research* 343; Brett Trueman, 'Why do Managers Voluntarily Release Earnings Forecasts?' (1986) 8 *Journal of Accounting and Economics* 53; William Ruland, Samuel Tung and Nashwa George, 'Factors Associated with the Disclosure of Managers' Forecasts' (1990) 65 *Accounting Review* 710; Baruch Lev and Stephen Penman, 'Voluntary Forecast Disclosures, Non-Disclosure, and Stock Prices' (1990) 28 *Journal of Accounting Research* 49.
62. Bipin Ajinkya, Sanjeev Bhojraj and Partha Sengupta, 'The Association Between Outside Directors, Institutional Investors and the Properties of Management Earnings Forecasts' (2005) 43 *Journal of Accounting Research* 343, 428.
63. Bipin Ajinkya, Sanjeev Bhojraj and Partha Sengupta, 'The Association Between Outside Directors, Institutional Investors and the Properties of Management Earnings Forecasts' (2005) 43 *Journal of Accounting Research* 343; Brett Trueman, 'Why do Managers Voluntarily Release Earnings Forecasts?' (1986) 8 *Journal of Accounting and Economics* 53; William Ruland, Samuel Tung and Nashwa George, 'Factors Associated with the Disclosure of Managers' Forecasts' (1990) 65 *Accounting Review* 710.
64. Ron Kasznik and Baruch Lev, 'To Warn or Not to Warn: Management Disclosures in the Face of an Earnings Surprise' (1995) 70 *Accounting Review* 113.

choose not to provide public earnings guidance because of litigation risks, concerns about increased pricing volatility or an inability to predict future earnings.[65]

The extent of outside[66] ownership and new capital raisings have been found to be important factors driving the provision of management forecasts, with analyst forecast error playing a less significant role.[67] Studies suggest that management forecasts are more accurate than analyst forecasts in the absence of management guidance.[68] They also suggest that management forecasts reduce analyst forecast dispersion and price volatility,[69] result in lower discounting of future earnings,[70] reduce information asymmetry,[71] and are informative for company valuations.[72] Evidence suggesting associations between the provision of earnings guidance and improved aggregate returns[73] and or reductions in the costs of capital is increasing.[74] Balakrishnan et al. suggest that managers can causally influence their cost of capital by voluntarily

65. Bipin Ajinkya, Sanjeev Bhojraj and Partha Sengupta, 'The Association Between Outside Directors, Institutional Investors and the Properties of Management Earnings Forecasts' (2005) 43 *Journal of Accounting Research* 343, 427–428; Douglas Skinner, 'Earnings Disclosures and Stockholder Lawsuits' (1997) 23 *Journal of Accounting and Economics* 249; Leonard Soffer, S Ramu Thiagarajan and Beverly Walther, 'Earnings Preannouncement Strategies' (2000) 5 *Review of Accounting Studies* 5.
66. 'Outside ownership' is defined as shareholdings by parties that are not company directors or officers.
67. Bipin Ajinkya, Sanjeev Bhojraj and Partha Sengupta, 'The Association Between Outside Directors, Institutional Investors and the Properties of Management Earnings Forecasts' (2005) 43 *Journal of Accounting Research* 343, 428; William Ruland, Samuel Tung and Nashwa George, 'Factors Associated with the Disclosure of Managers' Forecasts' (1990) 65 *Accounting Review* 710, 720.
68. George Foster, 'Stock Market Reaction to Estimates of Earnings Per Share By Company Officials' (1973) 11 *Journal of Accounting Research* 25, 35; Nicholas Gonedes, Nicholas Dopuch and Stephen Penman, 'Disclosure Rules, Information Production and Capital Market Equilibrium: The Case of Forecast Disclosure Rules' (1976) 14 *Journal of Accounting Research* 89; James Patell, 'Corporate Forecasts of Earnings Per Share and Stock Price Behavior: Empirical Test' (1976) 14 *Journal of Accounting Research* 246, 246; Bikki Jaggi, 'A Note on the Information Content of Corporate Annual Earnings Forecasts' (1978) 53 *Accounting Review* 961, 966. See also John Poole, 'Improving the Reliability of Management Forecasts' (1989) 14 *Journal of Corporation Law* 547, 635.
69. Gregory Waymire, 'Earnings Volatility and Voluntary Management Forecast Disclosure' (1985) 23 *Journal of Accounting Research* 268.
70. Michael Clement, Richard Frankel and Jeffrey Miller, 'Confirming Management Earnings, Forecasts, Earnings Uncertainty and Stock Returns' (2003) 41 *Journal of Accounting Research* 653.
71. Maribeth Coller and Teri Yohn, 'Management Forecasts and Information Asymmetry: An Examination of Bid-Ask Spreads' (1997) 35 *Journal of Accounting Research* 181, 190.
72. Gregory Waymire, 'Additional Evidence on the Information Content of Management Earnings Forecasts' (1984) 22 *Journal of Accounting Research* 703; Brett Trueman, 'Why do Managers Voluntarily Release Earnings Forecasts?' (1986) 8 *Journal of Accounting and Economics* 53; Grace Pownall, Charles Wasley and Gregory Waymire, 'The Stock Price Effects of Alternative Types of Management Earnings Forecasts' (1993) 68 *Accounting Review* 896.
73. Gregory Waymire, 'Additional Evidence on the Information Content of Management Earnings Forecasts' (1984) 22 *Journal of Accounting Research* 703, 717; Carol Anilowski, Mei Feng and Douglas Skinner, 'Does Earning Guidance Affect Market Returns? The Nature and Information Content of Aggregate Earnings Guidance' (2007) 44 *Journal of Accounting & Economics* 36.
74. Yan Li and Holly Yang, 'Disclosure and the Cost of Equity Capital: An Analysis at the Market Level' (Working Paper, 1 January 2013) available at http://papers.ssrn.com/sol3/papers.cfm?abstract_id = 1965663.

providing more timely and informative earnings guidance.[75] As might be expected, share price responses to publicly disclosed guidance are stronger when issued by managers with an established reputation for forecasting accuracy and in environments of information uncertainty.[76] As a whole, these studies suggest that the voluntary provision of public guidance by listed companies enhances the IOSCO goals of investor protection and market fairness, efficiency and transparency, and should therefore be encouraged.

§14.05 REGULATORY AND ENFORCEMENT ISSUES

While most jurisdictions acknowledge the critical importance of continuous disclosure regulation and practice, all countries face significant challenges when seeking to embed a resilient culture of continuous public disclosure. Since the late 1980s, most of the major securities exchanges around the world have listed as for-profit self-regulatory organisations.[77] As listed corporations, most of these exchanges have retained front line responsibility for monitoring compliance with their disclosure listing rules, with the notable exception of the LSE. Consequently, the disclosure listing rules are supervised by exchanges that are themselves listed on the markets they regulate. The supervisory and regulatory functions of most of the largest security exchanges are contained within a subsidiary company as a means to enhance the independence of the supervising entity from the commercial businesses. However, these structures only partially mitigate the significant conflicts that arise. The group executives continue to have conflicting duties and are not always well motivated to enforce the disclosure listing rules. As a Singapore Exchange Limited website previously explained:

> the profit motive of a demutualised exchange creates a natural tension between its regulatory responsibilities and duty to the public, and its shareholders. This natural tension gives rise to ... conflict issues ... A mutual exchange needs to balance the interests of its 'member-owners' with the interests of the investing public in [its] decision-making and rule-making.[78]

The allocation of responsibilities between the security exchanges and national regulators remains a critical element of most company disclosure frameworks, but this area is fraught with difficulties. As outlined in Part III, monitoring and enforcement of company disclosure matters by the major exchanges across the jurisdictions reviewed appear to be limited. Many of the exchanges lack the power to supervise and enforce their own disclosure rules. The powers of most are restricted to compulsory suspension or cancellation of listings, and these extreme measures are rarely used in practice,

75. Karthik Balakrishnan, Mary Brooke Billings, Bryan Kelly and Alexander Ljungqvist, 'Shaping Liquidity: On the Causal Effects of Voluntary Disclosure' (2014) 69 *Journal of Finance* 2237.
76. Holly Yang, 'Capital Market Consequences of Managers' Voluntary Disclosure Styles' (2011) 53 *Journal of Accounting & Economics* 167.
77. World Federation of Exchanges, *2009 Cost and Revenue Survey* (October 2010) 5.
78. SGX Ltd, 'Rule Making and SRO', viewed 7 June 2012, http://www.sgx.com/wps/wcm/connect/cp_en/site/regulation/rulemaking_and_sro/Rule-making+and+SRO+Page?presentationtemplate=design_lib/PT_Printer_Friendly. The website with this commentary is no longer available.

especially against larger corporations.[79] Only a handful of the exchanges reviewed implement formal disciplinary procedures applicable to company disclosure matters and have powers to censure or fine the relevant company. Thus even if the exchanges choose to become more active in supervising and enforcing company disclosure, the mechanisms for doing so may be limited.

The incentives of security exchange executives to actively monitor and enforce the disclosure listing rules are arguably minimal. Most of the largest security exchanges must compete aggressively with other trading platforms in their home nation and globally. Hence the exchanges can justifiably argue that the resources required for regulatory activities place them at a competitive disadvantage vis- à-vis alternate trading platforms that are not required to operate monitoring and supervisory arms.[80] A large share of the revenue and profit of these entities is derived from companies with the largest market capitalisations in the form of listing fees, clearing and settlement charges, and capital raising income. A delisting or suspension of one of these companies for a breach of the listing rules would result in a significant loss of income, particularly if the delisted or suspended company were to shift its listing to another security exchange. Moreover, most of the trading fees are paid by the largest participants. The primary focus of the traditional security exchanges within competitive environments is therefore to retain and grow their listed corporate base and to attract the highest volume traders, which are typically the largest financial institutions.[81]

The SEC noted in 2004 that failings or perceived failings with respect to securities exchanges fulfilling their self-regulatory obligations had sparked significant debate as to the efficacy of the regulatory processes.[82] In 2009, a report from the Organisation for Economic Co-operation and Development noted that exchanges were becoming increasingly uneasy about the prospect of having to continue performing their traditional regulatory and other corporate governance enhancing functions amid a shrinking revenue base.[83] These concerns about the extent and quality of exchange oversight continue to expand as financial markets fragment, the number of alternate security trading platforms grows, the levels of high frequency trading increase, and the federal supervisory budgets are reduced or threatened.[84] Consequently, at a time when

79. Adam Pritchard, 'Self Regulation and Securities Markets' (Spring 2003) *Regulation* 32; Craig Pirrong, 'The Self-Regulation of Commodity Exchanges: The Case of Market Manipulation' (1995) 38 *Journal of Law and Economics* 141.
80. Centre for Financial Market Integrity, *Self-Regulation in Today's Securities Markets: Outdated System or Work in Progress?* (2007) 8.
81. See, e.g., Michael Lewis, *Flash Boys* (W.W. Norton & Company, Inc, New York, 2015).
82. United States Securities and Exchange Commission, 'Self-Regulatory Organizations – Various Amendments; Proposed Rule' (8 December 2004 Release No. 34-50699; 17 CFR Parts 240, 242). See also Peter DeMarzo, Michael Fishman and Kathleen Hagerty, 'Self-Regulation and Government Oversight' (2005) 72 *Review of Economic Studies* 687; Karessa Cain, 'New Efforts to Strengthen Corporate Governance: Why Use SRO Listing Standards?' (2003) *Columbia Business Law Review* 619. Cain found that exchanges rarely deny listings as a means to signal their quality reputation.
83. Organisation for Economic Co-operation and Development, Directorate for Financial and Enterprise Affairs Steering Group on Corporate Governance, *The Role of Stock Exchanges in Corporate Governance* (2 July 2009) 4.
84. See, e.g., Tom Lin, 'The New Investor' (2013) 60 *UCLA Law Review* 678; Michael Lewis, *Flash Boys* (W.W. Norton & Company, Inc, New York, 2015).

increased surveillance of financial market activity is critical, the income of the major securities exchanges and the resources of some of the leading securities regulators are under pressure, potentially undermining the role of these entities as effective regulators and enforcers of company disclosure matters.

It appears that the securities exchanges are increasingly relying on the same empirical processes to detect possible insider trading as those used to monitor compliance with continuous disclosure obligations. All of the jurisdictions reviewed operate stockwatch programmes. Some also use price query processes that, when triggered, send a letter to the relevant company asking it to confirm whether it is in compliance with disclosure obligations. It is important to understand the role and limitations of these stockwatch programmes and price query systems. First, stockwatch programmes and price query notices only operate when there is unexplained and sharp short-term price or volume movement, so the spectrum of disclosure events they encompass is restricted. Further, if and when the materiality thresholds and security price movement parameters of these programmes are set at higher levels, the percentage of suspicious trades that activate the stockwatch programmes declines.[85]

Second, the stockwatch processes are limited with respect to the nature of information encompassed. Private or selective disclosure of material information is the most material informational risk faced by investors who rely on public disclosures. Many instances of trading on privately obtained or selectively disclosed information lead to gradual or steady share price movements over a period of days or months prior to its public release, particularly when the privately disclosed information involves a series of information items that cumulatively feed into a listed company's results or earnings forecasts. However, stockwatch programmes are not triggered when share prices respond to material price-sensitive information in a manner other than in a spiked pattern.

Third, the stockwatch and query processes are limited in consequence. These programmes only operate when short-term share price movements or trading volumes suggest material price-sensitive news has not been disclosed. By this time, uninformed investors that traded during the relevant period have already suffered a loss (or have missed a potential gain), which means that any benefits from the stockwatch programmes are indirect at best. Benefits of stockwatch programmes are negligible when a company responds to a query indicating it has not complied with disclosure obligations, or it makes a subsequent announcement, and no further investigation or enforcement action is then taken by the exchange. The stockwatch processes are only productive for investors as a whole if sustained monitoring and enforcement by the relevant exchange encourages companies to continuously disclose in future and or reduces the level of disclosure omissions that would otherwise occur. These outcomes are only likely when regulators have the capacity to examine the circumstances of individual queries, and are willing and able to initiate appropriate enforcement actions when contraventions of the disclosure listing rules occur.

85. For example, the ASX materiality and price movement parameters were outlined and discussed earlier in this chapter.

Finally, stockwatch processes operate on an *ex post facto* or hindsight basis. When the materiality of information is determined based on the level of near term share price movement, this shifts the burden to regulators, investors and stakeholders to establish misconduct after the event using relatively limited tools. In effect, the stockwatch programmes require regulators to establish that 'inside information' was *not* disclosed after the non-disclosure has already occurred, with evidence being limited to short-term security price movements following public release of the information.

The use of stockwatch programmes by security exchanges (and some federal regulators) as a primary means to monitor compliance with continuous disclosure regimes is problematic. This approach shifts the focus of regulators away from disclosure as a positive, proactive and broad obligation intended to assist a wide spectrum of interested persons and ensure a competitive market, to a narrow spectrum of disclosure circumstances that are deemed to be sufficiently 'suspicious' to justify a price query or initiate some form of enforcement.

Scholars have examined federal regulatory structures on varying bases, including consideration of the size and funding of individual regulators and the number of enforcement actions initiated.[86] However, the efficacy of security exchanges as monitors and enforcers of disclosure listing rules is an area that has received less focus. Security exchanges continue to play an important role as front line supervisors of company disclosure law and practice, with leading roles as regulator and supervisor of continuous disclosure frameworks in most of the jurisdictions examined. Thus, the legitimacy and efficacy of the role of exchanges as regulators of securities law requires deeper consideration and debate, with a focus on whether these structures serve the national public interest.

86. See, e.g., Howell Jackson and Mark Roe, 'Public and Private Enforcement of Securities Laws: Resource-Based Evidence' (2009) 93 *Journal of Financial Economics* 207.

PART V

Company Disclosure: Best Practice and Conclusion

> Boards of directors are accountable to their shareholders and both have to play their part in making that accountability effective. Boards of directors need to do so through the quality of the information which they provide to shareholders, and shareholders through their willingness to exercise their responsibilities as owners ...[I]f standards of financial reporting and of business conduct more generally are not seen to be raised, a greater reliance on regulation may be inevitable. Any further degree of regulation, would, in any event, be more likely to be well directed, if it were to enforce what has already been shown to be workable and effective by those setting the standard.[1]

INTRODUCTION

Disclosure regulation within financial markets is often a tool wielded by policy makers following periods of financial crises. This pattern was established in the 1930s when substantive company disclosure regulation was introduced in the US following a severe financial market crash and a sustained period of economic depression. More recently, regulation designed to enhance the transparency of financial institutions was passed in some countries in the wake of the GFC. However, enacting disclosure regulation is only the first of many steps necessary to achieve effective corporate disclosure and communication.

Chapter 15 highlights positive initiatives for inclusion within best practice company disclosure frameworks. These best practice guidelines reflect real world examples of structures, processes and practices used by leading corporations and

1. Report of the Committee on the Financial Aspects of Corporate Governance (1 December 2012) [3.4],[3.6] available at www.jbs.ac.uj/cadbury/reprot/index.html.

national regulators, as well as recommendations drawing on this author's many years of experience analysing company disclosures across major financial markets. The best practice company disclosure framework is discussed within two sections: regulatory structures and disclosure conduct.

Chapter 16 provides a concise summary of the book's arguments and concludes.

CHAPTER 15

Best Practice Company Disclosure Frameworks

> Regulators, under unprecedented pressure, face a range of demands, often contradictory in nature: be less intrusive – but more effective; be kindlier and gentler – but don't let the bastards get away with anything; focus your efforts – but be consistent; process things quicker – and be more careful next time; deal with important issues – but don't stray outside your statutory authority; be more responsive to the regulated community – but don't get captured by industry.[1]

§15.01 BEST PRACTICE COMPANY DISCLOSURE: REGULATORY STRUCTURES

[A] Regulator Transparency

A culture of public communication, transparency and accountability should start at the top of the disclosure regulatory hierarchy. All regulators of disclosure matters should be as open and continuously engaged with their various stakeholders (including the general public) as possible. Security exchanges and taxpayer-funded regulators must ensure that their supervisory and enforcement operations appear to be, and indeed are, fair, consistent and transparent. In the modern era, this requires websites that are user friendly and functional, with search engines that enable people to find relevant information quickly. The roles and powers should be clearly explained on the websites of the national regulators and security exchanges, including the allocation of responsibilities and the nature of the relationships between the exchanges and regulators. The rules, supervisory processes, and enforcement powers relating to disclosure matters should be outlined, and the details of any enforcement actions should be readily accessible. For example, the HKSE and JPX provide details of disclosure related processes and disciplinary proceedings on their websites. The SEC also provides

1. Malcolm Sparrow, *The Regulatory Craft* (Brookings Institution Press, Washington DC, 2000) 17.

disclosure guidance and outlines its enforcement actions across the various disclosure regimes. These digital processes raise awareness of disclosure issues and promote better disclosure standards for minimal cost.

The capacity and ability of regulators to supervise company disclosure regimes, and to successfully initiate enforcement actions when required, are essential ingredients of effective disclosure frameworks. Nevertheless, the efficacy of company disclosure regulators should not be assessed solely or predominantly on the number of successful enforcement outcomes. The absolute number of such actions is limited given typical resource constraints. Moreover, the disclosure events that can be pursued by regulators, particularly those involving more severe forms of enforcement such as litigation, generally reflect the most egregious conduct rather than common practice. The main focus of all disclosure regulators should be to promote a positive culture of public disclosure across entire markets by emphasising the long-term benefits of effective corporate communication that build and sustain a reputation of reliability, transparency and trust. Building and nurturing such disclosure cultures should be a high priority for all regulators, and all available tools should be harnessed to achieve this objective. For example, the SEC supervisory processes are broadly transparent. Publication of queries to listed companies and the company responses provides a good example of a relatively low cost procedure that alerts companies and others to potential disclosure issues.

A publicly funded central facility that provides easy access to national company periodic reports and continuous disclosure is important. The EDGAR website run by the SEC in the US is a good model for other jurisdictions to consider. Similar facilities that provide details on open access webcasts by listed companies should also be established to promote greater transparency and equity in relation to company briefings. These combined facilities would greatly assist investors to make well-informed and timely decisions and manage their company security holdings within savings and retirement portfolios. These facilities would also provide an independent record of companies embracing digital technologies to provide public access to substantive high quality information on a timely and consistent basis.

Most of the leading global exchanges operate tiered markets, with a main market for larger, more established companies, and additional secondary markets for smaller or growth companies. The listing requirements and ongoing obligations are generally less onerous for companies listed on the lower tier markets, because these markets are intended to provide flexible capital raisings and securities trading mechanisms for developing companies. The FSE uses a different model that other exchanges might consider implementing to enhance market transparency and company disclosure standards. It operates a single market, but companies can choose the listing standard with which they wish to adhere. Companies may list on the FSE under the general listing category with disclosure obligations that merely comply with EC standards, or may choose the premium listing category with higher disclosure standards, in the expectation that this provides long-term reputational and valuation benefits. This voluntary disclosure structure allows savers to invest in companies with their preferred disclosure standard and associated risk. Companies with the highest disclosure standards are – all other things being equal – likely to attract a premium rating and valuation, and this competitive process motivates other companies to opt for the higher disclosure standards. Hence this structure promotes better public disclosure practices as a positive feature of listing that ultimately benefits corporations and their investors and stakeholders.

[B] Regulatory Priorities

There has been a renewed focus over the last decade by most national regulators on enforcement of insider trading. For example, the FSA 2013 annual report states that '[o]ver the last 12 months the FSA conducted four criminal trials, prosecuting more individuals for insider trading this year than any other.'[2] Similarly a paper that discusses market cleanliness in the UK states that there were no convictions for insider trading in the years from 2004 to 2008, but twenty-three convictions during the period from 2009 to 2013.[3] The FSA was criticised by the House of Commons Treasury Committee and by various government reports for its 'light touch' regulatory approach following the GFC.[4] Alexander suggests that a tougher approach has since been taken by regulators that 'aims to expose and deter market abuse which has been rife in UK financial markets for many years' including the transfer of inside information.[5]

An increasing emphasis by regulators on insider trading may be misconceived, because it changes the supervisory and disclosure cultures and frameworks in a subtle but profoundly important way. Continuous disclosure regimes are related to, but distinct from, insider trading rules. The nature of insider trading regulation is negative, reactive, and narrowly focused, while continuous disclosure frameworks are positive, proactive and broad in nature. Insider trading regulation can only be applied after the relevant event, when any investor losses or shifts in wealth have already occurred. Insider trading litigation is broadly analogous to sending in the ambulance when disclosure accidents have occurred. These disclosure accidents include failures to periodically or continuously disclose material information, or incidents of selective disclosure of information to some investors or segments of the market. National regulators are limited in the number and type of court actions they can initiate, because litigation is risky, expensive and time-consuming. Large scale insider trading cases can take many years, and the final decisions are often delivered well after the relevant events. Furthermore, insider trading enforcement actions are generally motivated by deterrence rather than compensation. Favourable insider trading judgments typically do not provide compensation to investors and stakeholders who have suffered losses.

2. Financial Services Authority, *FSA Annual Report 2012/2013* 39.
3. Jim Goldman, Stefan Hunt, Paul Minter, Felix Suntheim and Qamar Zaman, 'Why Has the FCAs Market Cleanliness Statistic for Takeover Announcements Decreased Since 2009?' *Financial Conduct Authority Occasional Paper No. 4* (July 2014).
4. See, e.g., Kern Alexander, 'UK Insider Dealing and Market Abuse Law: Strengthening Regulatory Law to Combat Market Misconduct' in Stephen Bainbridge (ed.), *Research Handbook on Insider Trading* (Edward Elgar, Cheltenham UK, 2013) 424.
5. See, e.g., Kern Alexander, 'UK Insider Dealing and Market Abuse Law: Strengthening Regulatory Law to Combat Market Misconduct' in Stephen Bainbridge (ed.), *Research Handbook on Insider Trading* (Edward Elgar, Cheltenham UK, 2013) 424.

Recoveries realised by investors and taxpayer-funded regulators are often minimal in comparison to the amounts of wealth that are transferred on a day-to-day basis when insider trading events occur.

National company and securities regulators funded by taxpayers have limited funds, so they need to establish clear priorities and strategies. Best practice regulatory frameworks must ensure that available resources (including manpower, skills, knowledge and financial resources) are allocated as efficiently as possible to achieve regulatory objectives. As discussed more fully in the next chapter, the most efficient way to minimise most forms of market abuse and the level of insider trading across the market is to promote, monitor and enforce the existing periodic and continuous disclosure regulation that requires public disclosure of company information on a regular, comprehensive and timely basis. Assuming the FSA 2013 annual report and the FCA 2014 annual report fairly reflect the regulatory priorities in the UK, the quality and timeliness of listed company disclosure are not high on the agenda.[6] The disclosure priorities and allocation of regulatory resources in some of the jurisdictions reviewed may therefore require some recalibration, with a shift of resources to enable more intense supervision and enforcement of company disclosure frameworks. While best practice regulatory structures should include misconduct litigation such as insider trading, all company and securities regulators should prioritise and emphasise compliance with, and enforcement of, periodic and continuous disclosure obligations. Multifaceted regulatory approaches that vigorously promote a culture of high quality disclosure are likely to achieve disclosure policy goals and minimise losses suffered by investors and others more effectively than a dominant reliance on insider trading litigation. Scarce resources (particularly taxpayer monies) are better spent on programmes that proactively encourage high quality disclosure practices and prevent disclosure accidents from happening in the first place.

[C] Regulatory Review Programmes

National regulators outside of the US have used various approaches to enhance the quality of company disclosures. A common theme of these endeavours is an emphasis on corporate reporting that presents information in a clear, concise and effective manner. This process has been assisted by the plain English movement, which promotes documents that are written and expressed in such a way that readers can readily understand them. Policy guidance urging the use of clear, concise and effective disclosure is important, but without more, is unlikely to drive significantly improved company disclosure cultures and practices. Within best practice company disclosure regulatory structures, policy guidance should be supplemented by substantive regulatory initiatives. For example, regular reviews of publicly available company reports and disclosures by independent bodies are an essential feature of a best practice

6. The annual reports do not contain any discussion of listed company disclosure related matters, other than to highlight a positive trend in commissioned market cleanliness studies that examine possible suspicious trading in the two days prior to announcements of mergers and acquisition transactions. These studies are explained in Ch. 14.

disclosure framework. These review programmes should be multilayered and should include proactive monitoring and a broad range of supervisory functions, including education, policy guidance, and published discussions of identified risks and issues.

The corporate disclosure review programmes in Canada discussed in Chapter 6 provide a sound model for other jurisdictions to consider because the review processes operate as a virtuous cycle that promotes enhanced public reporting. These review programmes include full and targeted reviews of disclosures. The survey methodologies use a risk-based filter and quantitative and qualitative criteria. The review category outcomes are clearly specified and consistently applied. The programme sampling and outcome methodologies, the layout and content of the review reports, and the guidance and disclosure principles are consistent from year to year, providing clear disclosure policy standards and feedback. The review reports document the disclosure outcomes and discuss disclosure deficiencies in detail, providing an independent public record of progress achieved. They also highlight recurring problems and difficult issues for policy and scholarly consideration.

The Canadian disclosure review programmes include proactive measures such as early discussion with companies identified as potentially at risk of breaching the disclosure rules, with subsequent reviews of their filings. The regulatory responses are flexible, targeted and proportionate when non-compliance is uncovered. Enforcement actions are initiated using an extensive armoury of options and processes. When minor issues arise, companies are asked to make changes to disclosures in upcoming filings. When disclosure deficiencies are sufficiently significant to require refiling, the company's name, the date of refiling, a description of the disclosure deficiencies and the press release incorporating the revisions are posted on the regulatory website for three years. These postings highlight consistent offenders in the public arena and thereby operate as a 'name and shame' deterrent. Only the most serious deficiencies are referred to the enforcement area for action, reducing the required level of regulatory resources dedicated to litigation.

As discussed in Chapter 10, the HKEC also reviews company reports and disclosures on an annual basis. Its processes share some of the features of the Canadian programmes, with additional positive elements. The companies reviewed are selected using a risk-based approach that includes impact and probability criteria. The HKEC also selects a general accounting theme and an industry theme to examine each year. The accounting themes it has reviewed include business combinations and investments in associates and joint ventures, accounting for financial instruments, segment disclosure, accounting for goodwill and intangible assets, and accounting for impairment of assets. The industry themes reviewed include toll road infrastructure projects, companies with a major or principal business of mining activities, companies with a major or principal business involving property construction or investment in properties, businesses involved in telecommunications and internet services, and companies whose major or principal businesses are power and utilities.

The HKEC publishes an annual review report that identifies and discusses accounting and specialist industry disclosure issues. All of the HKEC reports note that some companies repeat information from the financial statements in narrative form within the MD&A sections, without further explanation or analysis. They repeatedly highlight that companies with substantial fluctuations in turnover, operating results, net asset values and segment results often provide little explanation or discussion. They recommend that companies expand their MD&A to explain how the reported and prospective financial positions, liquidity and operations have been, or will be, affected. They call for discussion in the MD&A to be consistent with the financial statements, and for outlines to improve readers' understanding of the nature and impact of significant events and material balances and transactions. They also emphasise that financial information prepared in accordance with accounting standards is the most important section of the financial reports.[7]

General corporate disclosure reviews can be enhanced by specialist or targeted surveys. For example, the OSC examined disclosures containing forward-looking information in 2012 in recognition of the critical importance of this type of information to investors.[8] Its report notes that only a third of companies reviewed provided a comparison of actual results with previously disclosed guidance. It identifies four areas for improvement:

(1) clear identification of forward-looking information;
(2) disclosure of the underlying material factors or assumptions;
(3) updates to forward-looking information; and
(4) discussion of actual results following disclosure of forward-looking information or estimates.[9]

To assist companies, the OSC report provides specific examples of boilerplate disclosure and preferred entity-specific disclosure. More generally, it recommends timely updating of earnings guidance following changes in managerial expectations. It also encourages the use of financial and non-financial key performance indicators. It suggests that companies present forward-looking information in reports in a separate section, including a table that sets out the company's objectives, specific assumptions and risks.[10] These recommendations reflect best practice.

National and global regulators accumulate extensive knowledge and experience about superior corporate disclosure techniques, form, and content. This knowledge should be systemically documented and communicated in the form of detailed and published feedback. Otherwise, the benefits of comprehensive monitoring are likely to dissipate over time. Regular and systematic empirical reviews of company reports and disclosures, such as those published by the CSA and HKEC, provide an invaluable independent record of company disclosure developments and issues. Such programmes are likely to promote and sustain high quality disclosure standards at a

7. Hong Kong Exchanges and Clearing Limited, *Financial Statements Review Programme Report 2012* (January 2013) 29.
8. Ontario Securities Commission (OSC), *Forward-Looking Information Disclosure* (OSC Staff Notice 51-721) 4, 7.
9. Ontario Securities Commission (OSC), *Forward-Looking Information Disclosure* (OSC Staff Notice 51-721) 3.
10. Ontario Securities Commission (OSC), *Forward-Looking Information Disclosure* (OSC Staff Notice 51-721) 20.

relatively minimal cost, particularly when supported by carefully calibrated supervisory and enforcement structures.

§15.02 BEST PRACTICE COMPANY DISCLOSURE: DISCLOSURE CONDUCT

[A] Disclosure Conduct: Periodic Reporting

This author's examination of disclosures found similar issues to those highlighted in the regulator review reports outlined in Part III, including poorly written MD&A, commentary referencing non-compliant financial measures, and a lack of comprehensive and specific risk disclosures. The examination also identified significant issues with the full year reporting processes, long-term performance commentary and analysis, and reporting formats that hinder, rather than promote, comparative analysis. The ensuing discussion discusses best practice mechanisms and conduct to address these issues.

[B] MD&A

Corporate directors and managers need sharply focused strategies and well implemented plans to remain competitive and achieve optimal performance, especially during challenging periods. There are significant benefits for managers and their stakeholders when corporate reporting is presented in a clear and consistent manner. Well-written commentary on important items and trends, combined with transparent and frank strategic and performance analysis, conveys a message to readers that the senior executives understand the status and position of the company, and its immediate and longer-term challenges. Clear disclosure and communication of company strategies and plans improves market confidence, encourages ongoing investment, and promotes and builds stakeholder trust and confidence.

The US has acknowledged the importance of high quality MD&A in company periodic reports for many decades. The MD&A in the full year reports in the US must address segmental performance, industry and economic factors affecting the company performance, the drivers of the changes in financial conditions or results, and the effects of discontinued operations. The reports must also discuss the income statement, including commentary on cost of sales, changes in the gross and net margins, contribution by business segment, capital commitments, risks and uncertainties, inflationary impacts, use of working capital, and unusual or infrequent events or transactions. The MD&A must include analysis of the company's balance sheet, including the end of period positions and ongoing drivers of liquidity, capital resources, off-balance sheet arrangements, transactions with related parties, proposed transactions, critical accounting estimates, and financial instrument exposures. The mandated MD&A in the quarterly reports, while more limited than in the full year reports, requires analysis of the quarter and year-to-date operations and cash flows, changes in results not related to ongoing business operations, and seasonal aspects affecting the results, operations or cash flow. These MD&A categories provide necessary contextual information for company managers and directors, and for outsiders, to interpret the financial statements and better understand the company's environment and its position and prospects.

Discussion and analysis of a company's historical and expected financial performance and operations within all periodic reports should include, at a minimum, the following information:

- an outline of the company's strategies, objectives and key performance indicators;
- MD&A of the company's performance against the stated criteria during the reporting period;
- the causes of material changes to line items of the financial statements;
- segmental information and analysis;
- disclosure of significant factors and events, including unusual events, non-recurring items and new developments;
- information concerning the company's liquidity and its ongoing ability to generate sustainable positive cash flows;
- foreign currency and translation effects;
- discussion and analysis of material trends, uncertainties and risks;
- commentary and analysis on longer-term trends and performance;
- forward-looking commentary and guidance; and
- commentary on the broader environment in which the company operates, including macroeconomic factors, industry trends and issues, sustainability issues, and relevant policy developments.

Best practice company reports provide MD&A and financial notes that are balanced and proportionate, with the level of detail reflecting the materiality or significance of the item, matter, or area discussed. Such reports frame the MD&A around the financial statements, with detailed notes and explanation of the reported numbers in the income statement, balance sheet, and cash flow statement. As regulatory reviews note repeatedly, period-to-period movement should be presented in numerical form, leaving scope within the commentary to explain or analyse the changes. Detailed analysis is then provided of important components that led to the result, including revenue and expense items, and business segment and product contributions. Key items on the balance sheet and cash flow statement are explained, including the debt, cash and liquidity positions and tables showing the scale and maturity profiles of significant debt items and capital commitments. The general commentary sections include discussion of company strategies within a broader context, including business and industry trends and seasonal factors.

Listed companies should publicly release all of the information that investors and other stakeholders need to value a company's securities, monitor its developments, and assess its financial and social performances. The nature and scope of additional information required for this purpose may vary by company and sector. Specialist sectors should provide sufficient information to enable all outsiders to assess their performance. For example, financial group reports should include clear capital outlines, detailed risk management plans and processes, and extensive data tables encompassing loan books, loan types, provisioning, margins, credit growth, domestic and country exposures, derivative positions, market share trends, and credit ratings. Similarly, resource company reports should include definition sections, five year historical production tables (including the volume and value of the primary products, as well as targeted and expected production volumes), average commodity prices and exchange rates for the period, clear summaries of the historical and forward derivative positions, detailed project and risk outlines and assessments, and sensitivity tables and analysis showing the historical and expected future relationships between commodity volume, price and exchange rate movements and financial outcomes. It is especially critical for resource companies to provide long-term performance reporting, including specific financial, social responsibility and sustainability goals, metrics and outcomes, given the typical length of resource and resource project cycles. The overarching principle that should motivate the content of MD&A in periodic reports and continuous disclosures should be communication that enables timely and well-informed decision making.

[C] Reporting in Compliance with Accounting Standards

Most jurisdictions have enacted some rules that prohibit or limit the use of non-compliant financial measures. Some countries require companies to provide tables that reconcile the non-compliant financial measures to the reported figures and an outline of the calculation methodologies. Some jurisdictions require companies to explain why the adopted non-compliant financial measures are useful. Some also require companies to provide warnings that these measures may not be comparable to similarly named financial measures used by other companies. These various rules are important and should be consistently applied and enforced. Some listed companies reference the same non-compliant financial measures and performance indicators over long periods and clearly explain the calculation methodologies and reasons for using these measures. Others provide this information in a separate explanatory appendix or as outlines on the company website. These practices are commendable, but are not universal. The empirical reviews outlined in Part III consistently highlighted issues concerning the use of unexplained references to non-compliant financial measures and the provision of management commentary with minimal, if any, connection to the financial statements.

Given the growing scale and adverse impact of issues involving the use of non-compliant financial measures, stricter regulatory protocols may be required. Best practice company disclosure frameworks should provide financial information and MD&A using consistent financial measures and terminology that is well-understood, integrated, and consistent across time and markets. This may require company disclosure that consistently reports and references financial measures calculated in compliance with accounting standards, including in the financial statements, financial notes, MD&A, performance tables, continuous disclosures, and information available on the company website. However, companies should be permitted to provide supplemental information (including discussion of non-compliant financial measures) on websites and during investor presentations.

[D] Risk Disclosures

Risk management is a critical limb of all business strategies and operations, and detailed disclosure of a company's risks and risk management plans is essential for outsiders to assess its financial position and prospects. Best practice reporting requires clear outlines of a company's foreseeable and likely risks and its established processes to manage these risks. These outlines should be company-specific and should explain how the company has prioritised, and is managing, the identified risks across its individual businesses and the organisation as a whole. The risk disclosure content should clearly reflect the materiality of the risks.

IOSCO indicates that risk disclosures should include:

- an outline of the assumptions underpinning management forecasts;
- disclosure of off-balance sheet transactions;
- information regarding the estimates, assumptions, methodologies and sensitivities associated with its adopted accounting policies; and
- detailed information about the company's exposure to financial market risks and its management of these risks, including those relating to interest rates, foreign currency exchange, commodity prices, liquidity, and derivative instruments.[11]

IOSCO also includes disclosure of corporate governance practices in its risk metrics, including information about the company's directors and senior management, independence of the directors, existence and operation of an audit committee, members of the compensation committee, and adoption of a code of ethics.[12] These IOSCO risk disclosure principles and recommendations are sound, but should be supplemented by broader commentary and analysis. Best practice risk disclosures require consideration of the relevant industry and macroeconomic risks, and the established strategies and processes to mitigate these risks. Where possible, companies should quantify the probability and likely consequences of all of the identified risks. Comprehensive analysis and discussion of risks is especially important during periods of significant company, industry and economic uncertainty.

11. Technical Committee of the International Organization of Securities Commission, *Principles For Periodic Disclosure By Listed Entitles* Final Report (February 2010) 7-28.
12. Technical Committee of the International Organization of Securities Commission, *Principles For Periodic Disclosure By Listed Entitles* Final Report (February 2010) 7-28.

[E] Full Year Reporting

Disclosure policy documents and corporate governance codes often highlight and discuss the virtues of equal access rights to company information and transparency in financial markets. However, the full year reporting processes require urgent reform to enable these principles to be reflected in practice. All listed companies should produce and release one set of comprehensive year-end accounts with substantive and accurate financial notes and MD&A. The US periodic reporting framework provides a good example for others to follow. The full year reports are focused and comprehensive, with broadly equivalent content required in the 10-Ks and annual reports. These full year reports appear, on average, to be more informative, and clear, concise and effective from a reasonable investor perspective than those in other jurisdictions. While these reports are not integrated in the manner proposed by the IIRC, they are often supported by CSR or sustainability reports prepared in compliance with the Global Reporting Initiative guidelines.[13]

[F] Long-Term Performance Reporting

Best practice disclosure frameworks should provide sufficient information to allow company insiders and external stakeholders to understand a company's strategies, goals and targets, and how it is faring against these plans and targets at any point in time. To achieve these aims, listed companies should clearly outline their short and long-term performance objectives and targets in periodic reports and on company websites. A company's board and executives should then provide progress reports that discuss actual performance and achievements against the identified goals and targets each period. These progress reports should provide updated short and long-term plans, financial and non-financial targets and key performance indicators. Any ongoing changes to the definitions and calculation methodologies of the targets or indicators should be explained and justified.

The author recommends the introduction of mandatory ten year performance tables within full year reports as a relatively simple and low cost measure to provide a clear focal point for assessing its competitive long-term performance trends and issues. The three statements required in a set of financial accounts (the profit and loss account, balance sheet, and cash flow statement) are intended to provide an integrated picture of the company's financial position. Comprehensive performance commentary and analysis should therefore include key performance indicators for all of the financial statements and important financial, shareholder and productivity measures. In a best practice environment, commentary and analysis should also include relevant corporate social responsibility and sustainability metrics. Ideally, the mandated content in the performance tables should contain a series of performance indicators, including:

13. Global Reporting Initiative, 'GRI Empowering Sustainable Decisions', viewed 29 June 2015, https://www.globalreporting.org/information/Pages/default.aspx.

- revenue indicators;
- profit indicators (including gross margin, earnings before interest and tax, EPS and diluted EPS);
- dividend details (including dividends paid and the dividend payout ratio);
- annual returns (including the security price at the end of each period and the dividends paid);
- productivity metrics (including return on equity, return on assets, short and long-term gearing ratios, cash usage or generation, and any hedging details);
- share details (including the shares on issue and total shareholder return for the period);
- debt indicators (including the current, long-term and total debt levels);
- cash flow indicators (including liquid assets and net cash flow generated or used);
- capital indicators (including the company's cost of capital and returns on equity and capital employed);
- corporate social responsibility and sustainability indicators (including metrics across the areas of employees, human rights, supplier relationships, community activities, and the environment).

The ten year compound growth rate for relevant figures should be shown on the right-hand side of the table. The metrics included in the performance table and the period covered should be mandated and all of the figures in the table should be calculated in accordance with accounting standards. As discussed previously, empirical research finds that when performance metrics and time periods are not prescribed, those included are often those that portray a company in the most positive light. The purpose and utility of all of the key performance metrics and indicators, and their definition and calculation methodologies, should be outlined. If companies wish to add lines to the bottom of the table in order to provide supplementary numbers, this should be permitted provided the alternative figures are calculated on a consistent basis and the calculation methodology is clearly explained. Company managers are best positioned to provide the proposed data on a reliable, comparable and timely basis.

The potential benefits of mandated long-term performance tables are significant. Comprehensive performance tables are a powerful tool to assess the performance of individual companies and compare outcomes across an industry and market. Company directors and managers require an understanding of the performance trends and their comparative position to be able to plan for the future with a positive but realistic mindset. All company directors and senior executives should comprehend and be able to explain the performance record of the company and its industry. A suggested test of the depth of their understanding of the business is whether they can explain the following in thirty minutes in clear terms:

- the operational and financial trends over the last decade;
- the most important metrics to assess the company's performance and competitive position;

- the company's goals and priorities over the next year and decade; and
- specific plans to achieve these objectives.

Performance tables provide essential context for considering a company's performance, including its achievements and areas that require improvement. While the provision of historical performance data does not of itself enable users to accurately predict future performance, a clear understanding of the past performance of a company is necessary to consider its competitive and future performance. It is vital for all participants to have access to sufficient information to understand the historical developments of a company, its current financial and operational positions, and the negative and positive aspects of its performance trends. Ten years of data reveals short and longer-term trends (whether upward, static or downward), the volatility of reported historical results, the cash flow usage or generation of the business, the debt profile and management record, the ability of the company to generate real returns above its cost of capital, and potential solvency issues. Ten year performance tables also provide a picture of the company's performance in its starkest form and enable company managers and boards and all other interested persons to cut through any noise. When important performance indicators show a consistent trend downwards or sideways, director response and stakeholder engagement is likely to be aroused and a variety of groups are likely to demand changes.

Senior executives should stand back regularly from the fray and all of the short-term noise that surrounds business and financial market environments to consider how to best construct and sustain a reputation of trust and reliability over the long-term. Company directors and managers should review the company's long-term performance table and ask themselves whether the company consistently does what it says it will do. More importantly, when the company does not or cannot do what it said it would do (as occurs at some point for most companies), how does it respond, and how does it communicate these responses to the market and to its many stakeholders.

[G] Standardised Reporting

Publicly available company information should be in a form that allows comparative analysis of individual company trends and performance against industry peers, and across the broader market. As some of the staff at the International Monetary Fund have suggested, disclosure regulation needs to include 'as much public reporting (within a consistent framework) as possible – to enhance market discipline as well as to enable effective monitoring.'[14] Consistent with these aims, the US has used periodic reporting templates for many decades. Companies are required to complete all of the

14. Ana Carvajal, Randall Dodd, Michael Moore, Erland Nier, Ian Tower and Luisa Zanforlin, International Monetary Fund (IMF), IMF Staff Position Note, 'The Perimeter of Financial Regulation' (26 March 2009). See also Louis Lowenstein, 'Financial Transparency and Corporate Governance: You Manage What You Measure' (1996) 96 *Columbia Law Review* 1335, 1361–1362; Merritt Fox, 'Required Disclosure and Corporate Governance' (1996) 62 *Law and Contemporary Problems* 113, 127; John McMillan, 'Market Design: The Policy Uses of Theory' (2003) 93 *American Economic Review* 139, 139; Donald Langevoort, 'Technological Evolution and the Devolution of Corporate Finance Reporting' (2004) 46 *William & Mary Law Review* 1, 32.

template sections (including commentary on the recurring and non-recurring elements of the reported result), thereby ensuring comprehensive and uncluttered information is presented in one document on a consistent basis each reporting period.[15] These reports are readable in sections or as a whole. This reporting framework enables all participants with a warrantable interest to engage in comparative analysis of individual companies, sectors, and financial markets. The provision of comprehensive information through non-discriminatory channels does not preclude companies from providing additional summary or tailored information within company announcements and on websites where this is considered necessary or useful for some investors or stakeholders.

[H] Disclosure Conduct: Continuous Disclosure

[1] Timeliness

Continuous disclosure obligations are intended to provide investors and stakeholders with materially price-sensitive information between reporting periods on a timely basis. The underlying rationale is that all investors should have access to such information at the same time. This rationale is reinforced by corporate governance principles designed to promote market transparency and fair treatment of shareholders. The continuous disclosure regimes are therefore only meaningful if company announcements are submitted to an exchange or regulatory information disseminator rapidly, so that all interested persons have public access to news and developments simultaneously.

Many corporate executives (and their legal advisers) indicate they are reluctant to continuously disclose matters while some of the relevant details and consequences remain uncertain. Some suggest that it is better to defer public disclosure until the outcomes are fully understood, with this preference often framed as a potential liability matter. However, this approach is inconsistent with the purposes of continuous disclosure obligations and the skills and experience of business people, investors and legal practitioners. Long time business people and financial market participants are well used to dealing with uncertainties and incomplete information, as business environments and financial markets are inherently dynamic and, at times, volatile and unpredictable. Business strategy and planning and company securities valuation are primarily focused on future events. As such, these processes involve judgments, estimates, forecasts and assumptions based on the best available information at a particular point in time. These judgments, estimates, forecasts and assumptions must be continually adjusted as events and circumstances change. Thus any notion that public disclosures should be delayed until every detail and consequence is known is misconceived and out of touch with commercial and market realities.

15. See United States Securities and Exchange Commission, *SEC Filings And Forms (EDGAR)* at http://www.sec.gov/edgar.shtml.

Companies should provide frank public disclosure of known facts and provide the market with as complete a picture as possible in order to minimise potential liability for selective disclosure or the provision of misleading statements. Lawyers are well used to dealing with uncertainties and making judgment calls after weighing available evidence. They routinely provide advice and recommendations when the factual outlines are not entirely complete and the legal outcomes are still uncertain. These scenarios are handled with careful use of caveats and the application of assumptions and disclaimers. When dealing with company disclosure matters, lawyers should apply similar skills. When company disclosure events arise that are considered borderline with respect to the need to publicly disclose or when the content of disclosures involves uncertainties, they should advise clients that the risk of non-disclosure will generally significantly outweigh the risks of providing incomplete disclosure. They should assist clients to disclose in a prudent and measured way, but also in a manner that explains what is known by the company at the time of disclosure, and just as importantly, what is not known. If necessary, companies can explain or highlight incomplete or uncertain elements of a transaction or news in the public announcement, and provide additional details when appropriate. Companies should outline any assumptions made and the steps being taking to clarify the position. When companies are considering whether to publicly disclose a matter or event, and the extent of the explanation that should be provided, any matters or events involving large sums of money or capital, or large variations from period-to-period, should be considered material to reasonable investors, even if these matters or events are one-off, exceptional, or recurring. Liability for a breach of disclosure rules is far more likely to arise when companies either fail to disclose or delay disclosure of significant developments. Indeed, this author is not aware of any instance where liability has attached to a listed company or its directors when it had in good faith provided timely, complete and balanced disclosure of the circumstances, including the significant uncertainties and required assumptions.[16]

Executives and their lawyers should be aware of the power and informational imbalances in financial markets, including the risks that information deemed confidential by the company will leak to segments of the market, especially when private exchanges between company representatives and institutional participants are occurring regularly. Empirical studies confirm that material news is absorbed rapidly into security prices, with most of the value reflected within two hours. So when material company news is leaked, large transfers of wealth occur during short periods before public announcements are made. Consequently, when significant transactions, events or programmes are being negotiated or planned, companies should prepare and agree the general content of a public announcement prior to the final agreement, completion or sign-off by the board in readiness for public release. And if a public announcement is required due to leakage of confidential information, company executives should provide frank and balanced public commentary on what is known at that time and any steps being taken to ascertain further information and assurances. Companies can provide further details when available or determined.

16. If readers are aware of any instances to the contrary, the author is open to correction.

Some listed companies are genuinely striving to address equal access issues and concerns. As noted in Part III, BP Oil maintains a trading conditions web page that is updated on a specific day at the same time each week.[17] Other companies provide detailed public guidance and or analyst consensus information that is updated regularly on company websites and through exchange announcement services. These are efficient and fair practices that use digital capabilities to provide all participants with simultaneous access to material information.

[2] Forward-Looking Information

Best practice disclosure frameworks for the twenty-first century should encourage the provision of forward-looking information in periodic reports and on a continuous basis. They should also prohibit, or at least discourage, the use of sell-side analyst forecasts as a benchmark for determining the need for company disclosures or as a proxy for market expectations. Disclosure structures built around private exchanges between company managers and analysts (whether sell-side or buy-side) are inappropriate because they encourage short-term earnings management, promote unhealthy relationships with institutional segments of the market, and severely undermine public disclosure frameworks.

The OSC recommends timely updating of earnings guidance following changes in managerial expectations. It suggests that companies present forward-looking information in reports in a separate section, including a table that sets out the company's objectives, specific assumptions and risks.[18] It encourages the use of financial and non-financial key performance indicators. These recommendations reflect best practice. For example, some of the periodic reports reviewed indicated whether an annual earnings forecast remained valid or had been revised. Others indicated and explained whether the public guidance had been met, with accompanying explanations when specified targets were not satisfied. These are excellent practices that other companies should follow.

The form in which companies provide public guidance is important. The nature and scope of any public guidance should be clear and unambiguous, with the calculation methodology detailed, particularly when the profit measure is a non-compliant financial measure. The same guidance measure should be used within a financial year, and ideally from year to year. When companies change the public guidance measure or the items that are excluded from the measure within a financial year, it becomes difficult, and sometimes impossible, for users to determine the nature and level of the relevant measure. These issues become more challenging when companies forecast and report in multiple currencies.

17. BP Oil Global, 'Trading Conditions Update, 27 January 2015 at http://www.bp.com/en/global/corporate/investors/results-and-reporting/trading-conditions-update.html. This webpage includes suitable disclaimers with respect to the accuracy and completeness of the data provided.
18. Ontario Securities Commission (OSC), *Forward-Looking Information Disclosure* (OSC Staff Notice 51-721) 20.

Listed companies that use non-compliant financial measures for forward-looking estimates or guidance should be especially prudent and careful. Public guidance in the form of non-compliant financial measures should be permitted because some financial items such as asset write-downs and mark-to-market variations are difficult to predict and quantify. However, these measures should only be permitted when the calculation methodology is clearly outlined, the same financial measures are used consistently as guidance during an entire financial year, and the performance analysis in the periodic reports provides an outline that reconciles the publicly disclosed guidance to the actual results and the figures included in the financial statements.

To summarise, clear presentation and labelling of forward-looking information within listed company reports and announcements are critical features of an effective company disclosure framework. Best practice in this area requires the following:

- public guidance or earnings forecasts that are explained in a manner that clearly identifies what is and what is not included in the guidance financial measure;
- references to a consistent guidance measure during a financial year;
- timely and consistent updating of trading conditions and revisions of any public guidance;
- clear labelling of any announcements that contain forward-looking information (e.g., a public announcement that contains information about changes to expected earnings should be clearly labelled as a 'forecast revision'); and
- separate sections within periodic reports explaining forward-looking information.

§15.03 COMPANY WEBSITES

Company websites are a valuable communication tool that companies should use to assist investors, stakeholders and the public to better understand a company's operations, reporting content and processes, and position and prospects. In modern environments, company websites are a key source of information for many groups, so they should tell a company's story in a coherent, comprehensible and compelling form. Voluntary global standards and practices appear to be developing with respect to the structure and content of information provided on large company websites. Standard website features include the provision of result material, annual reports, financial calendars, and basic corporate governance information. However, companies are encouraged to use more innovative formats and tools on these sites and to provide comprehensive information on a multifaceted and multilayered basis to suit a broad audience.

Well structured corporate websites should enable readers to locate and download relevant documents quickly. To be fully effective, they must also provide material that extends and enhances the mandated information. All companies should provide long-term financial and sustainability performance tables, commentary and analysis. This information and analysis should be provided in various forms, including performance tables, graphs, and charts, with supporting summaries and analysis of the results and developing trends. The adopted financial and sustainability performance goals and metrics should be clear, the reasons for using these particular goals and metrics should be explained, and the MD&A should connect to the ongoing performance of these goals and metrics for the current reporting period and over the long-term. When done well, this performance analysis should tell the company's story clearly, concisely and accurately, without exaggeration, undue optimism, and unnecessary commentary and pictures. Company websites should also encourage and enable broad stakeholder engagement with continuous interactive functionality.

[A] Annual Reports

Most listed companies provide print and online versions of their annual reports on the company website. Digital features within most online versions of annual reports are presently limited to a contents table and pages formatted for online reading. Companies should embrace further digital features, such as interactive graphs, performance tables, sensitivity calculators, and analytical tools. All pictures should be removed from both the print and online versions and uploaded onto video and photo galleries on the company website, leaving viewers to peruse those of interest. This reduces the size and bulk of the reports and their download speed, it minimises print costs where applicable, and it allows readers to focus on the core information.

[B] Result Material

Most companies have dedicated web pages for result-related information. Some of these websites present the result material within annual categories; others subdivide the results by quarterly or half yearly material. Companies are increasingly providing pre-filled spreadsheets that can be downloaded and modified by users. These practices should be standard for all listed companies. Some companies also provide historical spreadsheets for long periods, providing valuable data for various analytical purposes. Regardless of the layout used, the result material on company websites should include press releases, periodic reports and related disclosures, and slides and webcasts (or audios or transcripts) of investor presentations, including of the question and answer sessions. Result web pages should also provide analytical tools such as graphs, summary tables, performance indicators, and valuation calculation tools. These tools are important to encourage all groups, including company boards and managers, as well as outsiders, to better understand the company's position and to focus on long-term performance trends.

[C] Financial Calendars

Many companies provide a financial calendar on their websites. These calendars typically include the dates of the relevant quarterly, half year and full year result announcements and the annual general meeting. Best practice also requires reasonable advance notice of the periodic report release dates and any webcast access details to company briefings to ensure fair access for all. While companies should include the webcast access details in the public result announcements, earlier notice is required to enable all interested investors and stakeholders to plan to listen to, or participate in, various corporate briefings, meetings and forums.

[D] Corporate Governance

Some companies maintain a dedicated corporate governance webpage and this should be followed as standard practice. Corporate governance websites should explain the role, purpose, and performance measures of the board of directors and senior management, and the membership, role and duties of the board committees. They should outline the company's strategies, goals, policies and guidelines. They should also explain the nature, timing and content of all investor and stakeholder meetings and forums.

Executive compensation disclosure has received particular attention in the years since the GFC. Corporate governance websites should provide detailed material concerning senior executive and director remuneration. IOSCO suggests that information on compensation should include a description of the procedures used to determine remuneration and explanations concerning alignment of the compensation with performance, investors' interests, and shareholder returns. IOSCO further suggests that companies should disclose their equity compensation plans, including any potential dilutive effects. Remuneration disclosure rules generally require this information to be outlined in the annual reports, but this material should be supplemented and explained on a web page dedicated to remuneration issues. Relevant sustainability material should be included, such as environmental assessments and management plans, project feasibility and monitoring reports, energy efficiency reports and carbon disclosure statements. Additional information may include specialist reports, regulatory documents, diversity reports, community complaints reports and social responsibility reports.

§15.04 COMMUNICATION FACILITIES AND FORUMS

Some listed companies enable public access to result briefings and other investor meetings by means of webcast or audio facilities, and some of these facilities allow interactive exchanges. Some provide general contact details on their websites with facilities for questions to be submitted, some provide email addresses and telephone numbers for individual directors, investor relations representatives, and independent bodies, and some provide contact numbers for people who have serious concerns about a company's operations or reporting processes. Many companies also provide Facebook and Twitter links on their websites. All of these features are important, but more is needed to establish corporate communication frameworks that are broadly effective. Investors and others with a warrantable interest in listed corporations need time and appropriate facilities and opportunities to consider and respond to information provided by company boards and executives. Modern communication modes should allow continuous exchanges of information and ideas among and between company insiders and outsiders. While these exchanges will increasingly rely on digital modes, digital communications should be supported by limited options to engage with company directors and managers and other investors and stakeholders at physical meetings. Open access meetings that include physical and online participation options are important to ensure public transparency and accountability, to enable all investor and stakeholder groups to deliberate on company matters and question boards and executives, to reduce selective disclosure occurrences, and to break down the many barriers that currently exist between private and public communication frameworks.

§15.05 AN EFFECTIVE CORPORATE DISCLOSURE AND COMMUNICATION MODEL FROM AN END USER'S PERSPECTIVE

One's view of disclosure frameworks depends, of course, on one's perspective. Policy makers propose and draft disclosure legislation and rules, regulators supervise and enforce these rules, and litigators initiate legal actions grounded on specified legal provisions or rules. The wording and interpretation of relevant provisions are critically important for litigators because legal actions have to be carefully pleaded and supported with evidence. Investors and other corporate stakeholders who rely on public disclosures view disclosure matters very differently. Few users of publicly available company information pause to consider the particular disclosure regime under which information is provided, or the individual provisions that may have been breached when required disclosures have not been made. People use company information for many purposes, including for investment, monitoring, regulation, governance, sustainability, social responsibility, statistical and issue-specific reasons.

Disclosure regimes are intended to enable well-informed decisions, so it is vital that policy makers, regulators, scholars and practitioners consider and critique disclosure regulation and practice primarily from a user perspective. For many investors, company information is only meaningful when viewed or processed as part of the full set of available information, including information provided in periodic reports and continuous disclosures, additional information disclosed by companies through briefings and websites, and information gathered from sources external to the company. Institutional and retail investors making decisions about listed company securities must combine and synthesise individual pieces of information about a company. They do this to build as complete a picture of the company's position and prospects as possible, in order to decide whether to buy, hold or sell securities. Importantly, most substantive information about listed companies that is used by investors engaged in fundamental analysis is provided by the relevant companies either directly or indirectly.

The role, purposes and objectives of a disclosure framework need to be clarified and understood in order for that framework to be effective. Disclosure regulation was first introduced in the US in the 1930s, so it has been in operation for approximately eighty-five years. Perhaps, as a result, the purposes of the regulation appear to be better understood than in other jurisdictions. Securities regulation in the US expressly states that securities transactions through exchanges are intended to serve the 'national public interest.' This principle is reflected in the Intercontinental Exchange (NYSE) rules, which explicitly require disclosure of all material price-sensitive information to shareholders and the public. The specific purposes and intended audience of the company disclosure frameworks in other countries are not as easily discernible.

Consistent with the aims of the main securities statutes in the US and the NYSE listing rules, the SEC promotes a public disclosure structure as the primary means of corporate communication. It directs companies to provide comprehensive and timely periodic reports to enable all interested persons to assess a company's performance and prospects. The US disclosure rules have developed over time into a periodic reporting framework that encompasses the following limbs:

- the full year company reporting processes are now effectively integrated;
- standard form reporting is used to ensure comprehensive reporting in accordance with accounting standards;
- full quarterly reporting, including financial statements and notes, has been in place for nearly fifty years;
- five year performance tables are required in the 10-Ks; and
- an online and hard copy federal company document repository is provided that is free and easy for the public to use.

The SEC has managed and adapted well in this difficult regulatory space. Among its many roles and responsibilities, it has prioritised company reporting standards and the quality of publicly available information. It operates in a manner consistent with the assumption that listed companies should use public disclosure to release the same financial information and MD&A to all market participants and interested persons at the same time. It has a good appreciation of the appropriate level and scope of regulatory engagement required to achieve financial disclosures that, in the author's view, are generally clear and effective. Its monitoring of company disclosures is systematic and regular, the exchange of queries and answers from submitting companies are available to the public once resolved, it provides detailed guidance and feedback to companies, and enforcement actions are initiated under the full suite of federal disclosure rules when required. The US is likely to have benefited economically as a nation from the strength of this reporting structure and its reputation for high quality disclosure standards.

The periodic reporting frameworks outside of the US reflect only some of the features of the US model. Other regulatory structures do not appear to operate as systematically, or at the same levels of intensity and transparency, as the SEC. Most countries outside of the US require companies to include some MD&A in the relevant preliminary full year, half year and quarterly reports. However, the required MD&A is often phrased in broad terms, allowing companies significant discretion over the content and form of the publicly available reports. While such frameworks enable companies to report in a manner they consider most appropriate, a lack of formal structure and prescribed content can present major difficulties for readers. Issues that commonly arise include a lack of important notes and MD&A in the disclosures, MD&A

that is poorly connected to the financial statements or that is written to present results in a positive light, the inclusion of lots of pictures that are expensive to print and that dilute the core message, large inconsistencies in the form and content of MD&A provided from period-to-period by individual companies, and marked differences in the form and content of MD&A and financial notes across sectors and the general market. Such variability in listed company reporting makes it difficult, and sometimes impossible, for persons relying on public disclosures to engage in meaningful or comparative performance analysis. In worst case scenarios, the publicly available reports are presented as marketing documents, with a large number of glossy photos, without comprehensive and tailored outlines of the company's strategies, risks, and plans, without substantive discussion and analysis, and without compliant or useful financial measures and commentary that explain the company's short-term and long-term performance and trends.

Some commentators suggest that the continuous disclosure requirements reduce or replace the need for the periodic disclosure regime. They argue that continuous disclosure means that the market is informed at all times and that no investor is disadvantaged by lack of access to material information.[19] These arguments imply that companies are releasing all of the substantive information, which would normally be included in comprehensive half year and quarterly reports, within continuous disclosure reports. Such arguments are not credible to people who use public disclosures on a regular basis. While the primary purpose of continuous disclosure regimes is to ensure that all investors and other stakeholders are provided with materially price-sensitive information between reporting periods, these frameworks are inherently limited with respect to the nature, scope, and consistency of information provided. As the SEC has noted, listed company executives retain significant discretion under continuous disclosure rules in relation to what must be disclosed publicly and additional information that is permitted to be disclosed privately to some market participants. For example, listed companies are not obliged under continuous disclosure regimes in any of the countries reviewed to provide financial statements or financial forecasts (albeit some companies do so voluntarily). One might characterise the purpose of continuous disclosure regimes as 'filling in the informational gaps' between reporting periods. So the key question that arises is how large a gap can these disclosures reasonably be expected to fill when the periodic reporting structures are deficient.

From a user's perspective, the overall effectiveness of company disclosure frameworks depends greatly on the quality and timeliness of the periodic reporting structure and content. Periodic reporting and continuous disclosure regimes are interdependent and both need to be functioning optimally for disclosure frameworks to be fully effective. It is the regular and relatively standardised periodic reports that provide the essential baseline information from which investors assess the episodic continuous disclosures. When substantive periodic reporting content is lacking, ad hoc disclosures do not fill informational gaps and users are left with an incomplete picture

19. See, e.g., Australian Securities Exchange, Continuous Disclosure: The Australian Experience (20 February 2002) 17.

of a company's position, performance and prospects. Continuous or ad hoc company information is only useful to investors and other stakeholders when it is timely and sufficiently integrated with the content provided in periodic reports, and it forms a complete, consistent, and clear mosaic of available information.

The analysis provided in this book suggests that no country has adequately considered the essential legal and practical limbs of an effective disclosure framework and how to ensure these limbs operate on an integrated basis. While the periodic reporting regime in the US is 'gold standard', there is a distinct lack of integration between the periodic and continuous disclosure regimes. In the US, the SEC is responsible for supervision and enforcement of periodic reporting and for monitoring and enforcement of Reg FD. It also oversees the activities of securities exchanges. However, as explained in Part III, continuous disclosure obligations in the US are generally confined to the listing rules of the exchanges and formal enforcement of these rules by the NYSE appears to be limited or non-existent. The linkages between the periodic reporting and continuous disclosure rules are therefore tenuous.[20]

All legislators, regulators and scholars are encouraged to reconsider the existing listed company disclosure frameworks comprehensively and holistically from the perspective of a reasonable user. A reasonable user of corporate communications in the twenty-first century should be characterised broadly, and the overarching goal that should be applied to assess the efficacy of these frameworks should be the long-term national public interest. It is critical that all groups involved with company disclosure matters debate and comprehend afresh:

- the various purposes of listed company disclosure regulation;
- the intended audience of listed company reports and disclosures;
- the links and gaps across periodic and continuous disclosure regimes, and how well these frameworks operate as a whole from a user's perspective; and
- the appropriate nature, scale and intersection of the private and public disclosure and communication structures presently used by listed companies.

Of these issues, the last question demands the greatest consideration and honesty.

20. Some of the apparent weaknesses in the continuous disclosure framework in the United States are mitigated by the existence of Regulation Fair Disclosure and the requirement for listed companies to notify certain events to the United States Securities and Exchange Commission on Form 8-K. However, the types of events encompassed within the 8-K notification framework are limited and the reporting timeframe is within four business days after occurrence of the event. A disclosure period of four days is not timely in modern financial markets for continuous disclosures. See United States Securities Exchange Commission, 'Form 8-K', viewed 18 July 2015, http://www.sec.gov/answers/form8k.htm.

CHAPTER 16
Conclusion

> A marketplace can only succeed if it has the trust and confidence of investors, companies, industry professionals and the public ... Improving the market is a never-ending journey which requires the help and support of all stakeholders.[1]

While many scholars continue to question the rationales and net benefits of mandatory disclosure regimes, all developed countries and many emerging financial markets now have established company disclosure frameworks. It is important to acknowledge the limitations of this regulation, as it is not a panacea for all disclosure and other issues that arise in financial markets. Notwithstanding this reality, empirical research suggests that ongoing endeavours to promote high quality company disclosure standards and practices are critically important. The author has reviewed interdisciplinary research on company disclosure matters for many years and has not found any empirical studies that suggest that:

- financial markets work best when listed companies retain full discretion over disclosure recipients, the content disclosed, and the timing of disclosure;
- the quality of public disclosure by listed companies does not matter;
- the long-term interests of corporations and nations are best served by private communications between company managers and select participants.

Instead, there are large bodies of interdisciplinary empirical work that highlight the positive effects and benefits of high quality disclosure by listed companies. Country-specific and global empirical studies of financial markets consistently find associations between improved corporate and national outcomes and high disclosure standards, vigorous enforcement of securities laws, broad investor participation, protection of minority shareholder rights, sound corporate governance and sustainability practices, and public trust. This evidence as a whole suggests there are compelling economic and

1. SGX Ltd, 'Regulator's Column', viewed 19 May 2015 http://www.sgx.com/wps/wcm/connect/sgx_en/home/regulation_v2/consultations_and_publications/Regulators/SGXs-role-in-detecting-insider-trading.

national imperatives for company disclosure frameworks that encourage broad participation and public trust in financial markets.

Company disclosure regulation across the examined jurisdictions requires listed companies to report periodically, and to continuously disclose between reporting periods. The periodic reporting regimes require full year reporting and either half year or quarterly reporting. The continuous disclosure regimes require timely disclosure of materially price-sensitive company information. These disclosure frameworks generally comprise federal or national law and exchange listing rules, with the monitoring and enforcement responsibilities shared between securities exchanges and national or state regulators. These operational frameworks result in large variations in the quantity and quality of public disclosure and communication across the globe. Publicly available company information is sometimes so sparse, sanitised and dated that a reasonable bystander might legitimately question the role, purpose and utility of the disclosure frameworks.

This book calls for policy makers and others to reconsider the efficacy of the periodic reporting and continuous disclosure frameworks from the end user's perspective. Effective company disclosure frameworks must provide publicly available corporate disclosures that are sufficiently timely, complete, accurate, and balanced, so that all diligent and competent persons can make well-informed decisions throughout a financial year. To achieve this goal, the periodic reporting and continuous disclosure processes must work well on an integrated basis.

While the periodic disclosure regimes outlined in Part III may at first glance appear similar, a more detailed review reveals critical differences. The areas containing the most differences and disagreements within the periodic disclosure realm include the:

- timing, structure and content of full year reporting;
- regularity of periodic reporting;
- level and quality of MD&A within the periodic reports (and more generally);
- use of, and reference to, financial measures that are not in accordance with accounting standards within the periodic reports (and more generally);
- use of standard form reporting; and
- provision of long-term performance measures and commentary.

There are substantive differences between the periodic reporting rules and practices in the US and other jurisdictions. The US was the first country to establish comprehensive periodic reporting rules and standards in the 1930s. While its company disclosure structure is not perfect, the legal framework reflects clarity of purpose. The explicit objective of the primary securities statute in the US is to enhance the national public interest, and the intended audience of disclosures made by NYSE listed companies includes 'the public'. These objectives provide a sound framework for considering the efficacy of disclosure law and practice. The MD&A within the quarterly and full year periodic reports in the US includes tailored outlines of the company's strategies, performance, risks, and opportunities. These reports are completed on standard forms that assist users to engage in comparative company, sectoral and market analysis. The content of these reports is well focused and uncluttered because the SEC does not permit companies to include pictures, disconnected commentary, or marketing material. This reporting format and the centralised and impartial nature of the EDGAR website provide reliable information for investors and others engaged in listed company analysis. While the disclosure structures outside of the US reflect some of these features, no other national periodic disclosure framework is as comprehensive, transparent or user friendly. Other jurisdictions have elected to take a 'lighter touch' approach with respect to company reporting and practice, and the gap between the disclosure standards and practices in the US and those in other jurisdictions continues to widen.

The issues of most contention and variation with respect to continuous disclosure regulation and practice include:

- the processes and decision making concerning the materiality of information;
- the timeliness of public disclosures;
- the provision of earnings guidance; and
- supervisory and enforcement issues.

Day-to-day decisions around what information is material and requires public disclosure, the timeliness of the public disclosures, and the provision of private and or public earnings guidance or otherwise, are generally made by the most senior executives of listed corporations in the jurisdictions examined. These disclosure decisions and obligations are monitored and supervised at first instance by the relevant securities exchange. However, the ability and willingness of the exchanges to monitor and enforce the continuous disclosure rules and standards appear weak in many of the countries examined. The utility of regulation that is intended to enhance financial market integrity and transparency is undermined by widespread non-compliance, and its effect is negligible without supervisory entities that have sufficient powers, resources and motivation. The primary monitoring tools used by all of the exchanges (and federal regulators) reviewed are price query and stockwatch programmes. These price query and stockwatch processes, which are triggered by unusual short-term security price or volume trends, are limited in both scope and consequence, particularly when selective disclosure is involved. When listed companies provide little substantive information between reporting periods and fail to publicly disclose events and circumstances that have impacted, or are continuing to affect, the company's operations and position, the entire market may be 'surprised' or the company's security price may already have absorbed the news because segments of the market were aware of the developments. For evidential reasons, regulators and private litigators are far more likely to initiate some form of action against a company when the former events occur. Most private exchanges between company executives and institutional participants are not documented or recorded, and without such documentation, it is difficult to determine whether certain information was obtained by means of private disclosure from the company or from other sources, and whether the news was already 'publicly known' within the definitions of the relevant disclosure rules.

Louis Brandeis famously stated more than a century ago that 'sunlight is said to be the best of disinfectants; electric light the most efficient policeman.'[2] He argued that the potent force of publicity should be used as a continuous remedial measure in the impending struggle for disclosure within financial markets that is real and useful for a broad audience.[3] These calls by Brandeis for 'light' in financial markets and for meaningful corporate disclosure within public spheres remain germane and important today. Indeed, the company disclosure, accountability and governance concerns that existed when company disclosure regulation was first introduced are increasingly compelling given the scale and importance of financial markets and large corporations today. Many corporate groups operate and report in multiple countries, the largest financial institutions have global investment mandates, and there are millions of end savers that own listed company securities (both directly and indirectly) as part of their retirement investment portfolios. Effective listed company disclosure is therefore vital in the twenty-first century to ensure efficient, fair and competitive financial markets and to optimise corporate and national outcomes.

However, as Brandeis noted, there are no easy pathways to promote or mandate effective disclosure and communication between listed corporations and their stakeholders. Disclosure regimes are highly political and power imbalances mean the strength and efficacy of disclosure regimes tend to be diluted over time.[4] Company disclosure policies and practices are generally determined as a result of political compromise.[5] Each participant group uses democratic processes to lobby for a regulatory environment that puts it in the best position. Many company managers prefer to retain full discretion over communication and governance processes. Moreover, large market participants often use their powerful financial positions to lobby against reforms that diminish their superior access to company managers and information. Other corporate investors and stakeholders call for rules to enable broadly equal access to listed company information.

Incentives are a critical element of corporate disclosure frameworks. Disclosure issues generally arise when company managers and directors are reluctant to explain the company's position in plain terms to the world at large. Public company directors and managers prefer to present company developments with which they are associated in the best possible light. They have compelling monetary and other incentives to restrict or delay the public dissemination of information when the content is negative, when public disclosures may reflect poorly on the management, or when there are conflicts of interest. Institutional investors generally hold majority stakes in listed companies and for practical purposes have 'control' of these companies. Hence senior executives can potentially 'manage' a company's disclosures and communication

2. Louis Brandeis, *Other People's Money* (National Home Library Foundation, Washington, 1914) 62.
3. Louis Brandeis, *Other People's Money* (National Home Library Foundation, Washington, 1914) Ch. V.
4. See Archon Fung, Mary Graham and David Weil, *Full Disclosure: The Perils & Promise of Transparency* (Cambridge University Press, New York, 2007) 125–126.
5. Archon Fung, Mary Graham and David Weil, *Full Disclosure: The Perils & Promise of Transparency* (Cambridge University Press, New York, 2007) 7.

exchanges by satisfying the demands of these investors. The most powerful investors are clearly incentivised to obtain information privately in order to gain informational advantages vis-à-vis other participants. Consequently, the most vulnerable parties in this power struggle are smaller institutional investors, retail investors, and those in the community who are, or may be, adversely affected by corporate developments. These groups must generally rely on public disclosures and are the least likely to get timely access to all material information.

In previous decades, the means by which companies could disseminate information to large numbers of investors and stakeholders were limited. Company managers tended to build close private relationships and exchange information with institutions deemed important. Other parties had to rely on the more restricted information released in the public arena. These hierarchical disclosure and communication models are not appropriate in modern financial markets. Policy makers, regulators and companies should not predetermine or limit the content and format of publicly available company information based on preconceptions about investor and stakeholder capacity and roles. Companies cannot patronise investors by disseminating only analyst-filtered information for fear that investors may be overwhelmed. Paternalistic notions still abound within highly respected circles, including that large portions of the population are naïve, irrational, unsophisticated, inexperienced and unable to comprehend company financial statements, disclosures and commentary expressed in plain terms. This may be a convenient way to frame arguments for those wishing to maintain informational advantages in financial markets, but these models do not accord with empirical evidence and observation. Broad generalisations applied to investor and stakeholder segments that lack the political clout of large financial institutions should be seen for what they are – arguments constructed by entrenched interests to retain privileges that tilt the wealth creation processes across financial markets in their favour.[6]

There are major tensions in regulatory structures that simultaneously govern intermediated and direct investment in listed company securities. Financial markets today can essentially be categorised as emphasising either public or private disclosure models. Company securities investment and transaction activity across all major financial markets is increasingly dominated by the largest financial institutions and asset managers.[7] This continuing concentration in the ownership and trading of listed company securities strengthens the institutional demands for a weakening of the public disclosure structures. The demarcations between the public and private disclosure frameworks across the countries examined remain entrenched and largely distinct,

6. Conduct that publicly demeans disenfranchised or disadvantaged classes of people in order to retain or enhance power and wealth has occurred throughout human history For example, privileged males claimed for many centuries that women were too emotional and unstable to be given the vote. Others asserted that non-white populations lacked the necessary education and mental capacity to operate effectively within democratic structures.
7. See, e.g., Mats Isaksson and Sserdar Çelik, 'Who Cares? Corporate Governance in Today's Equity Markets', (OECD Corporate Governance Working Papers, No. 8, OECD Publishing, 2013) 28–32, viewed 6 April 2015, http://dx.doi.org/10.1787/5k47zw5kdnmp-en; Michael Lewis, *Flash Boys* (W.W. Norton & Company, Inc, New York, 2015).

despite the digital revolution. Behind the public facade, the main game is increasingly returning to its roots; namely who among the largest financial participants can win the most valued access to corporate managers and privately obtained inside information. Private access to corporate executives is often paid for either directly (in the form of favours such as silence, positive commentary, or the provision of new capital) or indirectly (in the form of fees to intermediaries such as brokers or investment banks).

Many jurisdictions permit or even encourage regular private exchanges between corporate executives and select institutional participants. However, when listed companies regularly engage with select participants behind closed doors, this promotes distinctly tiered disclosure channels and results in weak and ineffective public disclosure frameworks. Empirical studies and market evidence suggest that corporate disclosure structures that predominantly rely on private exchanges between select participants are generally inefficient, unfair, opaque, and ultimately, toxic. Thus conduct that involves participant demands for superior prospective earnings related information by means of private meetings or exchanges should be treated with disdain by corporations as a futile exercise that detracts from the company's performance. The world has moved on, and listed corporations are increasingly acknowledging their influence and position in society and their essential contributions to the real economy and the broader community. These entities now operate within reporting environments that are increasingly framed by corporate governance and sustainability principles. These principles are purposively designed to enhance long-term performance by public reporting and communication processes that encompass ongoing dialogue and engagement with investors and stakeholders that extend well beyond Wall Street and the like.[8]

The primary role of financial markets is to enable intermediation between listed entities seeking capital for investment purposes and savers with excess capital to invest. Holistic analysis of disclosure regimes includes the costs and benefits of compliance with the regulation, and the comparative outcomes from voluntary disclosure environments including the costs that are associated with disclosure omissions or deficiencies. Financial markets that lack broad investor confidence and public trust, or that operate in a vacuum without clear links to the real economy, eventually falter. Liquidity and pricing issues typically arise, leading to capital withdrawals and higher funding costs. These indicators feed through into the real economy, and during significant financial market crashes or economic recessions, the economic and social costs borne by communities can be immense. The GFC and continuing financial challenges in some areas of the world remind the global community that the health of financial markets, real economies, and the lives of individuals are entirely interconnected.

8. See, e.g., Mats Isaksson and Sserdar Çelik, 'Who Cares? Corporate Governance in Today's Equity Markets' (OECD Corporate Governance Working Papers, No. 8, 2013, OECD Publishing) viewed 6 April 2015, http://dx.doi.org/10.1787/5k47zw5kdnmp-en. 28-32; Report of the Committee on the Financial Aspects of Corporate Governance (1 December 2012) [3.1-3.4].

To achieve their stated objectives, company disclosure frameworks must be more than mere platitudes. Best practice frameworks require strong ongoing support from policy makers, regulators, corporations, investors, stakeholders and the public and should be driven by clear objectives and principles that are consistently applied. These frameworks should be systematically monitored and supervised, including regular reviews of the content and quality of company disclosures by independent sources. The regulatory structures should also be reviewed on a rolling basis to ensure continued relevancy and suitability as financial market and corporate environments change. Optimal long-term benefits are only derived from corporate disclosure frameworks that encompass broad participation, investor confidence and continued public trust in the integrity of financial markets. Such confidence is generated by giving legal weight to principles and rules that provide all participants with a right to comprehensive information on a timely basis, and that ensure minority shareholders rights are protected and market misconduct is enforced.

Company disclosure frameworks work best when listed companies adopt a normative culture of continuous public disclosure. Such cultures are only possible when directors and senior executives acknowledge the substantial benefits derived from timely and frank communication about company developments and performance. Good corporate disclosure and communication is ultimately built on trust and resilience. As in most long-term human relationships, building commitment and trust between a company and its core investors and stakeholders requires considerable time and effort. This trust is fragile, especially when developments are poorly communicated and market participants believe a company has not been entirely open and honest. Listed companies are generally very willing to communicate with stakeholders publicly when things are going well and performance trends are positive. Most are more reluctant to openly discuss negative events and developments. Consequently, the core culture and character of a company are typically best identified and assessed by its ability to simultaneously manage business issues and maintain open communication in a balanced and forthright manner with stakeholders during adverse events and challenging periods.

The primary tests of effective digital company reporting and communication in modern financial markets include the ease with which information can be sourced and downloaded electronically, the quality and timeliness of publicly accessible company reports and disclosures, and the adequacy of online facilities and forums that allow interactive dialogue between companies, shareholders and other stakeholders.[9] Listed

9. Listed companies have made large cost savings during recent decades from regulatory changes that permit electronic dissemination of reports. Some of these costs have been shifted to investors and other stakeholders, as these participants are now required to download and potentially company reports and information from electronic files stored on individual company websites, exchange websites, or independent websites such as EDGAR in the US or an RIS in Europe. These costs can be significant when corporate reports are hundreds of pages long and they contain lots of ink intensive graphs and pictures. While some jurisdictions enable investors to order hard copies of the annual reports either from a public website or from companies, other jurisdictions provide hard copies only to existing investors upon request. Furthermore, investors and stakeholders are not provided with hard copies of other reports such as preliminary final, half-year or quarterly reports.

companies have made large cost savings during recent decades from regulatory changes that permit electronic dissemination of reports and disclosures. Some of these savings should be redirected to harness the potential of digital communication.[10] Digital advances have radically changed modern communication models and the way that companies, investors, and stakeholders interact and compete. Global communities and modern financial markets have embraced technological change and entire populations are increasingly dependent on digital interfaces. Listed company disclosure and communication, and the associated regulatory frameworks, need to reflect these momentous societal changes in order to remain relevant and credible.

10. For example open access to briefings and other major meetings that discuss the position and prospects of listed companies should be standard practice and all listed companies should provide detailed financial and non-financial information on their websites, with a particular focus on long term performance commentary and analysis.

APPENDIX:

The Author's Empirical Review: Selected Companies Listed on Major Exchanges in North America, Europe and Asia

> What is required of financial reporting is that it should be honest and that it should present a balanced picture of the state of the company's affairs. The integrity of the reports depends on the integrity of those who prepare and present them ... Integrity means both straightforward dealing and completeness.[1]

1. UNITED STATES

Case Studies

A. *Microsoft Corporation*

Microsoft Corporation (Microsoft) is a large global software company. The review of the Microsoft disclosures included the information provided on the company website and the documents on the EDGAR website maintained by the SEC.

Website

The Microsoft investor relations web pages provide links to the following areas: company information, earnings and financials, annual reports, SEC filings, events, stock information, investor services, governance & citizenship, and contacts.[2] The company information web pages provide a company overview and strategy discussion,

1. Report of the Committee on the Financial Aspects of Corporate Governance (1 December 2012) [3.1-3.2] available at www.jbs.ac.uj/cadbury/report/index.html.
2. Microsoft Corporation, 'Microsoft Investor Relations', viewed 20 May 2015, http://www.microsoft.com/investor/default.aspx.

segment information, white papers and case studies.[3] The company overview and strategy pages include a video of the chief executive office (CEO) discussing the group transformation and a video from the chief financial officer (CFO) presenting its economic transformation.

The governance and citizenship web pages provide information and links to documentation concerning the group goals, the board of directors, shareholder accountability, the annual shareholder meetings, company policies and guidelines, a governance fact sheet, and frequently asked questions and answers.[4] The company goals pages provide high-level commentary concerning the purpose of corporate governance, the role of board oversight, and the benefits of shareholder accountability. The board of directors' web pages explain the role, membership and duties of the board committees, and include director biographies and videos of interviews with individual directors. They also provide contact details for shareholders who want to communicate directly with the board, a board committee, or an individual director.[5] The shareholder accountability pages include governance material and details of director and executive compensation. The company annual reports are available back to 1996. The stock information pages include dividend and stock histories, stock split information, a result calendar, and an investments calculator.

The earnings and financial web pages provide earnings releases, financial statements, MD&A of the performance, key performance indicators (KPIs), and segment results.[6] The financial statement web pages allow users to view or download the annual and quarterly financial statements back to 1996. Viewers can scan or download spread sheets containing the quarterly income statements, yearly income statements, segment history, and unearned revenue for the twenty year period from 1995 to 2015. The result announcement material for the full year and quarters includes press releases, webcasts, slides and transcripts. The MD&A provides charts of the relevant trends. Users are also provided with various types of charts of the revenue, operating income and diluted earnings per share trends for selected periods.[7] The KPI pages include bookings growth, unearned revenue, product revenue mix, revenue growth, and unit sales. The segmental results include downloadable Excel spreadsheets.

3. Microsoft Corporation, 'Company Overview and Strategy', viewed 20 May 2015, http://www.microsoft.com/investor/CompanyInfo/Overview/default.aspx.
4. Microsoft Corporation, 'Overview', viewed 20 May 2015, http://www.microsoft.com/investor/CorporateGovernance/Overview/default.aspx.
5. Microsoft Corporation, 'Contact the Board of Directors', viewed 20 May 2015, http://www.microsoft.com/investor/CorporateGovernance/BoardOfDirectors/contact_board.aspx.
6. Microsoft Corporation, 'Earnings Release FY15 Q3', viewed 20 May 2015, http://www.microsoft.com/investor/EarningsAndFinancials/Earnings/PressReleaseAndWebcast/FY15/Q3/default.aspx.
7. Microsoft Corporation, 'Trended Historical Financials', viewed 20 May 2015, http://www.microsoft.com/investor/EarningsAndFinancials/TrendedHistory/AnnualStatements.aspx.

Preliminary Final & Annual Reports

The Microsoft 10-K for the year ended 30 June 2012 was filed with the SEC on 26 July 2012. The annual report mailed to security holders was filed with the SEC on 19 October 2012. Despite the three-month time lag, the differences in the two reports are minimal. The 2012 annual report includes an introductory letter from the CEO, selected financial data sections for five years, important shareholder information, and a business description. Both the 10-K and annual reports include detailed presentations of the financial and operational positions of the group, and of the key market risks. There are no pictures in either report and the reports are full pages. Most of the MD&A content is framed around the financial statements, with detailed notes and explanation of the reported numbers. A brief outline of the business and industry trends, key opportunities and investments, and the industry and seasonal factors provides initial context. The income trends for the most recent three years are then discussed, including the revenue and income changes for the three years by sector and major expense items. The commentary discusses the key items on the balance sheet and cash flow statement including cash, investments, debt, dividends, capital commitments and liquidity. The financial statements are provided towards the end of the report, with notes that discuss specific items. The form, headings and content of the 2013 and 2014 full year reports are similar to the 2012 reports.

Interim Reports

The Microsoft 10-Q quarterly report for the period ended 31 December 2012 contains interactive spread sheet data and an electronic table of contents. The full set of financial statements and notes are outlined initially. The notes to the accounts provide detailed outlines of the derivative positions, assets and liabilities at fair value, debt maturities, face value and effective interest rates, and segment revenue and income. The MD&A includes a summary of the financial condition and operations; quantitative and qualitative disclosures of market risk, including foreign currency, interest rate, equity and commodity risks;[8] confirmation that the financial reporting and disclosure controls and procedures were reviewed; other information including a note on legal proceedings and an outline of the risk factors; and details of unregistered sales of equity securities and use of proceeds.

The quarterly result material on the website for the third quarter of 2015 is well presented and supported.[9] The result document includes the advance webcast details. The result web pages provide the earnings call slides, the earnings call transcript, the financial statements, the press release, the 10-Q, and an outlook file. The outlook file provides a clearly labelled table with the projected revenue growth by segment, gross

8. A value-at risk model (VaR) is used to estimate the one day VaR for each of the risk categories with the high low and average amounts over the quarter.
9. Microsoft Corporation, 'Earnings Release FY15 Q3', viewed 20 May 2015, http://www.microsoft.com/investor/EarningsAndFinancials/Earnings/PressReleaseAndWebcast/FY15/Q3/default.aspx.

margin and cost levels, likely restructuring costs, tax rate, and expected capital expenditure and unearned revenue for the final quarter of 2015.

Continuous Disclosures

Interested parties can subscribe to RSS feeds for investor relations upcoming events and announcements and news centre releases.[10]

Citizenship Reports

The Microsoft 2012 citizenship report indicates that citizenship governance matters were moved during the year to a new Regulatory and Public Policy committee. This committee is charged with 'overseeing public issues that may affect the company's operations or performance in areas like human rights, climate change, and responsible sourcing.'[11] A large portion of the report outlines the philanthropic endeavours of the group and interactions with its various communities. Focus areas include employee relationships, the environment, human rights, responsible sourcing and governance. Most of the commentary is high level, but some performance metrics are provided.

When reviewed in May 2015, the citizenship material had been moved to an independent section of the group website.[12] The citizenship web pages are now arranged under headings for Youth Spark, Working Responsibly, Servicing Communities and NonProfits. The 2014 citizenship report is more comprehensive, integrated and coherent than the 2012 report. The focus areas have been revised to ethical business conduct and governance, our people, serving communities, human rights, responsible sourcing and environmental sustainability. The report provides the prior year goals for each area, its performance against these goals, and the future goals. An internal assessment was done during the year for compliance with the Global Reporting Initiative (GRI) guidelines. A table lists compliance with items of the GRI 4 index.

B. Citigroup Inc

Citigroup Inc (Citigroup) is a large global financial group.

Website

The Citigroup home page is arranged under the headings of consumer businesses, institutional businesses, investor relations, and about us.[13] The consumer and

10. Microsoft Corporation, 'RSS Feeds', viewed 20 May 2015, http://www.microsoft.com/investor/InvestorServices/RSS/default.aspx.
11. Microsoft Corporation, *Microsoft 2012 Citizenship Report* 4
12. Microsoft Corporation, 'Corporate Citizenship', viewed 20 May 2015, http://www.microsoft.com/about/corporatecitizenship/en-us/.
13. Citigroup Inc, 'Citi', viewed 20 May 2015, http://www.citigroup.com/citi/.

institutional web pages provide a descriptive overview of the businesses within these areas. The 'about us' web pages provide access to a mission statement, a map highlighting country-specific presence, outlines of the board and group leaders, some historical material, governance information, and a link to a global citizenship area. The governance pages provide access to various governance documents, including details of the board and board committees, corporate governance guidelines, company policies, a code of conduct, and regulatory filings. A link to an ethics hotline is also provided.[14] The citizenship web pages provide access to the citizenship reports and various technical documents and information.

The investor relations home page provides access to recent presentations, notification of upcoming events, and the most recent annual report and proxy statements.[15] The financial information pages include the earnings releases, supplementary material, spread sheets, webcasts and transcripts of investor presentations, press releases, SEC filings, other regulatory filings, and credit ratings.[16] There are earnings release presentations for shareholders and fixed income investors. The quarterly earnings result material includes the media release, the financial results, an Excel spreadsheet, the presentation slides, the conference call transcript, and a webcast.[17] The investor presentations are listed chronologically. The other regulatory filings available include the Call Reports and the Basel II and Basel III disclosure reports. The company news releases are provided in chronological order, with search functionality by year or business segment.[18]

Preliminary Final and Annual Reports

The Citigroup 10-K and annual reports for the year ended 31 December 2012 were filed simultaneously on 1 March 2013. The initial pages contain an executive summary and a five year summary of selected financial data. The pages dealing with risk management are clear and they encompass specific global developments and issues. The financial results are explained in detail. The report on the EDGAR website has interactive data, allowing the report components to be downloaded as Excel spread sheets. The annual report consists of the 10-K and 20 additional pages including a short letter from the CEO, followed by general outlines of the main business with some pictures. The performance table in the annual report is for three years.

14. Citigroup Inc, 'Governance Documents', viewed 20 May 2015, http://www.citigroup.com/citi/investor/corporate_governance.html.
15. Citigroup Inc, 'Investor Presentations', viewed 20 May 2015, http://www.citigroup.com/citi/investor/overview.html.
16. Citigroup Inc, 'Investor Presentations', viewed 20 May 2015, http://www.citigroup.com/citi/investor/pres.htm#.
17. Citigroup Inc, 'Quarterly Earnings Releases and Supplements', viewed 20 May 2015, http://www.citigroup.com/citi/investor/qer.htm.
18. Citigroup Inc, 'Featured News', viewed 20 May 2015, http://www.citigroup.com/citi/news/news_list_view.html.

The Citigroup 2014 annual report also comprises the 10-K report with cover pages added. The cover pages include a three year performance table, a letter from the CEO, some pictures and broad overviews.

Interim Reports

The Citigroup 10-Q for the three months to 31 March 2013 was filed on 3 May 2013. It begins with a short executive summary. A significant proportion of its content concerns risk reporting and analysis. Comparative data is generally limited to quarter-on-quarter changes. Similarly, the earnings report, presentation and conference call transcript for the first quarter of 2015 contain MD&A on the financial performance for the quarter, with limited content on the group's strategy and prospects.

Citizenship Reports

The main focuses of the Citigroup 2012 global citizenship report are supporting consumers; governance, ethics and government relations; environmental sustainability; employee matters; and regional citizenship. The report provides a useful upfront summary of achievements and challenges in each of the main areas.[19] A section entitled 'key performance indicators' provides metrics across the focus areas for periods up to 8 years.[20] The 2013 citizenship report[21] states that 'corporate citizenship is a unifying theme across our business operations and global locations.'[22] This report indicates that the citizenship policies, programs and initiatives focus on three areas, namely promoting financial inclusion and economic progress, advancing environmental sustainability, and valuing employees.

2. CANADA

Case Studies

A. Royal Bank of Canada

The Royal Bank of Canada (RBC) is Canada's largest bank measured by market capitalisation and assets. The RBC is listed on the TSX and has a foreign issuer listing on the NYSE.

19. Citigroup Inc, *2012 Global Citizenship Report* 2-3.
20. Citigroup Inc, *2012 Global Citizenship Report* 4-11.
21. Citigroup Inc, *2013 Global Citizenship Report,* viewed 21 May 2015, *http://www.citigroup.com/citi/about/global_citizenship.html.* The 2014 report was not available on the website when viewed on 21 May 2015.
22. Citigroup Inc, *2013 Global Citizenship Report* 4.

Website

The vertical headings on the RBC home page are Canada, United States, International, and about RBC. The 'about RBC' web pages provide a corporate profile and access to information about corporate governance, the company's history, investor relations, the media newsroom, RBC social media, economics, publications, a community and sustainability area, and diversity.[23] The corporate profile pages provide outlines of the group's vision and values, its business segments, an overview, and regulatory filings including the Basel II and Basel III disclosures.[24] The corporate governance pages provide information on the corporate governance framework, the board of directors, the board committees, the executive officers, company policies, a reporting hotline, and contact details.[25] The historical pages include a celebratory review, virtual exhibits, and milestone commentary.[26] The RBS social media page provides links to RBS social media sites and projects including Facebook, Twitter, YouTube, and LinkedIn.[27] The economics pages provide research on the economy, financial markets, Canadian housing, key indicators, forecasts and special reports.[28] The diversity pages include a presidential message, discussion on why diversity matters, high level objectives and reports.[29] Other pages explain how people may report a fraudulent email or security concern and how to make a complaint.

The investor relations home page provides links to a corporate overview, financial information, events and presentations, debt and equity information, and the latest annual report.[30] The corporate overview pages include information on business segments and acquisitions. The financial information pages include the quarterly release dates and call times, the quarterly results, the annual reports and regulatory filings. The events and presentation pages provide information on upcoming events, conferences, investor days, quarterly presentations and the annual general meeting. The debt and equity information pages provide share, debt and dividends details, historical prices, and an investment calculator. The company result information is organised chronologically. The quarterly result material includes the press release, the

23. Royal Bank of Canada, 'Investor Relations', viewed 24 May 2015, http://www.rbc.com/investorrelations/.
24. Royal Bank of Canada, 'Corporate Profile', viewed 24 May 2015, http://www.rbc.com/aboutus/index.html.
25. Royal Bank of Canada, 'Corporate Governance', viewed 24 May 2015, http://www.rbc.com/governance/index.html.
26. Royal Bank of Canada, 'Celebrating our History', viewed 24 May 2015, http://www.rbc.com/history/index.html.
27. Royal Bank of Canada, 'RBC Social Media', viewed 24 May 2015, http://www.rbc.com/social/index.html.
28. Royal Bank of Canada, 'Economics', viewed 24 May 2015, http://www.rbc.com/economics/index.html.
29. Royal Bank of Canada, 'Diversity', viewed 24 May 2015, http://www.rbc.com/diversity/index.html.
30. Royal Bank of Canada, 'Investor Relations', viewed 24 May 2015, http://www.rbc.com/investorrelations/.

report to shareholders, the slides, the webcast, the speakers' notes, financial supplements, and regulatory capital disclosures.[31] The archived documents extend back to 2006. A document titled 'RBC at a Glance' highlights the group's results for the quarter, including overviews of the company and business segments, the group's key strategic goals, financial highlights including segmental and geographical results, and the shareholder performance trends for the prior five quarters.[32]

The community and sustainability web pages include content on the group's approach, reporting and performance, community, the environment, social finance, and news.[33] The reporting and performance pages provide links to reports on corporate integrity, economic impact, the marketplace, the workplace, the environment, and the community. The 'our approach' pages include recognition in the form of awards received, a list of stakeholders, and the group's pledges and priorities.[34]

Preliminary Final & Annual Reports

The RBC fourth quarter results to 31 October 2012 include the financial statements, MD&A focusing on quarter-on-quarter and year-on-year comparatives, and some key ratios and financial metrics. The report includes access details to the quarterly conference call and webcast presentation. The quarterly reports are limited to near term financial data and explanation. For broader context, readers must turn to the full year reports. The RBC 2012 annual report provides an upfront summary table with earnings and other metrics for three years. Key events during the year are outlined and the results are explained and compared to defined financial performance targets. A performance overview is provided, including segmental and geographic reporting. Reporting of the business segments includes outlook and priority commentary. The assumptions used in the management-reporting framework are explained, including the relevant performance measures and calculation methodologies. The section on risk management is extensive, including the main risk categories and risk processes.

The RBC 2014 annual report is comprised of a detailed financial report (similar to the 10-Ks in the US) with letters from the CEO and Chairperson and cover pages that highlight the group's strategic goals, long-term financial performance metrics and community engagement. A ten year financial performance table is provided at the end of the report, including balance sheet and income statement items, profitability measures, key ratios, share information and capital measures.

31. Royal Bank of Canada, 'Quarterly Information', viewed 24 May 2015, http://www.rbc.com/investorrelations/quarterly-financial-statements.html.
32. Royal Bank of Canada, 'Quarterly Information', viewed 24 May 2015, http://www.rbc.com/investorrelations/quarterly-financial-statements.html.
33. Royal Bank of Canada, 'Community & Sustainability', viewed 24 May 2015, http://www.rbc.com/community-sustainability/index.html.
34. Royal Bank of Canada, 'Our Approach', viewed 24 May 2015, http://www.rbc.com/community-sustainability/our-approach.html.

Interim Reports

The report for the second quarter of 2012 includes an upfront summary with selected income, balance sheet, cash flow, market share, segmental and business numbers, and comparative prior period figures. The MD&A outlines and discusses changes to key income and balance sheet items. Segmental reporting, trend analysis and some risk data are included. Summary financial notes are also provided, including financial instrument fair value outlines.

The results for the first quarter of 2015 provide similar information and adopt a similar layout to the 2012 reports. They include a shareholder report with financial statements, and moderately detailed financial notes and commentary; the press release; the result slides and speaker notes; the webcast audio; supplementary financial information, including detailed data on the segmental results, on and off balance sheet exposures, capital management, credit quality and credit risk exposures; and a regulatory index that references documents that satisfy specific regulatory requirements.

Continuous Disclosures

Company news releases from 2012 to the present are available from the RBC website.[35]

Corporate Responsibility Reports

The CEO states in the Corporate Responsibility Report (CRR) for 2012 that the 'competitiveness of a company and the health of the communities around it are mutually dependent, and that there is a competitive advantage in building a social value proposition into corporate strategy.'[36] This is described as the new bottom line. The report contains sections dealing with corporate integrity, economic impact, marketplace, workplace, environment, community, public accountability statements and vital statistics. A table highlights where the responsibilities and accountabilities for corporate integrity, economic impact, marketplace, workplace, environment and community lie within the group.[37] The group priorities, performance highlights, and plans for the following year are outlined for each focus area. A vital statistics section at the end of the report provides performance metrics for the prior three years across each of the focus areas.[38]

The focus areas in the 2014 CRR are the same as those in the 2012 report, but the structure of this report differs. This report is framed around the priority goals, KPIs, and

35. Royal Bank of Canada, 'Latest News', viewed 24 May 2015, http://www.rbc.com/investorrelations/news.html.
36. Royal Bank of Canada, *2012 Corporate Responsibility Report and Public Accountability Statement* 7.
37. Royal Bank of Canada, *2012 Corporate Responsibility Report and Public Accountability Statement* 17.
38. Royal Bank of Canada, *2012 Corporate Responsibility Report and Public Accountability Statement* 115-118.

performance against these goals and metrics. In 2014, the public accountability statement required under Canadian law is presented as a separate report from the CRR. It discusses the group's community development, access to financial services, initiatives to support small businesses and micro-credit, the number of employees, taxes paid, debt financing provided in each state, branch openings, closings and relocations, and the number of automatic teller machines installed and removed.[39]

B. Teck Resources Limited

Teck Resources Ltd (Teck) is a diversified resource company headquartered in Vancouver. Teck is listed on the TSX and has a foreign issuer listing on the NYSE.

Website

The Teck home page provides links to the annual reports, the latest events and news, and contact details.[40] There are also headings for 'about', media, investors, products, diversified mining and responsibility. The 'about' web pages provide a brief history of the group, the names and biographies of the company directors, and the names of company officers. The media area provides company news releases from 2006 to the present. It also includes a range of videos and links to the company's social media outlets through Twitter, Facebook and LinkedIn. The diversified mining web pages provide an overview of the product areas, with links to further pages for more detail, including definitions, the annual year-end reserve and resource statements, and a five-year production table of the principal products.[41] The focus areas in the 'responsibility' web pages are sustainability, safety and health, corporate governance, community investment, recycling and zinc, and health pages. These pages outline the company's commitments and case studies.[42]

The investor web pages provide access to a short business overview, news, financial reports, presentations and webcasts, a calendar, shareholder information, and an interactive analyst center.[43] The financial reporting web pages include the quarterly reports, annual reports, and public filings. The quarterly result material includes the reports, webcasts, audios, the presentation slides, and transcripts.[44] The presentation and webcast pages include presentations in slide and webcast form. The

---

39. Royal Bank of Canada, 2014 *Public Accountability Statement.*
40. Teck Resources Ltd, 'Teck', viewed 25 May 2015, http://www.teck.com/Generic.aspx?portalName=tc.
41. See, e.g., Teck Resources Ltd, 'Our Steelmaking Coal Business', viewed 25 May 2015, http://www.teck.com/Generic.aspx?PAGE=Teck+Site%2fDiversified+Mining+Pages%2fCoal&portalName=tc..
42. Teck Resources Ltd, 'Responsibility', viewed 25 May 2015, http://www.teck.com/Generic.aspx?PAGE=Teck+Site/Responsibility&portalName=tc.
43. Teck Resources Ltd, 'Investors', viewed 25 May 2015, http://www.teck.com/Generic.aspx?PAGE=Teck+Site/Investors&portalName=tc.
44. Teck Resources Ltd, 'Quarterly Reports', viewed 25 May 2015, http://www.teck.com/Generic.aspx?PAGE=Teck+Site%2fInvestors+Pages%2fFinancial+Reporting+Pages%2fQuarterly+Reports&portalName=tc.

shareholder information pages include the company share price charts, the company's dividend history, and shareholder contacts. The interactive analyst center, which is maintained by third parties, includes onscreen and downloadable financial data, including annual and quarterly figures for the last three to four years. Some basic chart facilities are also provided.[45]

Preliminary Final & Annual Reports

The results for the quarter and year to 31 December 2012 include minimal notes and prior year comparative figures. The front pages of the 2012 annual report contain a letter from the Chairman and full page pictures. The business outlines provide detailed information including tonnages, the 5-year production record and expected share of production for 2013, and the average commodity prices and exchange rates. The financial overview provides summary data for three years and MD&A on the gross profit, expenses, financial position and liquidity. A summary of capital expenditure commitments and a table showing debt maturities and other contractual commitments are also included. Discussion on the company's outlook is generally limited to high-level commentary. However the report provides estimated production tonnages and exchange rate sensitivity analysis.

The structure and content of the 2014 annual report resemble a 10-K report prefaced with front pages containing pictures and high level commentary. The segmental reports include some five year charts, and the financial statements and segmental results provide comparative figures for three years. The outlook statement includes production estimates and a sensitivity table showing the estimated effect of changes in commodity prices and the US dollar exchange rate.

Interim Reports

The report for the third quarter of 2012 provides unaudited financial statements, including segmental reporting, financial notes and limited MD&A. The report for the first quarter of 2015 includes more comprehensive and useful MD&A and advance details of the result webcast. It includes discussion that explains the impact of various factors on the results, including segmental, product, volume, pricing and expense details. It includes an outlook statement that discusses the external environment and the likely impact of key factors. It also includes commentary on the use of non-compliant financial measures, reasons why the company uses these measures and why they are useful to investors, and tables that reconcile these measures to the reported numbers.

45. See, e.g., Teck Resources Ltd, 'Interactive Analyst Center', viewed 25 May 2015, http://apps.indigotools.com/IR/IAC/?Ticker=TCK%2FB&Exchange=TSX#.

Continuous Disclosure

The news area of the Teck website provides access to company releases from 2006 to the present.[46]

Sustainability Reports

Annual sustainability reports are available from the Teck website for the last 12 years. The Teck 2012 sustainability report is arranged into five focus areas; community, our people, water, biodiversity, and energy and materials stewardship. Case studies are provided in each section. The community section shows the economic value generated and distributed by country of operation. The group provides community investment beyond the scope of normal business operations, which it categorises as philanthropic investment, community and infrastructure development, or commercial initiative.[47] In 2011, Teck developed a comprehensive sustainability strategy including medium-term goals through to 2015 and longer-term goals until 2030.[48] A performance overview table, an independent assurance report, and a global reporting initiative index are provided at the rear of the report.[49] The performance overview table provides some metrics across the focus areas for three years. The appendices provide data tables, an outline of the communities of interest, the company memberships, external standards and commitments, and a goals dashboard. Appendix D shows progress on the short-term sustainability goals across each of the focus areas.

At the time the website was reviewed, the most recent sustainability report was for 2013. The structure and content of the 2013 report is similar to the 2012 report. Most of the content is high level commentary, with more specific metrics at the end of the report. The report states that its audience is our communities of interest (COIs): any individuals or groups that may be affected by, have an interest in, or have the ability to influence our activities. This includes our employees, local communities, society at large, government, Indigenous People, media, and those with business interests in our company (e.g., shareholders, business partners or industry associations).

3. GERMANY

Case Studies

The companies selected for review are Siemens AG, a large global industrial company, and Deutsche Bank, the largest financial institution in Germany.

46. Teck Resources Ltd, 'News Releases', viewed 25 May 2015, http://www.teck.com/Generic.aspx?PAGE=Teck+Site%2fInvestors+Pages%2fNews&portalName=tc.
47. Teck Resources Ltd, *Teck 2012 Sustainability Report* 35-36. The group's stated aim is to donate 1% of annual pre-tax earnings to community investments, on a rolling average basis.
48. Teck Resources Ltd, *Teck 2012 Sustainability Report* 15.
49. Teck Resources Ltd, *Teck 2013 Sustainability Report*, viewed 25 May 2015.

A. *Siemens AG*

Siemens AG (Siemens) describes itself as an integrated technology company. Siemens is listed on the FWB and on the NYSE as a foreign issuer.

Website

The Siemens home page headings include products and solutions, corporate information, and news.[50] It also connects to a 'Siemens at a glance' document, publications and events, share information, a private investor area, corporate governance material, debt, ratings, and a financial calendar.[51] The Siemens 'at a glance' web pages provide factual information, a brief strategic overview, and a company presentation. Content on the corporate governance web pages is limited to technical documents. A multiyear overview provides a limited 5 year performance table (with seven line items). The consensus figures include estimated orders by segment, revenue, profits, restructure charges, reconciliation items, and consolidated net income and earnings per share figures for the next quarter and for the fiscal 2015 and 2016 years. The publications and events web pages provide annual reports, interim reports, quarterly earnings releases, financial results, consensus figures, company presentations, and ad hoc announcements with search functionality back to 2006.[52] When this author reviewed the web site in 2013, webcasts or audios of presentations and events were available back to 2006. In May 2015, equivalent material was more difficult to locate. Investor kits allow users to select desired documents in pdf format, but the only webcast found was the analyst call for the second quarter 2015 result.[53]

Preliminary Final & Annual Reports

The Siemens earnings announcement for the fourth quarter to 30 September 2012 is a short report without financial statements. Advance access details to webcasts of the analyst and media meetings are provided. The first 80 pages of the Siemens 2012 annual report provide pictures with high-level commentary on the focus areas of proximity, ideas, strengths, networking, and diversity. The financial report provides

50. Siemens, 'Siemens Global Website Investor Relations', viewed 25 May 2015, http://www.siemens.com/entry/cc/en/. These pages are in English, but links to equivalent websites in German are provided.
51. Siemens, 'Siemens Global Website Investor Relations', viewed 25 May 2015, http://www.siemens.com/investor/en.
52. Siemens, 'Publications & Events', viewed 25 May 2015, http://www.siemens.com/investor/en/publications_calendar.php.
53. This webcast was accessed from the investor relation home page: Siemens, 'Siemens Global Website Investor Relations', viewed 25 May 2015, http://www.siemens.com/investor/en.
    Interestingly, the company recommends that professionals select the financial calendar, the financial result, the quarterly earnings release and the analyst call presentation from the investor kits, and recommends that private investors' select the financial calendar, the annual and interim reports, the shareholder letter, and the company information sheet.

summary data, a letter to shareholders, corporate governance and combined management reports, the financial statements and additional information. The financial report includes a performance table with five years of data. The management report includes broad commentary on the business and economic environments, financial performance measures, financial performance, net assets position, overall assessment, sustainability, and expected developments and risks. The assessment section explains the key performance metrics used by management and discusses the group strategy, competitive position, and risks. Some sustainability metrics are included in the management report.

The form and content of the 2014 annual report is similar to the 2012 report, but the assessment content is weaker. A five year financial performance table is included. The strategy and performance commentary in the report is broad.

Interim Reports

The quarterly report for the three months to 31 December 2012 provides upfront financial key figures with prior year comparatives. The presentation and content is similar to the quarterly reports in the US, with detailed notes, MD&A and a set of financial statements.

The quarterly reports for the first and second quarters of 2015 provide limited financial information and MD&A. The second quarter report includes a short outlook statement with an expected earnings per share figure. The presentation webcast includes the question and answer session.

Continuous Disclosures

The ad hoc announcements are available on the website, but the nature and scope of these announcements are limited. There are only fifteen releases for the five years to 25 May 2015.[54]

Sustainability Reports

The Siemens 2012 sustainability report contains pictures and high-level discussion about the need for sustainable business. The second half provides more specific material including project outlines. It includes a three-year performance table across the various focus areas. The report complies with the United Nations Global Compact and the GRI G3.0 guidelines, and an independent assurance statement is included.[55]

---

54. Siemens, 'Ad Hoc Announcements', viewed 25 May 2015, http://www.siemens.com/investor/en/publications_calendar.php?pftab=1.
55. see Siemens, 'Siemens Global Website', viewed 26 June 2013, http://www.siemens.com/sustainability/en/sustainability/reporting/current-report.htm.

In 2014, the sustainability report is included within ten pages of the annual report. Most of the content is broad commentary. Some additional information is provided in a supplemental document.[56]

B. *Deutsche Bank AG*

Deutsche Bank AG (Deutsche Bank) is the largest banking and financial services company in Germany. Deutsche Bank has a primary listing on the FWB and is a foreign issuer on the NYSE.

Website

The Deutsche Bank investor relations home page provides access to reporting and events, corporate governance, supervisory boards, management, Deutsche Bank share information, the annual general meeting, ratings, bondholder information, and a responsibility area.[57] It also includes links to the company releases, a financial calendar and details of the annual general meeting. The corporate governance web pages provide mandated documents, company codes, and corporate governance statements.[58] The supervisory board pages provide pictures and details of the board members and its committees. Similarly, the management board pages provide pictures and details of the board members and its group executive committee. The Deutsche Bank share information pages provide information on issued shares, share price charts, dividends, a performance calculator, the share buyback program, the shareholder structure, the global registered shares, and recent capital raisings.[59] They also name the analysts and provide a consensus document. At the time of review, a consensus document dated 12 May 2015 included forecast income statements, balance sheets, ratios and per share data for the next quarter and for 2015, 2016 and 2017. The minimum, maximum and average figures and the number of forecasts included in the consensus figures were provided for each line item.[60] The annual general meeting pages provide access to the relevant documents and videos of the meetings. The bondholder pages provide access to prospectuses, news, presentations, reports, and the credit analysts.[61] The responsibility web pages include a data center and information on strategy, responsible business, society, our people, and the environment.[62]

56. Siemens, *Additional Sustainability Information to the Siemens Annual Report 2014.*
57. Deutsche Bank, 'Deutsche Bank Investor Relations', viewed 26 May 2015, https://www.db.com/ir/index_e.htm.
58. Deutsche Bank, 'Corporate Governance', viewed 26 May 2015, https://www.db.com/ir/en/content/corporate_governance.htm.
59. Deutsche Bank, 'Ordinary Share', viewed 26 May 2015, https://www.db.com/ir/en/content/ordinary_share.htm.
60. Deutsche Bank, 'Analysts and Earnings Estimates', viewed 26 May 2015, https://www.db.com/ir/en/content/analysts.htm.
61. Deutsche Bank, 'News Corner', viewed 26 May 2015, https://www.db.com/ir/en/content/news-corner-2015.htm.
62. Deutsche Bank, 'Deutsche Bank Investor Relations', viewed 26 May 2015, https://www.db.com/ir/index_e.htm. The differences between these two sets of releases are not clear.

These pages provide overviews, pictures, and links to other web pages and documents. The data center provides access to news, facts and figures, the corporate responsibility reports, and company brochures.

The reporting and events web pages provide company releases that are categorised by the company as either investor relation releases or ad hoc releases.[63] They also include company presentations, company reports, and a financial calendar. Tabs for the latest result material are provided on the right hand side. The result information includes the reports, supplementary information and a spreadsheet, the presentation and videos of the analysts call, and the press conference. When the website was reviewed, replay of the videos of the analyst calls was permitted for a year and registration was required to listen. The archived reports include regulatory filings, including the annual stress test disclosures.

Preliminary Final & Annual Reports

The Deutsche Bank 2012 annual report is 532 pages long, including full-page pictures throughout. The initial pages provide high-level statements about future transformation. A five-year financial performance table is included at the end of the report.

The 2014 annual report is more than five hundred pages long and its structure is cumbersome and repetitive. The financial report includes an operating and financial review section that provides commentary on the external environment, the banking industry and the company's performance. One section provides the key financial performance indicators of the group for the next two years, with some commentary on progress made. An outlook section is also included, but much of the commentary is broad and this author found it difficult to discern the established goals and pathways to achieve the stated financial targets.

Interim Reports

The Deutsche Bank report for the second quarter of 2012 is more succinct than the annual report. It explains the year-on-year changes and includes an outlook statement.

The first quarter report for 2015 provides detailed numbers, but the nature and scope of the MD&A in the report and accompanying presentation are limited.

Continuous Disclosures

The Deutsche Bank company announcements since 2000 are available from the website.[64]

63. Deutsche Bank, 'Deutsche Bank Investor Relations', viewed 26 May 2015, https://www.db.com/ir/index_e.htm.
64. Deutsche Bank, 'Deutsche Bank Resposibilty', viewed 26 May 2015, https://www.db.com/cr/index_en.htm.

Corporate Responsibility Reports

The Deutsche Bank 2012 corporate responsibility report (CRR) points to research that places the financial sector at the bottom of all sectors on being trusted 'to do what is right' for the second consecutive year.[65] It acknowledges the need to bring about 'deep cultural change' at the bank and describes how the business is 'balancing financial returns with ... [a] contribution to society and a healthy environment.'[66] The focus areas of the bank are responsible business, sustainable operations, and people and society. The responsible business section provides outlines concerning reputational risk, banking services for individuals and businesses, asset and wealth management, financing social and environmental change, advising corporate clients, and ensuring strong governance. Facts and figures and supplementary material are provided at the end of the report, including an independent assurance statement, a performance table for three years, a GRI Index, and a table that shows the group at a glance.

The Deutsche Bank 2014 CRR uses the same focus areas as in the 2012 report. Most of the report content is broad commentary. However, some three year goals are described alongside the 2014 performance and a three year performance table is included at the end of the report with financial and non-financial metrics.[67]

4. UNITED KINGDOM

Case Studies

Oil, financial services and retailing are important sectors represented on the LSE. Accordingly, the two companies selected for review are BP Plc and Sainsbury Plc.

A. BP Plc

BP Plc (BP) is a large global oil company. BP has a primary listing on the LSE and is listed on the NYSE as a foreign issuer.

Website

The BP investors home page is arranged with headings for about BP, products & services, sustainability, investors, and Gulf of Mexico restoration. It provides access to important quick links, share information, upcoming events, and key downloads.[68] The about BP web pages provide a range of information including an introduction to the group, its strategy, operations and structure, historical material, technology commentary, and an overview of energy economics. The strategy pages include the KPIs that

65. Deutsche Bank, *Corporate Responsibility Report 2012* 4.
66. Deutsche Bank, *Corporate Responsibility Report 2012* cover page.
67. Deutsche Bank, *Corporate Responsibility Report 2014* 85.
68. BP, 'Investors', viewed 26 May 2015, http://www.bp.com/en/global/corporate/investors.html.

are used to determine remuneration and assess the company's performance.[69] These indicators are described alongside 5 year graphs, but the calculation methodologies are not outlined and the items excluded from the underlying profit figures as 'non-operational' are not immediately explained or reconciled to the reported numbers.[70] The product and services web pages can be filtered by product or service and by country. One of the quick links from the home page provides access to a trading conditions page. This page explains that the 'trading conditions update is produced in order to provide disclosure to investors and potential investors of current trading conditions, and to ensure that they all receive equal access to the same information, at the same time.'[71] The trading conditions data is updated on a weekly basis every Friday at 15.30 UK time providing all interested parties with simultaneous and regular business data for various purposes, including valuation of the company's securities. The sustainability web pages provide material on safety, the energy future, the environment, society, how the group operates, case studies and reports.[72] The archived sustainability reports extend back to 1998. Country reports are also available for Angola, Australia, Azerbaijan, Georgia and Oman, and these are supported by externally verified site reports.

The investors web pages provide links to presentations, results and reporting, annual reports, a financial calendar, regulatory news and filings, share information, the annual general meeting, shareholder information, governance, socially responsible investing, and investor tools.[73] The presentations web pages include transcripts and webcasts of investor days and project or strategy meetings. The results and reporting pages provide result material. The quarterly result material includes the report, the press release, supplementary information, the slides, a transcript of the management presentation and a webcast. In addition, historical quarterly and annual information can be downloaded in pdf or Excel for the years 2010 to 2014. The share information includes the company listing details, issued shares and share capital. Annual reports are available back to 2006. The governance web pages outline the governance principles and various mandated reports.[74] The socially responsible investment page provides access to the company's sustainability reports, presentations, briefings and speeches, standards and codes of conduct, case studies, and a charting tool.[75] The investor toolkit web pages provide share price charts and some graphs with limited functionality and explanation.

69. BP, 'Our Key Performance Indicators', viewed 26 May 2015, http://www.bp.com/en/global/corporate/about-bp/our-strategy/key-performance-indicators.html.
70. A page is referenced for an IFRS equivalent number but the relevant document is not.
71. BP, 'Trading Conditions Update', viewed 26 May 2015, http://www.bp.com/extendedsectiongenericarticle.do?categoryId=9016864&contentId=7030494.
72. BP, 'Sustainability', viewed 26 May 2015, http://www.bp.com/en/global/corporate/sustainability.html.
73. BP, 'Investors', viewed 26 May 2015, http://www.bp.com/en/global/corporate/investors.html.
74. BP, 'Governance', viewed 26 May 2015, http://www.bp.com/en/global/corporate/investors/governance.html.
75. BP, 'Socially Responsible Investment', viewed 26 May 2015, http://www.bp.com/en/global/corporate/investors/socially-responsible-investment.html.

Interim Reports

The BP report for the six months to 31 July 2012 presents the financial results and MD&A within clearly identified segments. The report is brief. Most of the commentary references financial measures on an underlying basis, with reconciliations to the reported numbers within the financial statements. Comparative figures are limited to the prior year. The risk commentary is largely descriptive, except the litigation outline.

The report for the first quarter of 2015 provides a reasonable level of financial information but the information is poorly connected and the MD&A in the report and presentation is limited. The supplementary information provides explanations of terminology and reconciliations between the underlying and reported profit measures.[76]

Preliminary Final & Annual Reports

The commentary in the BP results for the fourth quarter and full year 2012 highlights financial measures on an underlying basis. The differences include fair value adjustments and non-operational items. One of the largest of the non-operational items is the cost associated with the Gulf of Mexico spill.

The commentary in the BP 2012 annual report is general, including the discussion in the Chairman's and CEO's letters. The report includes a section entitled 'Our key performance indicators', which highlights the KPIs that the board and management use to assess performance, including financial and non-financial metrics. The financial commentary is more detailed and a comprehensive five-year financial performance summary is provided.[77] Financial statements are provided for three years.

The structure and content of the 2014 annual report are similar to the 2012 report.[78] A KPI section and a five year financial performance table are included, but there is minimal MD&A that connect these indicators and long-term performance trends to the stated strategy, vision, goals and plans of the group. Some of the risk factor disclosures are useful, while others are highly generic. Some outlook commentary is included in the business segment reports, but its value is limited given its highly general nature.

Continuous Disclosures

The regulatory news filings can be filtered by type of disclosure and or date, and by word(s) in the title or body of the disclosures.[79]

76. It is not clear why the company does not reference this document in the report and on the company website.
77. BP, *Annual Report and Form 20-F 2012* 34-35.
78. BP Annual Report and Form 20-F 2014.
79. BP, 'Regulatory News Service and Filings', viewed 26 May 2015, http://www.bp.com/en/global/corporate/investors/regulatory-news-service-and-filings.html.

Sustainability Reports

Much of the content of the BP 2012 sustainability report discusses the general energy markets and internal management processes. A five-year sustainability performance table is provided at the rear of the report with safety, environment, employees, production, and community contribution metrics. An independent assurance opinion is provided.

The 2014 sustainability report is coherently structured and is reasonably focused and engaging. A five year performance table outlines the key indicators across the areas of safety, the environment, people and performance. The focus area commentary outlines 'what we said we would do', 'where we are today' and 'what we plan to do next', with varying degrees of specificity.

B. J Sainsbury Plc

J Sainsbury Plc (Sainsbury) is a major UK retailer that provides a range of ancillary services, including financial services.

Website

The Sainsbury home page is arranged with headings including about us, responsibility, investor centre and company blog. This page also provides links to the latest group stories, group reports, and the company's Twitter feed.[80] The 'about us' web pages provide brief outlines of the management and board, the company strategy and objectives, its values and commitments, its business structure and property, and some history.[81]

The responsibility web pages provide case studies, fact sheets and general information on the company's approach, values and progress, and the organisations with which it engages.[82] The 'our approach' pages explain how the group manages its sustainability commitments. They make a business case for the group's sustainability commitments, they explain how the governance structures at board and operating levels assist to direct and implement their sustainability plan, and they note that a focus on the most material issues and opportunities helps the group to make a more direct link between the commercial strategy and the challenges faced regarding responsible operations.

The investor centre pages provide access to share price information, financial performance analysis, annual reports, results and presentations, corporate governance material, a shareholder centre, a financial calendar, an investment case, analyst

80. J Sainsbury plc, 'Home', viewed 28 May 2015, http://www.j-sainsbury.co.uk/home/.
81. J Sainsbury plc, 'About us', viewed 28 May 2015, http://www.j-sainsbury.co.uk/about-us/.
82. J Sainsbury plc, 'Responsibility', viewed 28 May 2015, http://www.j-sainsbury.co.uk/responsibility/.

consensus figures, securitisation reports, green loan details, and investor news.[83] The share price information pages provide historical details, share price charts, an investment calculator, and a list of the major shareholders. The financial performance pages provide a summary of the income statements for the last two years, some financial performance metrics for the same period, and some data for a four year period. The nature of these figures and metrics are limited and many are calculated on an underlying basis, with only some reconciled to the reported results.[84] The annual reports pages provide access to the sustainability plan, the annual report, the group bank report and the accompanying Pillar 3 disclosure statement. The results and presentations pages include access to quarterly trading statements, preliminary results, the annual general meeting disclosures, company presentations and analyst seminars. This material can be filtered by type of report and relevant year.[85] The corporate governance web pages provide broad overviews and access to director and management biographies and terms of reference documentation. The shareholder centre pages include a warning from the FSA regarding unsolicited calls, they explain how to manage and view shareholder information online, and they provide historical dividend details.[86] The financial calendar includes historical and future events. This web page allows users to add the future events to their own calendars and provides links to historical documentation.[87] The investment case web pages provide high level outlines of the business strategy, a company overview, and the chairman's statement in the annual report. An 'analyst consensus' page provides the average, minimum and maximum analyst estimates for the group profit before tax, earnings per share and dividends per share for the current and next year. The company indicates that it seeks to keep the figures updated and consistent, but notes that it is under no obligation to do so. When viewed, the figures were dated 1 May 2015.[88] The securitisation web page provides access to bond holder reports relating to a refinancing transaction in 2006. The green loan page outlines the use of a commercial loan to invest in carbon reduction and other sustainability projects.[89] The investor news web pages provide news with picture boxes and headings and access to news released through the regulated news service (RNS). The RNS news can be filtered by type and announcement title and content.

83. J Sainsbury plc, 'Investor Centre', viewed 31 May 2015, http://www.j-sainsbury.co.uk/investor-centre/.
84. See, e.g., J Sainsbury plc, 'Financial Performance', viewed 31 May 2015, http://www.j-sainsbury.co.uk/investor-centre/financial-performance/5-year-summary/#tabbed_section.
85. J Sainsbury plc, 'Shareholder Centre', viewed 31 May 2015, http://www.j-sainsbury.co.uk/investor-centre/shareholder-centre/.
86. J Sainsbury plc, 'Results and Presentations', viewed 31 May 2015, http://www.j-sainsbury.co.uk/investor-centre/results-and-presentations/?articles_category = &articles_date = #form_filter_media.
87. J Sainsbury plc, 'Financial Calendar', viewed 31 May 2015, http://www.j-sainsbury.co.uk/investor-centre/financial-calendar/.
88. J Sainsbury plc, 'Analyst Consensus', viewed 31 May 2015, http://www.j-sainsbury.co.uk/investor-centre/analyst-consensus/.
89. J Sainsbury plc, 'Green Loan', viewed 31 May 2015, http://www.j-sainsbury.co.uk/investor-centre/green-loan/.

Preliminary Final & Annual Reports

The Sainsbury preliminary results for the year to 17 March 2012 include advance access details to the result presentation and webcast. The content of this report is similar to the 2012 half year report. The Sainsbury 2012 annual report contains full page pictures. The discussion in the CEO and chairman's letters is upbeat but vague. KPIs for five years are provided,[90] but most of the financial indicators are measures that are not in accordance with IFRS. For example, the figure for underlying profit before tax excludes profit or loss on disposal of profits, investment property fair value movements, financing fair value movements, International Accounting Standard (IAS) pension financing credit, impairment of goodwill and one-off items. The non-financial KPIs are broad statements rather than specified metrics.

The preliminary results for the year to 14 March 2015 include the result announcement, presentation slides and supplementary information, and the analyst webcast and transcript.[91] The MD&A in the result announcement, presentation and supplementary documentation includes some trend analysis and explanations of the factors impacting the results. However, the information presented is not easy to integrate and this task is made more difficult by repeated use of underlying figures as the primary information. While these figures are generally explained, the reconciliation processes are cumbersome and explanations regarding the excluded items are relatively brief. Similarly, the guidance commentary and items are difficult to apply and assess on a combined basis. The structure and content of the 2014 annual report is similar to the 2012 report.

Interim Reports

The Sainsbury half yearly report for the six months to 29 September 2012 has limited financial notes and MD&A. The MD&A provides vague discussion about the group's aspirations and values. The commentary discusses the underlying results for the period.[92] The content of the Sainsbury IMS statement for the 14 weeks to 5 January 2013 is limited to quarterly sales growth percentages and supermarket numbers. While the IMS provides broad trend indicators, the commentary is too general to determine or assess the company's financial or operational positions.

The material for the fourth quarter of 2015 includes the trading statement, a corporate responsibility and sustainability update, and an analyst call webcast and

90. The five-year earnings per share and diluted earnings per share records are not included in the table.
91. J Sainsbury plc, 'Fourth Quarter Trading Statement', viewed 1 June 2015, http://www.j-sainsbury.co.uk/investor-centre/results-and-presentations/2015/fourth-quarter-trading-statement/.
92. Reconciliations to figures that comply with accounting standards are provided in the financial statements.

transcript.[93] The content highlights broad performance trends relative to the general industry.

Sustainability Reports

The Sainsbury sustainability plan is rather vague in terms of strategy and details. The group vision is to 'be the most trusted retailer where people love to work and shop.'[94] The stated goal of the group is to 'make all our customers' lives easier every day by offering great quality and service at fair prices.' The priorities and focus of the sustainability plan are great food; compelling general merchandise and clothing; complementary channels and services; developing new business; and growing space and creating property value.[95] The highlighted corporate responsibility categories are: best for food and health; sourcing with integrity; respect for our environment; making a positive difference to our community; and a great place to work.

The 2014 sustainability report is presented as an update on progress so far.[96] The focus areas remain the same as in 2012, but the structure and content of this report are clear and informative. The front of this report lists 20 specific goals across the focus areas to be achieved by 2020. These goals are well connected to the group businesses and likely stakeholder sustainability concerns.[97] The report provides overviews of the company's suitability strategy, its business case, its framework for governance and delivery of its commitments, and its progress so far. The progress so far is summarised in a performance table that outlines the specific commitments and the progress achieved during each of the last three years. The remainder of the report explains these achievements in more detail.

5. JAPAN

Case Studies

The two companies chosen for review are Sumitomo Mitsui Financial Group and Sony Corporation because two of the largest sectors represented on the TSE are banks and electrical appliances.

93. J Sainsbury plc, 'Preliminary Results Announcement', viewed 28 May 2015, http://www.j-sainsbury.co.uk/investor-centre/results-and-presentations/2015/preliminary-results-announcement/.
94. Sainsbury, *20 x 20 Sustainability Plan* 3, viewed 27 June 2013, http://www.j-sainsbury.co.uk/responsibility/.
95. Sainsbury, *20 x 20 Sustainability Plan* 3, viewed 27 June 2013, http://www.j-sainsbury.co.uk/responsibility/.
96. Sainsbury, *Our 20 Sustainability Commitments To Help Us All Live Well For Less – An Update On Our Progress So Far*, 1 June 2015, available at http://www.j-sainsbury.co.uk/investor-centre/reports/2014/20x20-sustainability-plan-2014-update/.
97. Importantly, the sustainability targets are sufficiently clear and specific for all stakeholders to assess the priorities and performance of the company.

A. *Sumitomo Mitsui Financial Group*

Sumitomo Mitsui Financial (Sumitomo) is the largest financial services group in Japan. Sumitomo has a primary listing on the TSE and is listed on the NYSE as an American Depositary Receipt.

Website

The Sumitomo home page connects to a company profile, investor relations, corporate social responsibility, and news releases.[98] The company profile pages include a message from top management, a company overview, and information about the group mission, the corporate management system, the executives, the organisation and the credit ratings.[99] The message from top management includes an update and progress on achievement of key financial metrics. The company overview provides brief outlines of the group's subsidiary companies. The mission statement contains three high level goals. The corporate management system pages provide access to commentary from the annual report on corporate governance, compliance, internal audit and the risk management policy. The executive page includes the names, titles and responsibilities of the directors and senior executives. The organisation page provides a high level organisation chart.

The investor relations web pages provide links to financial information, stock information, debt investors, a company calendar, and the disclosure policy.[100] They also provide access to the latest news releases. The financial information web pages include the financial results and investor presentations, annual reports and SEC filings, financial highlights, fixed income investor presentations, investor presentations at small meetings, capital ratio information, a road map to risk management disclosure, and general meeting information.[101] The result material for the second quarters and full year include the financial results, supplementary information a presentation and video, a data book, and the press announcement. The result material for the first and third quarters is more limited and includes the financial results, an overview, and a presentation at a broker conference.[102] The group provides two financial reports; one in accordance with IFRS, and the other in accordance with Japanese generally accepted accounting principles (JGAAP). The supplementary information provides detailed financial notes. The data book provides additional material including trend analysis. The financial results include the financial statements with limited notes and MD&A. The supplementary information and data book provide more detailed financial notes.

98. Sumitomo Mitsui Financial Group, 'Home', viewed 1 June 2015, www.smfg.co.jp/english/.
99. Sumitomo Mitsui Financial Group, 'Company Profile', viewed 1 June 2015, http://www.smfg.co.jp/english/aboutus/.
100. Sumitomo Mitsui Financial Group, 'IR Information', viewed 1 June 2015, http://www.smfg.co.jp/english/investor/.
101. Sumitomo Mitsui Financial Group, 'Financial Information', viewed 1 June 2015, http://www.smfg.co.jp/english/investor/financial/statement.html.
102. Sumitomo Mitsui Financial Group, 'Financial Results & Investor Presentations', viewed 1 June 2015, http://www.smfg.co.jp/english/investor/financial/latest_statement.html.

The author found it difficult to dissect the key factors impacting the financial performance and future growth prospects from this result material. The presentation content is clear, but is very brief for the first and third quarters and is still relatively short for the second quarter and full year. The presentations for fixed income investors provide a clearer picture of the competitive position of the group. The risk management disclosure web pages allow access to documents that explain the group's risk governance and risk management strategies, capital adequacy, and framework for managing varying types of risk.[103] The stock information provides information on the shares, principal shareholders, dividends, the American Depository Receipts and analyst names. The debt investor web pages are similar to those in the investor pages but there are tailored presentations and information on the debt and capital securities.

The CSR web pages include information from the recent CSR reports. These reports are available on the website back to 2006. The areas of focus in the 2012 report are: support for reconstruction following the earthquake in Japan, the environment, improving the lives of senior citizens, and contributions to enhance the globalisation of Japan. These areas of focus remain the same in the 2014 report. When reviewed on 1 June 2015, the website outlined various processes and certifications awarded, but specific goals, key metrics and performance analysis were not found.[104]

Preliminary Final & Annual Reports

The Sumitomo preliminary final results for the year to 31 March 2012 include a report of the consolidated results in compliance with JGAAP, supplementary information, a performance overview, a Q&A document, the presentation slides, a data book, and the press conference announcement. The report includes key performance metrics, an operating and financial review, a group organisation chart, an outline of the management policy, and the consolidated and non-consolidated financial statements with notes. The operating and financial review presents the results in summary form and risk factors, and it includes an earnings forecast and outlook statement for the next year. The management policy pages include targeted indices for the core Tier one ratio, profitability metrics, an overseas banking ratio, a high level strategic statement, and issues to be addressed. The letters from the President and CEO in the Sumitomo 2012 annual report outline the group strategy. The overview explains the business segments. A set of five year consolidated and non-consolidated financial statements are provided with notes. The risk management plan and processes are explained in detail. The end of the report includes comprehensive financial and corporate data.

The 20-F report for the year to 31 March 2014 is listed on the company website as the annual report. This report provides a more integrated and comprehensive picture of the group's strategies, businesses, activities, risks and financial position than the other

103. Sumitomo Mitsui Financial Group, 'Road Map to Risk Management Disclosure', viewed 1 June 2015, http://www.smfg.co.jp/english/investor/financial/link.html.
104. Sumitomo Mitsui Financial Group, 'Corporate Social Responsibility', viewed 1 June 2015, http://www.smfg.co.jp/english/responsibility/.

reports and website material. It also provides greater clarity around the performance trends and drivers over the prior three to five years.

Interim Reports

The interim report for the six months to 30 September 2012 was submitted to the SEC on Form 6-K. This report outlines the economic and regulatory environments and provides detailed financial notes and MD&A. The 6-K for the six months to 30 September 2015 provides similar content.

The quarterly report for the nine months to 30 December 2012 includes financial statements, supplementary data and limited MD&A. The result material for the nine months to 31 December 2014 is similar, with limited MD&A and presentation content.

Continuous Disclosure

News releases are available on the website back to 2004.

Corporate Social Responsibility Reports

The 2012 CSR report includes a summary table with the targets and performance achieved across each of the focus areas. A range of data is provided but a large portion of the report concerns earthquake reconstruction programs. The focus areas of the 2014 CSR report are the same as those in the 2012 report, but the content is largely descriptive and the stated goals are broad.

B. Sony Corporation

Sony Corporation (Sony) has a primary listing on the TSE and is listed on the NYSE as an American Depositary Receipt.

Website

The Sony home page is arranged with headings for corporate information, news releases, investor relations, and CSR.[105] The corporate information page is very short. A webcast explains the group strategy and measures to return the group to profitability following a series of losses. The investor relations web pages provide access to material relating to the corporate strategy, events, financial information, news, and information on corporate stocks and bonds.[106] A strategy statement from the President and CEO on 18 February 2015 provides an update on the turnaround plans. This statement provides

105. Sony Corporation, 'home', viewed 1 June 2015, http://www.sony.net/.
106. Sony Corporation, 'Investor Relations', viewed 1 June 2015, http://www.sony.net/SonyInfo/IR/?j-short=IR.

a frank appraisal of the performance over the first three years of the restructuring plan, why the performance targets were not achieved, and the revised vision, specific plans and financial targets for the next three years. A web page provides access to material from investor days in 2014 and 2015, including presentations from senior executives and webcasts of these events.[107] The events web page is arranged chronologically, with links to individual event details. The result material includes the earnings announcement and report, supplementary information, presentations and a webcast and audio.[108] The stock and corporate bonds web pages provide information about the shares issued and ownership, the stock price, the bonds issued, and ratings. The CSR and environment area provides material on the management, product responsibility, responsible sourcing, training, development technology for sustainable development, and news releases.

Preliminary Final & Annual Reports

The Sony preliminary final results for the year ended 31 March 2012 include financial statements and segmental reporting by business segment, product category and geography. The results are reported in yen and US dollars. The financial notes, MD&A and presentation slides are limited in content. The report includes an outlook segment with revenue and profit forecasts for the next year.

The annual report for 2012 is short despite including business and CSR reviews. It includes a five-year financial performance table and a set of financial statements including three years of data. The report is in the traditional format with full-page pictures and high-level commentary. The strategy outline includes specific targets for the next year. The 20-F form submitted to the SEC for the 2012 year contains more comprehensive financial notes than the annual report.

The preliminary result material for the year to 31 March 2015 is similar in content to the 2012 report.[109] The presentation slides provide useful data to understand the result drivers. When the website was reviewed on 1 June 2015, the annual report and 20-K for the year to 31 March 2015 were not available. The 20-K for the year to 31 March 2014 contains most of the information on the website in an integrated form. It explains the history and development of the company. It provides a business overview including detailed segmental and geographical impacts, an organisational structure, and the major risks. It outlines the board practices, the directors and senior management, the capital structure, and the major shareholders. It provides a five year financial performance table and it outlines and discusses the financial performance for the prior three years.

107. Sony Corporation, 'Sony IR Day', viewed 1 June 2015, http://www.sony.net/SonyInfo/IR/library/irday/.
108. Sony Corporation, 'FY2014 Earnings Announcement', viewed 1 June 2015, http://www.sony.net/SonyInfo/IR/info/presen/index.html.
109. Sony Corporation, 'IR Events', viewed 1 June 2015, http://www.sony.net/SonyInfo/IR/info/calendar/index.html.

Interim Reports

The Sony quarterly reports for 2012 provide consolidated financial statements and segmental results by business segment and geography. Each report references an annual forecast and explains whether it remains unchanged or has been revised. For example, the report for the third quarter of 2012 indicated that the forecast remained unchanged, but an announcement on 25 April 2013 revised the forecasts upwards. This announcement is clearly labeled as a 'forecast revision'.[110]

The result material for the third quarter of 2014 includes the earnings release, presentation slides and a webcast including the question and answer session, supplementary information, financial targets for the mobile communications segment and a 2014 financial year forecast revision announcement.[111] This material includes the financial statements and limited financial notes and MD&A. The earnings release includes an outlook statement with specific forecasts and this is updated in a forecast revision announcement.

Continuous Disclosure

News releases are available from the website from 2002.[112]

Corporate Social Responsibility Reports

The Sony 2012 CSR report is included within the annual report. The focus areas include corporate governance, compliance, human resources, sourcing, services, environment, and community involvement processes. Specific targets are included in the environment section. The focus areas in the 2014 CSR report remain the same as those in the 2012 report. Most of the content is commentary, with occasional performance indicators and discussion.

6. HONG KONG

Case Studies

The two companies selected for review are PetroChina Limited and China Mobile because these are two of the largest companies listed on the HKEx by market capitalisation.

110. Sony Group, 'Investor Relations', viewed 29 June 2013, http://www.sony.net/SonyInfo/IR/financial/fr/index.html.
111. Sony Corporation, 'Events Materials', viewed 1 June 2015, http://www.sony.net/SonyInfo/IR/library/presentation/index.html.
112. Sony Corporation, 'IR News', viewed 1 June 2015, http://www.sony.net/SonyInfo/IR/news/2015.html.

A. PetroChina Company Limited

PetroChina Company Limited (PetroChina) is a global oil and gas producer and distributor. PetroChina is incorporated in the People's Republic of China with A shares listed on the Shanghai Stock Exchange, H shares listed on the HKEx, and American Deposit Shares representing H shares listed on the NYSE.

Website

The PetroChina home page includes headings for 'about us', investor relations, news and bulletins, products and services, society and environment, and work and career.[113] The content in the 'about us' area includes a company profile, the director and executives names, an organisational chart, core business outlines, the business strategy, and a research and development framework. The products and services pages provide overviews of the products, services and brands. The news and bulletin pages include news releases, business announcements and corporate announcements.[114] The society and environment pages provide access to the sustainability reports and broad overviews on health, safety and the environment.

The investor relations pages include information on the corporate governance structure, the company stock, periodic reports, result announcements, roadshows, prospectuses, and frequently asked questions and answers.[115] The corporate governance pages include information concerning shareholder meetings, directors and the board, the supervisory committee, performance assessment and incentives, disclosure, and code of ethics. The differences in corporate governance practices for the group and a company listed as a US domestic issuer under the NYSE corporate governance rules are clearly explained. The annual, half yearly and quarterly periodic reports are available for review or downloading. The result announcements are divided into annual and interim results. The annual results announcement is a summary of the annual report and the interim result announcements form a summary of the six monthly interim report.[116] The roadshow page includes headings for the press conferences and behind these headings are the press releases, results announcements, presentations, and audio webcasts with English translations. The audios do not include the question and answer sessions.[117] The outlook content in the presentation is general.

113. Petrochina Company Limited, 'Home', viewed 2 June 2015, http://www.petrochina.com.cn/ptr/.
114. Petrochina Company Limited, 'Investor Relations', viewed 2 June 2015, http://www.petrochina.com.cn/ptr/tzzgx/tzzgx.shtml.
115. Petrochina Company Limited, 'News & Bulletin', viewed 2 June 2015, http://www.petrochina.com.cn/ptr/xwygg/xwygg.shtml.
116. Petrochina Company Limited, 'Announcement of Results', viewed 2 June 2015, http://www.petrochina.com.cn/ptr/ndyjgb/dqbg_list.shtml.
117. See, e.g., Petrochina Company Limited, '2014 Annual Results Announcement', viewed 2 June 2015, http://mms.prnasia.com/00857/20150326/audio/default.htm.

Preliminary Final & Annual Reports

The PetroChina 2012 annual report includes upfront key financial data, a five-year table of income statement prepared under IFRS, three years of summary income statement figures under Chinese accounting standards (CAS), and a few pictures. The Chairman's report provides high-level commentary. The business operating review outlines market and business developments. It also provides MD&A of the financial position and the operating results. An initial set of financial statements complies with China accounting standards and another is prepared in accordance with IFRS. Both sets of financials report are given in Renminbi (Rmb) and include financial notes.

The 2014 annual report is similar in structure and content to the 2012 report. The company's 'story' for investors and other stakeholders is explained only at a high level. A five year performance table is included but the performance trends are not discussed. The most comprehensive and highest quality information on the company is found in the 20-F reports. At the time of review, the latest 20-F report available was for 2013.[118]

Interim Reports

The PetroChina half year report to 31 June 2012 includes two sets of unaudited financial statements; one prepared in accordance with CAS, the other in compliance with IFRS. The financial statements include prior period comparatives and some financial notes. The MD&A in the Directors' Report includes market and production content. It also provides commentary on the income, cash flow and capital expenditure items. The PetroChina report for the nine months to 30 September 2012 provides a summary of the results upfront, plus a short business review. A full set of financial statements under IFRS is included with limited notes.

The 2014 half year report includes financial statements in accordance with CAS and IFRS and limited MD&A and financial notes. The report for the first quarter of 2015 includes financial statements with very limited MD&A and financial notes.

Continuous Disclosures

Some news releases, corporate announcements and business announcements are available from the PetroChina website.

Sustainability Reports

The 2012 PetroChina sustainability report focus areas include corporate governance, sustained energy supply, operational safety, customer service, employee development, and society contributions. The report includes case studies, the objectives and plans for

118. See, e.g., '2013 United States Securities And Exchange Commission Form 20-F', viewed 2 June 2015, http://www.petrochina.com.cn/ptr/ndbg/201404/252d8f90385d457487103d8a9b2a0577.shtml.

the year relating to economic outcomes, safety, environment, employees, and public welfare, and a five year statistical table.

The structure and content of the 2014 sustainability report are similar to the 2012 report. The five year statistical table comprises business statistics (labelled as economic statistics), two safety statistics (death rate caused by accidents and total accident rate), three employee statistics (number of employees, percentage of employees receiving occupational health checks and percentage of non-Chinese nationals), four public welfare statistics (donations for poverty alleviation, education, disaster relief and environmental protection), and three environmental statistics (energy conserved, water conserved, and oil discharged in waste water).

B. China Mobile Limited

China Mobile Limited (China Mobile) is a Chinese state-owned telecommunication company that was incorporated in Hong Kong in 1997. China Mobile has a primary listing on the HKEx and is listed on the NYSE as a foreign issuer.

Website

The home page of China Mobile is arranged with headings for 'about China Mobile', investor relations, media centre, and our business.[119] The 'about China Mobile' pages include an overview, a chairman's statement, and information on the board of directors, milestones, credit ratings, corporate governance, and sustainable development.[120] The credit ratings page shows the change in ratings for the period 2003 to the present. The corporate governance web pages provide well-written commentary on the role and function of directors, shareholder rights, shareholder value and communication, attention to other stakeholders, the board of directors, the board committees with descriptions of each committee, its membership, responsibilities and work done in 2014. This page also discusses the role of management and employees, the internal and external audit and control frameworks, and the differences between the company's corporate governance processes and those required by the NYSE.[121] The sustainable development page provides an overview and access to the sustainability reports from 2006 to the present. The media centre contains press releases, news highlights, and photo and video galleries. The 'our business' pages provide a business review, a financial review and outlines of the key products and services, and the network and technologies.

The investor relations web pages provide operation data, stock information, financial reports, presentations and webcasts, announcements, SEC filings, circulars,

119. China Mobile, 'home', viewed 2 June 2015, http://www.chinamobileltd.com/en/global/home.php.
120. China Mobile, 'About China Mobile', viewed 2 June 2015, http://www.chinamobileltd.com/en/about/overview.php.
121. China Mobile, 'Corporate Governance', viewed 2 June 2015, http://www.chinamobileltd.com/en/about/cg.php.

analyst coverage and frequently asked questions.[122] The data pages provide operations data by month and operations and financial data by quarter and year from 1998.[123] The stock information pages provide a stock quote and chart, dividend and stock price histories, a company calendar, share information, and a novel share price chart with the timing of announcements, reports and circulars marked, and the summary details when highlighted.[124] The financial reports are presented as annual sets from 2006 to 2014 including the interim report, annual report and 20-F report. The presentations and webcast page includes the annual and interim presentations and webcasts arranged chronologically. The webcasts do not include the question and answer sessions.

Preliminary Final & Annual Reports

The China Mobile preliminary final results for the year ended 31 December 2012 contain a chairman's statement, financial statements and minimal notes. A video and slides of the results presentation are provided in English. The 2012 China Mobile annual report includes a letter from the chairman, a business review with high-level commentary on the strategy and outlook, and a financial review with MD&A of the operating results. The financial statements are in Rmb, are prepared in accordance with IFRS, and include prior year comparatives. A five-year table of the income statement is provided at the rear of the report. The report includes a few pictures. The China Mobile 20-F for 2012 includes a summary performance table incorporating income statement and balance sheet data for six years. It also includes a detailed risk outline, with consideration given to general industry risks and risks specific to the telecommunications industry in mainland China. A section entitled 'information on the company' explains the business model in more detail than the annual report and the financial statements and notes are more expansive and specific.

The presentation and content of the 2014 annual report are similar to the 2012 report. The contextual information is well-written but limited. The most substantive and useful information about the group is contained within the 2014 20-F. However, this report does not comprehensively discuss or analyse the profit and earnings per share trends over the prior five years, nor how the company expects to improve these outcomes going forward.

Interim Reports

The China Mobile interim report for the six months to 30 June 2012 includes a Chairman's statement with high-level commentary, unaudited financial statements, and limited financial notes. The China Mobile results for the three months to 31 March

122. China Mobile, 'Investor Relations', viewed 2 June 2015, http://www.chinamobileltd.com/en/ir/operation.php.
123. China Mobile, 'Operation Data', viewed 2 June 2015, http://www.chinamobileltd.com/en/ir/operation.php.
124. China Mobile, 'Stock Information', viewed 2 June 2015, http://www.chinamobileltd.com/en/ir/stockinfo.php?section = shareinfo.

2013 include summary financial and operating data and commentary. Operating revenue, operating profit, and profit attributable to equity shareholders are included. These figures are described as KPIs based on the group's unaudited management accounts, and investors are cautioned not to unduly rely on the data. No quarterly reports or data could be found for 2014.

The structure and content of the interim report for 2014 are similar to the 2012 interim report. No MD&A is included other than the Chairman's statement.

Continuous Disclosures

The company announcements are available back to 2000. The nature and scope of these releases are limited.

Sustainability Reports

The focus areas of the China Mobile 2012 sustainability report include corporate governance, sustained energy supply, operational safety, customer service, employee development, and societal contributions. The report includes a performance table with an outline of the key issues, achievements in 2012, and a column for looking forward to 2013. It provides a 2012 sustainability performance summary, with metrics across the focus areas and an independent assurance report.

The 2014 sustainability report is framed around three goals, namely responsible business, inclusive growth, and sustainable values. The responsible business focus includes compliance with corporate governance standards, the provision of a reliable network and trustworthy consumption. Inclusive growth encompasses growth with employees, win-win development with industry, and sharing with the community. Sustainable values include innovation and transformation, information and wellbeing, and green and future. A sustainability performance summary is provided at the rear of the report, with three years of data for various metrics.

7. AUSTRALIA

Case Studies

The two largest sectors represented on the ASX by market value are resources and finance. Thus, the two companies selected for review are BHP Billiton and Commonwealth Bank.

A. *BHP Billiton Plc; BHP Billiton Limited*

BHP Billiton Limited (BHP) is the largest resource group in the world by market value. BHP has dual listings on the ASX and LSE.[125]

Website

The BHP home page is arranged with headings for 'about us', business, society, people and careers, and investors and media.[126] The 'about us' web pages provide information on the company, leadership and strategy. The leadership page outlines the directors and management. The overviews of the company and its strategy are short but well-written. The business pages provide summaries of the coal, copper, iron ore and petroleum and potash businesses, including the executives and main assets. They also provide an overview on marketing and a global location map.[127] The society pages provide information on 'our contribution', the environment, operating with integrity, community and sustainability reports, community and sustainability news, climate change, indigenous communities, and regulatory information.[128] The content on most of these pages is tailored and integrated, with links to specific project information and news. The regulatory information is arranged by project within the product groups.[129] For example, the Mt Arthur Coal pages include the environmental management plans, environmental monitoring information, annual environmental management reports, independent environmental audits, the annual *Environment Protection and Biodiversity Conservation Act 1999* (Cth) compliance documents, blast information, community information including complaints reports, the Mt Arthur coal community consultative committee meeting documents, coal transport information, environment protection licence pollution studies and reduction programs, the Mt Arthur coal open cut mine modification project exhibition documents, project exhibitions, assessments and approvals, and the sustainable development policy.[130]

The investors and media web pages include news, shareholder information, owner relations, an image gallery, demerger information, reports and presentations, debt investors, a calendar, and 2014 annual reporting and key contacts.[131] The news can be filtered by year or activity. The shareholder information includes a share price

125. The review of this company was begun prior to the demerger of South32, approved by BHP Billiton shareholders on 6 May 2015.
126. BHP Billiton, 'Resourcing the Future', viewed 2 June 2015, http://www.bhpbilliton.com/home/Pages/default.aspx.
127. BHP Billiton, 'Businesses', viewed 2 June 2015, http://www.bhpbilliton.com/home/businesses/Pages/default.aspx.
128. BHP Billiton, 'Society', viewed 2 June 2015, http://www.bhpbilliton.com/home/Society/Pages/default.aspx.
129. BHP Billiton, 'Society', viewed 2 June 2015, http://www.bhpbilliton.com/home/Society/Pages/default.aspx.
130. BHP Billiton, 'Society', viewed 2 June 2015, http://www.bhpbilliton.com/home/Society/Pages/default.aspx.
131. BHP Billiton, 'Regulatory Information', viewed 3 June 2015, http://www.bhpbilliton.com/home/society/regulatory/Pages/default.aspx.

chart and information concerning online services, dividends, meetings including the annual general meetings, capital management including share buyback details, and frequently asked questions.[132] The owner relations pages provide documents relating to shale assets acquired by the company in Arkansas, Louisiana and Texas in the US. The image gallery can be filtered by 'People & Company' and 'Location & Operations'. The demerger page provides information concerning the demerger of South32, approved by BHP Billiton shareholders on 6 May 2015. The reports and presentation web pages provide access to all of the company reports and presentations, with search functionality by report type, presentation type, year, location, and business.[133] The debt investor pages provide credit ratings and documentation arranged by country. The calendar outlines future events.[134] The annual reporting pages provide access to sections of the 2014 annual report and 2014 sustainability report.[135] The key contacts page provides phone and email contacts for shareholders and the media by country group. When reviewed on 3 June 2015, no performance information or analysis (financial or non-financial) was found on the website beyond that included in the interim and annual reports, which is curious given the long economic, business and project cycles of resource companies.

Preliminary Final & Annual Reports

The BHP preliminary final report for 2012 includes financial statements and limited financial notes and commentary. The BHP 2012 annual report provides an upfront key information section. The content includes a brief summary of the business, the chairman's review and CEO report, selected key measures, and an outline of the risks. The key measures include a 5 year financial performance table with indicators from the income statement, balance sheet and other financial information.[136] A table of operational performance indicators for three years is also provided, including a range of production data and single injury frequency and community investment metrics. The main body of the report provides business information, an operating and financial review, corporate governance information, and a directors' report. The financial statements for three years and notes are at the rear. The report does not contain pictures.[137] The use of headings, shadowing and black and orange colours enhances the readability of the online version.

The preliminary result material for the year ended 30 June 2014 includes the news release, the result presentation, webcast and transcript, and an additional

132. BHP Billiton, 'Shareholder Information', viewed 3 June 2015, http://www.bhpbilliton.com/home/investors/shareholderinfo/Pages/default.aspx.
133. BHP Billiton, 'Reports & Presentations', viewed 3 June 2015, http://www.bhpbilliton.com/home/investors/reports/Pages/default.aspx.
134. No access details were found.
135. BHP Billiton, 'Annual Report 2014', viewed 3 June 2015, http://www.bhpbilliton.com/home/investors/annualreporting2014/Pages/default.aspx.
136. The section entitled 'other financial information' includes figures not in accordance with IFRS and readers are referred to a future section for a reconciliation.
137. In contrast, the summary review 2012 provides lots of glossy pictures and high-level commentary. The intended audience of this glossy brochure is not clear.

presentation on unlocking shareholder value. Access details to the presentation webcast are provided. The nature and scope of the MD&A and financial notes are limited and as such, it is not possible to fully integrate the MD&A and financial statements. The result release focuses primarily on underlying figures without complete reconciliations or reasons for using these figures. The comparative figures are limited to the prior two years, and some of these figures are restated without notes explaining why the restatements were made. This author found the result presentation difficult to follow because of the exclusion of a large number of items from the underlying figures. The prospective commentary and guidance indicators are ambiguous and difficult to apply. More positively, the slides include an excellent sensitivity table that outlines the estimated impact of factors on net profit.

The presentation and content of the 2014 annual report is similar to the 2012 annual report. The report is arranged in nine sections including a strategic report, asset outlines, a corporate governance statement, the remuneration report, the directors' report, legal proceedings, financial statements, glossary, and shareholder information. Most of the report is commentary. A KPI section includes total shareholder return and underlying EBIT, but no reported profitability or earnings per share measures. Similarly, the business sections of the reports use these underlying figures without entry point reconciliations.[138] One can legitimately question the 'exceptional' nature of some of the excluded items and the appropriateness of MD&A that references primary non-compliant measures, particularly when the reader is left to make the relevant connections and reconciliations. A five year summary table provides the most useful performance data in the report, as it includes key items from the reported income statement over the prior five year period, and additional non-compliant figures such as underlying EBITDA and EBIT. The 2014 20-F report submitted to the SEC uses a similar format and provides similar content to the annual report, but includes additional contextual information and financial notes.

Interim Reports

The BHP report for the six months ended 31 December 2012 includes condensed financial statements. The balance sheet notes are limited and only high level risk commentary is provided. The segmental results are reported by revenue and underlying EBIT. Most of the MD&A refers to underlying profit figures with readers referred to footnotes on other pages for the relevant definitions. The period covered in the report is restricted to two years and the MD&A is limited, but a short outline of the impact of volume changes, prices, exchange rates and costs is included. The supplementary information provides customer segment and product segment reporting. Explanation with respect to $3.5 billion in exceptional items and impairments is brief.

The result material for the six months ended 31 December 2014 includes the news release and the result presentation, webcast and transcript. The presentation and

138. The reader of the key performance indicator section is referred to section 1.11 for reconciliations of underlying EBIT to profit from operations. Section 1.11 then refers the reader to section 1.15.3 for an outline of the exceptional items.

content provided are similar to that contained in the 2012 material and the preliminary final result for the year to 30 June 2014.

Continuous Disclosures

While the website provides news releases, these do not include all of the ASX and LSE announcements.

Sustainability Reports

The areas of focus in the BHP 2012 sustainability report are people, environment, society, and governance. The report provides a performance table that outlines specific 2012 targets and outcomes, with indicators reflecting whether the target was achieved or not. Specific targets for the period 2013 to 2017 are also provided. Performance data is provided at the end of the report with varying content and time periods. The report is prepared in accordance with the Global Reporting Initiative Framework and the International Council on Mining and Metals Sustainable Development Framework, and an independent assurance opinion is included.

The 2014 sustainability report contains well-written commentary but limited specific or identifiable long-term goals, targets and performance analysis. A performance table at the start of the report provides general targets and performance commentary, and targets based on percentage movement from base figures that are not immediately explained in close proximity. Moreover, a performance table at the end of the report provides only two years of data. The only five year performance data included relates to employee occupational illness, total energy use, and greenhouse gas emissions (GHG). The goals for the first two measures are to respectively prevent and manage occupational illness and progress energy efficiency measures. The GHG target is to maintain 2017 levels to the baseline established in 2006.[139]

B. Commonwealth Bank of Australia Limited

The Commonwealth Bank of Australia Limited (CBA) is the largest bank and financial group in Australia.

Website

The investor relations home page of the CBA website is arranged with headings for careers, 'who we are', investors, and media & news.[140] The 'who we are' area provides

139. BHP Billiton, *Value Through Performance Sustainability Report 2014* 27. The author could not find the baseline 2006 greenhouse gas emission figure in this report.
140. Commonwealth Bank of Australia Ltd, 'Shareholders', viewed 3 June 2015, https://www.commbank.com.au/about-us/investors/shareholders.html.

a company overview and information about the management team, the group approach to diversity, international branches, and corporate governance.[141] The company overview page includes information about the company, its sustainability and community approaches, and its consumer commitments. The content of some of these pages overlaps. The profile information includes broad commentary that explains the company history, its structure, businesses, international network, some key facts and figures, and a broad strategic statement. The management team pages include biographies and photos of the senior executives. The corporate governance pages include the corporate governance statement and the risk management and governance process outlines from the annual report, the shareholder communication guidelines, the codes of conduct policies, the employee statement of professional practice, the anti-bribery and corruption policy and framework, the whistleblower program, and information with a heading 'How we implement sustainable business practices'.[142] The sustainability web pages explain the company's approach, focus areas, news and reporting.

The shareholders centre pages include the results, presentations and speeches, a financial calendar, annual reports, regulatory disclosures, dividends information, annual general meeting documentation, announcements, and the share register profile.[143] Result information is available from 1998. The material available for each year includes the half year and preliminary full year result documents.[144] The result material includes announcements, media releases, and analyst and media presentations and webcasts. Excel and pdf templates (released in advance), downloadable excel spreadsheets, and a result glossary are also provided for more recent results.[145] The Excel spreadsheets include prior year comparatives. The presentations and speeches are listed chronologically, with many of the available documents concerning quarterly trading updates.[146] The reasons for including the quarterly updates as presentations rather than as result material are unclear. The media releases include a cash earnings figure and various contextual and trend data. The regulatory material includes disclosures relating to the Basel III standards, capital instruments, and insurance capital adequacy. The annual general meeting material includes the notice, proxy votes, chairman's address and webcast. The ASX announcements on the website are published from 2001 onwards.

141. Commonwealth Bank of Australia Ltd, 'Who We Are', viewed 3 June 2015, https://www.commbank.com.au/about-us/who-we-are.html?ei=mv_who-we-are.
142. Commonwealth Bank of Australia Ltd, 'How We Implement Sustainable Business Practices', viewed 3 June 2015, https://www.commbank.com.au/about-us/who-we-are/sustainability/sustainable-business-practices.html.
143. Commonwealth Bank of Australia Ltd, 'Shareholders', viewed 3 June 2015, https://www.commbank.com.au/about-us/investors/shareholders.html.
144. Commonwealth Bank of Australia Ltd, '2015 Results', viewed 3 June 2015, https://www.commbank.com.au/about-us/shareholders/financial-information/results.html.
145. Commonwealth Bank of Australia Ltd, '2015 Results', viewed 3 June 2015, https://www.commbank.com.au/about-us/shareholders/financial-information/results.html.
146. See, e.g., Commonwealth Bank of Australia Ltd, '2014 Presentations & Speeches', viewed 3 June 2015, https://www.commbank.com.au/about-us/shareholders/financial-information/2014-presentations-speeches.html.

Preliminary Final & Annual Reports

The content and layout of the CBA preliminary final results for the year to 30 June 2012 are similar to the annual report. Two versions of the report are provided; a pdf version for printing and an html version for reading online. While the 2012 CBA annual report contains no pictures, it provides charts and uses shades of yellow to enhance readability of the online version. The report provides an upfront group performance highlights section. The highlights section includes a KPI table for the year, market shares, and credit ratings. A paragraph explains that CBA reports on both a statutory and cash basis and why this is useful. A table is provided that reconciles the net profit after tax on a statutory and underlying basis. A summary table is included with the historical return on equity and return on assets calculations for seven years. The report provides a comprehensive five year performance table including performance ratios, productivity indicators, and a shareholder summary section.[147] The risk management section provides a general outline of risks and the high level risk management processes.

The presentation and content of the 2014 preliminary final and annual reports are similar to the 2012 reports. The preliminary final presentation provides valuable supplementary information to construct a picture of the group's position. The annual report includes a five year financial summary and shareholder contact details.

Interim Reports

The CBA half year report to 31 December 2012 provides comprehensive information. The presentation is similar to that adopted in the annual report, with initial group performance highlights, KPIs, and a shareholder summary for the half year and comparative prior year period. Additional information, such as strategic and market information, is included in the analyst presentation slides and webcast. This presentation includes discussion of sustainability issues and metrics, reflecting some integration of these processes.

The presentation and content of the CBA half year report to 31 December 2014 is similar to the 2012 half year report. The initial pages provide the equivalent of an executive summary, including performance tables and comparative analysis with prior six monthly periods. These pages include summaries of the main businesses, return analysis, KPIs, a shareholder summary, market shares and credit ratings. This provides a clear and concise picture of the group and its performance and position. The remainder of the report is presented in clear sections enhancing its readability. It includes returns on a cash basis and the equivalent returns on a statutory basis, and a full reconciliation in the appendices. The corresponding presentation slides are comprehensive, integrated and confident. They include detailed analysis of the group's external and internal environments and peer comparatives. They also include a report on the group sustainability commitments and a five year scorecard.

147. Commonwealth Bank Limited, *Annual Report 2012* 92-93.

Sustainability Reports

The focus areas of the CBA 2012 sustainability report are sustainable business practices, responsible financial services, engaged and talented people, community contribution and action, and environmental stewardship. A five year performance table is provided with metrics in each of the focus areas. A GRI Index is provided. The metrics in the performance table (referred to as a sustainability scorecard) are assured by an external party.

The full 2014 sustainability report is readable online and this author found its structure rather cumbersome.[148] The focus areas remain the same as in 2012 with similar performance indicators. The sustainability performance data is downloadable in an Excel spreadsheet, allowing users to analyse long-term trends.

8. SINGAPORE

Case Studies

The companies selected for review are Singapore Telecommunications Ltd and Keppel Corporation, two of the largest entities listed on the SGX.

A. Singapore Telecommunications Limited

Singapore Telecommunications Limited (Singtel) is the largest listed company on the Singapore Exchange.

Website

The Singtel home page is arranged with headings for our company, investor relations, news room, careers, sustainability, and tenders.[149] The 'our company' pages provide brief overviews of the group, including its vision and core values, an organisational chart, the directors and management, the subsidiaries, associates and partners, the corporate governance framework, and the global offices.[150] The corporate governance web pages outline the board committee members and the terms of reference and policy documents. The news room web page provides the company announcements arranged chronologically.[151] The content provided in the sustainability pages is generally limited

148. A spreadsheet of the sustainability performance data, the assurance report and the GRI Index report were downloadable when the website was reviewed during June 2015, but not the full report.
149. Singapore Telecommunications Limited, 'Company Profile', viewed 6 June 2015, http://info.singtel.com/about-us/company-profile.
150. Singapore Telecommunications Limited, 'Company Profile', viewed 6 June 2015, http://info.singtel.com/about-us/company-profile.
151. Singapore Telecommunications Limited, 'News Releases', viewed 6 June 2015, http://info.singtel.com/about-us/news-releases. It is not clear whether these news announcements include all of the stock exchange announcements.

to broad commentary, but some projects and activities are highlighted. Sustainability reports are available from 2010.

The investor relations web pages include the financial results, stock exchange announcements, investor calendar, annual reports and shareholder meetings, fact sheets and presentations, basic share and dividend information, financial summaries, frequently asked questions, and investor contacts.[152] The quarterly result material includes the news releases, MD&A, the announcements, presentation slides with audio, and audios and transcripts of the analyst conference calls. Most of this material is available from 2000 to the present.[153] Detailed spreadsheets of the financial reports, including the financial statements and key telecommunication inputs, can also be downloaded. Stock exchange announcements can be viewed back to 2005.[154] The annual report and shareholder meetings web pages provide access to the annual reports as complete documents or in sections, and to the annual general meeting and extraordinary general meeting documentation.[155] The factsheets and presentation pages include pdf versions of investor day, group and divisional presentations.[156] The financial summary web page provides five year income statement, balance sheet, cash flow, per share and key ratio data.[157]

Preliminary Final & Annual Reports

The Singtel result material for the fourth quarter and full year ended 31 March 2013 includes the preliminary final report, MD&A and presentation slides. The preliminary final report contains the financial statements and limited notes. The media release and presentation include revenue, EBIT and EBITDA guidance for the 2014 year. The MD&A material includes detailed financial analysis. The early pages of the Singtel 2013 annual report contain pictures and high-level commentary. A five-year financial performance table is provided, including key ratios and earnings per share.[158] The financial notes are extensive.

The result material for the further quarter and year ended 31 March 2015 is similar in content and presentation to the 2013 material. The combined information is

152. Singapore Telecommunications Limited, 'Investor Relations', viewed 6 June 2015, http://info.singtel.com/about-us/investor-relations.
153. Singapore Telecommunications Limited, 'Financial Results', viewed 6 June 2015, http://info.singtel.com/about-us/investor-relations/financial-results.
154. Singapore Telecommunications Limited, 'Stock Exchange Announcements', viewed 6 June 2015, http://info.singtel.com/about-us/investor-relations/stock-exchange-announcements#content-top.
155. Singapore Telecommunications Limited, 'Annual Reports & Shareholder Meetings', viewed 6 June 2015, http://info.singtel.com/about-us/investor-relations/annual-reports.
156. Singapore Telecommunications Limited, 'Factsheets & Presentations', viewed 6 June 2015, http://info.singtel.com/about-us/investor-relations/factsheets-presentations.
157. Singapore Telecommunications Limited, 'Financial Summary', viewed 6 June 2015, http://info.singtel.com/about-us/investor-relations/financial-summary. The inclusion of this data on the website is commendable because most of this data shows generally negative trends.
158. Singapore Telecommunications Limited, *Singapore Telecommunications Limited Annual Report 2013* 40. The financial performance table includes earnings per share and underlying earnings per share figures.

presented coherently and includes detailed information on the internal and external environments. The news release and presentation contain an outlook section that includes guidance on capital expenditure, free cash flow, dividends, revenue and EBITDA. The performance analysis is generally limited to the prior comparative quarter and year. The 2014 annual report is arranged in sections, including an overview, a business review, sustainability and governance, performance, financials and additional information. The overview contains pictures and broad commentary, with most of the metrics limited to two years. Similarly, the sustainability section contains specific metrics but only for two years. The performance section includes a five year financial summary and discussion, but the MD&A describes the historical performance for each year rather than the five year trends. When the website was reviewed on 6 June 2015, specific plans to achieve the stated key performance metrics and improve financial performance going forward were not found.

Interim Reports

The Singtel reports for the second and third quarter of 2013 use a similar layout and provide similar content to that provided for the fourth quarter. The content and presentation of the result material for the third quarter ending December 2014 is similar to the 2013 material and the material for the fourth quarter of 2014.

Continuous Disclosures

The company announcements made through the SGX are available on the website back to 2005.[159]

Sustainability Reports

The focus areas included in the Singtel 2012 sustainability report are marketplace, people, environment, and community. The targets in each focus area for the next year are identified alongside the performance achieved in 2012. Specific targets for the following year and the next five years are also outlined. The focus areas in the 2014 sustainability report remain the same as in 2012. The focus area commentary includes tables with the 2014 targets and performance and the 2015 plans. A summary table provides some specific indicators. Some of the reported indicators within the focus areas include three to five years of data, while others show only the 2014 figures.

---

159. Singapore Telecommunications Limited, 'Stock Exchange Announcements', viewed 6 June 2015, http://info.singtel.com/about-us/investor-relations/stock-exchange-announcements#content-top.

B. *Keppel Corporation*

The business segments of Keppel Corporation (Keppel) include offshore and marine, infrastructure, property and investments.

Website

The Keppel home page is arranged with headings for about us, our people, our businesses, investor centre, media centre, sustainability, and contact us.[160] The 'about us' web pages indicate the group's vision and mission in broad terms, the names of its directors, senior management and a technology advisory panel, the group structure, a global footprint map and some history.[161] The pages for 'our people' discuss the group's core values, the talent management processes, and the Keppel community. The pages for 'our business' provide a broad overview of the main businesses of the group.[162] The sustainability pages provide information and overviews on the management of sustainability, corporate governance, the environment, product excellence, safety and health, labour practices and human rights, community and society.[163] The overviews are supported by features stories, showcase project descriptions, awards and accolades, and policy statements.

The investor centre web pages provide key financials, result releases and webcasts, financial reports, dividend information, a depositary bank, corporate governance, a calendar, frequently asked questions, and contacts.[164] The key financials provide summary figures for the first quarter of 2015 and the comparative 2014 results, as well as the net order book and contracts secured for the last ten years. The result releases and webcasts pages are arranged chronologically. The quarterly result releases are presented within annual blocks from 2005, including financial results, presentation slides, webcast of the presentations, and transcripts of the question and answer sessions.[165] Registration is required to listen to the webcasts. The financial reports page provides access to the annual reports from 2006. The content on the corporate governance pages provides outlines of compliance with the corporate governance principles and the risk management framework.[166]

160. Keppel Corporation, 'Home', viewed 7 June 2015, http://www.kepcorp.com/en/home.aspx.
161. Keppel Corporation, 'About Us', viewed 7 June 2015, http://www.kepcorp.com/en/content.aspx?sid = 92.
162. Keppel Corporation, 'Our Businesses', viewed 7 June 2015, http://www.kepcorp.com/en/content.aspx?sid = 51.
163. Keppel Corporation, 'Sustainability', viewed 7 June 2015, http://www.kepcorp.com/en/content.aspx?sid = 47.
164. Keppel Corporation, 'Investor Centre', viewed 7 June 2015, http://www.kepcorp.com/en/content.aspx?sid = 47.
165. Keppel Corporation, 'Result Releases & Webcasts', viewed 7 June 2015, http://www.kepcorp.com/en/content.aspx?sid = 73.
166. Keppel Corporation, 'Corporate Governance', viewed 7 June 2015, http://www.kepcorp.com/en/content.aspx?sid = 70.

Preliminary Final & Annual Reports

The Keppel preliminary full year results for 2012 include financial statements, notes, and summary management commentary. The results packs include presentation slides, webcasts, and a transcript of the question and answer sessions. The Keppel 2012 annual report includes financial highlights for two years. Many of these figures are calculated on an underlying basis with revaluations, impairments and divestments excluded. Similarly the 'figures at a glance' table and the ten-year chart of revenue and net profit exclude these amounts. To reconcile the underlying and reported figures, readers must turn to the five-year performance table at the end of the report.[167] The report includes pictures, a group overview, an operating and financial review, financial statements and notes.

The 2014 preliminary full year result material provides similar content and uses the same headings as the prior quarters and years. The 2014 annual report also uses a similar structure to the 2012 report, but most of the financial measures referenced are from the financial statements.[168] The strategic statements are very broad, including the rationales for the diversified businesses model. Most of the trend analysis is for three years, including the tables in the KPI page and the business reviews.

Interim Reports

The Keppel 2012 half year and quarterly reports include a CEO address, financial statements, notes and limited MD&A. The result material for the first quarter of 2015 is similar in content and format to the 2012 quarterly reports, including issued share capital details and segmental results. The presentation includes ten year charts of the group's net profit and earnings per share.

Continuous Disclosures

Media releases and SGX announcements are available on the website back to 1997.

Sustainability Reports

The Keppel 2012 sustainability report contains a three-year performance table with metrics for each of the main focus areas of environment, safety, labour and community. The focus area commentary includes highlights and a performance overview. The performance overviews include specific items, with columns headed 'what we said in 2012', 'what we did in 2012', and 'what we plan to do'. A GRI content index and an independent assurance statement are included at the end of the report.[169]

167. Keppel Corporation, *Shaping the Future Report to Shareholders 2012* 219.
168. The EVA measures are not fully explained.
169. The Global Reporting Initiative Statement indicates that the Sustainability Report fulfils the requirements of Application Level B+ of the G3.1 Guidelines.

When the site was viewed, the most recent sustainability report was for 2013.[170] This report includes a performance data table for three years, with performance indicators across the areas of environment, safety, labour, and community. These indicators are specific but relatively narrowly based.[171] The commentary throughout the report is mainly general, but the focus area section includes some specific discussion of goals, performance and plans.

170. Keppel Corporation, 'Sustainability Reports', viewed 7 June 2015, http://www.kepcorp.com/en/content.aspx?sid = 2935.
171. For example, the labour and human rights performance indicators include investment in training, training hours per employee, sustainable engagement score, group employee turnover rate, local hires, senior management hired locally. The only community performance indicator is philanthropic investments.

Reference List

Articles

Agapova, Anna, Madura, Jeff and Mailibayeva, Zhanel, 'Does Regulation Fair Disclosure Reduce Information Quality of Managerial Guidance?' (2012) 47 *Financial Review* 273.

Ajinkya, Bipin, Bhojraj, Sanjeev and Sengupta, Partha, 'The Association Between Outside Directors, Institutional Investors and the Properties of Management Earnings Forecasts' (2005) 43 *Journal of Accounting Research* 343.

Anilowski, Carol, Feng, Mei and Skinner, Douglas, 'Does Earning Guidance Affect Market Returns? The Nature and Information Content of Aggregate Earnings Guidance' (2007) 44 *Journal of Accounting & Economics* 36.

Arlen, Jennifer and Carney, William, 'Vicarious Liability for Fraud on Securities Markets: Theory and Evidence' (1992) *University of Illinois Law Review* 691.

Armstrong, Christopher, Guay, Wayne and Weber, Joseph, 'The Role of Information and Financial Reporting in Corporate Governance and Debt Contracting' (2010) 50 *Journal of Accounting and Economics* 179.

Ausubel, Lawrence, 'Insider Trading In a Rational Expectations Economy' (1990) 80 *American Economic Review* 1022.

Ayres, Ian and Choi, Stephen, 'Internalizing Outsider Trading' (2002) 101 *Michigan Law Review* 313.

Bailey, Warren, Li, Haitao, Mao, Connie and Zhong, Rui, 'Regulation Fair Disclosure and Earnings Information: Market, Analyst, and Corporate Responses' (2003) 58 *Journal of Finance* 2487.

Bainbridge, Stephen, 'Contemporary Issues in the Law of Business Organizations: Mandatory Disclosure: A Behavioural Analysis' (2000) 68 *University of Cincinnati Law Review* 1023.

Baker, Carol, 'Company Report- Written to Order' (2008) 29 *Credit Control* 6.

Balakrishnan, Karthik, Billings, Mary Brooke, Kelly, Bryan and Ljungqvist, Alexander, 'Shaping Liquidity: On the Causal Effects of Voluntary Disclosure' (2014) 69 *Journal of Finance* 2237.

Ball, Ray and Brown, Philip, 'An Empirical Evaluation of Accounting Income Numbers' (1968) 6 *Journal of Accounting Research* 159.

Ball, Ray, 'International Financial Reporting Standards (IFRS): Pros and Cons for Investors' (2006) 36 (Special issue) *Accounting and Business Research* 5.

Barber, Brad and Odean, Terrance, 'Online Investors: Do the Slow Die First?' (2002) 15 *Review of Financial Studies* 455.

Barron, Orie, Kile, Charles and O'Keefe, Terrence, 'MD&A Quality and Analysts' Earnings Forecasts' (1999) 16 *Contemporary Accounting Research* 75.

Barry, Brian, 'The Securities and Exchange Commission's Regulation Fair Disclosure: Parity of Information or Parody of Information?' (2002) 56 *University of Miami Law Review* 645.

Barry, John, 'The Economics of Outside Information and Rule 10b-5' (1981) 129 *University of Pennsylvania Law Review* 1307.

Barth, Mary, Konchitchki, Yaniv and Landsman, Wayne, 'Cost of Capital and Earnings Transparency' (2013) 55 *Journal of Accounting and Economics* 206.

Beaver, William, 'The Information Content of Annual Earnings Announcements' (1968) 6 *Journal of Accounting Research* 67.

Beaver, William, Lambert, Richard and Morse, Dale, 'The Information Content of Security Prices' (1980) 2 *Journal of Accounting and Economics* 3.

Benartzi, Shlomo and Thaler, Richard, 'Myopic Loss Aversion and the Equity Premium Puzzle' (1995) 110 *Quarterly Journal of Economics* 73.

Benston, George, 'Required Disclosure and the Stock Market: An Evaluation of the Securities Exchange Act of 1934' (1973) 63 *American Economic Review* 132.

Beny, Laura, 'Do Insider Trading Laws Matter? Some Preliminary Comparative Evidence' (2005) 7 *American Law and Economics Review* 144.

Beny, Laura, 'Insider Trading Law and Stock Markets Around the World: An Empirical Contribution to Theoretical Law and Economics Debate' (2007) 32 *Journal of Corporation Law* 237.

Beny, Laura, 'Do Investors in Controlled Firms Value Insider Trading Laws? International Evidence' (2008) 4 *Journal of Law, Economics & Policy* 267.

Bernard, Victor and Thomas, Jacob, 'Post-Earnings-Announcement Drift: Delayed Price Response or Risk Premium?' (1989) 27 *Journal of Accounting Research* 1.

Bertomeu, Jeremy, 'Discussion of Earnings Manipulation and the Cost of Capital' (2013) 51 *Journal of Accounting Research* 475.

Beyer, Anne, Cohen, Daniel, Lys, Thomas and Walther, Beverly, 'The Financial Reporting Environment: Review of the Recent Literature' (2010) 50 *Journal of Accounting and Economics* 296.

Bhattacharya, Utpal and Hazem, Daouk, 'The World Price of Insider Trading' (2002) 62 *Journal of Finance* 75.

Bhattacharya, Utpal, Hazem, Daouk, and Welker, Michael, 'The World Price of Earnings Opacity' (2003) 78 *Accounting Review* 641.

Bhattacharya, Utpal and Hazem, Daouk, 'When No Law is Better Than a Good Law' (2009) 13 *Review of Finance* 577.

Black, Bernard, 'The Legal and Institutional Precondition for Strong Securities Markets' (2001) 48 *UCLA Law Review* 781.

Bloomfield, Robert, Libby Robert, and Nelson, M, 'Confidence and the Welfare of Less-Informed Investors' (1999) 24 *Accounting, Organizations and Society* 623.

Botosan, Christine, 'Evidence that Greater Disclosure Lowers the Cost of Equity Capital' (2000) 12 *Bank of America Journal of Applied Corporate Finance* 60.

Botosan, Christine, 'Disclosure and the Cost of Capital: What Do We Know?' (2006) *Accounting and Business Research International Accounting Policy Forum* 31.

Bowen, Robert, Davis, Angela and Matsumoto, Dawn, 'Do Conference Calls Affect Analysts' Forecasts?' (2002) 77 *Accounting Review* 285.

Bowen, Robert, Davis, Angela and Matsumoto, Dawn, 'Do Firms Strategically Emphasize Performance Metrics in their Earnings Press Releases?' (2005) 80 *Accounting Review* 1011.

Boyle, James, 'A Theory of Law and Information: Copyright, Spleens, Blackmail, and Insider Trading' (1992) 80 *California Law Review* 1413.

Bozec, Yves and Bozec, Richard, 'Corporate Governance Quality and the Cost of Capital' (2011) 2 *International Journal of Corporate Governance* 217.

Bradley, Caroline, 'Disorderly Conduct: Day Traders and the Ideology of "Fair and Orderly Markets"' (2000) 26 *Journal of Corporation Law* 63.

Bratton, William, 'Does Corporate Law Protect the Interests of Shareholders and Other Stakeholders?: Enron and the Dark Side of Shareholder Value' (2002) 76 *Tulane Law Review* 1275.

Bratton, William and Wachter, Michael, 'The Case Against Shareholder Empowerment' (2010) 158 *University of Pennsylvania Law Review* 653.

Brav, Alon and Heaton, JB, 'Market Indeterminacy' (2003) 28 *Journal of Corporation Law* 517.

Brountas, Paul Jr, 'Rule 10b-5 and Voluntary Corporate Disclosures to Securities Analysts' (1992) 92 *Columbia Law Review* 1517.

Brown, James R, Martinsson, Gustav and Petersen, Bruce C, 'Law, Stock Markets, and Innovation' (2013) *68 Journal of Finance* 1517.

Brown, Philip, Foo, Mark and Watson, Iain, 'Trading by Insiders in Australia: Evidence on the Profitability of Directors' Trades' (2003) 21 *Company and Securities Law Journal* 248.

Brudney, Victor, 'Insiders, Outsiders, and Informational Advantages Under the Federal Securities Laws' (1979) 93 *Harvard Law Review* 322.

Brown, Stephen, Hillegeist, Stephen and Lo, Kin, 'Conference Calls And Information Asymmetry' (2004) 37 *Journal of Accounting and Economics* 343.

Brown, Stephen and Hillegeist, Stephen 'How Disclosure Quality Affects the Level of Information Asymmetry' (2007) 12 *Review of Accounting Studies* 443.

Brown, Stewart, 'Earnings Changes, Stock Prices, and Market Efficiency' (1978) *Journal of Finance* 17.

Brown, Timothy, 'Advantageous Comparison and Rationalization of Earnings Management' (2014) 52 *Journal of Accounting Research* 849.

Bryan, Stephen, 'Incremental Information Content of Required Disclosures Contained in Management Discussion and Analysis' (1997) 72 *Accounting Review* 285.

Bushee, Brian and Goodman, Theodore, 'Which Institutional Investors Trade Based on Private Information About Earnings and Returns?' (2007) 45 *Journal of Accounting Research* 289.

Bushee, Brian and Leuz, Christian, 'Economic Consequences of SEC Disclosure Regulation: Evidence From the OTC Bulletin Board' (2005) 38 *Journal of Accounting and Economics* 233.

Bushman, Robert M and Smith, Abbie, 'Transparency, Financial Accounting Information, and Corporate Governance' (2003) 9 *Economic Policy Review* 65.

Bushman, Robert, Piotroski, Joseph and Smith, Abbie, 'What Determines Corporate Transparency?' (2004) 42 *Journal of Accounting Research* 207.

Cain, Karessa, 'New Efforts to Strengthen Corporate Governance: Why Use SRO Listing Standards?' (2003) *Columbia Business Law Review* 619.

Calabresi, Guido and Melamed, A Douglas, 'Property Rules, Liability Rules and Inalienability: One View of the Cathedral' (1972) 85 *Harvard Law Review* 1089.

Campbell, John, Chen, Hsinchun, Dhakiwal, Dan, Lu, Hsin-min and Steele, Logan, 'The Information Content of Mandatory Risk Factor Disclosures in Corporate Filings' (2014) 19 *Review of Accounting Studies* 396.

Carlton, Dennis and Fischel, Daniel, 'The Regulation of Insider Trading' (1983) 35 *Stanford Law Review* 857.

Chang, Millicent, Hillman, Richard and Watson, Iain, 'Are Corporate Governance Mechanisms Effective in Reducing Insider Trading Profits?' (2005) 23 *Company and Securities Law Journal* 165.

Cheffins, Brian, 'Law As Bedrock: The Foundations of an Economy Dominated By Widely Held Public Companies' (2003) 23 *Oxford Journal of Legal Studies* 1.

Chipman, John and Moore, James, 'The New Welfare Economics 1939-1974' (1978) 19 *International Economic Review* 547.

Choi, Stephen, 'Regulating Investors Not Issuers: A Market-Based Proposal' (2000) 88 *California Law Review* 279.

Choi, Stephen, 'Selective Disclosure in the Public Capital Markets' (2002) 35 *UC Davis Law Review* 533.

Choi, Stephen, 'Law, Finance, and Path Dependence: Developing Strong Securities Markets' (2002) 80 *Texas Law Review* 1657.

Choi, Stephen and Pritchard, AC, 'Behavioral Economics and the SEC' (2003) 56 *Stanford Law Review* 1.

Choi, Stephen and Talley, Eric, 'Playing Favorites With Shareholders' (2002) 75 *Southern California Law Review* 271.

Clarke, Roger, Krase, Scott and Statman, Meir, 'Tracking Errors, Regret and Tactical Asset Allocation' (1994) 20 *Journal of Portfolio Management* 16.

Clarkson, Peter, Kao, Jennifer and Richardson, Gordon, 'The Voluntary Inclusion of Forecasts in the MD&A Section of Annual Reports' (1994) 11 *Contemporary Accounting Research* 423.

Clement, Michael, Frankel, Richard and Miller, Jeffrey, 'Confirming Management Earnings, Forecasts, Earnings Uncertainty and Stock Returns' (2003) 41 *Journal of Accounting Research* 653.

Coffee, John Jnr, 'Market Failure and the Economic Case for a Mandatory Disclosure System' (1984) 70 *Virginia Law Review* 717.

Coffee, John Jnr, 'Liquidity versus Control: The Institutional Investor as Corporate Monitor' (1991) 91 *Columbia Law Review* 1277.

Coffee, John Jnr, 'Brave New World? The Impact(s) of the Internet on Modern Securities Regulation' (1997) 52 *Business Lawyer* 1195.

Coffee, John Jnr, 'Understanding Enron: 'It's About The Gatekeepers, Stupid' (2002) 57 *Business Lawyer* 1403.

Coffee, John Jnr, 'What Caused Enron? A Capsule Of Social and Economic History of the 1990s' (2003) 89 *Cornell Law Review* 269.

Coffee, John Jnr, 'Gatekeeper Failure and Reform: The Challenge of Fashioning Relevant Reforms' (2004) 84 *Boston University Law Review* 301.

Cohen, Lauren, Malloy, Christopher and Pomorski, Lukasz, 'Decoding Inside Information' (2012) 57 *Journal of Finance* 1009.

Cole, Cathy and Jones, Christopher, 'Management Discussion and Analysis: A Review and Implications for Future Research' (2005) 24 *Journal of Accounting Literature* 135.

Coller, Maribeth and Yohn, Teri, 'Management Forecasts and Information Asymmetry: An Examination of Bid-Ask Spreads' (1997) 35 *Journal of Accounting Research* 181.

Corgill, Dennis, 'Insider Trading, Price Signals and Noisy Information' (1996) 71 *Indiana Law Journal* 355.

Cornell, Bradford and Sirri, Erik, 'The Reaction of Investors and Stock Prices to Insider Trading' (1992) 47 *Journal of Finance* 1031.

Cox, James, 'Insider Trading and Contracting: A Critical Response to the "Chicago School"' (1986) 4 *Duke Law Journal* 628.

Cox, James. 'Premises for Reforming the Regulation of Securities Offerings: An Essay' (2000) 63 *Law and Contemporary Problems* 11.

Cremers, Martijn and Ferrell, Allen, 'Thirty Years of Shareholder Rights and Firm Value' (2014) 69 *Journal of Finance* 1167.

Cronqvist, Henirk and Siegel, Stephan, 'The Genetics of Investment Biases' (2014) 133 *Journal of Financial Economics* 215.

Dallas, Lynne, 'Two Models of Corporate Governance: Beyond Berle and Means' (1988) 22 *University of Michigan Journal of Law Reform* 19.

Dallas, Lynne, 'Short-Termism, the Financial Crisis, and Corporate Governance' (2012) 37 *Journal of Corporation Law* 265.

Davies, Paul, 'Liability for Misstatements to the Market: Some Reflections' (2009) 9 *Journal of Corporate Law Studies* 295.

Debreceny, Roger and Rahman, Asheq, 'Firm-Specific Determinants of Continuous Corporate Disclosures' (2005) 40 *International Journal of Accounting* 249.

De Bondt, Werner and Thaler, Richard, 'Does the Stock Market Overreact?' (1985) 40 *Journal of Finance* 793.

De Bondt, Werner and Thaler, Richard, 'Further Evidence On Investor Overreaction And Stock Market Seasonality' (1987) 42 *Journal of Finance* 557.

De Franco, Gus, Lu, Hai and Vasvari, Florin, 'Wealth Transfer Effects of Analysts Misleading Behavior' (2007) 45 *Journal of Accounting Research* 71.

De Marzo, Peter, Fishman, Michael and Hagerty, Kathleen, 'Self-Regulation and Government Oversight' (2005) 72 *Review of Economic Studies* 687.

Demsetz, Harold, 'The Private Production of Public Goods' (1970) 13 *Journal of Law and Economics* 293.

Dhaliwal, Dan, Li, Oliver, Tsang, Albert and Yang, Yong, 'Voluntary Nonfinancial Disclosure and the Cost of Equity Capital: The Initiation of Corporate Social Responsibility Reporting' (2011) 86 *Accounting Review* 59.

Diamond, Douglas and Verrechia, Robert, 'Disclosure, Liquidity, and the Cost of Capital' (1991) 46 *Journal of Finance* 1325.

Donald, Christopher, 'A Critique of Arguments for Mandatory Continuous Disclosure' (1999) 62 *Saskatchewan Law Review* 85.

Doyle, Jeffrey, Jennings, Jared and Soliman, Mark, 'Do Managers Define Non-GAAP Earnings To Meet Or Beat Analyst Forecasts?' (2013) 56 *Journal of Accounting and Economics* 40.

Du, Julian and Wei, Shang-jin, 'Does Insider Trading Raise Market Volatility?' (2004) 114 *Economic Journal* 916.

Durnev, Art and Amrita, S Nain, 'Does Insider Trading Regulation Deter Private Information Trading? International Evidence (2007) 15 *Pacific Basin Financial Journal* 409.

Durnev, Art, Morck, Randall and Yeung, Bernard, 'Value Enhancing Capital Budgeting and Firm-Specific Stock Return Variation' (2004) 59 *Journal of Finance* 65.

Dye, Ronald, 'Disclosure of Nonproprietary Information' (1985) 23 *Journal of Accounting Research* 123.

Dyer, Boyd, 'Economic Analysis, Insider Trading, and Game Markets' (1992) 1 *Utah Law Review* 1.

Easley, David, Hvidkjaer, Soeren and O'Hara, Maureen, 'Is Information Risk a Determinant of Asset Returns?' (2002) 62 *Journal of Finance* 2185.

Easley, David and O'Hara, Maureen, 'Information and the Cost of Capital' (2004) 59 *Journal of Finance* 1553.

Easterbrook, Frank, 'Insider Trading, Secret Agents, Evidentiary Privileges, and the Production of Information' (1981) *Supreme Court Review* 309.

Easterbrook, Frank and Fischel, Daniel, 'Corporate Control Transactions' (1982) 91 *Yale Law Journal* 698.

Easterbrook, Frank and Fischel, Daniel, 'Mandatory Disclosure and the Protection of Investors' (1984) 70 *Virginia Law Review* 669.

Eckstein, T Andrew, 'The SEC's New Regulation FD: A Return to the Parity Theory' (2001) 69 *University of Cincinnati Law Review* 1289.

Elliott, John, Morse, Dale and Richardson, Gordon, 'The Association Between Insider Trading and Information Announcements' (1984) 15 *RAND Journal of Economics* 521.

Epstein, Marc and Palepu, Khrishna, 'What Financial Analysts Want' (1999) 80 *Strategic Finance* 48.

Ertimur, Yonca, Sletten, Ewa and Sunder, Jayanthi, 'Large Shareholders and Disclosure strategies: Evidence from IPO Lockup Expirations' (2014) 58 *Journal of Accounting and Economics* 79.

Eyssell, Thomas, 'Corporate Insiders and the Death of the Firm: Evidence on the Incidence of Insider Trading in Corporate Dissolutions' (1991) 26 *Financial Review* 517.

Fama, Eugene, 'Efficient Capital Markets: A Review of Theory and Empirical Work' (1970) 25 *Journal of Finance* 383.

Fama, Eugene, 'Market Efficiency, Long-Term Returns, and Behavioural Finance' (1998) 49 *Journal of Financial Economics* 283.

Fama, Eugene and Laffer, Arthur, 'Information and Capital Markets' (1971) 44 *Journal of Business Law* 289.

Fernandes, Nuno and Ferreira, Miguel, 'Insider Trading Laws and Stock Price Informativeness' (2009) 22 *Review of Financial Studies* 1845.

Fidrmuc, Jana, Goergen, Marc and Renneboog, Luc, 'Insider Trading, News Releases, and Ownership Concentration' (2006) 61 *Journal of Finance* 2931.

Findlay, Scott and Mathew, Prem, 'An Examination of the Differential Impact of Regulation FD on Analyst's Forecast Accuracy' (2006) 41 *Financial Review* 9.

Firth, Michael, Lin, Chen, Liu, Ping and Xuan, Yuhai, 'The Client is King: Do Mutual Fund Relationships Bias Analyst Recommendations?' (2013) 51 *Journal of Accounting Research* 165.

Fisch, Jill and Sale, Hillary, 'The Securities Analysts as Agent: Rethinking the Regulation of Analysts' (2003) *88 Iowa Law Review* 1035.

Fishe, Raymond and Robe, Michael, 'The Impact of Illegal Insider Trading in Dealer and Specialist Markets: Evidence From a Natural Experiment' (2004) 71 *Journal of Financial Economics* 461.

Fischel, Daniel, 'Symposium on Insider Trading: Insider Trading and Investment Analysts: An Economic Analysis of *Dirks v Securities and Exchange Commission*' (1984) 13 *Hofstra Law Review* 127.

Foster, George, 'Stock Market Reaction to Estimates of Earnings Per Share By Company Officials' (1973) 11 *Journal of Accounting Research* 25.

Fox, Merritt, 'Required Disclosure and Corporate Governance' (1996) 62 *Law and Contemporary Problems* 113.

Fox, Merritt, 'Regulation FD and Foreign Issuers: Globalisation's Strains and Opportunities' (2001) 41 *Virginia Journal of International Law* 653.

Fox, Merritt, 'The Issuer Choice Debate' (2001) 2 *Theoretical Inquiries in Law* 563;

Fox, Merritt, 'Civil Liability and Mandatory Disclosure' (2009) 109 *Columbia Law Review* 237.

Fox, Merritt, Morck, Randall, Yeung, Bernard and Durnev, Artyom, 'Law, Share Price Accuracy, and Economic Performance: The New Evidence' (2003) 102 *Michigan Law Review* 331.

Francis, Jennifer, Huang, Shawn, Khurana, Inder and Pereira, Raynolde, 'Does Corporate Transparency Contribute to Efficient Resource Allocation?' (2009) 47 *Journal of Accounting Research* 943.

Francis, Jennifer, Nanda, Dhananjay and Wang, Xin, 'Re-Examining the Effects of Regulation Fair Disclosure Using Foreign Listed Forms to Control for Concurrent Shocks' (2006) 41 *Journal of Accounting and Economics* 271.

Francis, Jennifer, Philbrick, Douglas and Schipper, Katherine, 'Shareholder Litigation and Corporate Disclosures' (1994) 32 *Journal of Accounting Research* 137.

Frank, Robert, 'If Homo Economicus Could Choose His Own Utility Function, Would He Want One with a Conscience?' (1987) 77 *American Economic Review* 593.

Frankel, Richard, Johnson, Marilyn and Skinner, Douglas, 'An Empirical Examination of Conference Calls as a Voluntary Disclosure Medium' (1999) 37 *Journal of Accounting Research* 133.

Frankel, Richard, McNichols, Maureen and Wilson, G Peter, 'Discretionary Disclosure and External Financing' (1995) 70 *Accounting Review* 135.

Frost, Carol, Gordon, Elizabeth and Hayes, Andrew, 'Stock Exchange Disclosure and Market Development: An Analysis of 50 International Exchanges' (2006) 44 *Journal of Accounting Research* 437.

Fu, Renhui, Kraft, Arthur and Zhang, Huai, 'Financial Reporting Frequency, Information Asymmetry, and the Cost of Equity' (2012) 54 *Journal of Accounting and Economics* 132.

Georgakopoulos, Nicholas, 'Insider Trading as a Transaction Cost: A Market Microstructure Justification and Optimization of Insider Trading Regulation' (1993) 26 *Connecticut Law Review* 1.

Gilson, Ronald and Kraakman, Reinier, The Mechanisms of Market Efficiency Twenty Years Later: The Hindsight Bias' (2003) 28 *Journal of Corporation Law* 715.

Gomes, Armando, Gorton, Gary and Madureira, Leonardo, 'SEC Regulation Fair Disclosure, Information and the Cost Of Capital' (2007) 13 *Journal of Corporate Finance* 300.

Gonedes, Nicholas, Dopuch, Nicholas and Penman, Stephen, 'Disclosure Rules, Information Production and Capital Market Equilibrium: The Case of Forecast Disclosure Rules' (1976) 14 *Journal of Accounting Research* 89.

Gordon, Jeffrey and Kornhauser, Lewis, 'Efficient Markets, Costly Information and Securities Research' (1985) 60 *New York University Law Review* 761.

Goshen, Zohar and Parchomovsky, Gideon, 'The Essential Role Of Securities Regulation' (2006) 55 *Duke Law Journal* 711.

Graham, John, Harvey, Campbell and Rajgopal, Shiva, 'The Economic Implications of Corporate Financial Reporting' (2005) 40 *Journal of Accounting and Economics* 3.

Graham, John, Harvey, Campbell and Rajgopal, Shiva, 'The Economic Implications of Corporate Financial Reporting' (2005) 40 *Journal of Accounting and Economics* 3.

Green, T Clifton, Jame, Russell, Markov, Stanimir and Subasis, Musa, 'Access to Management and the Informativeness of Analyst Research' (2014) 114 *Journal of Financial Economics* 239.

Groysberg, Boris, Healy, Paul and Maber, David, 'What Drives Financial Analyst Compensation at High-Status Banks?' (2011) 49 *Journal of Accounting Research* 969.

Guiso, Luigi, Sapienza, Paola and Zingales, Luigi, 'Trusting the Stock Market' (2008) 63 *Journal of Finance* 2557.

Guttentag, Michael, 'An Argument for Imposing Disclosure Requirements on Public Companies' (2004) 32 *Florida State University Law Review* 123.

Haddock, David and Macey, Jonathan, 'A Coasian Model of Insider Trading' (1986) 80 *North Western University Law Review* 1449.

Haft, Robert, 'The Effect of Insider Trading Rules on the Internal Efficiency of the Large Corporation' (1982) 80 *Michigan Law Review* 1051.

Hail, Luiz and Leuz, Christian, 'International Differences in the Cost of Equity Capital: Do Legal Institutions and Securities Regulation Matter?' (2006) 44 *Journal of Accounting Research* 485.

Hakansson, Nils, 'Interim Disclosure and Public Forecasts: An Economic Analysis and a Framework for Choice' (April 1977) 52 *Accounting Review* 396.

Hakansson, Nils, 'On the Politics of Accounting Disclosure and Measurement: An Analysis of Economic Incentives' (1981) 19 *Journal of Accounting Research* 1.

Hales, Jeffrey, Kuang, Xi and Venkataraman, Shankar, 'Who Believes the Hype? An Experimental Examination of How Language Affects Investor Judgments' (2011) 49 *Journal of Accounting Research* 223.

Han, Jun and Tong Tan, Hun, 'Investors Reactions to Management Earnings Guidance: The Joint Effect of Investment Position, News Valance, and Guidance Form' (2010) 48 *Journal of Accounting Research* 123.

Harold, Demsetz, 'The Private Production of Public Goods' (1970) 13 *Journal of Law and Economics* 293.

Heflin, Frank, Subramanyam, Kenneth and Zhang, Yuan, 'Regulation FD and the Financial Information Environment: Early Evidence' (2003) 78 *Accounting Review* 1.

Hirshleifer, David, 'Investor Psychology and Asset Pricing' (2001) 56 *Journal of Finance* 1533.

Hirshleifer, Jack, 'The Private and Social Value of Information and Reward To Inventive Activity' (1971) 61 *American Economic Review* 561.

Hoffman, Elizabeth and Spitzer, Matthew, 'Entitlement, Rights and Fairness: An Experimental Examination of Subjects' Concepts of Distributive Justice' (1985) 14 *Journal of Legal Studies* 259.

Holland, John, 'Private Voluntary Disclosure, Financial Intermediation And Market Efficiency' (1998) 25 *Journal of Business Finance & Accounting* 29.

Hong, Harrison and Kubik, Jeremy, 'Analysing The Analysts: Career Concerns and Biased Earnings Forecasts' (2003) 58 *Journal of Finance* 313.

Hong, Harrison and Stein, Jeremy, 'A Unified Theory of Underreaction, Momentum Trading, and Overreaction in Asset Markets' (1999) 54 *Journal of Finance* 2143.

Hooghiemstra, Reggy, 'Letters to the Shareholders: A Content Analysis Comparison of Letters Written by CEOs in the United States and Japan' (2010) 45 *The International Journal of Accounting* 275.

Hovenkamp, Herbert, 'The First Great Law & Economics Movement' (1990) 42 *Stanford Law Review* 993.

Huberman, Gur and Regev, Tomer, 'Contagious Speculation and a Cure for Cancer: A Non-Event that Made Stock Prices Soar' (2001) 56 *Journal of Finance* 387.

Jackson, Howell and Roe, Mark, 'Public and Private Enforcement of Securities Laws: Resource-Based Evidence' (2009) 93 *Journal of Financial Economics* 207.

Jaggi, Bikki, 'A Note on the Information Content of Corporate Annual Earnings Forecasts' (1978) 53 *Accounting Review* 961, 966.

Jagolinzer, Alan, Larcker, David and Taylor, Daniel, 'Corporate Governance and the Information Content of Insider Trades' (2011) 49 *Journal of Accounting Research* 1249.

James, Boyle, 'A Theory of Law and Information: Copyright, Spleens, Blackmail, and Insider Trading' (1992) 80 *California Law Review* 1413.

Jayaraman, Sudarshan, 'The Effect of Enforcement on Timely Loss Recognition: Evidence From Insider Trading Laws' (2012) 53 *Journal of Accounting and Economics* 77.

Jennings, Richard, 'Book Review of *Insider Trading and the Stock Market* by Henry G Manne' (1967) 55 *California Law Review* 1229.

Jensen, Michael and Meckling, William, 'Theory of the Firm: Managerial Behaviour, Agency Costs and Ownership Structure' (1976) 3 *Journal of Financial Economics* 305.

Johnson, Alex Jr, 'An Appeal for the Liberal Use of Law and Economics: The Liberals Fight Back' (1989) 67 *Texas Law Review* 659.

Jutuah, David, 'Box Ticking Isn't Enough for Investors, warns PwC' (September 27, 2007) *Accountancy Age* 8.

Kahan, Marcel, 'Securities Law and the Social Costs of "Inaccurate" Stock Prices' (1992) 41 *Duke Law Journal* 977

Kahan, Marcel and Klausner, Michael, 'Path Dependence in Corporate Contracting: Increasing Returns, Herd Behavior and Cognitive Biases' (1996) 74 *Washington University Law Quarterly* 347.

Kahneman, Daniel, Knetsch, Jack and Thaler, Richard, 'Fairness as a Constraint on Profit Seeking: Entitlements in the Market' (1986) 76 *American Economic Review* 728.

Kahneman, Daniel and Tversky, Amos, 'Prospect Theory: An Analysis of Decision under Risk' (1979) 47 *Econometrics* 263.

Kaniel, Ron, Liu, Shuming, Saar, Gideon and Titman, Sheridan, 'Individual Investor Trading and Return Patterns Around Earnings Announcements' (2012) 57 *Journal of Finance* 639.

Kaplow, Louis and Shavall, Steven, 'Fairness versus Welfare' (2001) 114 *Harvard Law Review* 961.

Kassouf, Sheen, 'Towards a Legal Framework for Efficiency and Equity in the Securities Markets' (1974) 25 *Hastings Law Journal* 417.

Kasznik, Ron and Lev, Baruch, 'To Warn or Not to Warn: Management Disclosures in the Face of an Earnings Surprise' (1995) 70 *Accounting Review* 113.

Ke, Bin and Yu, Yong, 'The Effect Of Issuing Biased Earnings Forecasts On Analysts' Access To Management And Survival' (2006) 44 *Journal of Accounting Research* 965.

Kent, Daniel, Hirshleifer, David and Subrahmanyam, Avanidhar, 'Investor Psychology and Security Market under and Overreactions' (1998) 53 *Journal of Finance* 1839.

Kidd, Ronald, 'Insider Trading: The Misappropriation Theory Versus an "Access To Information" Perspective' (1993) 18 *Delaware Journal of Corporate Law* 101.

Kimbrough, Michael, 'The Effect Of Conference Calls On Analyst And Market Underreaction To Earnings Announcements' (2005) 80 *Accounting Review* 189.
Kitch, Edmund, 'The Theory and Practice of Securities Disclosure' (1995) 61 *Brooklyn Law Review* 763.
Kitch, Edmund, 'Proposals for Reform of Securities Regulation: An Overview' (2001) 41 *Virginia Journal of International Law* 629.
Klock, Mark, 'Mainstream Economics and the Case for Prohibiting Inside Trading' (1994) 10 *Georgia State University Law Review* 297.
Kobayashi, Bruce and Ribstein, Larry, 'Outsider Trading as an Incentive Device' (2006) 40 *UC Davis Law Review* 21.
Kothari, SP, Shu, Susan and Wysocki, Peter, 'Do Managers Withhold Bad News?' (2009) 47 *Journal of Accounting Research* 241.
Krawiec, Kimberly, 'Fairness, Efficiency and Insider Trading: Deconstructing the Coin of the Realm in the Information Age' (2001) 95 *North Western University Law Review* 443.
Kripke, Homer, 'The SEC, The Accountants, Some Myths and Some Realities' (1970) 45 *New York University Law Review* 1151.
Kross, William and Suk, Inho, 'Does Regulation FD Work? Evidence from Analysts' Reliance on Public Disclosure' (2012) 53 *Journal of Accounting and Economics* 225.
Laibson, David, 'Golden Eggs and Hyperbolic Discounting' (1997) 112 *Quarterly Journal of Economics* 443.
Lambert, Richard, Leuz, Christian and Verrecchia, Robert, 'Accounting Information, Disclosure, and the Cost of Capital' (2007) 45 *Journal of Accounting Research* 385.
Lambert, Richard, Leuz, Christian and Verrecchia, Robert, 'Information Asymmetry, Information Precision, and the Cost of Capital' (2012) 16 *Review of Finance* 1.
Landsman, Wayne, Maydew, Edward and Thornock, Jacob, 'The Information Content of Annual Earnings Announcements and Mandatory Adoption of IFRS' (2012) 53 *Journal of Accounting and Economics* 34.
Lang, Mark and Lundholm, Russell, 'Cross-Sectional Determinants of Analysts Ratings of Corporate Disclosures' (1993) 31 *Journal of Accounting* 246.
Lang, Mark and Maffett, Mark, 'Transparency and Liquidity Uncertainty in Crisis Periods' (2011) 52 *Journal of Accounting and Economics* 101.
Langevoort, Donald, 'Information Technology and the Structure of Securities Regulation' (1985) 98 *Harvard Law Review* 747.
Langevoort, Donald, 'Investment Analysts and the Law of Insider Trading' (1990) 76 *Virginia Law Review* 1023.
Langevoort, Donald, 'Theories, Assumptions and Securities Regulation: Market Efficiency Revisited' (1992) 140 *University of Pennsylvania Law Review* 851.
Langevoort, Donald, 'Words From on High about Rule 10b-5: Chiarella's History, Central Bank's Future' (1995) 20 *Delaware Journal of Corporate Law* 865.
Langevoort, Donald, 'Organized Illusions: A Behavioral Theory of Why Corporations Mislead Stock Market Investors (and Cause Other Social Harms)' (1997) 146 *University of Pennsylvania Law Review* 101.

Langevoort, Donald, 'Half-Truths: Protecting Mistaken Inferences by Investors and Others' (1999) 52 *Stanford Law Review* 87.

Langevoort, Donald, 'Revisiting Gilson and Kraakman's Efficiency Story' (2003) 28 *Journal of Corporation Law* 499.

Langevoort, Donald, 'Technological Evolution and the Devolution of Corporate Finance Reporting' (2004) 46 *William & Mary Law Review* 1.

La Porta, Rafael, Lopez-de-Silanes, Florencio, Shleifer, Andrei and Vishny, Robert, 'Legal Determinants of External Finance' (1997) 52 *Journal of Finance* 1131.

La Porta, Rafael, Lopez-de-Silanes, Florencio, Shleifer, Andrei and Vishny, Robert, 'Law and Finance' (1998) 106 *Journal of Political Economy* 1113.

La Porta, Rafael, Lopez-de-Silanes, Florencio, Shleifer, Andrei and Vishny, Robert, 'Investor Protection and Corporate Valuation' (2002) 62 *Journal of Finance* 1147.

La Porta, Rafael, Lopez-de-Silanes, Florencio, and Shleifer, Andrei, 'What Works in Securities Laws?' (2006) 61 *Journal of Finance* 1.

Latane, Henry and Jones, Charles, 'Standardized Unexpected Earnings – A Progress Report' (1977) 32 *Journal of Finance* 1457.

Lawrence, Alastair, 'Individual Investors and Financial Disclosure' (2013) 56 *Journal of Accounting and Economics* 130.

Lawson, Garry, 'The Ethics of Insider Trading' (1988) 11 *Harvard Journal of Law and Public Policy* 727.

Lee, Chun, Rosenthal, Leonard and Gleason, Kimberly, 'Effect of Regulation FD on Asymmetric Information' (2004) 60 *Financial Analysts Journal* 79.

Lee, Edward, Strong, Norman and Zhu, Zhenmei (Judy), 'Did Regulation Fair Disclosure, SOX, and Other Analyst Regulations Reduce Security Mispricing?' (2014) 52 *Journal of Accounting Research* 733.

Lee, Ian, 'Fairness and Insider Trading' (2002) 1 *Columbia Business Law Review* 119.

Leland, Hayne, 'Insider Trading: Should It Be Prohibited?' (1992) 100 *Journal of Political Economy* 859.

LeRoy, Stephen, 'Efficient Capital Markets and Martingales' (1989) 27 *Journal of Economic Literature* 1585.

Leuz, Christian and Verrecchia, Robert, 'The Economic Consequences of Increased Disclosure' (2000) 38 *Journal of Accounting Research* 91.

Lev, Baruch, 'Toward a Theory of Equitable and Efficient Accounting Policy' (1988) 63 *Accounting Review* 1.

Lev, Baruch and Penman, Stephen, 'Voluntary Forecast Disclosures, Non-Disclosure, and Stock Prices' (1990) 28 *Journal of Accounting Research* 49.

Lev, Baruch and Thiagarajan, S Ramu, 'Fundamental Information Analysis' (1993) 31 *Journal of Accounting Research* 190.

Levine, Ross, 'Law, Finance, and Economic Growth' (1999) 8 *Journal of Financial Intermediation* 8.

Levitt, Arthur L, 'The Importance of High Quality Accounting Standards' (1998) 12 *Accounting Horizons* 79.

Levmore, Saul, 'Securities and Secrets: Insider Trading and the Law of Contracts' (1982) 68 *Virginia Law Review* 117.

Levmore, Saul, 'In Defense of the Regulation of Insider Trading' (1988) 11 *Harvard Journal of Law & Public Policy* 101.

Levmore, Saul, 'Simply Efficient Markets and the Role of Regulation: Lesson from the Iowa Electronic Markets and the Hollywood Stock Exchange' (2003) 28 *Journal of Corporation Law* 589.

Lewellen, Wilbur, Park, Taewoo and Ro, Byung, 'Self-serving Behaviour in Managers' Discretionary Information Disclosure' (1996) 21 *Journal of Accounting and Economics* 227.

Li, Feng, 'The Information Content of Forward-Looking Statements in Corporate Filings – A Naïve Baysian Machine Learning Approach' (2010) 48 *Journal of Accounting Research* 1049.

Libin, Nancy and Wrona, James, 'The Securities Industry and the Internet: A Suitable Match?' (2001) *Columbia Business Law Review* 601.

Lin, Hsiou-Wei and McNichols, Maureen, 'Underwriting Relationships, Analysts Earning Forecasts And Investment Recommendations' (1998) 25 *Journal of Accounting & Economics* 101.

Lin, Tom, 'The New Investor' (2013) 60 *UCLA Law Review* 678.

Link, Benedikt, 'The Struggle for a Common Interim Reporting Frequency Regime in Europe' (2012) 9 *Accounting In Europe* 191.

Lopes, Alexandro and de Alencar, Roberta, 'Disclosure and Cost of Equity Capital in Emerging Markets: The Brazilian Case' (2010) 45 *International Journal of Accounting* 45.

Lopez-Fernandini, Camilia, 'Regulation FD of the SEC's Selective Disclosure and Insider Trading Rule: Finally, Full And Fair Disclosure' (2001) 53 *Administrative Law Review* 1353.

Lowenstein, Louis, 'Financial Transparency and Corporate Governance: You Manage What You Measure' (1996) 96 *Columbia Law Review* 1335.

McLean, R David, Zhang, Tianyu and Zhao, Mengxin, 'Why Does the Law Matter? Investor Protection and Its Effects on Investment, Finance, and Growth' (2012) 57 *Journal of Finance* 313.

McMillan, John, 'Market Design: The Policy Uses of Theory' (2003) 93 *American Economic Review* 139.

McNichols, Maureen and Trueman, Brett, 'Public Disclosure, Private Information Collection, And Short-Term Trading' (1994) 17 *Journal of Accounting and Economics* 69.

Macey, Jonathan, 'From Fairness to Contract: The New Direction of the Rules Against Insider Trading' (1984) 13 *Hofstra Law Review* 9.

Macey, Jonathan, 'Ethics, Economics and Insider Trading: Ayn Rand Meets the Theory of the Firm' (1988) 11 *Harvard Journal of Law & Public Policy* 785.

Macey, Jonathan, 'Administrative Agency Obsolescence and Interest Group Formation: A Case Study of the SEC at Sixty' (1994) 15 *Cardozo Law Review* 909.

Macey, Jonathan, 'Securities Trading: A Contractual Perspective' (1999) 50 *Case Western Reserve Law Review* 269.

Maffett, Mark, 'Financial Reporting Opacity and Informed Trading By International Institutional Investors' (2012) 54 *Journal of Accounting and Economics* 201.

Mahoney, Paul, 'Manager-Investor Conflicts In Mutual Funds' (2004) 18 *Journal of Economic Perspectives* 161.

Malkiel, Burton, 'Review of *Insider Trading and the Stock Market* by Henry Manne' (1968) 41 *Journal of Business* 263.

Manne, Henry, 'In Defense of Insider Trading' (1966) 44 *Harvard Business Review* 113.

Manne, Henry, 'Insider Trading and the Law Professors' (1975) 23 *Vanderbilt Law Review* 547.

Marques, Ana, 'Disclosure Strategies Among S&P Firms: Evidence on the Disclosure of Non-GAAP Financial Measures and Financial Statements in Earnings Press Releases' (2010) 42 *British Accounting Review* 119.

Masson, Robert and Madhavan, Ananth, 'Insider Trading and the Value Of the Firm' (1991) 39 *Journal of Industrial Economics* 333.

Massoud, Nadia, Nandy, Deborah, Saunders, Anthony and Song, Keke, 'Do Hedge Funds Trade on Private Information? Evidence From Syndicated Lending and Short-Selling' (2011) 99 *Journal of Financial Economics* 477.

Maug, Ernst, 'Insider Trading Legislation and Corporate Governance' (2002) 46 *European Economic Review* 1569.

Mayew, William, 'Evidence of Management Discrimination Among Analysts During Earnings Conference Calls' (2008) 46 *Journal of Accounting Research* 627.

Meier-Schatz, Christian, 'Objectives of Financial Disclosure Regulation' (1986) 8 *Journal of Comparative Business and Capital Market Law* 219.

Mendelson, Morris, 'Review: The Economics of Insider Trading Reconsidered' (1969) 117 *University of Pennsylvania Law Review* 470.

Meng, Fanpeng, 'A History of Chinese Companies Listing in Hong Kong and Its Implications for the Future' (2011) 11 *Journal of Corporate Law Studies* 243.

Miller, Gregory, 'Earnings Performance and Discretionary Disclosure Decisions' (2002) 40 *Journal of Accounting Research* 173.

Mitchell, Lawrence, 'Book review –The Cult of Efficiency' (1992) 71 *Texas Law Review* 217.

Moore, Jennifer, 'What is Really Unethical about Insider Trading?' (1990) 9 *Journal of Business Ethics* 171.

Morck, Randall, Yeung, Bernard and Yu, Wayne, 'The Information Content of Stock Markets: Why Do Emerging Markets Have Synchronous Stock Price Movements?' (2000) 58 *Journal of Financial Economics* 215.

Morris, Richard, 'Corporate Disclosure in a Substantially Unregulated Environment' (1984) 20 *Abacus* 52.

Morse, Dale, 'Price and Trading Volume Reaction Surrounding Earnings Announcements: A Closer Examination' (1981) 19 *Journal of Accounting Research* 374.

Ng, Jeffrey, 'The Effect of Information Quality on Liquidity Risk' (2011) 52 *Journal of Accounting and Economics* 126.

Nichols, D Craig and Wahlen, James, 'How Do Earnings Numbers Relate To Stock Returns? A Review Of Classic Accounting Research With Updated Evidence' (Dec 2004) *Accounting Horizons* 263.

North, Gill, 'A Theoretical Basis for Selective Disclosure Regulation' (2009) 32 *University of New South Wales Law Journal* 143.

North, Gill, 'Periodic Disclosure Regulation: Enhancements To Enable All Investors To Make Informed Decisions?' (2009) 27 *Company and Securities Law Journal* 23.

North, Gill, 'A Re-examination of the Manne Efficiency Theory and the Insider Trading and Company Disclosure Efficiency Rationales' (2011) 25 *Australian Journal of Corporate Law* 209.

North, Gill, 'Continuous Disclosure in Australia: The Empirical Uncertainties' (2011) 29 *Company and Securities Law Journal* 394.

North, Gill, 'Public Company Communication, Engagement and Accountability: Where Are We and Where Should We Be Heading?' (2013) 31 *Company and Securities Law Journal* 167.

North, Gill, 'Listed Company Disclosure and Financial Market Transparency: Is this a Battle Worth Fighting or Merely Policy and Regulatory Mantra?' (2014) 6 *Journal of Business Law* 484.

North, Gill, 'Timely Public Disclosure of Company Information: A Likely Precondition for Optimal Long-Term Corporate and National Outcomes' (2014) 32 *Company and Securities Law Journal* 560.

North, Gill and Buckley, Ross, 'A Fundamental Re-examination of Efficiency in Capital Markets in Light of the Global Financial Crisis' (2010) 33 *University of New South Wales Law Journal* 714.

North, Gill and Buckley, Ross, 'A Financial Transaction Tax: Inefficient or Needed Systemic Reform?' (2012) 43 *Georgetown Journal of International Law* 745.

Odean, Terrance, 'Volume, Volatility, Price and Profit When All Traders are Above Average' (1998) 53 *Journal of Finance* 1887.

Oever, Jonathan, 'Insider Trading and the Dual Role of Information' (1997) 106 *Yale Law Journal* 1325.

Orcutt, John L, 'Investor Skepticism v Investor Confidence: Why the New Research Analyst Reforms will Harm Investors' (2003) 81 *Denver University Law Review* 1.

Painter, Richard, 'Insider Trading And The Stock Market Thirty Years Later' (1999) 50 *Case Western Reserve Law Review* 305.

Pastena, Victor and Ronen, Joshua, 'Some Hypotheses on the Pattern of Management's Informal Disclosures' (1979) 17 *Journal of Accounting Research* 550.

Patell, James, 'Corporate Forecasts of Earnings Per Share and Stock Price Behavior: Empirical Test' (1976) 14 *Journal of Accounting Research* 246.

Penman, Stephen, 'An Empirical Investigation of the Voluntary Disclosure of Corporate Earnings Forecasts' (1980) 18 *Journal of Accounting Research* 132.

Penman, Stephen, 'Insider Trading and the Dissemination of Firm's Forecast Information' (1982) 55 *Journal of Business* 479.

Pham, Peter, Suchard, Jo-Ann and Zein, Jason, 'Corporate Governance and the Cost of Capital: Evidence from Australian Companies' (2012) *Journal of Applied Corporate Finance* 84.

Pirrong, Craig, 'The Self-Regulation of Commodity Exchanges: The Case of Market Manipulation' (1995) 38 *Journal of Law and Economics* 141.

Pompillo, David, 'On the Reach of Insider Trading Law' (2007) 25 *Company and Securities Law Journal* 467.

Poole, John, 'Improving the Reliability of Management Forecasts' (1989) 14 *Journal of Corporation Law* 547.

Posner, Eric, 'The Jurisprudence of Greed' (2003) 151 *University of Pennsylvania Law Review* 1097.

Pownall, Grace, Wasley, Charles and Waymire, Gregory, 'The Stock Price Effects of Alternative Types of Management Earnings Forecasts' (1993) 68 *Accounting Review* 896.

Pritchard, Adam, 'Self Regulation and Securities Markets' (Spring 2003) *Regulation* 32.

Radin, Arthur, 'Have We Created Financial Statement Overload?' (2007) 77 *CPA Journal* 6.

Reese, William and Weisback, Michael, 'Protection of Minority Shareholder Interests, Cross-Listings in the United States, and Subsequent Equity Offerings' (2002) 66 *Journal of Financial Economics* 65.

Rhee, Robert, 'The Madoff Scandal, Market Regulatory Failure and the Business Education of Lawyers' (2009) 35 *Journal of Corporation Law* 363.

Roberts, Russell, 'How Little We Know: The Challenges of Financial Reform' (November 2009) 6(11) *Economists' Voice* 1.

Rodrigues, Usah and Stegemoller, Mike, 'Placebo Ethics: A Study in Securities Disclosure Arbitrage' (2010) 96 *Virginia Law Review* 1.

Rogers, Jonathan and Stocken, Phillip, 'Credibility of Management Forecasts' (2005) 80 *Accounting Review* 1233.

Romano, Roberta, 'Empowering Investors: A Market Approach to Securities Regulation' (1998) 107 *Yale Law Journal* 2359.

Romano, Roberta, 'The Need for Competition in International Securities Regulations' (2001) 2 *Theoretical Inquiries in Law* 387.

Romer, David, 'Rational Asset-Price Movements without News' (1993) 83 *American Economic Review* 1112.

Rozeff, Michael and Zaman, Mir, 'Market Efficiency and Insider Trading: New Evidence' (1988) 61 *Journal of Business* 25.

Ruland, William, Tung, Samuel and George, Nashwa, 'Factors Associated with the Disclosure of Managers' Forecasts' (1990) 65 *Accounting Review* 710.

Russell, Scott, 'Regulation Fair Disclosure: The Death of the Efficient Capital Market Hypothesis and the Birth of Herd Behaviour' (2002) 82 *Boston University Law Review* 527.

Saari, Christopher, 'The Efficient Capital Markets Hypothesis, Economic Theory and the Regulation of the Securities Industry' (1977) 29 *Stanford Law Review* 1031.

Sadka, Ronnie, 'Liquidity Risk and Accounting Information' (2011) 52 *Journal of Accounting and Economics* 144.

Sappideen, Razeen, 'Securities Market Efficiency Reconsidered' (1988) 9 *University of Tasmania Law Review* 132.

Scheppele, Kim, '"It's Just Not Right": The Ethics of Insider Trading' (1993) 56 *Law & Contemporary Problems* 123.

Schotland, Roy, 'Unsafe At Any Price: A Reply to Manne, Insider Trading and the Stock Market' (1967) 53 *Virginia Law Review* 1425.

Schrand, Catherine and Zechman, Sarah, 'Executive Overconfidence and the Slippery Slope to Financial Misreporting' (2012) 53 *Journal of Accounting and Economics* 311.

Schwartz, Jeff, 'Fairness, Utility, and Market Risk' (2010) 89 *Oregon Law Review* 175.

Scott, Kenneth, 'Insider Trading: Rule 10b-5, Disclosure and Corporate Privacy' (1980) 9 *Journal of Legal Studies* 801.

Seligman, Joel, 'The Historical Need for a Mandatory Corporate Disclosure System' (1983) 9 *Journal of Corporation Law* 1.

Seligman, Joel, 'The Reformulation of Federal Securities Law Concerning Non-Public Information' (1995) 73 *Georgetown Law Journal* 1083.

Seyhun, H Nejat, 'Insider's Profits, Costs of Trading and Market Efficiency' (1986) 16 *Journal of Financial Economics* 189.

Seyhun, H Nejat, 'The Effectiveness of the Insider Trading Sanctions' (1992) 35 *Journal of Law and Economics* 149.

Seyhun, H Nejat and Bradley, Michael, 'Corporate Bankruptcy and Insider Trading' (1997) 70 *Journal of Business* 189.

Sharpe, William, 'Efficient Capital Markets: A Review of Theory and Empirical Work' (1970) 25 *Journal of Finance* 418.

Shiller, Robert, 'Market Volatility and Investor Behavior' (1990) 80 *American Economic Review* 58.

Shiller, Robert, 'Conversation, Information, and Herd Behavior' (1995) 85 *American Economic Review* 181.

Shiller, Robert, 'From Efficient Markets Theory to Behavioural Finance' (2003) 17 *Journal of Economic Perspectives* 83.

Shiller, Robert and Pound, John, 'Survey Evidence on Diffusion of Interest and Information among Investors' (August 1989) *Journal of Economic Behaviour and Organisation* 44.

Shleifer, Andrei and Summers, Lawrence, 'The Noise Trader Approach in Finance' (Spring 1990) *Journal of Economic Perspective* 19.

Sinha, Praveen and Gadarowski, Christopher, 'The Efficacy of Regulation Fair Disclosure' (2010) 45 *Financial Review* 331.

Skaife, Hollis, Veenman, David and Wangerin, Daniel, 'Internal Control Over Financial Reporting and Managerial Rent Extraction: Evidence From The Profitability of Insider Trading' (2013) 55 *Journal of Accounting and Economics* 91.

Skinner, Douglas, 'Earnings Disclosures and Stockholder Lawsuits' (1997) 23 *Journal of Accounting and Economics* 249.

Soffer, Leonard, Thiagarajan, S Ramu and Walther, Beverly, 'Earnings Preannouncement Strategies' (2000) 5 *Review of Accounting Studies* 5.

Soltes, Eugene, 'Private Interaction Between Firm Management and Sell-side Analysts' (2014) 52 *Journal of Accounting Research* 245.

Steinberg, Marc, 'Insider Trading, Selective Disclosure, and Prompt Disclosure: A Comparative Analysis' (2001) 22 *University of Pennsylvania Journal of International Economic Law* 635.

Steinberg, Marc and Myers, Jason, 'Lurking in the Shadows: The Hidden Issues of the Securities and Exchange Commission's Regulation FD' (2002) 27 *Journal of Corporation Law* 173.

Stigler, George, 'Public Regulation of the Securities Markets' (1964) 37 *Journal of Business* 117.

Stiglitz, Joseph, 'Using Tax Policy to Curb Speculative Short-Term Trading' (1989) 3 *Journal of Financial Services Research* 101.

Stiglitz, Joseph, 'Symposium on Bubble' (Spring 1990) *Journal of Economic Perspective* 13.

Stout, Lynn, 'The Unimportance of Being Efficient: An Economic Analysis of Stock Market Pricing and Securities Regulation' (1988) 87 *Michigan Law Review* 613.

Stout, Lynn, 'Derivatives and the Legal Origins of the 2008 Credit Crisis' (2001) 1 *Harvard Business Law Review* 1.

Stout, Lynn, 'The Mechanisms of Market Inefficiency: An Introduction to the New Finance' (2003) 28 *Journal of Corporation Law* 635.

Summers, Lawrence and Summers, Victoria, 'When Financial Markets Work Too Well: A Cautious Case For a Securities Transaction Tax' (1989) 3 *Journal of Financial Services Research* 261.

Swanson, Carol, 'Insider Trading Madness: Rule 10b5-1 and the Death of Scienter' (2003) 52 *Kansas Law Review* 147.

Tan, Hun-Tong, Ying Wang, Elaine and Zhou, Bo, 'When the Use of Positive Language Backfires: The Joint Effect of Tone, Readability, and Investor Sophistication on Earnings Judgements' (2014) 52 *Journal of Accounting Research* 273.

Tetlock, Paul C, Saar-Tsechansky, Maytal and Macskassy, Sofus, 'More than Words: Quantifying Language to Measure Firms' Fundamentals' (2008) 63 *Journal of Finance* 1437.

Thevenot, Maya, 'The Factors Affecting Illegal Insider Trading In Firms With Violations of GAAP' (2011) 53 *Journal of Accounting and Economics* 375.

Thurber, Stephen, 'The Insider Trading Compensation Contract as an Inducement to Monitoring by the Institutional Investor' (1994) 1 *George Mason University Law Review* 119.

Tomasic, Roman, 'Corporate Collapse, Crime and Governance - Enron, Anderson and Beyond' (2002) 14 *Australian Journal of Corporate Law* 183.

Tribe, Laurence, 'Constitutional Calculus: Equal Justice or Economic Efficiency?' (1985) 98 *Harvard Law Review* 592.

Trueman, Brett, 'Why do Managers Voluntarily Release Earnings Forecasts?' (1986) 8 *Journal of Accounting and Economics* 53.

Unger, Laura, 'Corporate Communications Without Violations' (1999) 51 *Administrative Law Review* 1119.

Vanstraelen, Ann, Zareski, Marilyn and Robb, Sean, 'Corporate Nonfinancial Disclosure Practices and Financial Analyst Forecast Ability Across Three European Countries' (2003) 14 *Journal of International Financial Management and Accounting* 249.

Verrecchia, Robert, 'Essays on Disclosure' (2001) 32 *Journal of Accounting and Economics* 97.

Vyas, Dushyantkumar, 'The Timeliness of Accounting Write-Downs by US Financial Institutions During the Financial Crisis of 2007-2008' (2011) 49 *Journal of Accounting Research* 823.

Walker, Martin and Louvari, Evagelia, 'The Determinants of Voluntary Disclosure of Adjusted Earnings Per Share Measures by UK Quoted Companies' (2003) 33 *Accounting and Business Research* 295.

Walsh, David, 'Price Reaction to Order Flow "News" in Australian Equities' (1997) 5 *Pacific-Basin Finance Journal* 1.

Wang, Clare, 'Accounting Standards Harmonization and Financial Statement Comparability: Evidence from Transnational Information Transfer' (2014) 52 *Journal of Accounting Research* 955.

Wang, William, 'Trading on Material Non-Public Information on Impersonal Stock Markets: Who is Harmed, and Who Can Sue Whom under SEC Rule 10b-5?' (1981) 54 *Southern California Law Review* 1217.

Wang, William, 'Stock Market Insider Trading: Victims, Violators And Remedies – Including an Analogy to Fraud in the Sale of a Used Car with a Generic Defect' (2001) 33 *Securities Law Journal* 381.

Watts, Ross, 'Systematic "Abnormal Returns" After Quarterly Earnings Announcements' (1978) *Journal of Financial Economics* 127.

Waymire, Gregory, 'Additional Evidence on the Information Content of Management Earnings Forecasts' (1984) 22 *Journal of Accounting Research* 703.

Waymire, Gregory, 'Earnings Volatility and Voluntary Management Forecast Disclosure' (1985) 23 *Journal of Accounting Research* 268.

Whincorp, Michael, 'Towards A Property Rights and Market Microstructural Theory of Insider Trading Regulation - The Case of Primary Securities Markets Transactions' (1996) 7 *Journal of Business and Finance Law* 212.

Williams, Jared, 'Financial Analysts and the False Consensus Effect' (2013) 51 *Journal of Accounting Research* 855.

Wurgler, Jeffrey, 'Financial Markets And The Allocation Of Capital' (2000) 58 *Journal of Financial Economics* 187.

Xu, Hao-Feng and Lin, Mei-Feng, 'Controlling Owner and Transparency: Information Transparency and Disclosure Rankings System' (2011) 29 *African Journal of Business Management* 11589.

Yang, Holly, 'Capital Market Consequences of Managers' Voluntary Disclosure Styles' (2011) 53 *Journal of Accounting & Economics* 167.

Yi, Linda, 'Road Shows On The Internet: Taking Individual Investors For A Ride On The Information Highway' (2002) 52 *Duke Law Journal* 243.

Young, Danqing and Guenther, David, 'Financial Reporting Environments and International Capital Mobility' (2003) 41 *Journal of Accounting Research* 553.

Zeikel, Arthur, 'On the Threat of Change' (Nov/Dec 1975) *Financial Analysts Journal* 17.

Books

Ariely, Dan, *The (Honest) Truth About Dishonesty: How We Lie to Everyone---Especially Ourselves* (HarperCollins, 2012).

Beaver, William, *Financial Reporting: An Accounting Revolution* (Prentice Hall, 3rd ed, 1998).

Berle, Adolf and Means, Gardiner, *The Modern Corporation and Private Property* (Transaction Publishers, 1932).

Brandeis, Louis, *Other People's Money* (National Home Library Foundation, Washington, 1914).

Coffee, John Jr., *Gatekeepers: The Professions and Corporate Governance* (Oxford University Press, 2006).

Easterbrook, Frank and Fischel, Daniel, *The Economic Structure of Corporate Law* (Harvard University Press, 1991).

Einhorn, David, *Fooling Some of the People All of the Time: A Long Short Story* (John Wiley & Sons, 2008).

Etzioni, Amitai, *The Moral Dimension: Toward a New Economics* (Free Press, 1988).

Fung, Archon, Graham, Mary and Weil, David, *Full Disclosure: The Perils & Promise of Transparency* (Cambridge University Press, New York, 2007).

Gauthier, David, *Morals By Agreement* (Oxford University Press, Oxford, 1986).

Graham, Benjamin, Dodd, David and Cottle, Sidney, *Security Analysis, Principles and Techniques* (McGraw-Hill; 4th ed, 1962).

Kaplow, Louis and Shavell, Steven, *Fairness versus Welfare* (Harvard University Press, 2002).

Keynes, John, *The General Theory of Employment, Interest and Money* (Macmillan, London, 1936).

Kripke, Homer, *The SEC And Corporate Disclosure: Regulation In Search Of A Purpose* (Harcourt Brace Jovanovich Publishers, New York, 1979).

Lewis, Michael, *Flash Boys* (W.W. Norton & Company, Inc, New York, 2015).

Lo, Andrew (ed), *Market Efficiency: Stock Marker Behaviour and Theory and Practice Volume I* (Edward Elgar Publishing, Lyme NH, 1997).

McRobert, Andrew and Hoffman, Ronnie, *Corporate Collapse: An Early Warning System for Lenders, Investors and Suppliers* (McGraw Hill, Sydney, 1997).

Manne, Henry, *Insider Trading and the Stock Marke*t (Free Press, 1966).

Popper, Karl L, *The Logic of Scientific Discovery* (Hutchinson & Co, 1959).

Posner, Richard, *Economic Analysis of Law* (Aspen Law & Business, 6th ed, 2003).

Sen, Amartya, *On Ethics and Economics* (Wiley-Blackwell, 1987).

Sunstein, Cass, *Free Markets and Social Justice* (Oxford University Press, 1997).

Walker, Gordon, Fisse, Brent and Ramsay, Ian, *Securities Regulation in Australia and New Zealand* (Lawbook Co, 1st ed, 1994).

Wang, William and Steinberg, Marc, *Insider Trading* (Oxford University Press, 2010).

Working Papers

Chan, Howard, Brown, Rob and Kee Ho, Yew, 'Initiation Of Analyst Coverage: Does It Add Value?' (Working Paper, Monash University, University of Melbourne, 20 May 2003).

Coval, Joshua, Hirshleifer, David and Shumway, Tyler, 'Can Individual Investors Beat the Market?' (Working Paper 04-025, Harvard University, September 2005).

Fong, Kingsley, Gallagher, David, Gardner, Peter and Swan, Peter, 'A Closer Examination Of Investment Manager Herding Behaviour' (Working Paper, University of New South Wales, 25 February 2004).

Ioannou, Ioannis and Serafeim, George, 'The Consequences of Mandatory Corporate Sustainability Reporting' (Working Paper 11-100, Harvard Business School, 26 October 2012).

Li, Yan and Yang, Holly, 'Disclosure and the Cost of Equity Capital: An Analysis at the Market Level' (Working Paper, 1 January 2013).

Lo, Andrew, 'Reconciling Efficient Markets with Behavioral Finance: The Adaptive Markets Hypothesis' (Working Paper, 8 March 2005).

Matsumoto, Dawn, Pronk, Maarten and Roelofsen, Erik, 'Managerial Disclosure vs Analyst Inquiry: An Empirical Investigation of the Presentation and Discussion Portions of Earnings-Related Conference Calls' (Working Paper, 1 November 2006).

Schulmeister, Stephan, 'A General Financial Transactions Tax: A Short Cut of the Pros, the Cons and a Proposal' (Working Paper No 344, Austrian Institute of Economic Research, October 2009).

Speeches

D'Aloisio, Tony, Chairman Australian Securities and Investments Commission, 'Developments in the Global Regulatory System' (Speech Delivered at the Financial Services Council Annual Conference, Melbourne, 12 August 2010).

Burton, John, Chief Accountant United States Securities and Exchange Commission, 'FORECASTS: A Changing View From The Securities and Exchange Commission' (Speech delivered to Northwestern University Conference on Public Reporting of Corporate Financial Forecasts, 2 April 1973).

Cole, Margaret, Director of Enforcement, Financial Services Authority, 'Insider Dealing in the City' (Speech delivered at the London School of Economics, London, 17 March 2007).

Cox, Christopher, Chairman United States Securities and Exchange Commission, 'Plain Language and Good Business' (Speech delivered to the Center for Plain Language symposium, Washington DC, 12 October 2007).

Gibson, Belinda, Australian Securities and Investments Commissioner, 'Disclosure And The Role of ASX and ASIC' (Speech delivered at the Listed Companies Conference, 26 March 2008).

Gibson, Belinda, Australian Securities and Investments Commissioner, 'Facilitating Capital Raising for Corporate Australia' (Speech delivered at the Corporate Finance World Australia 2009 Conference, 10 November 2009).

Gibson, Belinda, Australian Securities and Investments Commissioner, 'Working In a Regulated Environment' (Speech delivered at the Law Society of Western Australia Summer School, 26 February 2010).

Glassman, Cynthia A, United States Securities and Exchange Commissioner, 'Does the SEC Disclosure Eschew Obfuscation? Res Ipsa Loquitor' (Speech presented at the Plain Language Associations International's Fifth International Conference, Washington DC, 4 November 2005).

Hamilton, Karen, 'Launch of "Enhanced Disclosure"' (Speech delivered at the Committee for Economic Development of Australia, Sydney, 19 July 2002).

Levitt, Arthur, 'Audit Committee Oversight, Selective Disclosure and Insider Trading' (Statement delivered at the Open Commission Meeting, 15 December 1999).

Lewis, Christopher, Founder of Center for Public Integrity, 'Legal Corruption and the Mercenary Culture' (Speech delivered at Edmond J Safra Center for Ethics, 18 April 2013).

Mayne, Eric and Lawrence, David, 'Update on the Transfer of Market Supervision' (Presentation delivered at the 2010 Annual Stockbrokers Conference, 8 June 2010).

Sommer AA Jnr, United States Securities and Exchange Commissioner, 'Forecasting: A Look at the Future' (Speech delivered to Corporate Financial Forecast and Disclosure Conference, Drexel University, Philadelphia, 29 March 1974).

Tanzer, Greg, Secretary General, International Organization of Securities Commissions, 'Building a Better Financial System: IOSCO's Role' (Speech delivered to Intergovernmental Working Group of Experts on International Standards of Accounting and Reporting, 12 October 2011).

Thomsen, Linda, Director Division of Enforcement, United States Securities and Exchange Commission, 'Insider Trading' (Testimony Before the US Senate Committee on the Judiciary, 26 September 2006).

Turner, Adair, Chairman, Financial Services Authority (Speech to the City Banquet, The Mansion House, London, 22 September 2009).

Unger, Laura, United States Securities and Exchange Commissioner, 'Fallout from Regulation FD: Has the SEC Finally Cut the Tightrope?' (Speech delivered at the Glassier LegalWorks Conference, 27 October 2000).

Other

Alexander, Kern, 'UK Insider Dealing and Market Abuse Law: Strengthening Regulatory Law to Combat Market Misconduct' in Stephen Bainbridge (ed), *Research Handbook on Insider Trading* (Edward Elgar, Cheltenham UK, 2013).

Allens Arthur Robinson, *Submissions to the Corporations and Markets Advisory Committee in Response to its Issues Paper on Aspects of Market Integrity* (10 March 2009).

Anisman, Philip, *Insider Trading Legislation: An Outline of the Issues and Alternatives* (1986).

Australasian Investor Relations Association, 'The What, When and Where of Consensus Estimates for Listed Entities in Australia' (Issues Paper, February 2010).

Australian Broadcasting Corporation Television, *Ivor Ries with a Reporting Season Forecast* (19 July 2009) Inside Business < http:/www.abc.net.au/insidebusiness/content/2009/s2629947.htm > .

Australian Financial Markets Association, *CAMAC Market Integrity Paper Responses* (10 March 2009).

Australian Investor Relations Association, *Snap Poll: One-on-One Meetings with Analysts & Fund Managers* (15 June 2005).

Australian Securities and Investments Commission, *"Heard It On The Grapevine..." Draft ASIC Guidance And Discussion Paper. Disclosure Of Information To Investors And Compliance With Continuous Disclosure And Insider Trading Provisions* (November 1999).

Australian Securities and Investments Commission, *Better Disclosure for Investors - Guidance Rules* (23 August 2000).

Australian Securities and Investments Commission, 'Promina Pays $100,000 Fine' (Press Release 07-69, 20 March 2007).

Australian Securities and Investments Commission, 'Our Financial Markets: The Big Issues' (ASIC Summer School Report, 18-20 February 2008).

Australian Securities and Investments Commission, 'Our Financial Markets: The Big Issues' (ASIC Summer School Report, 18-20 February 2008).

Australian Securities and Investments Commission, *ASIC Annual Report 09-10 A Year of Achievement.*

Australian Securities and Investments Commission, 'ASIC's Review of 30 June 2010 Financial Reports and Focuses for 31 December 2010' (Media Release 10-282AD, 22 December 2010).

Australian Securities and Investments Commission, Regulatory Guide 230: *Disclosing Non-IFRS Financial Information* (December 2011).

Australian Securities and Investments Commission, 'Improved Financial Information for Investors and Others' (Media Release 11-312MR, 21 December 2011).

Australian Securities and Investments Commission, Regulatory Guide 247: *Effective Disclosure in an Operating and Financial Review* (March 2013).

Australian Securities and Investments Commission, 'Findings from 30 June 2013 Financial Reports' (Media Release 13-341, 16 December 2013).

Australian Securities and Investments Commission, 'Findings from 31 December 2013 Financial Reports' (Media Release 14-141, 27 June 2014).

Australian Securities and Investments Commission, 'Findings from 30 June 2014 Financial Reports' (Media Release 14-332, 12 December 2014).

Australian Securities and Investments Commission, Regulatory Guide 170: *Prospective Financial Information.*

Australian Securities Exchange, *Memorandum of Understanding Between Australian Securities and Investments Commission and Australian Stock Exchange Limited* (30 June 2004).

Australian Securities Exchange Corporate Governance Council, *Corporate Governance Principles and Recommendations with 2010 Amendments* (3rd ed, 2014).

Australian Securities Exchange, ASX Guidance Note 8 *Continuous Disclosure Listing Rule 3.1* (June 2005).

Australian Securities Exchange, ASX Guidance Note 8 *Continuous Disclosure: Listing Rules 3.1-3.1B* (1 May 2013).

Australian Securities Exchange, ASX Guidance Note 8 *Continuous Disclosure: Listing Rules 3.1-3.1B* (1 July 2015).

Australian Securities Exchange Compliance, *Continuous Disclosure: An Abridged Guide* (March 2013).

Bafin, *Issuer Guidelines* (14 May 2009).

Canadian Institute of Chartered Accountants, *Building a Better MD&A, A Guide for Smaller Issuers* (November 2007).

Canadian Institute of Chartered Accountants, *Building a Better MD&A, Risk Disclosure* (March 2008).

Canadian Institute of Chartered Accountants, *CFO Beyond-GAAP Briefing: Forward-Looking Information* (May 2008).

Canadian Institute of Chartered Accountants, *MD&A Guidance on Preparation And Disclosure* (July 2009).

Canadian Securities Administrators, CSA Staff Notice 51-334: *Continuous Disclosure Review Program Activities for the Fiscal Year Ended March 31, 2011* (15 July 2011).

Canadian Securities Administrators, CSA Staff Notice 51-337: *Continuous Disclosure Review Program Activities for the Fiscal Year Ended March 31, 2012* (19 July 2012).

Canadian Securities Administrators, CSA Staff Notice 51-339: *Continuous Disclosure Review Program Activities for the Fiscal Year Ended March 31, 2013* (18 July 2013).

Canadian Securities Administrators, CSA Staff Notice 51-341: *Continuous Disclosure Review Program Activities for the Fiscal Year Ended March 31, 2014* (17 July 2014).

Carvajal, Ana, Dodd, Randall, Moore, Michael, Nier, Erland, Tower, Ian and Zanforlin, Luisa, International Monetary Fund Staff Position Note, 'The Perimeter of Financial Regulation' (26 March 2009).

Centre for Financial Market Integrity, *Self-Regulation in Today's Securities Markets: Outdated System or Work in Progress?* (2007).

Chartered Financial Analysts Institute, *European Investment Professionals Back Quarterly Reporting* (20 November 2003).

Chartered Secretaries Australia, *Market Integrity* (10 March 2009).

Commission of Experts of the President of the UN General Assembly on Reform of the International Monetary and Financial System, *Principles for a New Financial Architecture* (21 September 2009).

Commonwealth of Australia, HIH Royal Commission, *The Failure of HIH Insurance* (2003).

Companies and Securities Advisory Committee, Commonwealth of Australia, *Report on Continuous Disclosure* (1996).

Davies, Paul, Ferrarini, Guido, Hopt, Klaus, Pietrancosta, Alain, Skog, Rolf, Soltysinski, Satanislaw, Winter, Jaap and Wymeersch, Eddy, European Company Law Experts *Response to the European Commission's Green Paper* "The EU Corporate Governance Framework" (22 July 2011).

Department for Business Innovation & Skill United Kingdom, *Ensuring Equity Markets Support Long Term Growth: The Government Response to the Kay Review* (November 2012).

Dubow, Ben and Monteiro, Nuno, 'Measuring Market Cleanliness', Financial Services Authority Occasional Paper Series 23 (March 2006).

European Commission (2004) Directive 2004/109/EC of the European Parliament and of the Council, Official Journal of the European Union, L 390.

European Commission, Report from the Commission Staff Working Paper Impact Assessment (SEC(2011) 1280 final).

European Parliament, Directive 2013/50/EU amending 2004/109/EC and Directive 2003/71/EC.

Financial Conduct Authority, *The Full Handbook*

Financial Reporting Council, *The UK Corporate Governance Code* (September 2014).

Financial Services Authority, *FSA Annual Report 2012/13.*

Geddes, Victoria, FIRST Advisers, 'Opinion Restoring the Relevance of AGMS', *Company Director* 1 August 2010.

Global Reporting Initiative, 'GRI Empowering Sustainable Decisions', viewed 29 June 2015, https://www.globalreporting.org/information/Pages/default.aspx.

Global Reporting Initiative, 'GRI and Sustainability Reporting', viewed 29 June 2015, https://www.globalreporting.org/information/sustainability-reporting/Pages/gri-standards.aspx.

Goldman, Jim, Hunt, Stefan, Minter, Paul, Suntheim, Felix and Zaman, Qamar, 'Why Has the FCAs Market Cleanliness Statistic for Takeover Announcements Decreased Since 2009?' Financial Conduct Authority Occasional Paper No 4 (July 2014).

Government Commission, *German Corporate Governance Code* (as amended 5 May, 2015).

Grant, Jeremy, 'Singapore Exchange Tightens Listing Rules', *FT.com* 19 July 2012.

Hong Kong Exchanges and Clearing Limited, *Financial Statements Review Programme Report 2010* (August 2010).

Hong Kong Exchanges and Clearing Limited, *Financial Statements Review Programme Report 2012* (January 2013).

Hong Kong Exchanges and Clearing Limited, *Financial Statements Review Programme Report 2013* (February 2014).

House of Commons Treasury Committee, 'Banking Crisis: Reforming Corporate Governance and Pay in the City: Ninth Report of Session 2008 – 2009' (15 May 2009).

In the Matter of Bank of Boston Corporation, Administrative Proceeding File No. 3-8270 (1995) 14 March 2014, <http://www.sec.gov/litigation/aljdec/id81bpm.txt>.

In the Matter of Office Depot, Inc., Accounting and Auditing Enforcement Release No. 3198 (21 October 2010) http://www.sec.gov/litigation/admin/2010/34-63152.pdf.

In the Matter of Patricia A. McKay, Exchange Act. Release No. 63154 (21 October 2010) http://www.sec.gov/litigation/admin/2010/34-63154.pdf31.

In the Matter of Sony Corporation and Sumio Sano: Release No. 40305 (5 August 1998) < http://www.sec.gov/litigation/admin/3440305.txt > .

In the Matter of Stephen A. Odland, Exchange Act Release No. 63153 (21 October 2010) http://www.sec.gov/litigation/admin/2010/34-63153.pdf.

International Integrated Reporting Council, *Consultation Draft of the International Framework* (2013).

International Integrated Reporting Council, *The International Framework* (December 2013).

International Integrated Reporting Council, *Basis for Conclusions* (December 2013).

International Organization of Securities Commissions, *Objectives and Principles of Securities Regulation* (June 2010).

Isaksson, Mats and Çelik, Sserdar, 'Who Cares? Corporate Governance in Today's Equity Markets', (OECD Corporate Governance Working Papers, No. 8 2013, OECD Publishing).

Johnson, Steve, 'FSA Crackdown on Cash For CEO Access', *FT.com*, 4 March 2013.

Jordan, Pav and Sibonney, Claire, 'Canada Banks Propose TMX Deal To Rival LSE Bid', *Reuters.com* 14 May 2011.

Kohler, Alan, *Secrets and Lies* (2 December 2008) Business Spectator <http:// www.businessspectator.com.au/bs.nsf/Article/Secrets-and-lies-LWRDP?OpenDocument&src = srch> at 3 December 2008.

Law Council of Australia, *Response to CAMAC's Issues Paper: Aspects of Market Integrity* (10 March 2009).

Mazars, *Transparency Directive Assessment Report.*

Monteiro, Nuno, Zaman, Qamar and Leitterstorf, Susanne, 'Updated Measurement of Market Cleanliness', Financial Services Authority Occasional Paper Series 25 (March 2007).

National Investor Relations Institute, 'Most Corporate Conference Calls Are Now Open to Individual Investors and the Media' (Press Release, 29 Feb 2000).

National Investor Relation Institute, 'National Investor Relation Institute Releases Survey Result on the Impact of SEC Regulation Fair Disclosure' (Press Release, 2 July 2001).

New York Stock Exchange, *Listed Company Manual.*

Oakley, David, 'John Kay: Professor of Doom is "Waiting for the Next Crisis"', *FT.com*, 10 June 2013.

Ontario Securities Commission, *Corporate Finance Branch Report* (2009).

Ontario Securities Commission, *Forward-Looking Information Disclosure* (OSC Staff Notice 51-721, June 13, 2013).

Organisation for Economic Co-operation and Development, Directorate for Financial and Enterprise Affairs Steering Group on Corporate Governance, *The Role of Stock Exchanges in Corporate Governance* (2 July 2009).

Power, Ben, 'Aristocrat Under Scrutiny After Results Release', *Australian Financial Review* (Sydney), 20 February 2003.

Report of the Committee on the Financial Aspects of Corporate Governance (1 December 1992).

Representatives of the Australian Accounting Profession, *Aspects of Market Integrity* (31 March 2009).

Securities and Derivatives Industry Association, *Submission on CAMAC Issues Paper – Aspects of Market Integrity* (11 March 2009).

Securities and Exchange Surveillance Commission, *SESC Brochure* (October 2012).

Securities and Futures Commission and the Stock Exchange of Hong Kong Limited, *Memorandum of Understanding Governing Listing Matters* (28 January 2003).

Selb, Christine and Frean, Alexandra, 'Lehman Vice-President Lost Job After Raising Repo 105 Ethical Concerns', *The Australian* (Sydney), 17 March 2010.

Standing Committee on Legal and Constitutional Affairs, House of Representatives Commonwealth of Australia, *Fair Shares for All: Insider Trading in Australia* (1989).

Steinert-Threlkeld, Tom, 'LSE Faces Counterbid for TMX Group', *Securitiestechnology-monitor.com* (16 May 2011).

Technical Committee of the International Organization of Securities Commission, *Principles For Periodic Disclosure By Listed Entitles* Final Report (February 2010).

The Joint Ore Reserves Committee of the Australasian Institute of Mining and Metallurgy, Australian Institute of Geoscientists and Minerals Council of Australia (JORC), *Australasian Code For Reporting of Exploration Results, Mineral Resources and Ore Reserves- The JORC Code 2004 Edition* (December 2004).

The Kay Review of UK Equity Markets and Long-Term Decision Making: *Interim Report* (February 2012).

The Kay Review of UK Equity Markets and Long-Term Decision Making: *Final Report* (July 2012).

Tillman, Robert and Irgaard, Michael, *Control Overrides in Financial Statement Fraud: A Report to the Institute for Fraud Protection* (16 January 2007).

Toronto Stock Exchange, *TSX Company Manual.*

Unger, Laura, 'Conflicts of Interest Faced by Brokerage Firms and Their Research Analysts' (Written testimony to the Committee on Financial Services, United States House of Representatives, Washington DC, 31 July 2001).

United States Financial Crisis Inquiry Commission Report 47 (January 2011).

United States Financial Industry Regulatory Authority, 'FINRA Fines 10 Firms a Total of $43.5 Million for Allowing Equity Research Analysts to Solicit Investment Banking Business and for Offering Favorable Research Coverage in Connection With Toys"R"Us IPO' (Media Release, 11 December 2014).

United States Securities and Exchange Commission, *A Plain English Handbook: How to Create Clear SEC Disclosure Documents* (August 1988).

United States Securities and Exchange Commission, Securities Act Release No 33-6835 (18 May 1989) Financial Reporting Release No 36, Final Rule: *Disclosure in Management's Discussion and Analysis of Financial Condition and Results of Operations; Certain Investment Company Disclosures.*

United States Securities and Exchange Commission, 'Form 10-K', http://www.sec.gov/answers/form10k.htm.

United States Securities and Exchange Commission, 'Form 10-Q', http://www.sec.gov/answers/form10q.htm.

United States Securities and Exchange Commission, *Comments of 50 Individuals Received* (2000) <http://www.sec.gov/rules/proposed/s73199/0420b01w.html>.

United States Securities and Exchange Commission, *Proposed Rule: Selective Disclosure and Insider Trading* (2000).

United States Securities and Exchange Commission, *Final Rule, Selective Disclosure and Insider Trading* (2000).

United States Securities and Exchange Commission, Securities Act Release 33-8039 (4 December 2001) Financial Reporting Release 59, *Cautionary Advice Regarding the Use of "Pro-Forma" Financial Information in Earnings Releases.*

United States Securities and Exchange Commission, Securities Act Release 33-8040 (12 December 2001) Financial Reporting Release No 60, *Cautionary Advice Regarding Disclosure About Critical Accounting Policies.*

United States Securities and Exchange Commission, Securities Act Release 33-8056 (22 January 2002) Financial Reporting Release 61, *Disclosure Relating to Liquidity and Capital Resources, Off-Balance Sheet Arrangements, Trading Activities and Related Party Transactions.*

United States Securities and Exchange Commission, Securities Release 33-8098 (10 May 2002) International Series Release No 1258, Proposed Rule: *Disclosure in Management's Discussion and Analysis about the Application of Critical Accounting Policies.*

United States Securities and Exchange Commission, Securities Act Release No 33-8182 (28 January 2003) Financial Reporting Release No 67, Final Rule: *Disclosure in Management's Discussion and Analysis About Off-Balance Sheet Arrangements and Aggregate Contractual Obligations.*

United States Securities and Exchange Commission, Securities Release 33-8350 (29 December 2003) Financial Reporting Release 72, *Interpretation: Commission Guidance Regarding Management's Discussion and Analysis of Financial Conditions and Results of Operations.*

United States Securities and Exchange Commission, 'Self-Regulatory Organizations—Various Amendments; Proposed Rule' (Release No. 34–50699; 17 CFR Parts 240, 242, 8 December 2004).

United States Securities and Exchange Commission, *Regulation FD Compliance & Disclosure Interpretations* Question 101.02 (14 August 2009).

United States Securities and Exchange Commission, *Report on Review of Disclosure Requirements in Regulation S-K* (December 2013).

United States Securities and Exchange Commission, 'SEC Issues Staff Report on Public Company Disclosure' (Press Release 2013-269, 20 December 2013).

Wisenthal, Stephen, 'Brokers Say Reporting Season Too Short', *Australian Financial Review* (Sydney), 15 September 2004.

World Federation of Exchanges, *2009 Cost and Revenue Survey* (October 2010).

Table of Cases

Australia

United States

Table of Legislation

Index

D

INTERNATIONAL BANKING AND FINANCE LAW SERIES

1. Jan Job de Vries Robbe, *Innovations in Securitisation. Yearbook 2006*, 2006 (ISBN 90-11 - 2533-7).
2. Jim Bartos, *United States Securities Law: A Practical Guide*, Third edition, 2006 (ISBN 90-411-2362-8).
3. Hui Huang, *International Securities Markets: Insider Trading Law in China*, 2006 (ISBN 90-411-2557-4).
4. Barth et al., *Financial Restructuring and Reform in Post-WTO China*, 2007 (ISBN 90-411- 2573-6).
5. Zhongfei Zhou, *Banking Laws in China*, 2007 (ISBN 978-90-411-2519-4).
6. Jan Job de Vries Robbe & Paul Ali, *Expansion and Diversification in Securitization Yearbook 2007*, 2007 (ISBN 978-90-411-2661-0).
7. Ross Buckley, *International Financial System. Policy and Regulation*, 2008 (ISBN 978- 90-411-2746-4).
8. Jan Job de Vries Robbe, *Securitization Law and Practice: In the Face of the Credit Crunch*, 2008 (ISBN 978-90-411-2715-0).
9. Phoebus Athanassiou, *Hedge Fund Regulation in the European Union: Current Trends and Future Prospects*, 2009 (ISBN 978-90-411-2856-0).
10. Jan Job de Vries Robbe, *Structured Finance: On from the Credit Crunch: The Road to Recovery*, 2009 (ISBN 978-90-411-2787-7).
11. Gaetane Schaeken Willemaers, *The EU Issuer-Disclosure Regime: Objectives and Proposals for Reform*, 2011 (ISBN 978-90-411-3394-6).
12. Panagiotis Delimatsis & Nils Herger (eds), *Financial Regulation at the Crossroads: Implications for Supervision, Institutional Design and Trade*, 2011 (ISBN 978-90-411-3355-7).
13. Raffaele Scalcione, *The Derivatives Revolution: A Trapped Innovation and a Blueprint for Regulatory Reform*, 2011 (ISBN 978-90-411-3430-1).
14. Douglas Arner & Ross Buckley, *From Crisis to Crisis: The Global Financial System and Regulatory Failure*, 2011 (ISBN 978-90-411-3354-0).
15. Anton P. Trichardt, *Letters of Comfort: A Trans-Systemic Analysis*, 2012 (ISBN 978-90- 411-3600-8).
16. Eddy Wymeersch, *Alternative Investment Fund Regulation*, 2012 (ISBN 978-90-411-3690- 9).
17. Asif H. Qureshi & Xuan Gao (eds), *International Economic Organizations and Law: The Perspective and Role of the Legal Counsel*, 2012 (ISBN 97890-411-3427-1).
18. Rhys Bollen, *The Law and Regulation of Payment Services: A Comparative Study*, 2012 (ISBN 978-90-411-3818-7).
19. Ramandeep Kaur Chhina, *Standby Letters of Credit in International Trade*, 2012 (ISBN 978-90-411-4560-4).

20. Dirk A. Zetzsche (ed.), *The Alternative Investment Fund Managers Directive: European Regulation of Alternative Investment Funds*, 2012 (ISBN 978-90-411-4044-9).
21. Lorenzo Sasso, *Capital Structure and Corporate Governance: The Role of Hybrid Financial Instruments*, 2013 (ISBN 978-90-411-4843-8).
22. Pablo Iglesias-Rodríguez, *The Accountability of Financial Regulators: A European and International Perspective*, 2013 (ISBN 978-90-411-3874-3).
23. Seraina Neva Grünewald, *The Resolution of Cross-Border Banking Crises in the European Union: A Legal Study from the Perspective of Burden Sharing*, 2014 (ISBN 978-90-411-4909-1).
24. Megan Bowman, *Banking on Climate Change: How Finance Actors and Transnational Regulatory Regimes are Responding*, 2015 (ISBN 978-90-411-5223-7).
25. Jin Sheng, *China's Listed Companies: Conflicts, Governance and Regulation*, 2015 (ISBN 978-90-411-5925-0).
26. Sven Schelo, *Bank Recovery and Resolution*, 2015 (ISBN 978-90-411-4959-6).
27. Luis M. Hinojosa-Martínez & José María Beneyto (eds), *European Banking Union: The New Regime*, 2015 (ISBN 978-90-411-5263-3).
28. Gill North, *Effective Company Disclosure in the Digital Age*, 2015 (ISBN 978-90-411-3815-6)